Camping Utah

Help Us Keep This Guide Up to Date

Every effort has been made by the author and editors to make this guide as accurate and useful as possible. However, many things can change after a guide is published—campgrounds open and close, grow and contract; amenities and regulations change; facilities come under new management; and so on.

We would appreciate hearing from you concerning your experiences with this guide and how you feel it could be improved and kept up to date. While we may not be able to respond to all comments and suggestions, we'll take them to heart, and we'll also make certain to share them with the author. Please send your comments and suggestions to the following address:

GPP
Reader Response/Editorial Department
P.O. Box 480
Guilford, CT 06437

Or you may e-mail us at:

editorial@globepequot.com

Thanks for your input, and happy camping!

Camping Utah

A Comprehensive Guide to Public Tent and RV Campgrounds

Second Edition

Donna Lynn Ikenberry

FALCONGUIDES

GUILFORD, CONNECTICUT
HELENA, MONTANA
AN IMPRINT OF GLOBE PEQUOT PRESS

FALCONGUIDES®

Copyright © 2002, 2014 Globe Pequot Press

FalconGuides is an imprint of Globe Pequot Press.
Falcon, FalconGuides, and Outfit Your Mind are registered trademarks of Morris Book Publishing, LLC.
All photographs by Donna Lynn Ikenberry.

Maps: Alena Joy Pearce © Morris Book Publishing, LLC
Project editor: Julie Marsh
Layout: Maggie Peterson

Library of Congress Cataloging-in-Publication Data
Ikenberry, Donna Lynn.
        Camping Utah / Donna Lynn Ikenberry.—1st ed.
                 p. cm.—(A Falcon guide)
        ISBN 978-0-7627-1080-5
1.Camping—Utah—Guidebooks. 2. Camp sites, facilities, etc.—Utah—Directories. 3. Utah—Guidebooks.
I. Title. II. Series
GV1991.42.U8 I54 2001
647.9792.09.025—dc21

                                       2001040721

ISBN 978-0-7627-8353-3

For my husband, Mike Vining,
my brother, Don Ikenberry, and my sister-in-law, Yolie Gutierrez

Contents

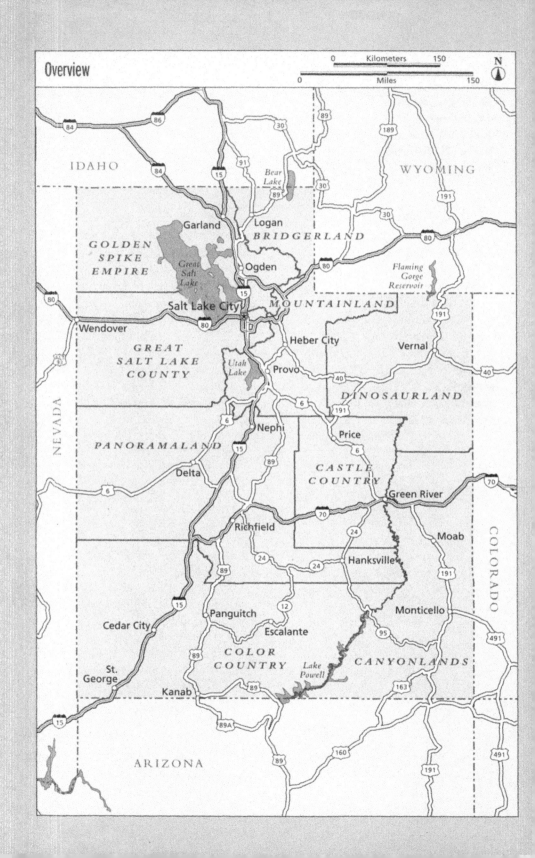

Acknowledgments

One of the best things about writing a book is being able to dedicate it to someone special. In this case, I'm dedicating my book to the two awesome men in my life, my husband, Mike Vining, and my brother, Don Ikenberry, and my sister-in-law, Yolie Gutierrez.

Both Mike and Don are amazing men. Mike is my soul mate, my best friend, my favorite traveling companion. Mike was with me as I checked out every Utah campground. He not only joined me on every occasion, but he chauffeured me around, driving thousands of miles, while I took notes, planned our routes, and put this book together.

Though Don wasn't there checking out campgrounds with me, he has always been the most supportive, loving brother. He and I have always been close, but we attained a new closeness when we took care of our dad during his final days on Earth. We both miss him so very much. Don's wife, Yolie, is the "sister" I never had. Don and Yolie are an amazing couple. We laugh a lot as they are always fun to be around. I couldn't love them more.

When I wrote the first edition of *Camping Utah*, my parents, Donald and Beverly Ikenberry, were alive and well and I talked to them daily. I always felt blessed by their endless love and support. My parents passed away in recent years and I miss them daily.

My family has gotten a lot bigger since I met and married Mike in 1999. Mike's mom, Arlene Vining, passed away more than a decade ago, but not before I got to know and love her. I am grateful for Mike's dad, Roger Vining, who is always positive and happy. I am grateful for my two stepdaughters, my six grandchildren, my two brothers-in-law, and their wives as well.

Additional thanks go to the folks at the USDA Forest Service, the Bureau of Land Management, the Bureau of Reclamation, the Utah State Parks Department, and the National Park Service, who so patiently answered my questions. I also want to thank the state of Utah for granting us free day-use entry to all of its state parks.

And of course, I am also indebted to Imee Curiel, Julie Marsh, and Ann Seifert at Globe Pequot Press for their help and support.

A nice hike leads to Morning Glory Bridge, located near Moab.

Introduction

When I originally said yes to writing a guide to Utah's public campgrounds in 1999, both disappointment and elation welled up inside me at the same time. Why? I was disappointed because I had told myself I'd take a break from writing books. I had spent every summer since 1986 working on either a new book or a book revision, and I felt as though I needed a break.

At the same time I was thrilled at the prospect of spending time in Utah, because it was a state I'd left pretty much unexplored. For years I had wanted to see the region, to get to know it intimately. I wanted to say I'd actually lived in the state for a few months.

I signed the contract knowing I would be driving thousands of miles over the period of a few months, but I also knew I'd spend time exploring the region both on foot and by bicycle. Utah is an outdoor enthusiast's paradise, and I knew I'd have to get off the beaten path on a regular basis. What I didn't know was that I would enter the state with my very own chauffeur and personal rock climbing guide.

A couple of months before arriving in Utah, Mike Vining and I got married on top of Mauna Kea, the highest point in Hawaii. We like to say we are on a fifty-year honeymoon, so I suppose you could say we spent the first part of that honeymoon in Utah, climbing magnificent rock, hiking many a trail, riding our bicycles both off and on the road, and observing wildlife. We checked out all of Utah's campgrounds together, with Mike doing more than just the driving—he checked out many a toilet for me, too.

Am I glad I made the decision to go ahead and write this book? I am. In fact, I wouldn't have missed it for anything.

Utah was all I had imagined and a whole lot more. A potpourri of landscapes, the Beehive State affords everything from world-famous redrock canyons to heaven-bound mountains, elaborate river systems, lonely desert, fertile valleys, and a maze of rock spires and pinnacles just waiting to be explored.

When my book came up for revision in 2013, Mike and I headed back to Utah, spending a total of two and a half months in this lovely state. We rechecked campgrounds, added some new ones to the list, deleted some that had closed, and took all new photographs. In addition to camping we spent time hiking and mountain biking, as well as kayaking, and while exploring we learned about the state all over again.

Several thousand years ago the place we today know as Utah was inhabited by nomadic desert peoples. About AD 1300 the Ancestral Puebloan Culture reached its peak; later, Native American tribes, including the Ute, Paiute, and Gosiute, lived here when early Spanish explorers happened upon the region. Once claimed by Mexico, in 1847 it was chosen by the members of the Church of Jesus Christ of Latter-day Saints, or Mormons, as a refuge from persecution. The Mormons lived in isolation until Utah became part of the United States in 1848 via the Treaty of Guadalupe Hidalgo, which ended the Mexican War.

The state is composed of portions of three major natural regions, or physiographic provinces: the Basin and Range Province (also known as the Great Basin), the Middle Rocky Mountains or Rocky Mountain Province, and the Colorado Plateau.

The Basin and Range Province covers about one-third of Utah. A region of shimmering white salt flats, gray plains, and high mountains, here rivers terminate not at the sea but in the Great Salt Lake Desert or the Great Salt Lake.

Utah's northeastern mountain ranges consist of the Uinta and the Wasatch Ranges. The Wasatch is known for its majestic granite peaks, its glacier-carved valleys, and its endless glacial lakes. The Uintas are older and one of the few major ranges in the Rocky Mountains that stretch in an east-to-west direction. The highest point, Kings Peak, is also, at 13,528 feet, the highest point in the state. The highest points in the Wasatch Range are Mount Timpanogos (11,750 feet) and Mount Nebo (11,877 feet). Given these facts it's easy to see how Utah got its name. The state's moniker comes from a Native American word meaning "those who dwell high up" or "mountain dwellers."

The Colorado Plateau is a rainbow of colors and unique physical characteristics. Here, uplifted plateaus rise to more than 11,000 feet. Carved by rivers and eroded by wind and water, there are hundreds of canyons garnished in yellows, purples, reds, and pinks. The Colorado River snakes through these colorful canyons, as do the Green River and some of the Colorado's other tributaries.

The Great Salt Lake is the largest and most famous lake in Utah. With several times more saline than the oceans, it is the largest inland body of salt water in North America. It is also the largest remnant of Lake Bonneville, which in prehistoric times blanketed much of Utah and Nevada.

Utah is a land of extremes—even the climate varies dramatically. The valleys and plateaus are hot and dry in summer, and in winter they are usually dry as well. The climate is pretty mild in the south and cold in the north. As you might expect, the mountains are cooler and receive more precipitation. Most of Utah claims an annual precipitation of 8 to 16 inches, though the Great Salt Lake Desert boasts 5 inches annually. The mountains average about 40 inches of precipitation a year, with most of it falling in the form of heavy winter snow. Snow in the Wasatch Mountains can be particularly heavy, with single storms dumping several feet. Annual snowfall can reach 30 feet. In summer local thunderstorms often drop enormous quantities of rain, creating flash floods.

Forests cover about one-fifth of Utah. The southwestern corner of the state is blanketed with desert plants such as the Joshua tree, mesquite, a variety of cacti, and creosote bush. Sagebrush, greasewood, and bluegrass are the most common plants in the canyon section of the Colorado Plateau. Adding color to the scene are prickly pear and Indian paintbrush.

Open woodlands cover the foothills and lower slopes up to about 7,000 feet. A potpourri of Rocky Mountain and Utah junipers, as well as pinyon trees and quaking aspens, is also found in scattered groves at about the same elevation. Mountain mahogany and Gambel oak are common, too. Along streams look for willows, mountain alder, dogwood, and box elder.

Conifer forests consist of lodgepole pine and ponderosa pine, along with aspen, Douglas fir, and limber pine. Higher up you'll find Engelmann spruce, subalpine fir, and white fir. Ironically, the Colorado, or blue spruce, which happens to be the state tree, is not a Utah native. As you travel through the forests, you'll notice that many trees are dying due to a pine beetle epidemic. Unfortunately, trees are dying throughout the Rocky Mountain region. Use care when traveling in the forest and do not camp near dead trees.

Hosting an abundance of colorful wildflowers in spring and summer, Utah is home year-round to a number of large mammals. These include mule deer, elk, moose, pronghorn, bison, black bears, Rocky Mountain bighorns, Rocky Mountain goats, and cougars. Smaller mammals include Canada lynx, bobcat, foxes (gray, red, and kit), coyotes, badgers, beavers, otters, raccoons, mink, ringtails, weasels, and martens, as well as prairie dogs, rabbits, squirrels, skunks, and porcupines.

North American beavers are always a treat to see while camping.

Reptiles are plentiful in the plateau areas of the state. In addition to two poisonous snakes—the western rattlesnake and the sidewinder—there are garter snakes, coachwhip snakes, and yellow-belly racers. The only poisonous lizard in the United States, the Gila monster, is found in southwestern Utah. Other reptiles include the horned and collared lizards and the desert tortoise.

There are seventeen kinds of toads, frogs, and salamanders in Utah. One of my favorites is the boreal toad, which is sometimes found up in the high country. Actually, they live in a variety of habitats, including ponds, lakes, meadows, woodlands, wetlands, even desert springs.

Utah's birdlife is stunning, especially in spring and fall when migratory birds pass through. Then, bird observers may see both the Canada and snow goose, and a variety of ducks, such as the redhead, canvasback, mallard, pintail, and shoveler. A number of waterbirds breed on Great Salt Lake islands, including the white pelican, the snowy egret, the double-crested cormorant, the green heron, and the white-faced ibis.

Game birds are sought after by hunters and birders alike. While you're out and about, look for ring-necked pheasants, both California and Gambel's quail, mourning doves, chukars, and both sage and ruffed grouse. Protected by law, there are both golden and bald eagles in the mountainous areas. Fifty-five species of fish are found in Utah's lakes and streams. The most popular game fish are brook, rainbow, brown, and cutthroat trout, as well as smallmouth and largemouth bass.

Obviously, Utah has an abundance of natural gifts to offer both visitors and those who live here. Fortunately, there are 329 public campgrounds from which to enjoy the wide variety of flora, fauna, wonderful vistas, and multitude of outdoor activities. Happy camping!

How to Use This Guide

This book was written with you, the camping enthusiast, in mind.

To keep this book as up to date as possible, I invite you to tell me about those campgrounds that we may have missed. I'd also appreciate knowing about any new campgrounds, and about those that may have been improved or have deteriorated. If any have closed, I'd like to know that, too. Please send your comments and suggestions to Donna Ikenberry, c/o Globe Pequot Press, PO Box 480, Guilford, CT 06437.

Choosing a Campground

Utah is a big place, with 329 public campgrounds to help you explore it. The campgrounds are managed by a number of agencies. Of the 329 campgrounds, 190 are managed by the USDA Forest Service and 44 are Utah state park campgrounds; the Bureau of Land Management cares for another 46. In addition, there are 40 national park, national monument, and national recreation area campgrounds, as well as 9 county and city campgrounds.

The Utah Department of Tourism has divided the state into nine travel regions. It's a good format, one that works; thus I've used the same travel regions to help you locate and select a campground in the area of your choice. These nine areas are known as Bridgerland, the Golden Spike Empire, Great Salt Lake Country, Mountainland, Dinosaurland, Panoramaland, Castle Country, Color Country, and Canyonlands.

For each chapter or area, I've included a map of the travel region, as well as a summary introducing you to the area. And of course, all of the public campgrounds found there are described as well.

Each campground description includes information on location, detailed instructions as to how to get there, number of sites, whether or not they can be reserved, cost, contact information, activities, and more. Read on for a better understanding of the information provided within some of these categories.

Location. The location gives the approximate site of the campground.

GPS. Global positioning system coordinates are provided for each campground. The GPS unit derives coordinate positions from satellites. These can be listed in degrees, minutes, and seconds, or the more common method written in decimal minutes. Descriptions in this book are written in decimal minutes. If you don't own a GPS, don't worry: You do not need a GPS to visit or locate any of these campgrounds.

Facilities. This includes everything from fire pits and water to toilets, showers, boat ramps, dump stations, and any other amenities worthy of notice.

Sites. Sites are listed as the number of basic sites found in each area. If there are double sites, triple sites, and group sites available, then those are listed as well. If hookups, both partial and full, are available, then those are also mentioned.

Sunset near Dead Horse Point (site 286)

Maximum RV length. Unless otherwise noted, this is the total length of the RV itself. If it is listed as "30 feet," that means a 30-foot motor home, a 30-foot travel trailer, or a 30-foot fifth-wheel trailer would fit in the space. In one case—Natural Bridges National Monument—the maximum length allowed is the combined length of both the tow vehicle and the trailer.

Fee. Because fees change from year to year, I have opted to use the following price-range code for one night's stay, based on 2013 prices:

$ = for campsites costing $10 or less

$$ = for campsites costing $11 to $20

$$$ = for campsites costing $21 to 30

$$$$ = for campsites costing $31 to $40

$$$$$ = for campsites costing $41 and higher

Many public campgrounds offer a reduced rate for folks with either an Access Pass or a Senior Pass. (Please note that none of Utah's state parks offers such a reduction.) An Access Pass is a free lifetime entrance pass available to citizens or permanent residents of the United States, regardless of age, who have been determined to be blind or permanently disabled. A Senior Pass is a lifetime entrance pass for those age 62 or older. It has a one-time processing charge of $10. Both passes also provide a 50 percent discount on federal use fees charged for facilities and services such as camping, swimming, parking, boat launching, or cave tours. They do not cover or reduce special recreation permit fees or fees charged by concessionaires. Half-price camping fees are available for basic or individual sites only; half-price camping is not available for double, triple, or group sites.

Maximum stay. Campers must limit their stay to the maximum number of days.

Road conditions. Road surfaces range from paved to gravel to dirt.

Management: The management agency the campground falls under, whether it is the state park service, forest service, etc., that maintains the grounds.

Reservations. If reservations are accepted, you'll find a number listed for you to call, or a website so you can go online to make reservations. Making reservations is a good idea, especially during the peak summer months, weekends, and holidays. Additional fees are required for reservations so it makes a campground stay more costly, but it ensures you of a place to camp, too.

Activities. I've listed popular activities to be enjoyed at each campground. Some offer nothing more than a nice place to relax and picnic, while others abound with opportunities for rock climbing, hiking, backpacking, boating, kayaking, canoeing, mountain biking, fishing, golfing, horseback riding, off-highway driving, and much more. In fact, geocaching, a fun activity for the whole family, is also available in some of Utah's state parks.

Season. A season is listed when there is one, though you should know that most of the campgrounds open when conditions allow it. If a campground that usually opens by Memorial Day is buried under 4 feet of snow one year, it will open at a later date than usual. On the other hand, if early snow falls in a region that is normally open until the end of October, you may find campgrounds there closed earlier than usual.

Finding the campground. Use these directions in conjunction with a detailed state map or the appropriate forest service or Bureau of Land Management map to find the sites. *The Utah Atlas & Gazetteer* by DeLorme was especially useful to us as we toured around the state.

About the campground: In this section you will learn all you need to know about what you will find in the campground and in the vicinity. It is an expansion on and elaboration of the activities listed earlier, as well as special notes so that you have a good idea of what to expect if you choose this campground. I have also tried to list anything that is accessible to people with disabilities, whether it is the toilet, campsite, or other amenities such as a fishing pier or picnic area.

Camping Utah Amenities Charts

Use the amenities charts to quickly find the campground that is right for you. Categories denote the availability of group sites, hookup sites, showers, drinking water, and dump stations. You'll also learn the total number of sites at each campground, the maximum length RV allowed, the kinds of toilets found there, and whether or not there are wheelchair-accessible sites. In addition, campers can quickly find out what kinds of recreation are enjoyed in each area, fee information, and whether or not a site can be reserved. A description of some of these categories follows.

Goblin Valley is an excellent place to camp and explore.

Hookups. When available, these are listed using the following code:
W = Water, E = Electric, and S = Sewer.

Toilets. These are also listed by code: F = Flush, V = Vault, and C = Chemical.

Drinking water. Water is always listed where available, but you should know that if water is available one week it may not be the next. Why? Because it may pass water-quality tests on one occasion, only to fail the next time around. Also, water is turned off in many areas in winter, so early- or late-season visitors may find it unavailable. Streams or creeks often flow through Utah's campgrounds: Be sure to treat such water before using it.

Recreation. Outdoor activities are listed by code: H = Hiking, C = Rock Climbing, M = Mountain Biking, S = Swimming, F = Fishing, B = Boating, L = Boat Launch, O = Off-highway Driving, R = Horseback Riding, K = Kayaking and Canoeing, and G = Golf.

On a Special Note

- Fireworks (firecrackers, rockets, or other explosives) are not allowed on national forest system land due to fire hazard. It is illegal to possess or ignite any type of firework on national forest system land. This includes sparklers.

- Discharge or use of firearms and other weapons are prohibited in campgrounds.

- Though I didn't list each specifically, many campgrounds do sell firewood. Firewood collecting is prohibited in many areas; besides, it's really best to leave the natural resources alone. Please plan on bringing your own firewood or buying some.

- In most campgrounds vehicles must be parked on roads or designated parking spurs only.

- Occupancy limits vary from campground to campground. Some may have a limit of one family or a total of ten people per single unit, and two families or twenty people per double unit. Please stick to the regulations for each individual campground.

- In some areas of Utah, particularly the Colorado Plateau, you'll find cryptobiotic crust covering the soil. A thin, dark organism, it blankets the arid landscape in preparation for future plant communities. Its crusty, lumpy top is born from a unification of mosses, algae, lichens, and fungi. The crusts can take a century to develop and mere seconds to destroy. Step on a crust and it'll be pulverized into dust. Please do not step on the crust—stay on trails or rocks instead.

- Dogs are allowed in most campgrounds, but there are some that prohibit them. Dogs should always be kept quiet, and they should always be on a leash and never allowed to chase the local wildlife. Campers need to clean up after their dogs, too.

- Generators should be used sparingly and never during quiet hours. Some campgrounds have certain times for generator use. Please obey the rules.

Playing in the Outdoors

A great outdoor experience can be had by just about anyone, but those who respect and appreciate the out-of-doors seem to gain a whole lot more from the encounter. Please do not leave garbage at your campsite (or on the trail), do not destroy the toilets that are there for our use, and remember: When you are out and about, take only pictures, leave only footprints. Do this, and you'll leave a treasure for future generations to enjoy.

Preparation

Some of the campgrounds in this guide are located off well-maintained, well-traveled paved roads. A cell phone is probably all you need in an emergency. But you should know that there are also campgrounds in more remote areas—places out of cell-phone range, where another car may pass by only rarely. For this reason you should make sure that your vehicle's tires and engine are in good shape. You'll want to top off the gas tank when leaving civilization for long, and you'll want to carry emergency vehicle gear. A jack and all the necessities for changing a flat tire are essential; you'll also want jumper cables, spare belts, and, when you're in snow country, tire chains (a must). Mike and I also carry a shovel and an axe. If a tree falls and blocks the road, we can cut the tree and keep going.

If you have your camping gear and food with you, you'll have fewer things to worry about should you break down in the boondocks. When traveling in remote areas, always carry food, water, a sleeping bag or blankets, matches, a flashlight, and a first-aid kit. Most important, if you'll be away for a while, notify friends or family of your intended destination and time of return.

Camping

Low-impact camping is a necessity, whether you are camping in the wilderness or at a developed campground like the ones found in this guide. If trash pickup isn't available—and it's not at many campgrounds—then always pack out what you brought in. If you build a campfire, conserve on wood, and keep it small. Of course, you should heed all regulations regarding wood gathering, fires, and smoking.

Once you choose a campsite, keep it neat and tidy. If you find trash around the site, pick it up and pack it out. If you have a pet, keep it on a leash and keep it quiet. Do not let it roam around, bothering others. It's important to respect those who are in the surrounding sites. If you need to hear music, keep it low. If you want to walk around, stay on main pathways—do not cut across your neighbor's site.

All food should be stored in closed containers, inside your vehicle. Bears are smart critters, and in some places they've been known to recognize an ice chest. If there are smart bears around your area, cover the coolers so they are not visible.

Arch from Arches Trail

Although some campgrounds offer showers, many do not. If you need to wash off, do so away from natural bodies of water, such as lakes or streams. You should also bathe away from the drinking-water spigots in the campground. A plastic bucket or a black shower bag is good for bathing.

Most public campgrounds have stay limits that range from a few days to a month or so, with the average stay being around fourteen days. Please adhere to the limit and plan your stay accordingly.

Getting Ready to Enjoy the Great Outdoors

When I'm out hiking a trail or rock climbing or mountain biking, I often see folks who've forgotten a few of the basics—things like food and water and maybe even a jacket or some other piece of warm clothing. Certainly by the end of their recreational pursuit, they must be thinking that being outdoors isn't any fun at all.

To best enjoy and savor the day, always bring water on a hike; a few snacks or a lunch will be handy, too. Also, it is best to dress in layers of clothing. Don't don a T-shirt and then throw on a big parka. Instead dress in layers, wearing a breathable fabric next to your skin. Fleece is a nice second layer, with a breathable, rainproof jacket and pants for outerwear. Footwear depends on the activities you enjoy. Walking

RV passing through tunnel near Red Canyon

shoes are fine for short trails, but if you are going to be taking long hikes, hiking boots will offer more protection. They are also more comfortable.

If you will be hiking, mountain biking, or rock climbing, and you'll be away from your vehicle for any length of time, a small day pack should provide room enough for a few necessities such as money, keys, sunglasses, a map, water, snacks, a camera, binoculars, and a lightweight jacket. Longer trips will require more gear and a bigger pack.

Safety

Nature is unpredictable; thus you always need to use common sense and good judgment when spending time in the outdoors. If you leave your campsite to spend time in the backcountry, you are taking some risks, but you will reap riches beyond measure. Besides, the drive from your home to the campground was probably even more of a risk!

Hypothermia. Hypothermia occurs when you lose body heat faster than you can generate it, resulting in a decline in core body temperature. Common causes are exposure to cold, physical exhaustion, and too little food intake. Contributing factors may include exposure to wind, rain, or snow; dehydration; wearing damp or wet clothing; and prolonged inactivity.

The best treatment for hypothermia is prevention. Wear layers of clothing, stripping them off before you break a sweat and adding them to keep out the cold. Snack throughout the day on high-energy foods such as fruit, granola, trail mix, soup, and sandwiches. Drink plenty of fluids to prevent dehydration.

If someone in your hiking party is suffering from hypothermia, stop and get that person dry and warm. Hot fluids can help restore body heat. If the patient is unconscious, try zipping two sleeping bags together and have two helpers lie with the patient, one on either side. Do not give liquids to a person who is unconscious.

Heat exhaustion. Exposure to hot ambient air temperatures, when combined with too much sun or strenuous exercise, will lead to an elevated body temperature. Protect yourself from overheating by wearing a hat or draping a wet bandanna over your head and the back of your neck. Water intake is the most important factor in preventing heat-related illnesses. The human body doesn't signal that it's thirsty until it's too late. An adult may need a gallon and a half of water a day when exercising in hot weather. Drink plenty of water before you get thirsty, and drink frequently. Plain water is best, though electrolyte-replacement drinks are effective in extremely hot weather or during strenuous activity. Do not take salt tablets.

Lightning. Take extra precautions when dealing with stormy skies. According to the National Oceanic and Atmospheric Association (NOAA), about 300 people in the United States die each year from lightning strikes. Many more are injured, some permanently. To avoid being struck by a lightning bolt, watch the weather. Spring and summer are the busiest seasons for lightning, though discharges can occur any time of year, even during snowstorms. Most lightning storms occur in mid- to late afternoon. Storms are usually preceded by wind and the approach of dark, towering clouds. Lightning may travel far ahead of the storm.

If you're out hiking, seek shelter away from open ground or exposed ridges. Dropping even a few yards off a ridgetop will reduce your risk. In the forest stay away from single, tall trees. On open ground find a low spot free of standing water. Stay out of shallow caves, crevasses, or overhangs. During a lightning storm assume a low crouch with only your feet touching the ground. Put a sleeping pad or pack (be sure it has no frame or other metal in it) beneath your feet for added insulation against shock. Do not huddle together; members of a group should stay at least 30 feet apart. This way, if someone is hit, the others can give CPR and first aid for burns and shock.

In a tent get in the crouch position. Stay in your sleeping bag and keep your feet on a sleeping pad. Signs of an imminent lightning strike include hair standing on end; an itchy feeling—one hiker described it as "bugs crawling all over"—on your skin; an acrid, "hot metal" smell; and buzzing or crackling noises in the air. Tuck into a crouch immediately if any of these signs are present.

Bears. What should you do if you meet a black bear on the trail? Most bears will detect you before you ever detect them, and will leave the area. If you do meet a bear before it has had time to leave, stay calm. Talk aloud to let the bear know that you are present, and back away slowly, facing the animal all the while. Avoid direct eye contact, which bears may perceive as a threat. Give the bear plenty of room to escape; if you're on a trail, step off the path on the downhill side. Then slowly leave the area. Don't run—this will prompt the bear to chase you. Besides, you can't outrun a bear. There's no sense in trying.

Water. By now most backcountry visitors have heard about the protozoan Giardia lamblia. It won't kill you, but in some cases you may wish it had. Symptoms include severe abdominal cramps, gas and bloating, loss of appetite, and acute diarrhea. Fortunately, not all water is contaminated, but you can't tell by looking. No matter how pure the water looks, never drink from any spring, stream, river, or lake without treating the water first. It's better to be safe than sick.

There are several methods for treating water. First, you can boil all water—a good method if you want hot drinks or a boiled dinner, but a lousy idea if you need a cool drink right away. At altitudes below 4,000 feet, boiling for a minimum of one minute should suffice. Add several minutes of boiling time for higher altitudes; experts recommend a minimum of five minutes anywhere in Utah, due to high elevation. Increase time for very high elevations or whenever the water is cloudy or muddy. Some hikers find a water purifier more convenient. This is the method I use: Run water through the purifier and it's ready to drink. In emergencies, commercial water purification chemicals will do.

Altitude or mountain sickness. Altitude or mountain sickness can be a problem for some campers. It usually takes about two or three days to acclimatize to high altitude. If you or someone in your party feels a bit nauseated or dizzy, or experiences a headache or loss of appetite, you'll all need to stop and rest. Drink water, and make sure to get plenty of sodium and high-energy foods. If symptoms don't go away, your only option is to descend to a lower elevation where there's more oxygen. Never ascend if you are suffering from mountain sickness.

Biting insects. Ticks themselves are harmless, but the diseases they carry can be deadly—including Lyme disease, Colorado tick fever, and Rocky Mountain spotted fever. After traveling in tick country, watch for symptoms of tickborne disease, including a high fever, arthritis-like pain in the bones and joints, or a rash. During tick season (spring and summer), stay out of tall grass or brushy areas, and inspect yourself and clothing after each outing. Look for ticks nightly before going to bed. Carefully inspect legs, groin, armpits, ears, and scalp.

To remove a loose tick, flick it off with a fingernail. If the tick is firmly embedded in your skin, use tweezers to pinch a small area around its mouth and pull it out. (You may have to remove a tiny chunk of skin to get all of the tick.) Try not to squeeze the tick's body, since this increases the risk of infection. Clean the wound with an antiseptic.

Mosquitoes are more of a nuisance than a danger. Most North American mosquitoes can transmit a form of encephalitis, however, which is potentially fatal. The best way to avoid mosquito-borne diseases is to avoid being bitten. Bug sprays with N, N-diethyl-3-methylbenzamide (DEET) work well, but there are more natural sprays and creams as well. Wear long pants, a long-sleeved shirt, ankle-high shoes, and a cap that covers your ears. Try not to camp near stagnant water or fields of damp or dewy grass.

Map Legend

══80══	Interstate Highway
══91══	US Highway
══24══	State Highway
— - — - —	State Border
————	Region Boundary
⬤	Body of Water
▭	National Forest
▭	National Park

✳	Capital
○	City/Town
❶	Camping Locator

Bridgerland

Located in Utah's Rocky Mountain Province, Bridgerland is situated smack dab in the north-central part of the state. Bordered on the north and east by the neighboring states of Idaho and Wyoming, respectively, it is also flanked on the west by the Golden Spike Empire travel region and on the south by the travel region known as Mountainland.

A photographer's delight, Bridgerland is a place of unparalleled beauty, a place where anglers fly fish "blue-ribbon" streams and folks come to canoe along the Bear River. In addition, rock climbers come to scale various routes in Logan Canyon, while mountain bikers and hikers hit some of the area trails, and birders and scuba divers explore the lovely domain of Bear Lake.

Bridgerland is the smallest of Utah's nine travel regions—a mere 2,205 square miles. Even so, the place is packed with campgrounds, offering a total of eighteen sites for visitors to stay at and enjoy. Encompassing both Rich and Cache Counties, a potpourri of sites exists in places like the Uinta-Wasatch-Cache National Forest, both Hyrum and Bear Lake State Parks, and Birch Creek, a Bureau of Land Management site.

At Bear Lake State Park, campgrounds on the south and east sides of the natural lake make sailing, swimming, and scuba diving easily accessible. And in winter, ice fishing for the unique Bonneville cisco is popular. The lake is known as the Caribbean of the Rockies for its lovely turquoise-blue water; you may be tempted to ask the locals if they put blue dye in Bear Lake. Of course, residents will tell you that the unique color isn't caused by a dye. Instead, light rays reflect off limestone particles suspended in the water, changing the lake to random shades of blue.

The lake boasts year-round fun. Typical spring weather offers up migrating birds, while summer brings boaters and scuba divers. The raspberry harvest occurs in August, with a rodeo, a parade, and fireworks to celebrate the annual event. Bear Lake Raspberry Days are usually held the first week of August. In fall you can enjoy foliage colors at their best, while winter offers snowmobiling and skiing through miles of famous Utah powder snow.

Hyrum Lake State Park is a popular place, too. The Little Bear River supplies the 450-acre reservoir, where water sports and fishing are big attractions. Visitors can also enjoy a few sandy beaches, though there are no lifeguards. During freeze-up, from about the middle of December through late March, some visitors fish through the ice, while others ice skate or sail their iceboats across the lake.

1

Several campgrounds are situated near the community of Logan, known for its music festivals and high-quality arts. In July and August the Utah Festival Opera Company performs in the beautifully restored Ellen Eccles Theatre, while the Utah Music Festival brings chamber music to the area from late June through August. In addition, summer visitors find a bevy of musicals, comedies, and dramas in the historic Old Lyric Repertory Theatre in downtown Logan.

Logan Canyon is a delight, a place that could take days to explore. In fact, during our first visit my husband and I spent three days driving what for many is less than a 1-hour drive. US 89 meanders more than 20 miles into the Bear River Range, a northern branch of the Wasatch Mountains. The route is particularly beautiful in fall, when the colors are vibrant and photogenic.

For more information contact Bridgerland Travel Region, 160 N. Main St., Logan; (801) 752-2161 or (800) 882-4433; http://utahtravelcenter.com/travelregions /bridgerland.htm.

		Total Sites	Group Sites	Hook-up Sites	Hookups	Max. RV Length	Dump Station	Toilets	Showers	Drinking Water	ADA Compliant	Fees	Reservations	Recreation
1	Hyrum Lake State Park	34	1	9	WE	Any	•	F	•	•	•	$$-$$$$$	•	FSBLK
2	Pioneer	18				20		V		•		$$		FHRO
3	Friendship	6	1			None		V				$-$$$$$	•	FHRO
4	Spring	3				None		V				$		F
5	Bridger	10				20		F		•		$$		CHMF
6	Spring Hollow	15	2			20		V		•		$$-$$$$$	•	CHMF
7	Guinavah-Malibu	43	3			25		F		•		$$-$$$$$	•	CHMF
8	Preston Valley	6				20		F		•		$$		CMF
9	Lodge	10				20		V		•		$$		CMFO
10	Wood Camp	6				20		V				$$-$$$$		CMHF
11	Lewis M. Turner	10				20		F				$$		M
12	Tony Grove Lake	40				30		V			•	$$-$$$$	•	HFR
13	Red Banks	12				20		V		•		$$		HFM
14	Sunrise	27				25		V		•		$$	•	
15	Rendezvous Beach	147	4	106	WES	Any	•	F	•	•	•	$$-$$$$$	•	FSBLK
16	Eastside	101	2			Any		V		•		$-$$$$$	•	FBSLK
17	Birch Creek	*				20		V				None		F
18	Monte Cristo	47	2			25/45		V		•		$$-$$$$$	•	HMO

Hookup: W = Water, E = Electric, S = Sewer   * = Dispersed Camping, no designated sites
Recreation: H = Hiking, C = Rock Climbing, M = Mountain Biking, S = Swimming, F = Fishing, B = Boating, L = Boat Launch, O = Off-highway Driving, R = Horseback Riding, K = Kayaking and Canoeing, G = Golf
Toilets: F = Flush, V = Vault, C = Chemical
Per-night campsite cost: $ = $10 or less $$ = $11 to $20 $$$ = $21 to 30 $$$$ = $31 to $40 $$$$$ = $41 and higher

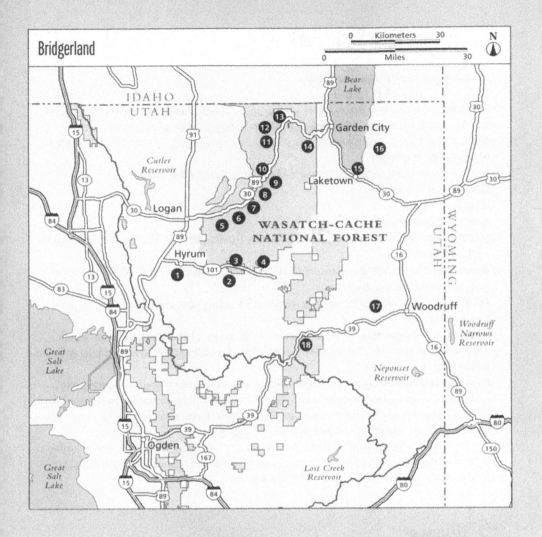

1 Hyrum Lake State Park

Location: Just south of downtown Hyrum
GPS: N41 37.669'/W111 51.994'
Facilities: Fire pits, picnic tables, partial hookups, flush toilets, showers, drinking water, dump station, boat ramps and docks, ADA sites, plus volleyball and horseshoes for the group site
Sites: 22 basic sites, 9 partial-hookup sites, 1 group site (maximum 100 people), and 2 cabins
Maximum RV length: Any
Fee: $$ for basic and partial-hookup sites; $$$$$ for group site and cabins
Maximum stay: 14 days
Elevation: 4,700 feet
Road conditions: Paved
Management: Hyrum State Park, 405 W. 300 South, Hyrum; (435) 245-6866; http://stateparks .utah.gov/parks/hyrum
Reservations: In the Salt Lake area, call (801) 322-3770; elsewhere, (800) 322-3770; http:// utahstateparks.reserveamerica.com
Activities: Fishing, swimming, boating, waterskiing, ice skating, and picnicking
Season: Year-round
Finding the campground: From the junction of UT 101 and UT 165 at the east end of Hyrum, drive west on UT 101 for 1.7 miles, then turn left (south) onto 400 West; you'll reach the entrance station in another 0.4 mile.
About the campground: Nestled in Cache Valley, a scenic mountain valley, and located on the south shore of Hyrum Lake, this year-round park offers the usual summer activities plus ice fishing for trout and yellow perch in winter. Lake View Campground is located along the south shore of the lake. Maple trees, willows, and pines shade the wide, graveled sites.

The 400-plus-acre reservoir provides an abundance of recreational opportunities. In addition to boating and swimming, visitors will enjoy the many bird species found here, including grebes, egrets, herons, pelicans, and an assortment of songbirds.

2 Pioneer

Location: In the Uinta-Wasatch-Cache National Forest, about 8 miles east of Hyrum
GPS: N41 37.690'/W111 41.578'
Facilities: Fire pits, picnic tables, drinking water, and vault toilets
Sites: 18 basic sites
Maximum RV length: 20 feet
Fee: $$ for basic sites
Maximum stay: 7 days
Elevation: 5,200 feet
Road conditions: Paved to the campground, then gravel

Management: Logan Ranger District, 1500 E. Hwy. 89, Logan; (435) 755-3620; www.fs.usda .gov/main/uwcnf/home
Reservations: None
Activities: Fishing and picnicking; opportunities for hiking, horseback riding, and off-roading nearby
Restrictions: ATVs not allowed
Season: May through October
Finding the campground: From the junction of UT 165 and UT 101 on the east edge of Hyrum, drive paved UT 101, also called Blacksmith Fork Canyon Road, east for 8 miles.
About the campground: An assortment of miniature roses, box elders, willows, and maple trees serves to decorate this lush campground. Located along the Blacksmith Fork, it's a good place for trout fishing or a picnic. Although 20-foot RVs are allowed, please note that the only turnaround is located to the left (south), where you'll find sites 6 through 15.

3 Friendship

Location: In the Uinta-Wasatch-Cache National Forest, about 11 miles east of Hyrum
GPS: N41 39.670' / W111 39.905'
Facilities: Fire pits, picnic tables, and vault toilets; no garbage service (pack it out)
Sites: 5 basic sites and 1 group site (maximum 25 people)
Maximum RV length: None (trailers not recommended due to rough road; best for tents and truck campers)
Fee: $ for basic sites; $$$$$ for group site
Maximum stay: 7 days
Elevation: 5,600 feet
Road conditions: Gravel
Management: Logan Ranger District, 1500 E. Hwy. 89, Logan; (435) 755-3620; www.fs.usda .gov/main/uwcnf/home
Reservations: For the group site only, call (877) 444-6777 or TDD (877) 883-6777; www .recreation.gov
Activities: Fishing and picnicking; hiking, horseback riding, and ATVing nearby
Season: May through October
Finding the campground: From the junction of UT 165 and UT 101 on the east edge of Hyrum, head east on paved UT 101, also called Blacksmith Fork Canyon Road. Travel 7.2 miles to a gravel road heading north and then east up the Left Fork Blacksmith Fork Canyon. There are signs for both the Friendship and Spring Campgrounds along the way. (**Note:** The road is very rough and not advisable for trailers.) You'll reach the campground after 3.6 miles.
About the campground: Shady sites rest along the Left Fork Blacksmith Fork, offering a place to enjoy some trout fishing and have a picnic under the maple trees. Sites are small, so tents and vans are best.

4 Spring

Location: In the Uinta-Wasatch-Cache National Forest, approximately 12 miles east of Hyrum
GPS: N41 39.725'/W111 39.244'
Facilities: Fire pits, picnic tables, and vault toilets
Sites: 3 basic sites
Maximum RV length: None (RVs not recommended)
Fee: $ for basic sites
Maximum stay: 7 days
Elevation: 5,500 feet
Road conditions: Gravel
Management: Logan Ranger District, 1500 E. Hwy. 89, Logan; (435) 755-3620; www.fs.usda
.gov/main/uwcnf/home
Reservations: None
Activities: Fishing and picnicking
Season: May through October
Finding the campground: From the junction of UT 165 and UT 101 on the east edge of Hyrum, head east on paved UT 101, also called Blacksmith Fork Canyon Road. Travel 7.2 miles to a gravel road heading north and then east up the Left Fork Blacksmith Fork Canyon. There are signs for both the Spring and Friendship Campgrounds along the way. (**Note:** The road is very rough and not advisable for trailers.) You'll reach the campground after 4.5 miles.
About the campground: Small sites, best for tents, are shaded with maples and box elders, while the Left Fork Blacksmith Fork offers a place to enjoy some trout fishing and have a picnic.

5 Bridger

Location: In the Uinta-Wasatch-Cache National Forest, approximately 6 miles east of Logan
GPS: N41 44.870'/W111 44.037'
Facilities: Fire pits, picnic tables, drinking water, and flush toilets
Sites: 10 basic sites
Maximum RV length: 20 feet
Fee: $$ for basic sites
Maximum stay: 7 days
Elevation: 5,000 feet
Road conditions: Paved
Management: Logan Ranger District, 1500 E. Hwy. 89, Logan; (435) 755-3620; www.fs.usda
.gov/main/uwcnf/home
Reservations: None
Activities: Rock climbing, hiking, mountain biking, fishing, and picnicking
Season: May through September
Finding the campground: From the junction of US 89 and US 91 in Logan, travel east on paved US 89 for 5.5 miles to the campground, which is on the south side of the road.
About the campground: Located in beautiful Logan Canyon, a place with an abundance of

Broadtail hummingbirds are always a joy to watch in flight.

campgrounds, this is a wonderful place from which to climb, hike, bike, fish for trout, or just sit and enjoy a picnic. Box elders, maples, and miniature roses shade the campsites and add to the lovely scene, with the Logan River roaring nearby.

Logan Canyon is a climber's paradise, with its sheer-walled limestone and quartzite cliffs offering up more than 300 mostly bolted routes, ranging in difficulty from 5.5 to 5.14. See *Rock Climbing Utah*, a FalconGuides book by Stewart Green, for more information.

6 Spring Hollow

Location: In the Uinta-Wasatch-Cache National Forest, about 7 miles east of Logan
GPS: N41 45.194'/W111 43.010'
Facilities: Fire pits, picnic tables, drinking water, and vault toilets
Sites: 12 basic sites, 1 double site, and 2 group sites (maximum 75 people each)
Maximum RV length: 20 feet
Fee: $$ for basic sites; $$$$ for double site; $$$$$ for group sites
Maximum stay: 7 days
Elevation: 5,100 feet
Road conditions: Paved
Management: Logan Ranger District, 1500 E. Hwy. 89, Logan; (435) 755-3620; www.fs.usda .gov/main/uwcnf/home

Reservations: Call (877) 444-6777 or TDD (877) 833-6777; www.recreation.gov
Activities: Climbing, hiking, mountain biking, fishing, photography, and picnicking
Season: May through October
Finding the campground: From the junction of US 89 and US 91 in Logan, travel east on paved US 89 for 6.5 miles to the campground, which is on the south side of the road.
About the campground: Located in the stunning realms of Logan Canyon, where campgrounds are plentiful, this is a great place from which to climb, hike, bike, and fish. The Logan River borders the north side of the shady campground, while Spring Hollow Creek rushes through it. Sites 1 to 6 are best for trailers, and sites 7 to 13 are best for tents and very small trailers due to narrow and windy roads with thick vegetation. Two trails begin here: The Riverside Nature Trail is for hikers and travels east to the Guinavah-Malibu Campground. Head back down the river, and you'll enjoy 4 miles along the River Trail, which is open to both bicyclists and hikers.

7 Guinavah-Malibu

Location: In the Uinta-Wasatch-Cache National Forest, approximately 7 miles east of Logan
GPS: N41 45.727' / W111 42.127'
Facilities: Fire pits, picnic tables, drinking water, and flush toilets
Sites: 37 basic sites, 3 double sites, and 3 group sites (maximum varies from 50 to 150 people)
Maximum RV length: 25 feet
Fee: $$ for basic sites; $$$$ for double sites; $$$$$ for group sites
Maximum stay: 7 days
Elevation: 5,100 feet
Road conditions: Paved and dirt
Management: Logan Ranger District, 1500 E. Hwy. 89, Logan; (435) 755-3620; www.fs.usda .gov/main/uwcnf/home
Reservations: Call (877) 444-6777 or TDD (877) 833-6777; www.recreation.gov
Activities: Climbing, hiking, mountain biking, fishing, photography, and picnicking
Restrictions: Campground gate locked at 10 p.m. each night
Season: May through October
Finding the campground: From the junction of US 89 and US 91 in Logan, travel east on paved US 89 for 7.4 miles to the campground, which is on the south side of the road.
About the campground: Here in the kingdom of Logan Canyon, where the scenery is stunning, campgrounds are numerous, and outdoor activities are plentiful, you'll find more than enough to do in the way of climbing, hiking, biking, and fishing. The Logan River cuts through the campground, while cottonwood, box elder, and maple trees serve to shade it. The complex actually consists of two campgrounds: Guinavah offers basic sites 12 to 40 plus group sites B and C, while Malibu consists of group site A and basic sites 1 to 11. One trail begins in the campground, and another starts just across the street. The Riverside Nature Trail is for hikers and travels west to the Spring Hollow Campground. Across the road you'll find the Wind Caves Trail. It leads 1.3 miles to a triple arch and natural limestone cave.

8 Preston Valley

Location: In the Uinta-Wasatch-Cache National Forest, approximately 10 miles east of Logan
GPS: N41 46.407'/W111 39.281'
Facilities: Fire pits, picnic tables, flush toilets, and drinking water
Sites: 6 basic sites
Maximum RV length: 20 feet
Fee: $$ for basic sites
Maximum stay: 7 days
Elevation: 5,200 feet
Road conditions: Paved
Management: Logan Ranger District, 1500 E. Hwy. 89, Logan; (435) 755-3620; www.fs.usda
.gov/main/uwcnf/home
Reservations: None
Activities: Climbing, mountain biking, fishing, and picnicking
Season: May through October
Finding the campground: From the junction of US 89 and US 91 in Logan, travel east on paved
US 89 for 10.4 miles to the campground, which is on the south side of the road.
About the campground: This small campground is located about midway through glorious Logan
Canyon, with easy access to rock climbing and fishing. Deciduous trees shade the sites, while the
Logan River flows nearby. Please note that RVers should stay away from sites 1 and 2, because
there is no place for trailers to turn around.

Climbers should note that Logan Canyon is a paradise of sheer-walled limestone and quartzite
cliffs offering up more than 300 mostly bolted routes. Routes range in difficulty from 5.5 to 5.14;
see Stewart Green's book *Rock Climbing Utah* for more information.

9 Lodge

Location: In the Uinta-Wasatch-Cache National Forest, approximately 13 miles east of Logan
GPS: N41 46.651'/W111 37.223'
Facilities: Fire pits, picnic tables, drinking water, and vault toilets
Sites: 10 basic sites
Maximum RV length: 20 feet
Fee: $$ for basic sites
Maximum stay: 7 days
Elevation: 5,500 feet
Road conditions: Paved to the campground, then gravel
Management: Logan Ranger District, 1500 E. Hwy. 89, Logan; (435) 755-3620; www.fs.usda
.gov/main/uwcnf/home
Reservations: None
Activities: Climbing, mountain biking, fishing, off-highway driving, and picnicking
Season: May through October

Finding the campground: From the junction of US 89 and US 91 in Logan, drive east on paved US 89 for 11.5 miles, then turn right (south) onto a narrow paved road for 1.3 miles to the campground. Just prior to reaching the campground there's a fork; go right, then make a sharp right turn into the campground. A sign points the way.

About the campground: Popular with ATVers, this shaded campground offers box elder and other deciduous trees as well as the waters of the Right Hand Fork. It's a good place from which to base activities such as rock climbing, fishing, and exploring off the main highway. There are many places to mountain bike, including a ride to Ephraim's Grave—the site at which the largest grizzly bear in America was killed—and a trip to the top of Logan Peak. For more information see the FalconGuides book *Mountain Biking Utah*, by Gregg Bromka.

10 Wood Camp

Location: In the Uinta-Wasatch-Cache National Forest, about 13 miles east of Logan
GPS: N41 47.841'/W111 38.677'
Facilities: Fire pits, picnic tables, and vault toilets
Sites: 5 basic sites and 1 double site
Maximum RV length: 20 feet
Fee: $$ for basic sites; $$$$ for double site
Maximum stay: 7 days
Elevation: 5,400 feet
Road conditions: Paved to the campground, then dirt
Management: Logan Ranger District, 1500 E. Hwy. 89, Logan; (435) 755-3620; www.fs.usda .gov/main/uwcnf/home
Reservations: None
Activities: Climbing, mountain biking, hiking, fishing, photography, and picnicking
Season: May through October
Finding the campground: From the junction of US 89 and US 91 in Logan, drive east on paved US 89 for 12.5 miles. The campground is on the north side of the road.
About the campground: You won't find drinking water here, but you will find the Logan River and shady sites for fishing. Best of all, the Jardine Juniper Trailhead is just 100 yards away. A sign points the way.

The Jardine Trail leads to a gnarled, 3,200-year-old juniper. The trail is about 4 or 5 miles long and accessible to hikers, mountain bikers, and horseback riders. It's a great hike, climbing approximately 1,800 feet while gaining the ridge, then descending a short distance to the tree.

11 Lewis M. Turner

Location: In the Uinta-Wasatch-Cache National Forest, about 22 miles northeast of Logan
GPS: N41 53.120'/W111 34.287'
Facilities: Fire pits, picnic tables, non-potable water, and flush toilets
Sites: 10 basic sites
Maximum RV length: 20 feet
Fee: $$ for basic sites
Maximum stay: 7 days
Elevation: 5,600 feet
Road conditions: Paved
Management: Logan Ranger District, 1500 E. Hwy. 89, Logan; (435) 755-3620; www.fs.usda .gov/main/uwcnf/home
Reservations: None
Activities: Photography, mountain biking, and picnicking
Restrictions: ATVs not allowed
Season: June through October
Finding the campground: From the junction of US 89 and US 91 in Logan, head east on paved US 89 for 21.7 miles. At this point make a left (southwest) at the sign for Tony Grove. The road forks immediately; keep straight (northwest) to reach the campground in 0.4 mile.
About the campground: Set among aspens this partially open campground makes a great base camp for exploring the nearby area. It's also a fine place from which to watch for wildlife and have a picnic. If you want to do some mountain biking, check out Gregg Bromka's FalconGuides book *Mountain Biking Utah*.

12 Tony Grove Lake

Location: In the Uinta-Wasatch-Cache National Forest, approximately 28 miles northeast of Logan
GPS: N41 53.543'/W111 38.328'
Facilities: Fire pits, picnic tables, vault toilets, ADA sites; no trash service (pack it out)
Sites: 35 basic sites, 1 double site, and 4 tents-only sites
Maximum RV length: 30 feet
Fee: $$ for basic and tent sites; $$$$ for double site
Maximum stay: 7 days
Elevation: 8,033 feet
Road conditions: Paved
Management: Logan Ranger District, 1500 E. Hwy. 89, Logan; (435) 755-3620; www.fs.usda .gov/main/uwcnf/home
Reservations: Call (877) 444-6777 or TDD (877) 833-6777; www.recreation.gov
Activities: Hiking, fishing, horseback riding, photography, and picnicking

Red-naped sapsucker adult feeds its hungry chick.

Season: July through September

Finding the campground: From the junction of US 89 and US 91 in Logan, head east on paved US 89 for 21.7 miles, then make a left (southwest) at the sign for Tony Grove. Keep left at the fork (which you'll reach almost immediately) and continue another 6.6 miles, mostly heading west on the paved road. You'll reach the campground just before the road ends at Tony Grove Lake.

About the campground: Grouse, moose, and a whole lot more might await those who decide to camp at Tony Grove. Set among aspens, spruce, and other conifers, with some sites overlooking scenic Tony Grove Lake, this campground offers access into the Mount Naomi Wilderness.

Trails lead into the 45,000-acre preserve, which encompasses some of the most rugged and spectacular country in the Bear River Range. A trail leads about 2,000 feet up and nearly 3 miles to the top of 9,979-foot Mount Naomi, the highest in the northern part of the Wasatch Range. Climb in the summer months and you're sure to indulge in fields of wildflowers—you might even see some wildlife, too.

13 Red Banks

Location: In the Uinta-Wasatch-Cache National Forest, approximately 23 miles northeast of Logan

GPS: N41 53.914' / W111 33.890'

Facilities: Fire pits, picnic tables, drinking water, and vault toilets

Sites: 12 basic sites
Maximum RV length: 20 feet
Fee: $$ for basic sites
Maximum stay: 7 days
Elevation: 6,300 feet
Road conditions: Paved to the campground, then gravel
Management: Logan Ranger District, 1500 E. Hwy. 89, Logan; (435) 755-3620; www.fs.usda
.gov/main/uwcnf/home
Reservations: None
Activities: Hiking, fishing, mountain biking, and picnicking
Restrictions: ATVs not allowed
Season: June through October
Finding the campground: From the junction of US 89 and US 91 in Logan, travel east on paved
US 89 for 22.7 miles to the campground, which is on the north side of the road.
About the campground: Aspens, cottonwoods, and willows grace this spot, with the Logan River
flowing nearby. The campground is right next to the road and probably not the most quiet place
come summer, but the river should drown out some of the noise. The site was named for the steep
red bank of sandstone and conglomerate visible from the campground.

14 Sunrise

Location: In the Uinta-Wasatch-Cache National Forest, about 6 miles west of Garden City
GPS: N41 55.230'/W111 27.754'
Facilities: Fire pits, picnic tables, drinking water, and vault toilets
Sites: 27 basic sites
Maximum RV length: 25 feet
Fee: $$ for basic sites
Maximum stay: 7 days
Elevation: 7,600 feet
Road conditions: Paved
Management: Logan Ranger District, 1500 E. Hwy. 89, Logan; (435) 755-3620; www.fs.usda
.gov/main/uwcnf/home
Reservations: Call (877) 444-6777 or TDD (877) 833-6777; www.recreation.gov
Activities: Picnicking
Restrictions: ATVs not allowed
Season: June through September
Finding the campground: From the junction of UT 30 and US 89 in Garden City, drive west on
paved US 89 for about 6 miles to the campground, which is on the south side of the road.
About the campground: Shady sites are the norm in this beautiful—and popular—camping area
set among aspens and conifers. Look closely and you may catch a glimpse of Bear Lake. Ranging
from azure to turquoise to sky blue, the lake is more than 20 miles long and 8 miles wide. Once a
hunting and gathering grounds for Native Americans, it was later a meeting place for almost every
mountain man who trapped in the Rocky Mountains. Today it's a popular destination for campers.

RVs at Birch Creek Campground, Rendezvous Beach, have a lovely view of Bear Lake.

15 Rendezvous Beach: Bear Lake State Park

Location: About 8 miles south of Garden City
GPS: N41 50.772' / W111 20.946'
Facilities: Fire pits, picnic tables (some covered), full hookups, flush toilets, showers, drinking water, dump station, ADA sites, boat and watercraft rentals, snack bar, and boat ramps and docks
Sites: 37 basic sites, 106 full-hookup sites, and 4 group sites (maximum varies from 60 to 80 people)
Maximum RV length: Any
Fee: $$ for basic sites; $$$ for full-hookup sites; $$$$$ for group sites
Maximum stay: 14 days
Elevation: 5,900 feet
Road conditions: Paved
Management: Bear Lake State Park, 940 N. Bear Lake Blvd., Garden City; (435) 946-3343; www .stateparks.utah.gov/park/bear-lake-state-park
Reservations: In the Salt Lake area, call (801) 322-3770; elsewhere, (800) 322-3770; http:// utahstateparks.reserveamerica.com
Activities: Fishing, swimming, boating, waterskiing, and picnicking
Restrictions: Campground gate closed from 10:30 p.m. to 7 a.m.
Season: May 1 through September 30

Finding the campground: From the junction of UT 30 and US 89 in Garden City, drive south on UT 30 for 8.1 miles to the campground, which is on the east side of the road.

About the campground: Enter the park at Rendezvous Beach, along the south shore of Bear Lake where there's a wide sandy beach, and you'll find four campgrounds—Willow, Birch, Cottonwood, and Big Creek—for your enjoyment. Family reunions and other big group meetings are definitely popular here!

The Willow Campground offers three group sites. At Cottonwood you'll find thirty-seven sites scattered throughout an immense grove of cottonwoods. (**Note:** Vehicles line up in parking-lot fashion here; thus there won't be much space between you and your neighbor in the parking lot, but you can spread out under the trees.)

Birch Creek is the newest campground at Bear Lake and has full hookups in all sixty sites, plus covered picnic tables. Most sites have views of the lake.

Big Creek Campground is a nice place for RVers and others wanting a space among cottonwoods and wild roses. Forty-six sites, some of them huge, offer full hookups and either stove stands or BBQ grills. There are also five cabins for rent and one group site.

16 Eastside: Bear Lake State Park

Location: About 10 miles north of Laketown
South Eden: GPS: N41 55.832'/W111 16.988'
Cisco Beach—North: GPS: N41 57.257'/W111 16.637'
Rainbow Cove: GPS: N41 58.130'/W111 16.262'
North Eden: GPS: N42 00.064'/W111 15.647'
Facilities: Fire pits, picnic tables, vault toilets, drinking water (at South Eden only), and two boat-launching areas, one at Rainbow Cove and the other at First Point
Sites: 99 basic sites and 2 group sites (maximum 50 people each)
Maximum RV length: Any
Fee: $ for basic sites; $$$$$ for group sites
Maximum stay: 14 days
Elevation: 5,900 feet
Road conditions: Paved to the campgrounds, then gravel
Management: Bear Lake State Park, 940 N. Bear Lake Blvd., Garden City; (435) 946-3343; www .stateparks.utah.gov/park/bear-lake-state-park
Reservations: For sites at South Eden in the Salt Lake area, call (801) 322-3770; elsewhere, (800) 322-3770; http://utahstateparks.reserveamerica.com
Activities: Fishing, boating, swimming, waterskiing, scuba diving, and picnicking
Season: Year-round (Cisco Beach and Rainbow Cove); the others are open May 1 through October 31 and are closed for the winter season.
Finding the campground: From the junction of UT 30 and a paved road leading to the east shore of Bear Lake (a sign points the way), go north on the paved county road. You'll pass the South Eden, Cisco Beach, Rainbow Cove, and North Eden Campgrounds as you head north.
About the campground: Four primitive campgrounds along the east shore of Bear Lake offer camping in an open setting; most sites have great views of the lake. Bear Lake is popular for scuba divers, boaters, and anglers looking forward to trout, Bonneville cisco, and whitefish.

South Eden offers twenty reservable sites. There are also two group sites with pavilions.

Cisco Beach is famous among scuba divers, who enjoy the steep underwater drop-offs. The campground has fifty-six sites.

Farther north you'll find Rainbow Cove with thirteen sites; all but sites 1 through 4 are spacious. And for extra-large sites check out the ten sites at North Eden.

17 Birch Creek

Location: About 9 miles west of Woodruff
GPS: N40 30.092' / W112 33.480'
Facilities: Vault toilets
Sites: Dispersed camping
Maximum RV length: 20 feet
Fee: None
Maximum stay: 14 days
Elevation: 6,850 feet
Road conditions: Gravel
Management: Bureau of Land Management, Salt Lake Field Office, 2370 S. 2300 West, Salt Lake City; (801) 977-4300; www.blm.gov/ut/st/en/fo/salt_lake.html
Reservations: None
Activities: Fishing and picnicking
Season: May through October
Finding the campground: From the junction of UT 16 and 39 in Woodruff, drive west on UT 39 for 7.8 miles. A sign points the way north to Birch Creek Reservoir. Follow the maintained dirt road for 1.1 miles.
About the campground: According to the folks at the BLM, the campground is in need of deferred maintenance. Because there are no standard amenities, the campground is free. An unmaintained path leads to the west end of one reservoir, and another reservoir above and to the west, both of which are popular for rainbow and cutthroat trout fishing.

18 Monte Cristo

Location: In the Uinta-Wasatch-Cache National Forest, about 20 miles west of Woodruff
GPS: N41 27.819'/W111 29.849'
Facilities: Fire pits, picnic tables, drinking water, and vault toilets
Sites: 45 basic sites and 2 group sites (maximum 100 people each)
Maximum RV length: 25 feet (45 feet in group sites)
Fee: $$ for basic sites; $$$$$ for group sites
Maximum stay: 7 days
Elevation: 9,000 feet
Road conditions: Paved
Management: Ogden Ranger District, 507 25th St., Ste. 103, Ogden; (801) 625-5112; www .fs.usda.gov/main/uwcnf/home
Reservations: For group sites only, call (877) 444-6777 or TDD (877) 833-6777; www .recreation.gov
Activities: Hiking, off-highway driving, mountain biking, and picnicking
Restrictions: Horses restricted within the campground, but legal in dispersed campsites north of the campground; ATVs not allowed in the campground
Season: July through October
Finding the campground: From the junction of UT 16 and 39 in Woodruff, drive west on UT 39 for 20.2 miles to the campground, which is on the south side of the road.
About the campground: Aspen, spruce, and fir add to the already lovely high-elevation setting of this campground. Two group sites, available by reservation only, make this a nice spot for those who just want a base camp from which to explore, or a place for relaxing and picnicking.

There's a 16-mile loop that will be of interest to those with mountain bikes or ATVs. Ranging from 8,400 feet to 8,800 feet, the loop receives moderate use, while its series of ridge roads provides views of the Wasatch, Uinta, and Wellsville Mountains.

Golden Spike Empire

The Golden Spike Empire is a vast and varied place located in the northwest corner of Utah. One of nine state travel regions, it comprises 7,129 square miles and includes part of the Utah geologic regions known as the Great Basin, Wasatch Front Cities, and Rocky Mountain Province. Bordered by Nevada on the west, the Golden Spike Empire abuts Idaho on the north, while Utah travel regions Great Salt Lake Country, Mountainland, and Bridgerland snuggle up to it on the south and east sides. Four counties—Box Elder, Weber, Morgan, and Davis—call the place home.

In addition to grand desert and mountain scenes, there is an abundance of animal life. Visitors may see big-game species such as moose, elk, and mule deer, while the more fortunate may even see bighorn sheep and mountain goats. Smaller but no less significant mammals include marmots, snowshoe hares, porcupines, beavers, and several kinds of chipmunks and ground squirrels. Many bird species can be found here, too.

An extreme diversity in plant communities results from rapid changes in topography. As a result there's a wide array of plants to appreciate: everything from sagebrush and rabbitbrush in the desert, to oak woodlands on the western slopes of the Wasatch Mountains. Higher still, aspen woodlands lead to forests of Douglas fir, lodgepole pine, and spruce. Stunning canyons offer an array of maples, red-barked dogwood, cottonwoods, and many species of wildflowers.

Twenty-three campgrounds make exploring the Golden Spike Empire both fun and easy. These sites allow you to enjoy a mix of wildlife watching, history, and recreation at places such as Antelope Island State Park, or to thrill to a drive up the Ogden Canyon Scenic Byway, which leads to a multitude of pretty places including Pineview Reservoir. In addition, birders will find hundreds of species of song-, wading, and shorebirds at both the Farmington Bay Waterfowl Management Area and farther north at the Bear River Migratory Bird Refuge west of Brigham City.

A number of different agencies manage the campgrounds found here. Weber County Parks and Recreation manages the campgrounds at Weber County Memorial Park, North Fork Park, and Fort Buenaventura Park. The primitive campground at Clear Creek is the only Utah site managed by the Sawtooth National Forest, though

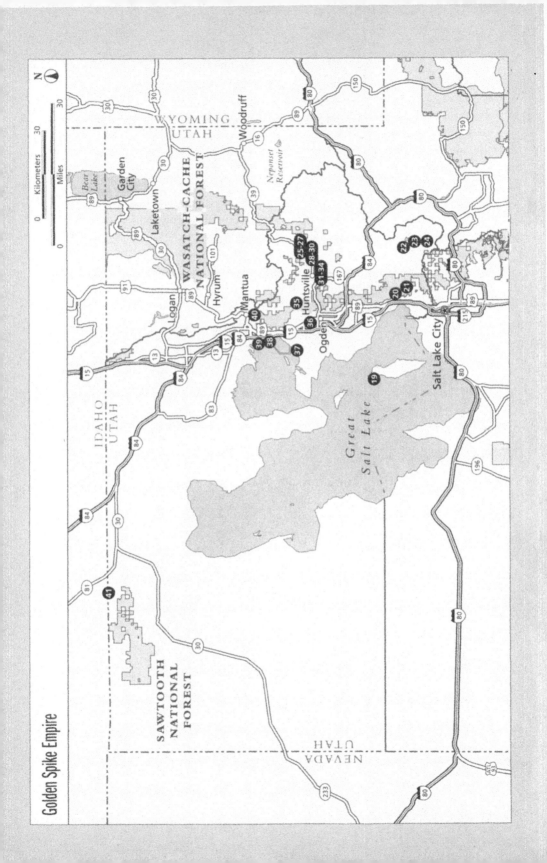

Golden Spike Empire

there are twelve campgrounds cared for by the Uinta-Wasatch-Cache National Forest. Several state parks take care of the remaining campgrounds.

The state parks in this region offer much in the way of water-related activities. Three campgrounds are located along Willard Bay, where water sports and bird watching are the main activities. The same is true for Antelope Island State Park, where folks also come to hike, mountain bike, and view bison and pronghorn. Three campgrounds at East Canyon State Park offer fishing opportunities for anglers and waterskiing for those who enjoy the sport.

Campgrounds in the Wasatch Mountain Range are numerous, especially along the South Fork Ogden River, where you can engage in hiking, biking, fishing, boating—or just relaxing and enjoying your surroundings.

While most of the campgrounds in the region are closed during winter, some remain open year-round. For additional information contact the Golden Spike Empire at 2501 Wall Ave., Ogden; (801) 627-8288 or (800) 255-8824; http://utahtravelcen ter.com/travelregions/goldenspike.htm.

		Total Sites	Group Sites	Hook-up Sites	Hookups	Max. RV Length	Dump Station	Toilets	Showers	Drinking Water	ADA Compliant	Fees	Reservations	Recreation
19	Antelope Island State Park	47	1			35	•	V		•	•	$$-$$$$$	•	MHRSBLK
20	Sunset	10				20		V		•		$$-$$$		MH
21	Bountiful Peak	35	1			24				•		$$-$$$$$	•	MHRO
22	Dixie	27		27	WES	40	•	F	•	•	•	$$-$$$$$	•	FSBLK
23	Big Rock	21				40		V			•	$$-$$$	•	FSBK
24	Rivers Edge	1	1			20		V				$$$$$	•	FSBK
25	Weber County Memorial Park	63	3			35		F		•	•	$$-$$$$$	•	FH
26	Willows	17				30		V		•		$$-$$$$		F
27	Upper Meadows	9				15		V		•		$$		F
28	Lower Meadows	23				35		V		•		$$-$$$$		F
29	Perception Park	27	3			35		V		•	•	$$-$$$$$	•	FH
30	South Fork	43				35		V		•	•	$$	•	F
31	Botts	7				20		V		•		$$-$$$$		F
32	Magpie	10				30		V		•		$$-$$$$		F
33	Jefferson Hunt	27				40		V		•		$$		FSBK
34	Anderson Cove	85	5			40	•	V		•	•	$$-$$$$$	•	FHSBMLK
35	North Fork Park	187	6			Any		F		•	•	$$-$$$$$	•	FHMR
36	Fort Buenaventura Park	16	2	4	E	35		V		•		$$-$$$$	•	FK
37	South Marina	30		24	WES	35	•	F	•	•	•	$$-$$$	•	FSBLK
38	Cottonwood	39		39	WES	Any	•	F	•	•	•	$$$	•	FSBLK
39	Willow Creek	39				Any	•	F	•	•	•	$$	•	FSBLK
40	Box Elder	30	4			30		F		•		$$-$$$$	•	F
41	Clear Creek	7				30		V		•		None		HO

Hookup: W = Water, E = Electric, S = Sewer

Recreation: H = Hiking, C = Rock Climbing, M = Mountain Biking, S = Swimming, F = Fishing, B = Boating, L = Boat Launch, O = Off-highway Driving, R = Horseback Riding, K = Kayaking and Canoeing, G = Golf,

Toilets: F = Flush, V = Vault, C = Chemical

Per-night campsite cost: $ = $10 or less $$ = $11 to $20 $$$ = $21 to 30 $$$$ = $31 to $40 $$$$$ = $41 and higher

19 Antelope Island State Park

Location: About 10 miles south of the fee station
GPS: N41 05.353'/W112 07.240'
Facilities: Fire pits, picnic tables, BBQ grills, ADA sites, tent pads (at White Rock), drinking water, and vault toilets in the campgrounds. Nearby there are showers, flush toilets, a marina, boat storage, boat launch, boat and watercraft rentals, visitor center, gift shop, a full-service grill, a dump station and ice machine. A concessionaire offers guided horseback rides, boat rentals, and cruises on the Great Salt Lake.
Sites: 34 basic sites, 12 tents-only sites, and 1 group site (maximum 80 people)
Maximum RV length: 35 feet
Fee: $$ for basic sites at Bridger Bay; $$$ for basic and tents-only sites (maximum 16 people) at White Rock; $$$$$$ for group site
Maximum stay: 14 days
Elevation: 4,200 feet
Road conditions: Paved at Bridger Bay; dirt at White Rock Bay
Management: Antelope Island State Park, 4528 W. 1700 South, Syracuse; (801) 773-2941; http://stateparks.utah.gov/park/antelope-island-state-park
Reservations: In the Salt Lake area call (801) 322-3770; elsewhere, (800) 322-3770; http://utahstateparks.reserveamerica.com
Activities: Mountain biking, hiking, horseback riding, swimming, boating, and picnicking
Restrictions: Horses are not allowed in Bridger Bay Campground, but are allowed at White Rock Bay Campground. Campground gate is closed from 10 p.m. to 6 a.m.
Season: Year-round
Finding the campground: Leave I-15 at exit 332 (UT 108), which leads to Syracuse. A sign points the way to the state park. Head west on UT 108 for 3.9 miles until you reach its junction with UT 127; stay straight, now traveling on UT 127, for another 3 miles to the fee station. Drive the 7-mile causeway to the island, where you'll find a marina, a boat ramp, a visitor center, and a gift shop. Make a right and drive an additional 2.7 miles to the Bridger Bay Campground. The campground at White Rock Bay is located a couple of miles to the southeast.
About the campground: Huge, open camp spaces make this a delight for RVers with monster rigs. There are nice views from this state park, with great trails as well. Though the amenities are primitive at both campgrounds, you will find full services at the day-use area.

A 7-mile causeway leads from the mainland to the largest of the ten islands found in the Great Salt Lake. Also the largest natural lake west of the Mississippi River, the lake and surrounding areas teem with wildlife. Antelope Island is 15 miles long and 4.5 miles wide. There are opportunities to view wildlife such as pronghorn, bison, and jackrabbits, as well as the chance to do some saltwater bathing, bird watching, hiking, biking, and horseback riding, or to explore historical sites. For those who like to hike to high points, there's a 4.5-mile trail leading to the top of Frary Peak—at 6,596 feet the highest point on the island.

20 Sunset

Location: In the Uinta-Wasatch-Cache National Forest, about 6 miles east of Farmington
GPS: N41 0.205'/W111 50.395'
Facilities: Fire pits, picnic tables, drinking water, and vault toilets
Sites: 9 basic sites and 1 double site
Maximum RV length: 20 feet
Fee: $$ for basic sites; $$$ for double site
Maximum stay: 7 days
Elevation: 6,400 feet
Road conditions: Gravel
Management: Salt Lake Ranger District, 6944 S. 3000 East, Cottonwood Heights; (801) 999-2103; www.fs.usda.gov/main/uwcnf/home
Reservations: None
Activities: Mountain biking, hiking, and picnicking
Season: June through September
Finding the campground: From I-15 go east at exit 327 (Lagoon Drive, UT 225) in Farmington and continue east on UT 225 for 0.4 mile to Main Street. Now make a right (south) onto Main and travel another 0.3 mile, then go left (east) onto 600 North for 0.2 mile. There's a sign reading "Scenic Byway." At the T junction go left (north, then east) onto 100 East and continue up the paved road. Though unsigned as such, the road later becomes FR 007 and is quite steep, narrow, and winding. (Trailers over 24 feet are not recommended.) It turns to gravel after 1.6 miles. Continue an additional 3.6 miles on the gravel road to the campground, which is on your right. The campground sign is tucked away in the trees, so look closely or you'll miss the turnoff.
About the campground: Small sites are tucked away in the oak and maple forest found here, so car or tent camping is best; the place just isn't suited for trailers. Mountain biking and hiking are popular in this canyon.

21 Bountiful Peak

Location: In the Uinta-Wasatch-Cache National Forest, about 10 miles southeast of Farmington
GPS: N40 58.840'/W111 48.269'
Facilities: Fire pits, picnic tables, drinking water, and vault toilets
Sites: 30 basic sites, 4 double sites, and 1 group site (maximum 100 people)
Maximum RV length: 24 feet
Fee: $$ for basic sites; $$$ for double sites; $$$$$ for group site
Maximum stay: 7 days
Elevation: 7,500 feet
Road conditions: Gravel
Management: Salt Lake Ranger District, 6944 S. 3000 East, Cottonwood Heights; (801) 999-2103; www.fs.usda.gov/main/uwcnf/home

Reservations: For the group site only, call (877) 444-6777 or TDD (877) 833-6777; www
.recreation.gov
Activities: Mountain biking, hiking, horseback riding, off-highway driving, and picnicking
Season: June through September
Finding the campground: From I-15 go east at exit 325 (Lagoon Drive, UT 225) in Farmington
and continue east on UT 225 for 0.4 mile to Main Street. Now make a right (south) onto Main
and travel another 0.3 mile, then go left (east) onto 600 North for 0.2 mile. There's a sign reading
"Scenic Byway." At the T junction go left (north, then east) onto 100 East and continue up the
paved road. Though unsigned as such, the road later becomes FR 007 and is quite steep, narrow, and winding. (Trailers over 24 feet are not recommended.) It turns to gravel after 1.6 miles.
Continue an additional 6.3 miles on the gravel road to a fork; keep right (south) and drive another
0.8 mile to the campground.
About the campground: Conifers, aspens, and some nice views of Bountiful Peak and the surrounding area are yours for the asking at this pleasant campground. ATVs are popular here, with
nearby Skyline Drive being a frequent destination. There's also a trail to the top of Bountiful Peak,
a favorite for hikers and horseback riders, and Farmington Flats is a popular mountain bike ride.
Check out FalconGuides' *Mountain Biking Utah* by Gregg Bromka, for more information.

22 Dixie: East Canyon State Park

Location: About 12 miles southeast of Morgan
GPS: N40 55.473'/W111 35.434'
Facilities: Fire pits, covered picnic tables, partial and full hookups, ADA sites, flush toilets, show-
ers, dump station, drinking water, a volleyball court, boat ramp, dry boat storage, and fish cleaning
station. A concessionaire offers a gas dock, snack bar, boat rentals, and a convenience store.
Sites: 11 partial-hookup sites; 9 full-hookup sites; 5 partial-hookup double sites; 2 full-hookup
double sites, 4 yurts, and 2 cabins
Maximum RV length: 40 feet
Fee: $$ for partial-hookup sites; $$$ for full-hookup sites; $$$$ for partial-hookup double sites;
$$$$$ for full-hookup double sites, yurts, and cabins
Maximum stay: 14 days
Elevation: 5,800 feet
Road conditions: Paved
Management: East Canyon State Park, 5535 S. Hwy. 66, Morgan; (801) 829-6866; www.state
parks.utah.gov/park/east-canyon-state-park
Reservations: In the Salt Lake area, call (801) 322-3770; elsewhere, (800) 322-3770; http://
utahstateparks.reserveamerica.com
Activities: Fishing, swimming, boating, waterskiing, bird watching, and picnicking
Restrictions: ATVs not allowed; campground gate closed from 10 p.m. to 6 a.m.
Season: Year-round
Finding the campground: From the junction of I-84 and UT 66 in Morgan, go southeast on UT 66
for 12 miles to the park entrance.

RVs find a scenic spot at Dixie Campground, East Canyon State Park.

About the campground: Set on a sunny, open slope overlooking 684-acre East Canyon Reservoir, this campground is a popular spot for those interested in water-related activities. It's also a delight for anglers, who vie for rainbow trout and kokanee salmon. Crawfishing and ice fishing are popular as well.

Look for wildlife while visiting the park. If you're lucky, you might see a mule deer, a badger, a fox, a great horned owl, or even a loon. Migrating birds often stop here on their journeys, so keep your binoculars ready.

23 Big Rock: East Canyon State Park

Location: About 17 miles southeast of Morgan
GPS: N40 52.775' / W111 34.850'
Facilities: Fire pits, covered picnic tables, ADA sites, tent pads, and vault toilets
Sites: 19 basic sites and 2 double sites
Maximum RV length: 40 feet
Fee: $$ for basic sites; $$$ for double sites
Maximum stay: 14 days

Mike Vining enjoys a hike along the Mormon Flat Trail, East Canyon State Park.

Elevation: 5,700 feet

Road conditions: Paved

Management: East Canyon State Park, 5535 S. Hwy. 66, Morgan; (801) 829-6866; www.state parks.utah.gov/park/east-canyon-state-park

Reservations: In the Salt Lake area, call (801) 322-3770; elsewhere, (800) 322-3770; http:// utahstateparks.reserveamerica.com

Activities: Fishing, swimming, boating, waterskiing, bird watching, and picnicking

Restrictions: ATVs not allowed

Season: Year-round

Finding the campground: From the junction of I-84 and UT 66 in Morgan, go southeast on UT 66 until it ends at UT 65 in 13.5 miles. Now go right (west, then south) on UT 65 for another 3.9 miles.

About the campground: Located on the south end of 680-acre East Canyon Reservoir, these large sites are not always close to the water. Whether or not you can access the lake from here depends on the water level. It's a popular spot for all sorts of water-related activities as well as fishing. Anglers often pursue trout and kokanee salmon.

24 Rivers Edge: East Canyon State Park

Location: About 17 miles southeast of Morgan
GPS: N40 52.580'/W111 34.907'
Facilities: Picnic tables (some covered), fire pits, BBQ grills, and vault toilets
Sites: 1 group site (maximum 75 people)
Maximum RV length: 20 feet
Fee: $$$$$ for group site
Maximum stay: 14 days
Elevation: 5,700 feet
Road conditions: Gravel
Management: East Canyon State Park, 5535 S. Hwy. 66, Morgan; (801) 829-6866; www.state parks.utah.gov/park/east-canyon-state-park
Reservations: In the Salt Lake area, call (801) 322-3770; elsewhere, (800) 322-3770; http://utahstateparks.reserveamerica.com
Activities: Fishing and picnicking, with swimming, boating, and waterskiing at the nearby reservoir
Season: Year-round
Restrictions: ATVs not allowed
Finding the campground: From the junction of I-84 and UT 66 in Morgan, go southeast on UT 66 until it ends at UT 65 in 13.5 miles. Now go right (west, then south) on UT 65 for another 4.1 miles.
About the campground: Located along the river a short distance from East Canyon Reservoir, this primitive group site is on the southern edge of the reservoir. (That's if there is much water in the reservoir.) There are two other group sites—Large Spring and Mormon Flat—located about 4 miles south of the reservoir off the gravel road to Mormon Flats. Large Spring (GPS: N40 49.161'/W111 34.976') offers a place to camp for a maximum of twenty-five people. Mormon Flat Group Site (GPS: N40 48.926'/W111 35.098') has space for a maximum of seventy-five people. It's at the trailhead for the Mormon Pioneer National Historic Trail, a lovely 4-mile-long trail leading to the top of Big Mountain.

25 Weber County Memorial Park

Location: Near Causey Reservoir, about 10 miles northeast of Huntsville
GPS: N41 17.822'/W111 35.732'
Facilities: Fire pits, picnic tables, ADA sites, flush toilets, and drinking water. Three group sites also have horseshoe pits, a volleyball court, and electricity.
Sites: 60 basic sites and 3 group sites (maximum 50 people each)
Maximum RV length: 35 feet
Fee: $$ for basic sites; $$$$$ for group sites
Maximum stay: 7 days
Elevation: 5,200 feet
Road conditions: Paved to the campground, then gravel

Management: Weber County Parks and Recreation, 1181 N. Fairgrounds Dr., Ogden; (801) 399-8491 or (800) 407-2757; www.co.weber.ut.us/parks/wmpark.php
Reservations: For group sites only, call (801) 399-8491; www.co.weber.ut.us/parks/reservations/avail.php
Activities: Fishing, hiking, volleyball, horseshoes, and picnicking
Season: May through October
Finding the campground: From the junction of UT 39 and 100 South in Huntsville, head east on UT 39 for 8.4 miles, then turn right (south) onto the paved road to Causey Reservoir; a sign points the way. You'll reach the campground after another 1.2 miles. The campground is just west of the reservoir.
About the campground: This county park is situated along the banks of the South Fork Ogden River, a short distance from Causey Reservoir, where you'll find trails for hikers leading from the north end of Causey Dam at Boy Scout Camp to Baldy Ridge, Bear Hollow, and Baldy Peak. All sites, including the group sites, are on the grass, with some trees for shade. Basic sites are scattered throughout the area, with some located near the river, which is popular with anglers targeting rainbow, cutthroat, and brown trout.

26 Willows

Location: In the Uinta-Wasatch-Cache National Forest, about 8 miles northeast of Huntsville
GPS: N41 17.508' / W111 38.071'
Facilities: Fire pits, picnic tables, stove stands, vault toilets, and drinking water
Sites: 17 basic sites, including some double sites
Maximum RV length: 30 feet
Fee: $$ for basic sites; $$$$ for double sites
Maximum stay: 7 days
Elevation: 5,300 feet
Road conditions: Paved to the campground, then gravel
Management: Ogden Ranger District, 507 25th St., Ste. 103, Ogden; (801) 625-5112; www.fs.usda.gov/main/uwcnf/home
Reservations: None
Activities: Fishing and picnicking
Restrictions: Campground gate closed from 10 p.m. to 7 a.m.
Season: May through September
Finding the campground: From the junction of UT 39 and 100 South in Huntsville, head east on paved UT 39 for 7.5 miles; the campground is on the south side of the road.
About the campground: Located along the South Fork Ogden River, this campground is a great place for fishing for rainbow, brown, and cutthroat trout; relaxing; and enjoying the cottonwoods and wild roses that inhabit the place.

27 Upper Meadows

Location: In the Uinta-Wasatch-Cache National Forest, approximately 8 miles northeast of Huntsville
GPS: N41 17.426'/W111 38.185'
Facilities: Fire pits, picnic tables, stove stands, vault toilets, and drinking water
Sites: 9 basic sites
Maximum RV length: 15 feet
Fee: $$ for basic sites
Maximum stay: 7 days
Elevation: 5,300 feet
Road conditions: Gravel
Management: Ogden Ranger District, 507 25th St., Ste. 103, Ogden; (801) 625-5112; www
.fs.usda.gov/main/uwcnf/home
Reservations: None
Activities: Fishing and picnicking
Restrictions: Campground gate closed from 10 p.m. to 7 a.m.
Season: May through September
Finding the campground: From the junction of UT 39 and 100 South in Huntsville, head east on paved UT 39 for 7.4 miles, then turn right (south) onto a gravel road leading to both the Upper Meadows and Lower Meadows Campgrounds. The Upper Meadows Campground is to the left (east) after you turn onto the gravel road.
About the campground: Resting in cottonwoods and other lush vegetation, this small campground is located in beautiful Ogden Canyon, along the South Fork Ogden River. A small campground best for tents and vans, it's a nice place for trout fishing and relaxing.

28 Lower Meadows

Location: In the Uinta-Wasatch-Cache National Forest, about 7 miles northeast of Huntsville
GPS: N41 17.205'/W111 38.598'
Facilities: Fire pits, picnic tables, stove stands, vault toilets, and drinking water
Sites: 23 basic sites, including some double sites
Maximum RV length: 35 feet
Fee: $$ for basic sites; $$$$ for double sites
Maximum stay: 7 days
Elevation: 5,300 feet
Road conditions: Gravel
Management: Ogden Ranger District, 507 25th St., Ste. 103, Ogden; (801) 625-5112; www
.fs.usda.gov/main/uwcnf/home
Reservations: None
Activities: Fishing and picnicking
Restrictions: Campground gate closed from 10 p.m. to 7 a.m.
Season: May through September

Finding the campground: From the junction of UT 39 and 100 South in Huntsville, head east on paved UT 39 for 7.4 miles, then turn right (south) onto a gravel road leading to both the Upper Meadows and Lower Meadows Campgrounds. Stay straight, then make a right (west) and parallel the river for 0.8 mile to the Lower Meadows Campground.

About the campground: Situated in beautiful Ogden Canyon and located along the South Fork Ogden River, this is a great place for trout fishing, relaxing, and enjoying the cottonwoods and other plants and trees that live here.

29 Perception Park

Location: In the Uinta-Wasatch-Cache National Forest, about 7 miles northeast of Huntsville
GPS: N41 17.358'/W111 38.418'
Facilities: Fire pits, picnic tables, BBQ grills, ADA sites, playground, vault toilets, and drinking water
Sites: 24 basic sites and 3 group sites (maximum 50 people each)
Maximum RV length: 35 feet
Fee: $$ for basic sites; $$$$$ for group sites
Maximum stay: 7 days
Elevation: 5,300 feet
Road conditions: Paved
Management: Ogden Ranger District, 507 25th St., Ste. 103, Ogden; (801) 625-5112; www .fs.usda.gov/main/uwcnf/home
Reservations: For group sites only, call (877) 444-6777 or TDD (877) 833-6777; www .recreation.gov
Activities: Fishing, hiking, and picnicking
Restrictions: Campground gate closed from 10 p.m. to 7 a.m.
Season: May through September
Finding the campground: From the junction of UT 39 and 100 South in Huntsville, travel east on paved UT 39 for 7.2 miles to the campground, which is on the south side of the road.
About the campground: The South Fork Ogden River, with its typical habitat of cottonwoods and a whole lot more, makes this a nice spot for camping. The forest service claims this is one of the nicest campgrounds providing barrier-free use around. Several spaces are wheelchair accessible, and an asphalt trail along the river allows for viewing of the rapids. In addition, there are several fishing docks with guardrails throughout the campground. From here, anglers may catch rainbow, brown, and cutthroat trout.

30 South Fork

Location: In the Uinta-Wasatch-Cache National Forest, about 6 miles northeast of Huntsville
GPS: N41 16.912'/W111 39.238'
Facilities: Fire pits, picnic tables, stove stands, ADA sites, vault toilets, and drinking water

Sites: 43 basic sites
Maximum RV length: 35 feet
Fee: $$ for basic sites
Maximum stay: 7 days
Elevation: 5,200 feet
Road conditions: Paved to the campground, then gravel
Management: Ogden Ranger District, 507 25th St., Ste. 103, Ogden; (801) 625-5112; www
.fs.usda.gov/main/uwcnf/home
Reservations: Call (877) 444-6777 or TDD (877) 833-6777; www.recreation.gov
Activities: Fishing and picnicking
Restrictions: Campground gate closed from 10 p.m. to 7 a.m.
Season: May through September
Finding the campground: From the junction of UT 39 and 100 South in Huntsville, travel east on paved UT 39 for 6.4 miles to the campground, which is on the south side of the road.
About the campground: The South Fork Ogden River and its typical cottonwood habitat are yours for the asking at this campground. If you like to fish, try catching rainbow, brown, and cutthroat trout.

31 Botts

Location: In the Uinta-Wasatch-Cache National Forest, approximately 6 miles northeast of Huntsville
GPS: N41 16.635'/W111 39.477'
Facilities: Fire pits, picnic tables, stove stands, vault toilets, and drinking water
Sites: 6 basic sites and 1 double site
Maximum RV length: 20 feet
Fee: $$ for basic sites; $$$$ for double site
Maximum stay: 7 days
Elevation: 5,200 feet
Road conditions: Paved to the campground, then gravel
Management: Ogden Ranger District, 507 25th St., Ste. 103, Ogden; (801) 625-5112; www
.fs.usda.gov/main/uwcnf/home
Reservations: None
Activities: Fishing and picnicking
Restrictions: Campground gate closed from 10 p.m. to 7 a.m.
Season: May through September
Finding the campground: From the junction of UT 39 and 100 South in Huntsville, travel east on paved UT 39 for 5.9 miles to the campground, which is on the south side of the road.
About the campground: This small campground, which I'd recommend for tents and vans only, is found along the South Fork Ogden River and offers typical cottonwood habitat. It's a good place to fish for trout or to just plain relax.

32 Magpie

Location: In the Uinta-Wasatch-Cache National Forest, about 5 miles northeast of Huntsville
GPS: N41 16.211'/W111 40.017'
Facilities: Fire pits, picnic tables, stove stands, drinking water, and vault toilets
Sites: 8 basic sites and 2 double sites
Maximum RV length: 30 feet
Fee: $$ for basic sites; $$$$ for double sites
Maximum stay: 7 days
Elevation: 5,200 feet
Road conditions: Paved to the campground, then gravel
Management: Ogden Ranger District, 507 25th St., Ste. 103, Ogden; (801) 625-5112; www .fs.usda.gov/main/uwcnf/home
Reservations: None
Activities: Fishing and picnicking
Restrictions: Campground gate closed from 10 p.m. to 7 a.m.
Season: May through September
Finding the campground: From the junction of UT 39 and 100 South in Huntsville, travel east on paved UT 39 for 5.2 miles to the campground, which is on the south side of the road.
About the campground: Tucked away in a mix of cottonwoods and box elders, with the South Fork Ogden River flowing nearby, this recently renovated campground is a nice place for RVers who would like to do some trout fishing or relaxing.

33 Jefferson Hunt

Location: In the Uinta-Wasatch-Cache National Forest, approximately 2 miles south of Huntsville
GPS: N41 14.957'/W111 46.108'
Facilities: Fire pits, picnic tables, stove stands, lantern stands, drinking water, and vault toilets
Sites: 27 basic sites
Maximum RV length: 40 feet
Fee: $$ for basic sites
Maximum stay: 7 days
Elevation: 5,000 feet
Road conditions: Gravel
Management: Ogden Ranger District, 507 25th St., Ste. 103, Ogden; (801) 625-5112; www .fs.usda.gov/main/uwcnf/home
Reservations: None
Activities: Fishing, swimming, boating, and picnicking
Restrictions: Campground gate closed from 10 p.m. to 7 a.m.
Season: May through September

Finding the campground: From the junction of UT 39 and 100 South in Huntsville, go south on paved UT 39 West for 1.4 miles. At a sign reading "Jefferson Hunt," go right (north) onto the paved (later gravel) road for an additional 0.2 mile.

About the campground: Both open and shady sites exist in this campground, with cottonwoods, willows, and Russian olives among the types of trees.

The campground is on the southeast end of Pineview Reservoir, where the South Fork of the Ogden River meets the reservoir, and is an excellent base from which to enjoy water sports such as windsurfing, swimming, and boating. The reservoir is also a great place for fishing. Anglers may catch rainbow, brown, and cutthroat trout, along with bullhead catfish, largemouth and smallmouth bass, bluegills, crappie, yellow perch, whitefish, and tiger muskies.

34 Anderson Cove

Location: In the Uinta-Wasatch-Cache National Forest, approximately 2 miles southwest of Huntsville
GPS: N41 15.006'/W111 47.171'
Facilities: Fire pits, picnic tables, stove stands, ADA sites, drinking water, dump station, vault toilets, horseshoe pits, volleyball courts, and boat ramp
Sites: 68 basic sites, including some double sites, 12 tents-only sites, and 5 group sites (maximum 100 people each)
Maximum RV length: 40 feet
Fee: $$$ for basic sites; $$ for tents-only sites; $$$$$ for double and group sites
Maximum stay: 7 days
Elevation: 5,000 feet
Road conditions: Paved; tent area is gravel
Management: Ogden Ranger District, 507 25th St., Ste. 103, Ogden; (801) 625-5112; www.fs.usda.gov/main/uwcnf/home
Reservations: Call (877) 444-6777 or TDD (877) 833-6777; www.recreation.gov
Activities: Fishing, hiking, swimming, boating, mountain biking, and picnicking
Restrictions: ATV travel is not allowed adjacent to Pineview Reservoir. Dogs are not allowed in the tent area. Campground gate is closed from 10 p.m. to 7 a.m.
Season: May through September
Finding the campground: From the junction of UT 39 and 100 South in Huntsville, go south and then west on paved UT 39 West for 2.3 miles.
About the campground: Lots of grass and a bounty of shade trees are the norm at this lovely campground, located along the south shore of Pineview Reservoir. Nearly all water activities are popular, as is fishing. Anglers may catch rainbow, brown, and cutthroat trout, along with bullhead catfish, largemouth and smallmouth bass, bluegills, crappie, yellow perch, whitefish, and tiger muskies.

There are some mountain bike trails nearby. Check out Gregg Bromka's FalconGuides book *Mountain Biking Utah* for more information.

35 North Fork Park

Location: Along the North Fork Ogden River, about 10 miles northeast of North Ogden
GPS: N41 22.214'/W111 54.351'
Facilities: Fire pits, picnic tables, flush toilets, drinking water, and horse corrals. Two ADA sites also have electricity. Six group sites have horseshoe pits and volleyball poles.
Sites: 181 basic sites and 6 group sites (maximum varies from 30 to 50 people)
Maximum RV length: Any
Fee: $$ for basic sites; $$$$$ for group sites
Maximum stay: 7 days
Elevation: 5,700 feet
Road conditions: Paved to the campground, then gravel
Management: Weber County Parks and Recreation, 1181 N. Fairgrounds Dr., Ogden; (801) 399-8491; www.co.weber.ut.us/parks/nfpark.php
Reservations: For group sites only, call (801) 399-8491; www.co.weber.ut.us/parks/reserva tions/avail.php
Activities: Fishing, hiking, mountain biking, horseback riding, volleyball, horseshoes, and picnicking
Season: May through October
Finding the campground: From the junction of Washington Boulevard and North Ogden Canyon Road in North Ogden, go east on North Ogden Canyon Road for about 7 miles. Turn left and head north-northwest on North Fork Road to the campground.
About the campground: There are six group areas here, each with its own horseshoe pit and volleyball poles. Several trails for nonmotorized vehicles are in the area, including the Ben Lommond Peak Trail, which begins here at the south end of the park near the horse corrals. This is one of the most popular and heavily used trails in the Ogden area, so be prepared for a crowd. Scenic vistas are your just reward for making the hike; it's 7.6 miles long one way and gains 2,880 feet.

36 Fort Buenaventura Park

Location: In downtown Ogden
GPS: N41 12.929'/W111 59.321'
Facilities: Fire pits, picnic tables, electric hookups, drinking water, vault toilets, playground, canoe rentals, and horseshoe pit
Sites: 10 basic sites, 4 electric-hookup sites, and 2 group sites (maximum 50 people each). In addition, the entire campground, including group sites and activity area, can be reserved.
Maximum RV length: 35 feet
Fee: $$ for basic sites; $$$ for electric-hookup sites; $$$$ for group sites
Maximum stay: 7 days
Elevation: 4,300 feet
Road conditions: Paved
Management: Fort Buenaventura Park, 2450 A Ave., Ogden; (801) 399-8491; www.co.weber .ut.us/parks/fortb/
Reservations: For group sites only, call (801) 399-8491

Ospreys nest throughout Utah, always choosing nesting sites near water.

Activities: Fishing, canoeing, and picnicking

Season: April through October

Finding the campground: When traveling from the south, exit I-15 at exit 342 in Ogden and drive east on 24th Street. There are signs pointing the way to the state park. After 1 mile turn right (south) onto paved A Avenue and follow it for just 0.2 mile before turning left (east) onto a paved road that leads to the park. (If you're traveling from the north, exit I-15 at exit 343 and go east toward City Center. Make a right at Washington Boulevard, another right onto 24th Street, and then a left onto A Avenue.)

About the campground: Though this campsite is in downtown Ogden, you'll hardly know it in this lush setting of box elders and cottonwoods. Once a Utah state park, the campground is now managed by Weber County.

While visiting the campground, be sure to check out Fort Buenaventura as well; it was re-created in 1980 on its original site. Mountain men rendezvous are reenacted at the fort on special occasions.

37 South Marina: Willard Bay State Park

Location: About 8 miles north of Ogden

GPS: N41 21.149' / W112 04.336'

Facilities: Fire pits, picnic tables (some covered), ADA sites, BBQ grills, flush toilets, showers, drinking water, full hookups, dump station, seasonal/transient boat slip rentals, and boat ramps

Sites: 24 full-hookup sites and 6 tents-only sites

Maximum RV length: 35 feet

Fee: $$ for tents-only sites; $$$ for full-hookup sites

Maximum stay: 14 days

Elevation: 4,200 feet

Road conditions: Paved

Management: Willard Bay State Park, 900 W. 650 North, #A, Willard; (435) 734-9494; www .stateparks.utah.gov/park/willard-bay-state-park

Reservations: You can make reservations if you are reserving the entire campground. In the Salt Lake area, call (801) 322-3770; elsewhere, (800) 322-3770; http://utahstateparks.reserveamerica.com

Activities: Fishing, swimming, boating, waterskiing, bird watching, and picnicking

Restrictions: Campground gate closed from 10 p.m. to 6 a.m.

Season: Year-round

Finding the campground: From exit 351 off I-15, north of Ogden and just south of Willard, drive south on UT 126 for a short distance, then make a right (west) onto 4000 North. Signs for the state park point the way. After 1.4 miles turn right (north) onto 2000 West. You'll reach the entrance station in an additional 1.3 miles.

About the campground: Located in one of two recreation areas along the east shore of Willard Bay, the South Marina Campground has six grassy tent sites with shade and twenty-four full-hookup sites. Each full-hookup site offers two side-by-side parking spaces with little shade. The entire campground can be reserved as a large group site (maximum 200 people); otherwise sites are available first-come, first-served.

Willard Bay, which rests atop the Great Salt Lake floodplain, is a great place for fishing. Anglers may hook kokanee salmon, largemouth bass, bluegills, crappie, yellow perch, and walleye.

38 Cottonwood: Willard Bay State Park North Marina

Location: About 15 miles north of Ogden

GPS: N41 25.218' / W112 03.197'

Facilities: Fire pits, covered picnic tables, full hookups, ADA sites, flush toilets, dump station, showers, drinking water, marina with boat ramps and docks

Sites: 39 full-hookup sites

Maximum RV length: Any

Fee: $$$ for full-hookup sites

Maximum stay: 14 days

Elevation: 4,200 feet

Road conditions: Paved

Management: Willard Bay State Park, 900 W. 650 North, #A, Willard; (435) 734-9494; www .stateparks.utah.gov/park/willard-bay-state-park

Reservations: In the Salt Lake area, call (801) 322-3770; elsewhere, (800) 322-3770; http:// utahstateparks.reserveamerica.com

Activities: Fishing, swimming, boating, waterskiing, bird watching, and picnicking

Restrictions: Campground gate closed from 10 p.m. to 6 a.m.

Season: Year-round

Finding the campground: From exit 357 off I-15 in Willard, head south on the west side of the interstate. The entrance station is just off the interstate, which means you should expect freeway noise.
About the campground: Full-hookup sites rest among an array of trees—including maple, box elder, cottonwood, and Russian olive. A sandy beach and a nature trail are bonuses for those who opt to camp here.

Though it may seem as though fishing, boating, and other water-related activities are favorites, birding is also popular: More than 200 species can be observed at or near the park. Still, anglers may snag kokanee salmon, largemouth bass, bluegills, crappie, yellow perch, and walleye.

39 Willow Creek: Willard Bay State Park North Marina

Location: About 15 miles north of Ogden
GPS: N41 25.218' / W112 03.197'
Facilities: Fire pits, picnic tables, ADA sites, flush toilets, dump station, showers, drinking water, boat ramps and docks
Sites: 39 basic sites
Maximum RV length: Any
Fee: $$ for basic sites
Maximum stay: 14 days
Elevation: 4,200 feet
Road conditions: Paved
Management: Willard Bay State Park, 900 W. 650 North, #A, Willard; (435) 734-9494; www.stateparks.utah.gov/park/willard-bay-state-park
Reservations: In the Salt Lake area, call (801) 322-3770; elsewhere, (800) 322-3770; http://utahstateparks.reserveamerica.com
Activities: Fishing, swimming, boating, waterskiing, bird watching, and picnicking
Restrictions: Campground gate closed from 10 p.m. to 6 a.m.
Season: Year-round
Finding the campground: From exit 357 off I-15 in Willard, head south on the west side of the interstate. The entrance station is just off the interstate, which means you should expect freeway noise.
About the campground: Dense vegetation and an array of trees—including maple, box elder, cottonwood, and Russian olive—provide the setting for this popular, shady campground. A sandy beach and a nature trail are bonuses for those who opt to camp here. Also, some sites have views of the bay.

Though it may seem as though fishing, boating, and other water-related activities are favorites, birding is also popular: More than 200 species can be observed at or near the park. Still, anglers may snag kokanee salmon, largemouth bass, bluegills, crappie, yellow perch, and walleye.

40 Box Elder

Location: In the Uinta-Wasatch-Cache National Forest, just south of Mantua
GPS: N41 29.728' / W111 57.110'
Facilities: Fire pits, picnic tables, flush toilets, and drinking water

Sites: 26 basic sites and 4 group sites (maximum varies from 50 to 125 people)
Maximum RV length: 30 feet
Fee: $$ for basic sites; $$$$ for group sites
Maximum stay: 7 days
Elevation: 5,100 feet
Road conditions: Paved to the campground, then gravel
Management: Logan Ranger District, 1500 E. Hwy. 89, Logan; (435) 755-3620; www.fs.usda
.gov/main/uwcnf/home
Reservations: Call (877) 444-6777 or TDD (877) 833-6777; www.recreation.gov
Activities: Fishing and picnicking
Season: May through October
Finding the campground: Leave US 91 at the exit for Mantua and the Box Elder Campground. Follow the signs for 0.8 mile on pavement to the campground, which is on the south side of US 91. A gravel road leads into the campground.
About the campground: Box Elder Creek sings through the thick vegetation of cottonwoods and box elders in this very shady campground, which is just west of Mantua Reservoir.

41 Clear Creek

Location: In the Sawtooth National Forest, approximately 39 miles west of Snowville
GPS: N41 57.190'/W113 19.341'
Facilities: Fire pits, picnic tables, vault toilets, and drinking water
Sites: 7 basic sites
Maximum RV length: 30 feet
Fee: None
Maximum stay: 14 days
Elevation: 6,300 feet
Road conditions: Gravel
Management: Minidoka Ranger District, 2609 Hiland Ave., Burley, ID 83318; (208) 678-0430;
www.fs.usda.gov/main/sawtooth/home
Reservations: None
Activities: Hiking, off-highway driving, and picnicking.
Season: June through October
Finding the campground: From Snowville, drive west on I-84 for about 2 miles to exit 5, then continue west on UT 30 for another 16 miles. Now keep straight on UT 42; after an additional 7.5 miles, UT 42 becomes ID 81. Go another 1.3 miles before turning left onto Strevell Road. Drive the maintained road for about 4 miles to the junction of FR 001. Go south, driving the gravel road approximately 8 more miles to the campground.
About the campground: Set on the slopes of the Raft River Range, this is a great base from which to explore the area, though trails are pretty much nonexistent. The grassy range runs east to west, which is quite rare in this part of the country.

Great Salt Lake Country

Great Salt Lake Country is just what its name implies—great. The place is also big, and it's remote: No doubt, it can feel mighty lonely out in its western realms. And while much of the place is accessible to visitors, the public isn't allowed at the following military-restricted areas—Dugway Proving Grounds, the Deseret Test Center, and the Wendover Range. Still, there are fourteen campgrounds to make exploring just that much easier.

Great Salt Lake Country, one of Utah's nine travel regions, is situated in the northern part of the state. Comprising 7,487 square miles, the place consists of two counties, Tooele and Salt Lake, and three Utah geographic areas—Great Basin, Wasatch Front Cities, and the Rocky Mountain Province. Bordered on the west by Nevada, it is surrounded on three sides by various other Utah travel regions. These are the Golden Spike Empire to the north, Mountainland to the east, and Panoramaland to the south.

Utah's capital, Salt Lake City, rests at the base of the lovely Wasatch Mountains. Wasatch, an Indian word meaning "high mountain pass," aptly describes the Wasatch Range, for it offers many such passes during its 200-mile journey from central Utah to Idaho.

Salt Lake City is a short drive from several wonderful campgrounds. These sites make great bases from which to explore the city; if you're more interested in the great out-of-doors, they're wonderful spots from which to explore the mountains. Climbers will find some superb rocks to scale here. There are wide ranges of both sport and traditional climbs in both Big and Little Cottonwood Canyons. Hikers, backpackers, horseback riders, mountain bikers, and anglers will also find plenty to keep them busy.

There's another haven for outdoor enthusiasts in the Deseret Peak Wilderness, located in the Stansbury Mountain Range. Trails lead to a bevy of high alpine lakes and glacial cirques. From Deseret Peak, at 11,031 feet, there are wonderful views of the Wasatch Mountains, the Great Salt Lake, and the Great Salt Lake Desert. Six campgrounds—Cottonwood, Intake, Boy Scout, Lower Narrows, Upper Narrows, and Loop—make exploring possible.

Out in the desert you'll find stretches of the original Pony Express Trail and a campground. Simpson Springs is within walking distance of a restored Pony Express station, a tribute to the hardy riders who routinely covered the ten-day, 1,838-mile distance from St. Joseph, Missouri, to Sacramento, California. Riders stopped at stations such as the one found here every 12 miles or so: Each rider would change horses about six times a day.

Of the fourteen campgrounds found in this travel region, twelve are managed by the Uinta-Wasatch-Cache National Forest; the Bureau of Land Management manages two of them. Though most are closed in winter, two can be visited year-round. Simpson Springs is available for camping all year, as is Vernon Reservoir, though Vernon is officially open from April through December. Try Vernon Reservoir in winter—it can be a nice place to go ice fishing, another one of the many activities enjoyed in the area.

For more information contact Great Salt Lake Country Travel Region, 90 S. West Temple St., Salt Lake City; (801) 521-2882 or (800) 541-4955; www.utahtravelcenter .com/travelregions/greatsaltlake.htm.

		Total Sites	Group Sites	Hook-up Sites	Hookups	Max. RV Length	Dump Station	Toilets	Showers	Drinking Water	ADA Compliant	Fees	Reservations	Recreation
42	Cottonwood	3				20		V				$$-$$$$$		FMHC
43	Intake	5				20		V				$$		CFMH
44	Boy Scout	9	1			20		V				$$-$$$$$	•	CHRFM
45	Lower Narrows	3				20		V				$$		CHRFM
46	Upper Narrows	8	2			20		V				$-$$$$$	•	CHRFM
47	Loop	13				20		V				$$-$$$		CHRFM
48	Clover Springs	11	1			30		V				$-$$	•	RFOH
49	Simpson Springs	21	1			30		V				$-$$$$$		HOM
50	Vernon Reservoir	10				40		V		•		None		FOBK
51	Tanners Flat	43	4			25		F & V		•	•	$$$-$$$$$	•	CHMF
52	Albion Basin	18				25		V		•		$$-$$$$$	•	HMC
53	Jordan Pines	4	4			25		V		•		$$$$$	•	CHMF
54	Spruces	94	2			40		F		•	•	$$$-$$$$$	•	HFCM
55	Redman	42	2			30		V		•		$$-$$$$$	•	CMFH

Hookup: W = Water, E = Electric, S = Sewer
Recreation: H = Hiking, C = Rock Climbing, M = Mountain Biking, S = Swimming, F = Fishing, B = Boating, L = Boat Launch, O = Off-highway Driving, R = Horseback Riding, K = Kayaking and Canoeing, G = Golf,
Toilets: F = Flush, V = Vault, C = Chemical
Per-night campsite cost: $ = $10 or less $$ = $11 to $20 $$$ = $21 to 30 $$$$ = $31 to $40 $$$$$ = $41 and higher

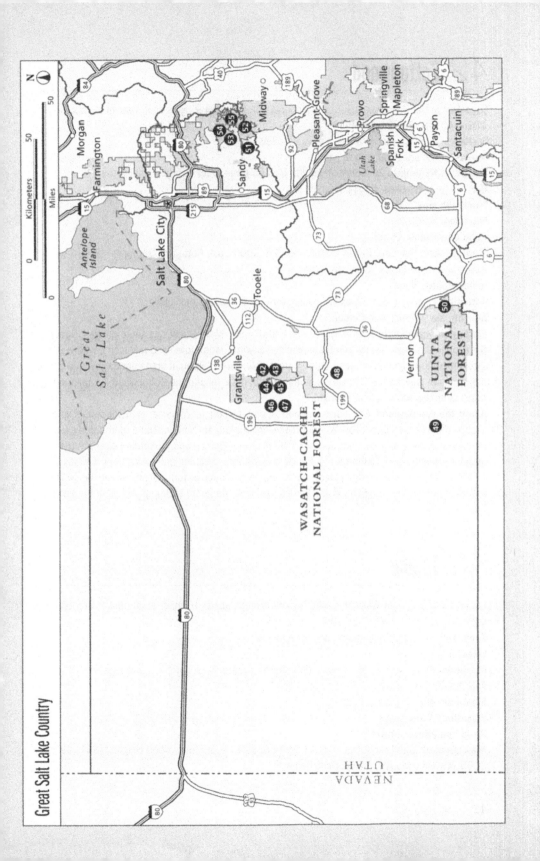

Great Salt Lake Country

42 Cottonwood

Location: In the Uinta-Wasatch-Cache National Forest, about 9 miles southwest of Grantsville
GPS: N40 30.092'/W112 33.480'
Facilities: Fire pits, picnic tables, and vault toilets
Sites: 2 basic sites and 1 triple site
Maximum RV length: 20 feet (total length; best for tents, truck campers, and vans)
Fee: $$ for basic sites; $$$$$ for triple site
Maximum stay: 7 days
Elevation: 6,200 feet
Road conditions: Gravel
Management: Salt Lake Ranger District, 6944 S. 3000 East, Cottonwood Heights; (801) 999-2103; www.fs.usda.gov/main/uwcnf/home
Reservations: None
Activities: Fishing, mountain biking, hiking, rock climbing, and picnicking
Season: May through mid-October
Finding the campground: From Grantsville and UT 138 (Main Street), go south on West Street. Signs point the way to North and South Willow Canyon Roads. Drive for 5 miles on paved West Street, then turn right (southwest) onto South Willow Canyon Road. It starts out narrow and paved, then turns to gravel after 3.3 miles; continue another 0.7 mile to the Cottonwood Campground, which is on the south side of the road.
About the campground: Box elders, dogwoods, and a whole lot more serve to shade this small, secluded place, with South Fork Willow Creek singing along its border. With a mere three sites, this would make a nice camping spot for a small group. Fishing and mountain biking are the most popular activities here, but farther up the canyon are rock climbing and hiking opportunities.

This is a tents-only kind of place with absolutely no place to turn trailers around. Water isn't available here in the campground, but you can get it at the guard station just west of the Intake Campground.

43 Intake

Location: In the Uinta-Wasatch-Cache National Forest, about 10 miles southwest of Grantsville
GPS: N40 29.847'/W112 34.305'
Facilities: Fire pits, picnic tables, and vault toilets
Sites: 5 basic sites
Maximum RV length: 20 feet (total length; best for tents, truck campers, and vans)
Fee: $$ for basic sites
Maximum stay: 7 days
Elevation: 6,300 feet
Road conditions: Gravel
Management: Salt Lake Ranger District, 6944 S. 3000 East, Cottonwood Heights; (801) 999-2103; www.fs.usda.gov/main/uwcnf/home

Reservations: None
Activities: Rock climbing, fishing, mountain biking, hiking, and picnicking
Season: May through September
Finding the campground: From Grantsville and UT 138 (Main Street), go south on West Street. Signs point the way to North and South Willow Canyon Roads. Drive for 5 miles on paved West Street, then turn right (southwest) onto South Willow Canyon Road. It starts out narrow and paved, then turns to gravel after 3.3 miles; continue another 1.4 miles to the Intake Campground, which is on the south side of the road.
About the campground: Box elders and miniature roses make this a shady place. Like most of the campgrounds here in the canyon, it's small and delightful but recommended for tents only, because there's no place to turn trailers around.

South Fork Willow Creek flows through the campground, making this a fun place for fishing. Mountain bikers can head up the canyon on their bicycles, while rock climbers will find some sport routes just up the canyon at the narrows. Hikers and horseback riders will find trails up the canyon at the Boy Scout and Loop Campgrounds.

Water isn't provided here in the campground, but it's available at the guard station just west of the campground.

44 Boy Scout

Location: In the Uinta-Wasatch-Cache National Forest, about 10 miles southwest of Grantsville
GPS: N40 29.660'/W112 34.733'
Facilities: Fire pits, picnic tables, tent pads, and vault toilets
Sites: 7 basic sites, 1 double site, and 1 group site (maximum 25 people)
Maximum RV length: 20 feet (narrow and winding road; not recommended for long RVs or trailers)
Fee: $$ for basic sites; $$$ for double site; $$$$$ for group site
Maximum stay: 7 days
Elevation: 6,500 feet
Road conditions: Gravel
Management: Salt Lake Ranger District, 6944 S. 3000 East, Cottonwood Heights; (801) 999-2103; www.fs.usda.gov/main/uwcnf/home
Reservations: For the group site only, call (877) 444-6777 or TDD (877) 833-6777; www.recreation.gov
Activities: Rock climbing, hiking, horseback riding, fishing, mountain biking, and picnicking
Season: May through September
Finding the campground: From Grantsville and UT 138 (Main Street), go south on West Street. Signs point the way to North and South Willow Canyon Roads. Drive for 5 miles on paved West Street, then turn right (southwest) onto South Willow Canyon Road. It starts out narrow and paved, then turns to gravel after 3.3 miles; continue another 2 miles to the Boy Scout Campground, which is on the south side of the road.
About the campground: A potpourri of deciduous trees and some pines shades this campground. South Fork Willow Creek flows through the campground, and hikers and horseback riders will find the Stansbury Front Trail, which leads 2.4 miles to Hickman Canyon.

If you'd rather do some rock climbing, check out the tough sport routes in the narrows, just up from the Upper Narrows Campground.

Water isn't available here in the campground, but it's provided at the guard station just west of the Intake Campground.

45 Lower Narrows

Location: In the Uinta-Wasatch-Cache National Forest, about 11 miles southwest of Grantsville
GPS: N40 29.523'/W112 35.522'
Facilities: Fire pits, picnic tables, and vault toilets
Sites: 3 basic sites
Maximum RV length: 20 feet (total length; best for tents, truck campers, and vans)
Fee: $$ for basic sites
Maximum stay: 7 days
Elevation: 6,800 feet
Road conditions: Gravel
Management: Salt Lake Ranger District, 6944 S. 3000 East, Cottonwood Heights; (801) 999-2103; www.fs.usda.gov/main/uwcnf/home
Reservations: None
Activities: Rock climbing, hiking, horseback riding, fishing, mountain biking, and picnicking
Season: May through September
Finding the campground: From Grantsville and UT 138 (Main Street), go south on West Street. Signs point the way to North and South Willow Canyon Roads. Drive for 5 miles on paved West Street, then turn right (southwest) onto South Willow Canyon Road. It starts out narrow and paved, then turns to gravel after 3.3 miles; continue another 2.7 miles to the Lower Narrows Campground, which is on the south side of the road. (*Note:* The road is narrow and winding and not recommended for trailers.)
About the campground: Park off the road and walk into this small campground, with South Fork Willow Creek providing the opportunity for anglers to do a little fishing. With only three shady sites, this would make a nice place for a small group to meet and enjoy the outdoors.

From the Boy Scout Campground nearby, there's a trail leading 2.4 miles to Hickman Canyon. It might be of interest for hikers and horseback riders. In addition, there are dirt roads for curious mountain bikers, and hard sport routes for rock climbers just up from the Upper Narrows Campground.

Water isn't available here in the campground, but you can get it at the guard station just west of the Intake Campground.

46 Upper Narrows

Location: In the Uinta-Wasatch-Cache National Forest, about 11 miles southwest of Grantsville
GPS: N40 29.514'/W112 35.667'
Facilities: Fire pits, picnic tables, and vault toilets
Sites: 6 basic sites and 2 group sites (maximum 30 and 50 people, respectively)
Maximum RV length: 20 feet (Total length; though there are group sites for up to 50 people, parking is at a premium. Don't bother bringing your RV.)
Fee: $ for basic sites; $$$$ to $$$$$ for group sites
Maximum stay: 14 days
Elevation: 6,900 feet
Road conditions: Dirt
Management: Salt Lake Ranger District, 6944 S. 3000 East, Cottonwood Heights; (801) 999-2103; www.fs.usda.gov/main/uwcnf/home
Reservations: For the group site only, call (877) 444-6777 or TDD (877) 833-6777; www.recreation.gov
Activities: Rock climbing, hiking, horseback riding, fishing, mountain biking, and picnicking
Season: May through September
Finding the campground: From Grantsville and UT 138 (Main Street), go south on West Street. Signs point the way to North and South Willow Canyon Roads. Drive for 5 miles on paved West Street, then turn right (southwest) onto South Willow Canyon Road. It starts out narrow and paved, then turns to gravel after 3.3 miles; continue another 2.9 miles to the Upper Narrows Campground, which is on the south side of the road. (**Note:** The road is narrow and winding and not recommended for trailers.)
About the campground: Park off the road and walk into this primitive campground, which is dispersed over a mile-long stretch of road. South Fork Willow Creek flows alongside the campground. You'll find shady sites near the parking area and just down a trail.

Hikers and horseback riders may want to check out the Stansbury Front Trail, which leads 2.4 miles to Hickman Canyon. It's back at the Boy Scout Campground. There are also trails leading from the Loop Campground, which is just up the canyon. Rock climbers will find twelve difficult sport routes at the narrows, which is just up from this campground.

Water isn't provided here in the campground, but it's available at the guard station just west of the Intake Campground.

47 Loop

Location: In the Uinta-Wasatch-Cache National Forest, about 12 miles southwest of Grantsville
GPS: N40 29.028'/W112 36.365'
Facilities: Fire pits, picnic tables, and vault toilets
Sites: 12 basic sites and 1 double site

Maximum RV length: 20 feet (total length; narrow and winding road; not recommended for long RVs or trailers)
Fee: $$ for basic sites; $$$ for double site
Maximum stay: 14 days
Elevation: 7,400 feet
Road conditions: Gravel
Management: Salt Lake Ranger District, 6944 S. 3000 East, Cottonwood Heights; (801) 999-2103; www.fs.usda.gov/main/uwcnf/home
Reservations: None
Activities: Rock climbing, hiking, horseback riding, fishing, mountain biking, and picnicking
Season: May through September
Finding the campground: From Grantsville and UT 138 (Main Street), go south on West Street. Signs point the way to North and South Willow Canyon Roads. Drive for 5 miles on paved West Street, then turn right (southwest) onto South Willow Canyon Road. It starts out narrow and paved, then turns to gravel after 3.3 miles; continue another 3.9 miles to the Loop Campground. (**Note:** The road is narrow and winding and not recommended for trailers.)
About the campground: Aspens, a variety of other deciduous trees, and conifers serve to shade these sites, some of which are partially open. It's a pretty place, with access to the Mill Fork Trailhead, which leads into the Deseret Peak Wilderness and offers exceptional hiking in the Stansbury Mountains.

Water is not available here in the campground, but you can get it at the guard station near the Intake Campground; you'll pass it en route to this campground.

48 Clover Springs

Location: On the north side of the Onaqui Mountains, about 23 miles southwest of Tooele
GPS: N40 20.821'/W112 33.036'
Facilities: Fire pits, picnic tables, vault toilets, horse feeding stations, a horse trough, and horse corrals; no trash service (pack it out)
Sites: 10 basic sites and 1 group site (maximum 50 people)
Maximum RV length: 30 feet
Fee: $ for basic sites; $$ for group site
Maximum stay: 14 days
Elevation: 6,000 feet
Road conditions: Paved to the campground, then gravel
Management: Bureau of Land Management, Salt Lake Field Office, 2370 S. 2300 West, Salt Lake City; (801) 977-4300; www.blm.gov/ut/st/en/fo/salt_lake.html
Reservations: For the group site only, call (801) 977-4300
Activities: Horseback riding, fishing, OHV riding, and hiking
Season: May through October

Finding the campground: Drive south from Tooele about 15 miles on UT 36, a paved road, and then head west on paved UT 199 for 7.8 miles to the campground, which is on the south side of the road.

About the campground: This is an equestrian-friendly campground, with specific sites for visitors with horses. Sites offer horse feeding stations, and there's a horse water trough nearby. Junipers present what little shade they can in this mostly open area.

Anglers may fish in the small stream here, while the area serves OHV riders and hikers as well.

49 Simpson Springs

Location: On the north side of the Simpson Mountains, about 58 miles southwest of Tooele
GPS: N40 02.135'/W112 46.972'
Facilities: Fire pits, BBQ grills, picnic tables, non-potable water, and vault toilets; no trash service (pack it out)
Sites: 20 basic sites and 1 large group site (maximum 250 people) near the livestock corrals, 0.25 mile west of the campground
Maximum RV length: 30 feet
Fee: $ for basic sites; $$$$$ for group site
Maximum stay: 14 days
Elevation: 5,100 feet
Road conditions: Gravel
Management: Bureau of Land Management, Salt Lake Field Office, 2370 S. 2300 West, Salt Lake City; (801) 977-4300; www.blm.gov/ut/st/en/fo/salt_lake.html
Reservations: None; for the group site only, a Special Recreation Permit (SRP) is required. Call (801) 977-4300 for more information.
Activities: Hiking, off-highway driving, and mountain biking
Restrictions: Horses not allowed in the campground (horse corral with water located 0.25 mile to the west)
Season: Year-round
Finding the campground: Drive south from Tooele about 33 miles on paved UT 36, then head southwest on the Pony Express Trail National Scenic Backway, which is maintained gravel. Drive for 24.7 miles to a Pony Express historic site and the campground.

About the campground: Located on the lower flank of the Simpson Mountains, there's a wide, sweeping view of the region north and west of here. It's Great Basin country, so expect juniper trees and sagebrush and not a whole lot more.

There's water at the campground, but it's posted as unsafe to drink. This could change in the future, but you should carry water just in case. It's a safe way to go anytime you're in a remote area such as this.

You'll see a restored Pony Express station near the campground, as well as the remains of a stone cabin built with stones from the original Pony Express station. During 1860 and 1861, horse riders rested here before they continued their 1,800-mile mail run.

50 Vernon Reservoir

Location: In the Uinta-Wasatch-Cache National Forest, about 6 miles southeast of Vernon
GPS: N39 59.512'/W112 23.106'
Facilities: Fire pits, covered picnic tables, drinking water, and vault toilets; no trash service (pack it out)
Sites: 10 basic sites
Maximum RV length: 40 feet
Fee: None
Maximum stay: 7 days
Elevation: 6,100 feet
Road conditions: Gravel
Management: Spanish Fork Ranger District, 44 W. 400 North, Spanish Fork; (801) 798-3571; www.fs.usda.gov/main/uwcnf/home
Reservations: None
Activities: Fishing, off-highway driving, kayaking, nonmotorized boating, and picnicking
Restrictions: Powerboats not allowed
Season: April through December
Finding the campground: Drive south from Vernon on UT 36, then turn right (southeast) onto FR 005. A sign points the way to Benmore. Travel the maintained gravel road for about 6 miles to the campground.
About the campground: Powerboats are not allowed on the lake, but folks with a canoe, kayak, or rowboat are welcome to cruise around to their hearts' content. Situated in a pinyon-juniper setting, the campground is open with very little vegetation. The road to the reservoir is accessible most of the year, making this a good place to go ice fishing come winter. Please note that although you can camp in winter, the water is turned off because of freezing conditions.

51 Tanners Flat

Location: In the Uinta-Wasatch-Cache National Forest, about 4 miles east of Sandy
GPS: N40 34.328'/W111 42.016'
Facilities: Fire pits, picnic tables, drinking water, ADA sites, flush and vault toilets, and an amphitheater; a volleyball court is also available (bring your own net and ball).
Sites: 34 basic sites, 3 double sites, 2 tents-only sites, and 4 group sites (maximum varies from 25 to 50 people)
Maximum RV length: 25 feet
Fee: $$$ for basic and tents-only sites; $$$$$ for double and group sites
Maximum stay: 7 days
Elevation: 7,200 feet
Road conditions: Paved

Management: Salt Lake Ranger District, 6944 S. 3000 East, Cottonwood Heights; (801) 999-2103; www.fs.usda.gov/main/uwcnf/home
Reservations: Call (877) 444-6777 or TDD (877) 833-6777; www.recreation.gov
Activities: Rock climbing, hiking, mountain biking, fishing, volleyball, and picnicking
Restrictions: Domestic animals not allowed in the Little Cottonwood Canyon watershed
Season: Late May through October
Finding the campground: From the junction of UT 210 and UT 209, just east of Sandy, go east on UT 210 for 4.3 miles. The campground is on the right (south) side of the road.
About the campground: Aspens, a variety of other deciduous trees, and some conifers serve to shade these sites. Four group sites make this a popular spot for big groups, whereas some enjoy the park and walk-in sites, which are more private than those you just park and camp right next to. Little Cottonwood Creek is a favorite of anglers, and nearby areas offer a multitude of activities for rock climbers, hikers, and mountain bikers. Of special interest is a trail open to hiking and biking up White Pine Canyon; it's just up the road from the campground.

52 Albion Basin

Location: In the Uinta-Wasatch-Cache National Forest, about 11 miles east of Sandy
GPS: N40 34.653' / W111 36.783'
Facilities: Fire pits, picnic tables, drinking water, and vault toilets
Sites: 16 basic sites, 1 double site, and 1 triple site
Maximum RV length: 25 feet
Fee: $$ for basic sites; $$$$ for double and triple sites
Maximum stay: 7 days
Elevation: 9,500 feet
Road conditions: Gravel
Management: Salt Lake Ranger District, 6944 S. 3000 East, Cottonwood Heights; (801) 999-2103; www.fs.usda.gov/main/uwcnf/home
Reservations: Call (877) 444-6777 or TDD (877) 833-6777; www.recreation.gov
Activities: Hiking, mountain biking, rock climbing, photography, and picnicking
Restrictions: Domestic animals not allowed in the Little Cottonwood Canyon watershed
Season: June (sometimes July due to snow) through September
Finding the campground: From the junction of UT 210 and UT 209, just east of Sandy, go east on UT 210 for approximately 11 miles. The road is paved for the first 8 miles or so, then turns to maintained gravel.
About the campground: Located in Little Cottonwood Canyon, the Albion Basin Campground is a good place from which to enjoy and explore the area. No doubt the place is a photographer's paradise, especially in summer when it sees an explosion of wildflowers. The basin hosts an annual Wasatch Wildflower Festival, usually in late July or early August. Moose, deer, and mountain goats also frequent the area.

53 Jordan Pines

Location: In the Uinta-Wasatch-Cache National Forest, about 13 miles southeast of Salt Lake City
GPS: N40 38.788' / W111 38.893'
Facilities: Fire pits, picnic tables, drinking water, and vault toilets
Sites: 4 group sites (maximum varies from 100 to 125 people)
Maximum RV length: 25 feet
Fee: $$$$$ for group sites
Maximum stay: 7 days
Elevation: 7,200 feet
Road conditions: Paved
Management: Salt Lake Ranger District, 6944 S. 3000 East, Cottonwood Heights; (801) 999-2103; www.fs.usda.gov/main/uwcnf/home
Reservations: Call (877) 444-6777 or TDD (877) 833-6777; www.recreation.gov
Activities: Rock climbing, hiking, mountain biking, fishing, and picnicking
Restrictions: Neither dogs nor horses allowed in Big Cottonwood Canyon; ATVs not allowed at campground
Season: June through September
Finding the campground: From the junction of UT 210 and UT 190, about 4 miles southeast of Salt Lake City, travel east on UT 190 for 9.3 miles and make a right (south). Drive another 0.2 mile to the campground.
About the campground: Jordan Pines consists of four group sites—Lodgepole, Limber Grove, Pine Grove, and Ponderosa Pine—which can each accommodate 100 to 125 people. The sites are available by reservation only.

Sites are both open and shady, with aspens and conifers making up most of the vegetation. Big Cottonwood Creek flows nearby, making this a nice spot for anglers, while there are nearby trails to delight hikers and a bounty of rock near the mouth of the canyon for rock climbers.

54 Spruces

Location: In the Uinta-Wasatch-Cache National Forest, about 14 miles southeast of Salt Lake City
GPS: N40 38.528' / W111 38.528'
Facilities: Fire pits, picnic tables, ADA sites, drinking water, flush toilets, and volleyball courts (bring your own net and ball)
Sites: 81 basic sites, 9 double sites, 2 triple sites, and 2 group sites (maximum 50 people each)
Maximum RV length: 40 feet
Fee: $$$ for basic sites; $$$$$ for double, triple, and group sites
Maximum stay: 7 days
Elevation: 7,400 feet
Road conditions: Paved
Management: Salt Lake Ranger District, 6944 S. 3000 East, Cottonwood Heights; (801) 999-2103; www.fs.usda.gov/main/uwcnf/home

Reservations: Call (877) 444-6777 or TDD (877) 833-6777; www.recreation.gov
Activities: Hiking, fishing, rock climbing, mountain biking, volleyball, softball, and picnicking
Restrictions: Dogs and horses not allowed in Big Cottonwood Canyon
Season: June through September
Finding the campground: From the junction of UT 210 and UT 190, about 4 miles southeast of Salt Lake City, travel east on UT 190 for 9.8 miles to the campground, which is on the south side of the road.
About the campground: This is a nice campground in a lush forest of aspen and conifers, with some meadow thrown in for good measure. There are volleyball courts for the overnight group areas.

Hikers will find a multitude of trails nearby, while anglers will find good fishing in Big Cottonwood Creek, and climbers will find both traditional and sport routes in the canyon.

55 Redman

Location: In the Uinta-Wasatch-Cache National Forest, about 17 miles southeast of Salt Lake City
GPS: N40 36.913' / W111 35.327'
Facilities: Fire pits, picnic tables, drinking water, and vault toilets
Sites: 36 basic sites, 2 double sites, 2 triple sites, and 2 group sites (maximum varies from 35 to 50 people)
Maximum RV length: 30 feet
Fee: $$ for basic sites; $$$$ for double sites; $$$$$ for triple and group sites
Maximum stay: 7 days
Elevation: 8,300 feet
Road conditions: Paved to the campground, then gravel
Management: Salt Lake Ranger District, 6944 S. 3000 East, Cottonwood Heights; (801) 999-2103; www.fs.usda.gov/main/uwcnf/home
Reservations: Call (877) 444-6777 or TDD (877) 833-6777; www.recreation.gov
Activities: Rock climbing, mountain biking, hiking, fishing, and picnicking
Restrictions: Dogs and horses not allowed in Big Cottonwood Canyon
Season: June through September
Finding the campground: From the junction of UT 210 and UT 190, about 4 miles southeast of Salt Lake City, travel east on UT 190 for 13.1 miles to the campground, which is on the south side of the road.
About the campground: A mix of aspens, conifers, and meadow makes this a nice place to camp, with tiny streams trickling through the area.

Hiking trails are found in the canyon, as is good fishing in Big Cottonwood Creek. The place is also a mecca for rock climbers, who come to participate in both traditional and sport climbing.

Mountainland

Mountainland is, well, chock-full of mountains. Of course, if you spend time in the place, you'll find that the region is more than just mountains. It's an area of unique diversity, one of those places where there is virtually something for everyone. You'll find things to do whether you're interested in hot-air ballooning, snowmobiling, horseback riding, sailing, windsurfing, and other water-related activities, rock climbing, hiking, backpacking, bird watching, wildlife watching, biking, and more.

Mountainland is the second smallest of Utah's travel regions, with 5,054 square miles tucked away in the northern part of the state. Bordered on the north by Wyoming and the state travel region called Bridgerland, the region snuggles up to Dinosaurland to the east, Castle Country and Panoramaland to the south, and Great Salt Lake Country and the Golden Spike Empire to the west. The region consists of three state geographic areas: the Great Basin, Wasatch Front Cities, and Rocky Mountain Province. It also includes all of Summit, Wasatch, and Utah Counties.

Located in the heart of the Rockies, Mountainland is an easily accessible place, traversed north to south by I-15 and east to west by I-80. Driving is a pleasure here, for a number of roads have been designated Scenic Byways and Scenic Backways. In summer drive the Mount Nebo Scenic Byway, a paved delight, and you'll climb to more than 9,000 feet while enjoying breathtaking views of Utah Valley and the Wasatch Mountains. Provo Canyon Scenic Byway is another must-see. Open year-round, this paved route winds past Bridal Veil Falls to Deer Creek Reservoir and on to Heber Valley. Another must-do is Mirror Lake Scenic Byway. It passes through heavily forested mountain terrain, climbing to 10,687 feet in its 65-mile length. (It is closed in winter.)

Mountainland might be a small travel region, but it is not small on campgrounds. You'll find sixty-three campgrounds in a potpourri of settings, most of them excellent places from which to explore the region.

There are fifty-two national forest campgrounds, all Uinta-Wasatch-Cache National Forest delights. In addition, there is one city-managed campground—Jolley's Ranch—and three county-managed campgrounds—Nunns Park, Willow Park, and Spanish Fork River Park—that add to the riches found here. There are seven state park campgrounds, two of which are found at Jordanelle Reservoir. With the exception of Wasatch Mountain State Park, Utah's largest state park with 22,000 acres, all the state parks provide a wonderful place from which to enjoy a multitude of water sports. In fact, in Utah Lake State Park you'll find the largest freshwater lake in the state.

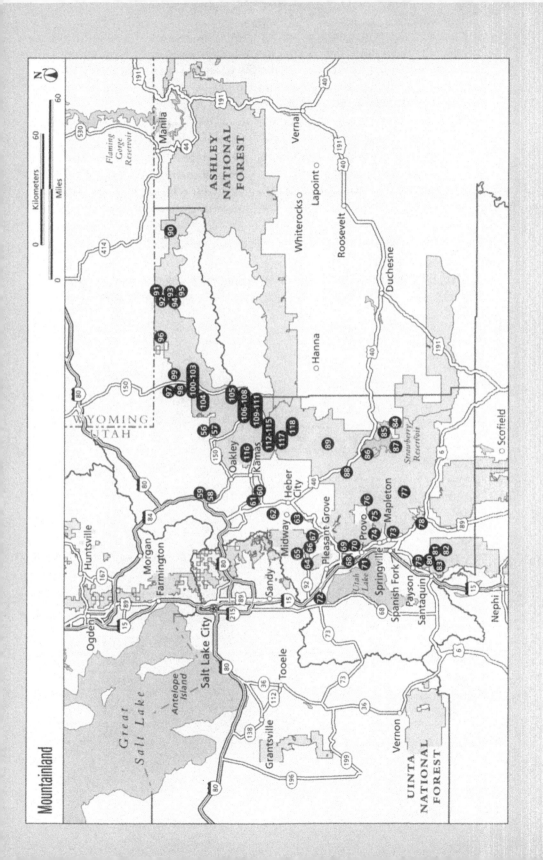

Mountainland

Fortunately, there are campgrounds close to Timpanogos Cave National Monument. A definite must-see, the cave is located deep inside majestic Mount Timpanogos. Here, visitors will have to earn seeing the beautiful cave formations: A 1.5-mile trail climbs more than 1,000 feet in elevation to the cave entrance. Be sure to pay for your ticket at the visitor center before climbing to the cave.

There's also a campground near the Sundance Resort, founded in 1969 by Robert Redford. In winter both alpine and Nordic skiing are popular; in summer enchanting musicals are performed in an outdoor theater amid spectacular mountain scenery.

Throughout Mountainland you'll have the opportunity to view wildlife. The region's many lakes, streams, and rivers are stocked with fish ranging from cutthroat and rainbow trout to mackinaw and brown trout, walleye, bluegills, and striped bass. The meadows and mountains are home to moose, elk, mule deer, black bears, mountain lions, mountain goats, bobcats, and a variety of birds, including grouse, partridge, and others too numerous to mention.

For more information on Mountainland, contact the travel region at 586 E. 800 North, Orem; (801) 229-3800; www.utahtravelcenter.com/travelregions/mountainland.htm.

		Total Sites	Group Sites	Hook-up Sites	Hookups	Max. RV Length	Dump Station	Toilets	Showers	Drinking Water	ADA Compliant	Fees	Reservations	Recreation
56	Smith and Morehouse	34				45		V		•		$$	•	FBLHMK
57	Ledgefork	73				Any		V		•		$$-$$$$	•	FBMHLK
58	Rockport State Park: South	100	3	34	WE	40	•	F & V	•	•	•	$$-$$$$$	•	FSBHMLK
59	Rockport State Park: North	19	2			Any		V		•		$$-$$$$$	•	FSBLK
60	Rock Cliff	6				None		F	•	•	•	$$	•	FHML
61	Hailstone	184		103	WE	Any	•	F	•	•	•	$$	•	FSBLHK
62	Wasatch Mountain State Park	125	4	121	WES	35	•	F	•	•	•	$$-$$$$$	•	GFMH
63	Deer Creek State Park	63		34	WES	Any	•	F & V	•	•	•	$$-$$$	•	FSBHMLK
64	Little Mill	37	1			30		V			•	$$-$$$$$	•	HCF
65	Granite Flat	55	3			30		V		•		$$-$$$$$	•	HMFK
66	Timpooneke	28	1			30		V		•		$$-$$$$$	•	HMFK
67	Mount Timpanogos	27				30		F		•		$$	•	H
68	Nunns Park	18				20		F & V		•		$$	•	MHF
69	Hope	26				20		V		•		$$-$$$$	•	MH

#	Name	Total Sites	Group Sites	Hook-up Sites	Hookups	Max. RV Length	Dump Station	Toilets	Showers	Drinking Water	ADA Compliant	Fees	Reservations	Recreation
70	Rock Canyon	4	4			20		V		•		$$$$$	•	HOM
71	Lakeshore	32		32	WE	Any	•	F	•	•	•	$$$-$$$$$	•	FSBMHLK
72	Willow Park	41	13			Any		F & V		•		$$-$$$$$	•	FKBHL
73	Whiting	28	2			35		V		•		$$-$$$$$	•	HMR
74	Jolley's Ranch	57		57	WE	50		F		•		$$	•	FM
75	Cherry	32	4			35		V				$$-$$$$$	•	FHMCRG
76	Balsam	26	1			20		V		•		$$-$$$$$	•	FHRM
77	Diamond	67	7			Any		F		•		$$-$$$$$	•	FHM
78	Spanish Fork River Park	11	2			Any		F		•		$$-$$$$$	•	FHM
79	Maple Lake	7				20		V				$$		HFK
80	Maple Bench	10				20		V		•		$$		HFK
81	Payson Lakes	111	3			45		F & V		•	•	$$-$$$$$	•	HRFSK
82	Blackhawk	38	23			40	•	F		•	•	$$-$$$$$	•	HMR
83	Tinney Flat	16	3			25		V		•		$$-$$$$$	•	FCH
84	Aspen Grove	57		1	WES	40		F		•	•	$$-$$$$	•	FBKL
85	Soldier Creek	166	1			Any	•	F		•		$$-$$$$$	•	FBLK
86	Strawberry Bay	288	7	27	WES	Any	•	F		•		$$-$$$$$	•	FBMHLK
87	Renegade Point	66				30		F		•		$$-$$$$	•	FBMHLK
88	Lodgepole	57	2			40	•	F		•		$$-$$$$$	•	HF
89	Currant Creek	102	4			40	•	F		•		$$-$$$$$	•	FBHRMLK
90	Hoop Lake	44				25		V		•		$$		FHRB
91	Statelilne	41				30	•	V		•		$$	•	FBHMKL
92	Bridger Lake	30				45		V		•		$$-$$$$		FBHMLK
93	Marsh Lake	46				45		V		•		$$-$$$$	•	FBOHMLK
94	China Meadows	9				20		V				$$		FHKMRO
95	Trailhead	11				30		V				$$		FHR
96	Little Lyman Lake	10				16		V		•		$$		FOH
97	East Fork Bear River	7				20		V		•		$$		FOM
98	Bear River	4				20		V		•		$$		FOM
99	Christmas Meadows	11				20		V		•		$$	•	FH

Hookup: W = Water, E = Electric, S = Sewer

Recreation: H = Hiking, C = Rock Climbing, M = Mountain Biking, S = Swimming, F = Fishing, B = Boating, L = Boat Launch, O = Off-highway Driving, R = Horseback Riding, K = Kayaking and Canoeing, G = Golf,

Toilets: F = Flush, V = Vault, C = Chemical

Per-night campsite cost: $ = $10 or less $$ = $11 to $20 $$$ = $21 to 30 $$$$ = $31 to $40 $$$$$ = $41 and higher

Hike Number	Hike Name	Total Sites	Group Sites	Hook-up Sites	Hookups	Max. RV Length	Dump Station	Toilets	Showers	Drinking Water	ADA Compliant	Fees	Reservations	Recreation
100	Stillwater	24	4			35		V		•		$$-$$$$$	•	F
101	Hayden Fork	9				20		V		•		$$		F
102	Beaver View	18				22		V		•		$$		F
103	Sulphur	22	1			22		V		•		$$-$$$$$	•	F
104	Butterfly Lake	20				25		V		•		$$		FKRH
105	Mirror Lake	78				40		V		•	•	$$-$$$$$	•	FBHRLK
106	Moosehorn	33				30		V				$$	•	FKH
107	Lost Creek	35				30	•	V		•		$$	•	FK
108	Lilly Lake	14				30		V		•		$$		FK
109	Trial Lake	60				35		V		•		$$	•	FH
110	Cobblerest	18				20		V				$$		FH
111	Shady Dell	20				25		V		•		$$-$$$$		FH
112	Soapstone	34				40	•	V		•		$$-$$$$$	•	F
113	Pine Valley North	3	3			30		V		•		$$$$$	•	FHMR
114	Lower Provo River	10				30		V				$$	•	FHRM
115	Shingle Creek	33				25		V		•		$$		FOMH
116	Yellow Pine	33				25		V				$$		FHMR
117	Mill Hollow	28				40		V		•		$$	•	FHKM
118	Wolf Creek	5	2			25		V		•		$$-$$$$$	•	H

Hookup: W = Water, E = Electric, S = Sewer

Recreation: H = Hiking, C = Rock Climbing, M = Mountain Biking, S = Swimming, F = Fishing, B = Boating, L = Boat Launch, O = Off-highway Driving, R = Horseback Riding, K = Kayaking and Canoeing, G = Golf,

Toilets: F = Flush, V = Vault, C = Chemical

Per-night campsite cost: $ = $10 or less $$ = $11 to $20 $$$ = $21 to 30 $$$$ = $31 to $40 $$$$$ = $41 and higher

56 Smith and Morehouse

Location: In the Uinta-Wasatch-Cache National Forest, about 13 miles northeast of Oakley
GPS: N40 46.154'/W112 06.440'
Facilities: Fire pits, picnic tables, drinking water, vault toilets, and a boat launch at nearby Smith and Morehouse Reservoir
Sites: 34 basic sites
Maximum RV length: 45 feet
Fee: $$ for basic sites
Maximum stay: 7 days
Elevation: 7,800 feet
Road conditions: Gravel to the campground, then paved
Management: Heber-Kamas Ranger District, 2460 S. Hwy. 40, Heber City; (435) 654-0470; www .fs.usda.gov/main/uwcnf/home
Reservations: Call (877) 444-6777 or TDD (877) 833-6777; www.recreation.gov
Activities: Fishing, boating, hiking, mountain biking, and picnicking
Restrictions: ATVs not allowed
Season: May through September
Finding the campground: From the small settlement of Oakley and the junction of UT 32 and Weber Canyon Road, drive northeast on paved Weber Canyon Road for 11.8 miles. Make a right (south) onto FR 33, a gravel road. A sign points the way to the Smith and Morehouse Recreation Area. After 1.8 miles you'll reach the campground.
About the campground: Set among aspens and pines, shaded sites and beautiful scenes make this a favorite place to visit. Nearby, Smith and Morehouse Reservoir offers fishing, boating, and more. The area is also a favorite for hikers and mountain bikers.

57 Ledgefork

Location: In the Uinta-Wasatch-Cache National Forest, approximately 15 miles northeast of Oakley
GPS: N40 44.111'/W111 05.974'
Facilities: Fire pits, picnic tables, drinking water, vault toilets, and a boat launch at nearby Smith and Morehouse Reservoir
Sites: 67 basic sites and 6 double sites
Maximum RV length: Any
Fee: $$ for basic sites; $$$$ for double sites
Maximum stay: 7 days
Elevation: 7,700 feet
Road conditions: Gravel to the campground, then paved
Management: Heber-Kamas Ranger District, 2460 S. Hwy. 40, Heber City; (435) 654-0470; www .fs.usda.gov/main/uwcnf/home
Reservations: Call (877) 444-6777 or TDD (877) 833-6777; www.recreation.gov
Activities: Fishing, boating, mountain biking, hiking, and picnicking

Restrictions: ATVs not allowed

Season: May through September

Finding the campground: From the small settlement of Oakley and the junction of UT 32 and Weber Canyon Road, drive northeast on paved Weber Canyon Road for 11.8 miles. Make a right (south) onto FR 33, a gravel road. A sign points the way to the Smith and Morehouse Recreation Area. You'll pass the Smith and Morehouse Campground and Smith and Morehouse Reservoir before reaching the campground at 3.8 miles.

About the campground: As at the Smith and Morehouse Campground, which is located nearby, these campsites are set among aspens and pines, with plenty of shade and beautiful scenery. Smith and Morehouse Reservoir is close to the campground and offers fishing and boating. The area is also a favorite of hikers and mountain bikers.

58 Rockport State Park: South Entrance

Location: About 40 miles east of Salt Lake City

GPS: N40 45.238' / W111 22.377'

Facilities: Fire pits, picnic tables (some covered), ADA sites, BBQ grills, partial hookups, flush and vault toilets, showers at Juniper Campground, drinking water, sewage disposal station, boat ramp, and boat docks

Sites: 54 basic sites (including some double sites), 34 sites with partial-hookups (some double sites), 6 walk-in tent sites, 3 boat-in sites, and 3 group sites (maximum varies from 40 to 75 people)

Maximum RV length: 40 feet

Fee: $$ for basic, walk-in, and boat-in sites; $$$ for partial-hookup sites; $$$$$ for group sites

Maximum stay: 14 days

Elevation: 6,000 feet

Road conditions: Paved

Management: Rockport State Park, 9040 N. State Hwy. 302, Peoa; (435) 336-2241; www.state parks.utah.gov/park/rockport-state-park

Reservations: In the Salt Lake area, call (801) 322-3770; elsewhere, (800) 322-3770; http:// utahstateparks.reserveamerica.com

Activities: Fishing, swimming, sailing, waterskiing, boating, hiking, mountain biking, birding, and picnicking. In winter, cross-country skiing and ice fishing are popular.

Restrictions: Campground gates closed from 11 p.m. to 6 a.m.

Season: Year-round

Finding the campground: About 8 miles south of Coalville, leave I-80 at exit 155 and head south on UT 32. After 5 miles, turn left (east) onto UT 302; you'll reach the park entrance after another 0.3 mile.

About the campground: From the southern entrance at Rockport State Park, six campgrounds and three group sites in a span of about 3 miles offer everything from primitive sites with vault toilets to partial-hookup sites with water and electricity and hot showers. There are a total of one hundred sites accessible from the south entrance, including boat-in sites and group sites. Listing the campgrounds from south to north: Cottonwood has twenty shady sites; Hawthorne is a group camping area; Crandall Cove has 10 sites; Crandall Group Site has a nice view of the lake; Twin Coves has twenty-four sites; Lariat Group Site is near the water; Juniper offers thirty-four partial-

Kayaking the lovely waters of Rockport State Park; Juniper Campground is visible in the background.

hookup sites; Cedar Point has six walk-in tent sites, available by reservation only; and just to the north there are three boat-in sites.

All these campgrounds are located along the shore of, or near, scenic Rockport Reservoir. Spanning more than 500 acres, the reservoir is a popular place for water sports, fishing, bird watching, and sunbathing. Most of the sites are partially shaded, and those that aren't offer covered picnic tables. Vault toilets are the norm at all but the Juniper Campground, where you will find flush toilets and hot showers.

59 Rockport State Park: North Entrance

Location: About 41 miles east of Salt Lake City
GPS: N40 47.568' / W111 24.473'
Facilities: Fire pits, picnic tables, BBQ grills, vault toilets, and drinking water
Sites: 17 basic sites and 2 group sites (maximum 75 people each)
Maximum RV length: Any
Fee: $$ for basic sites; $$$$$ for group sites
Maximum stay: 14 days
Elevation: 5,800 feet
Road conditions: Paved to the campground, then gravel

Management: Rockport State Park, 9040 N. State Hwy. 302, Peoa; (435) 336-2241; www.state parks.utah.gov/park/rockport-state-park

Reservations: In the Salt Lake area, call (801) 322-3770; elsewhere, (800) 322-3770; http://utahstateparks.reserveamerica.com

Activities: Fishing, swimming, sailing, waterskiing, boating, birding, and picnicking; cross-country skiing and ice fishing in winter

Season: Year-round

Finding the campground: About 8 miles south of Coalville, leave I-80 at exit 155 and head south on UT 32. After 0.6 mile turn left (east) onto Rockport Road, which parallels main highway UT 302; you'll reach the park entrance after another 0.4 mile.

About the campground: From the northern entrance at Rockport State Park, you'll find the Riverside Campground, as well as the Old Church and Riverside group areas. Riverside Campground sites are mostly in the open, but there are a few trees around. The Old Church Group Campground is located near the Old Church, originally built in 1892. The church was restored in 2005 and is now on the Summit County Historical Registry.

All the campgrounds are located on the opposite side of the Wanship Dam from scenic Rockport Reservoir. Spanning more than 500 acres, the reservoir is a popular place for water sports, fishing, bird watching, and sunbathing.

60 Rock Cliff: Jordanelle State Park

Location: About 14 miles northeast of Heber City

GPS: N40 36.285'/W111 20.312'

Facilities: Fire pits, picnic tables, ADA sites, flush toilets, showers, drinking water, fish cleaning station, and a small boat access ramp

Sites: 6 walk-in sites

Maximum RV length: None

Fee: $$ for walk-in sites

Maximum stay: 14 days

Elevation: 6,200 feet

Road conditions: Paved

Management: Jordanelle State Park, SR 319 #515 Box 4, Heber City, UT 84032; (435) 649-9540; www.stateparks.utah.gov/park/jordanelle-state-park

Reservations: In the Salt Lake area, call (801) 322-3770; elsewhere, (800) 322-3770; http://utahstateparks.reserveamerica.com

Activities: Fishing, hiking, mountain biking, and picnicking

Restrictions: Pets not allowed; campground gates closed from 10 p.m. to 6 a.m.

Season: Year-round

Finding the campground: From the junction of US 40 and UT 32, about 6 miles north of Heber City, drive north then east on UT 32 for 7.7 miles. The campground turnoff is on the north side of the highway; the entrance station is another 0.6 mile ahead.

About the campground: With its beautiful wetlands setting, this is a Utah state park treasure. RVs are not allowed—in fact, cars aren't even allowed, at least not next to each campsite. Instead, campers park and walk into the walk-in campground. Sites have all the usual amenities, and there are showers and flush toilets; you just have to walk to get to them.

(*Note:* In 2010 a water main broke and closed forty-four sites in the Riverbend, Aspen Grove, and Upland Meadows loops. They remain closed due to budget problems. It is not known when the campgrounds will reopen, so check if you are interested.)

Pets are not allowed in the campground due to the plentiful animal life found here. Birds are especially abundant, with nearly 200 different species passing through or residing in the area. The tall cottonwoods and aspens of the beautiful riparian area at Rock Cliff are home to owls, kestrels, woodpeckers, hawks, and eagles, as well as a variety of hummingbirds. Ospreys nest in the area, and in winter bald eagles can be found roosting in the woodlands.

The Nature Center is certainly one of the highlights of the area, with an elevated boardwalk and interpretive area accessible for those in wheelchairs (some of the campsites are accessible, too).

61 Hailstone: Jordanelle State Park

Location: About 9 miles north of Heber City
GPS: N40 37.213'/W111 25.419'
Facilities: Fire pits, picnic tables, tent pads, BBQ grills, ADA sites, flush toilets, showers, drinking water, dump station, partial hookups, mini-laundries, boat ramp and boat docks, fish cleaning station, and a marina with a restaurant, store, and rentals
Sites: 103 partial-hookup sites, 40 basic sites, 41 hike-in sites, and 2 cabins
Maximum RV length: Any
Fee: $$ for partial-hookup, basic, and hike-in sites; $$$$$ for cabins
Maximum stay: 14 days
Elevation: 6,200 feet
Road conditions: Paved
Management: Jordanelle State Park, SR 319 # 515 Box 4, Heber City, UT 84032; (435) 649-9540; www.stateparks.utah.gov/park/jordanelle-state-park
Reservations: In the Salt Lake area, call (801) 322-3770; elsewhere, (800) 322-3770; http://utahstateparks.reserveamerica.com
Activities: Fishing, swimming, boating, birding, hiking, and picnicking
Restrictions: Campground gate closed from 10 p.m. to 6 a.m.
Season: Year-round
Finding the campground: From Heber City drive north on US 40 for about 8 miles to exit 8 (Mayflower) and a sign pointing the way to the state park. From the exit it's another mile to the entrance station.
About the campground: A mix of wide-open sites should delight those camping on the west shore of scenic Jordanelle Reservoir. The place is popular with those who enjoy fishing, boating, water sports, swimming, hiking, and mountain biking. There are three separate campgrounds at Hailstone: one with water and electric hookups for RVers, another for camping without hookups, and yet another for walk-in tent campers. According to park personnel it's a 20-minute walk or so to the Keetley Hike-in Campground.

Dogs are allowed in the campground (on a leash, of course), but are not permitted on public beaches or adjacent waters.

62 Wasatch Mountain State Park: Pine Creek Campground

Location: About 3 miles northwest of Midway
GPS: N40 32.643'/W111 29.203'
Facilities: Fire pits, picnic tables, ADA sites, some tent pads, some BBQ grills, flush toilets, showers, full and partial hookups, drinking water, dump station, and a golf course
Sites: 57 partial-hookup sites, 64 full-hookup sites (including some double sites), 4 group sites (maximum varies from 75 to 100 people), and 2 cabins
Maximum RV length: 35 feet
Fee: $$ for partial-hookup sites; $$$ for full-hookup sites; $$$$$ for group sites and cabins
Maximum stay: 14 days
Elevation: 5,900 feet
Road conditions: Paved
Management: Wasatch Mountain State Park, PO Box 10, Midway, UT 84049; (435) 654-1791; www.stateparks.utah.gov/park/wasatch-mountain-state-park
Reservations: In the Salt Lake area, call (801) 322-3770; elsewhere, (800) 322-3770; http://utahstateparks.reserveamerica.com
Activities: Golfing, fishing, mountain biking, hiking, and wildlife watching
Restrictions: Campground gate closed from 10 p.m. to 6 a.m.
Season: April through October
Finding the campground: From the junction of UT 113 and UT 222 in Midway, drive 3.3 miles northwest via UT 222. En route you'll pass a visitor center for Wasatch Mountain and the golf course.
About the campground: Nestled in beautiful Heber Valley and tucked up against the Wasatch Mountains, you'll find three wonderful campground loops to satisfy all your needs. Mahogany offers all full-hookup sites, while Cottonwood has both partial- and full-hookup sites. Sites are fairly open, but some offer plenty of shade as well. The Oak Hollow Loop offers sites for tents, vans, and small motor homes, with water and electricity at each site. Vegetation is thick, so sites are pretty private here.

In addition to the sites listed above, there's a seventeen-site camping area at the Little Deer Creek Camp. It's 10 miles up a dirt road, the last 3 miles of which require high-clearance vehicles. You'll find water and flush toilets, but no showers or electricity.

A USGA-sanctioned golf course is a major attraction here. Hikers, horseback riders, and mountain bikers will want to check out the trails at nearby Dutch Hollow.

63 Deer Creek State Park

Location: About 12 miles northeast of Provo
GPS: N40 24.649'/W111 30.811'
Facilities: Fire pits, picnic tables (some covered), ADA sites, some BBQ grills, flush and vault toilets, showers, drinking water, dump station, and a boat ramp
Sites: 23 basic sites, 34 full-hookup sites, and 6 tents-only sites

Golfers can enjoy the scenery and the game at Wasatch Mountain State Park.

Maximum RV length: Any
Fee: $$ for basic and tents-only sites; $$$ for full-hookup sites
Maximum stay: 14 days
Elevation: 5,400 feet
Road conditions: Paved
Management: Deer Creek State Park, PO Box 257, Midway, UT 84049; (435) 654-0171; www
.stateparks.utah.gov/park/deer-creek-state-park
Reservations: In the Salt Lake area, call (801) 322-3770; elsewhere, (800) 322-3770; http://
utahstateparks.reserveamerica.com
Activities: Fishing, swimming, boating, hiking, mountain biking, birding, and picnicking
Restrictions: Dogs allowed only in the campground, not on the beach or in the water; camp-
ground gate closed from 10 p.m. to 6 a.m.
Season: Year-round
Finding the campground: From the junction of UT 52 and US 189 in Provo, travel northeast on
US 189 for 12 miles to the campground, which is on the left (north) side of the road.
About the campground: Deer Creek Reservoir lies in the southwest corner of lovely Heber Valley,
and these two campgrounds lie at the south end of the lake. The place is a mecca for outdoor
enthusiasts, especially those who enjoy water sports such as boating, windsurfing, swimming,
sailboating, and more. A fish cleaning station is available, and two concessionaires provide a restaurant, boat rentals, gasoline, and other items. Great Horned Owl is the eldest of the two campgrounds, with basic sites and nice views of the lake. Chokecherry offers covered picnic tables,

full-hookup sites, and access to Chokecherry Lake Trail, which leads down to the lake. If you enjoy hiking, horseback riding, and/or mountain biking, check out the Deer Creek Trail, an 8-mile segment of the much longer Provo-Jordan River Parkway Trail. Dogs are not allowed on the trail.

64 Little Mill

Location: In the Uinta-Wasatch-Cache National Forest, about 9 miles northeast of Pleasant Grove
GPS: N40 26.919'/W111 40.574'
Facilities: Fire pits, picnic tables, ADA sites, and vault toilets
Sites: 34 basic sites, 2 double sites, and 1 group site (maximum 50 people)
Maximum RV length: 30 feet
Fee: $$ for basic sites; $$$$ for double sites; $$$$$ for group site
Maximum stay: 7 days
Elevation: 6,000 feet
Road conditions: Paved
Management: Pleasant Grove Ranger District, 390 N. 100 East, Pleasant Grove; (801) 785-3563; www.fs.usda.gov/main/uwcnf/home
Reservations: Call (877) 444-6777 or TDD (877) 833-6777; www.recreation.gov
Activities: Hiking, rock climbing, fishing, and picnicking
Restrictions: Vehicle length restriction of 30 feet over the Alpine Scenic Loop (UT 92)
Season: June through October
Finding the campground: From the junction of UT 146 and UT 92, approximately 5 miles north of Pleasant Grove, travel east on UT 92 for 4.1 miles to the campground, which is on the right (south) side of the road. The North Mill Group Area is only 0.2 mile beyond, on the same side of the road.
About the campground: A shady, one-way road parallels the American Fork River for about 1 mile through this lengthy campground, with a forest of box elder, maple, and conifers to keep things cool. While some folks come to relax and fish, others come to enjoy nearby Timpanogos Cave National Monument, and some come to hike.

The place is especially favored among rock climbers, who try their best to stick to nearby walls. In fact, this campground offers several favorite rock climbing areas of its own. Diversion Wall is located here and offers an abundance of higher-level moderate to difficult routes.

65 Granite Flat

Location: In the Uinta-Wasatch-Cache National Forest, about 13 miles northeast of Pleasant Grove
GPS: N40 29.381'/W111 39.179'
Facilities: Fire pits, picnic tables, drinking water, and vault toilets
Sites: 44 basic sites, 8 double sites, and 3 group sites (maximum varies from 100 to 125 people)
Maximum RV length: 30 feet
Fee: $$ for basic sites; $$$$ for double sites; $$$$$ for group sites
Maximum stay: 7 days
Elevation: 6,800 feet

Road conditions: Paved
Management: Pleasant Grove Ranger District, 390 N. 100 East, Pleasant Grove; (801) 785-3563; www.fs.usda.gov/main/uwcnf/home
Reservations: Call (877) 444-6777 or TDD (877) 833-6777; www.recreation.gov
Activities: Hiking, mountain biking, fishing, kayaking, softball, horseshoe pits, and picnicking
Restrictions: ATVs/OHVs not allowed; vehicle length restriction of 30 feet over the Alpine Scenic Loop (UT 92).
Season: June through September
Finding the campground: From the junction of UT 146 and UT 92, approximately 5 miles north of Pleasant Grove, travel east on UT 92 for 5.2 miles to a fork. Turn left (north) onto UT 144 for 3.2 miles to the campground.
About the campground: Granite Flat is a delight for large groups, with three large areas to satisfy just about everyone's needs. Many sites are located in the shady realms of conifers, aspens, and other deciduous trees. Hikers will find the Box Elder Trailhead here, while anglers will find good fishing at both Silver Lake Flat and Tibble Fork Reservoirs, located nearby. Kayaking and canoeing at the lakes are equally fun. There's also a nice intermediate 8-mile mountain bike ride from Tibble Fork Reservoir past the campground and on up to Silver Lake Flat Reservoir.

66 Timpooneke

Location: In the Uinta-Wasatch-Cache National Forest, about 14 miles northeast of Pleasant Grove
GPS: N40 25.915'/W111 38.783'
Facilities: Fire pits, picnic tables, drinking water, and vault toilets
Sites: 20 basic sites, 7 double sites, and 1 group site (maximum 40 people)
Maximum RV length: 30 feet (bumper-to-bumper or combined vehicle/RV length)
Fee: $$ for basic sites; $$$$ for double sites; $$$$$ for group site
Maximum stay: 7 days
Elevation: 7,400 feet
Road conditions: Part paved, part gravel
Management: Pleasant Grove Ranger District, 390 N. 100 East, Pleasant Grove; (801) 785-3563; www.fs.usda.gov/main/uwcnf/home
Reservations: Call (877) 444-6777 or TDD (877) 833-6777; www.recreation.gov
Activities: Hiking, mountain biking, fishing, photography, and picnicking
Restrictions: ATVs/OHVs not allowed; vehicle length restriction of 30 feet over the Alpine Scenic Loop (UT 92)
Season: June through October
Finding the campground: From the junction of UT 146 and UT 92, approximately 5 miles north of Pleasant Grove, travel east on UT 92 for 8.7 miles to the campground, which is on the right (south). If you're looking for the group site, you'll find it 0.2 mile prior to the campground, on the left (north) side of the road.
About the campground: Situated on the north side of Mount Timpanogos, a beautiful mountain in the Wasatch Range, this shady campground offers a forest of deciduous trees and conifers, as well as a creek that flows through the campground and offers anglers the opportunity to fish for their meals. The group area is found nearby and offers the same amenities for large groups.

Gravel roads in the area are fun for mountain bikers, while hikers will love the views from the Timpooneke Trail, which leads to the top of Mount Timpanogos—at 11,750 feet the highest point in the Mount Timpanogos Wilderness. The trail is about 9 miles long and gains almost 4,900 feet in elevation.

67 Mount Timpanogos

Location: In the Uinta-Wasatch-Cache National Forest, about 12 miles northeast of Provo
GPS: N40 24.355'/W111 36.380'
Facilities: Fire pits, BBQ grills, picnic tables, drinking water, and flush toilets
Sites: 27 basic sites
Maximum RV length: 30 feet (bumper-to-bumper or combined vehicle/RV length)
Fee: $$ for basic sites
Maximum stay: 7 days
Elevation: 6,800 feet
Road conditions: Paved
Management: Pleasant Grove Ranger District, 390 N. 100 East, Pleasant Grove; (801) 785-3563; www.fs.usda.gov/main/uwcnf/home
Reservations: Call (877) 444-6777 or TDD (877) 833-6777; www.recreation.gov
Activities: Hiking, photography, and picnicking
Restrictions: ATVs not allowed; vehicle length restriction of 30 feet over the Alpine Scenic Loop (UT 92)
Season: June through October
Finding the campground: From the junction of US 189 and UT 52 on the north end of Provo, travel northeast on US 189 for 6.9 miles to the junction of UT 92. There's a sign reading "Sundance and Aspen Grove" at the junction. Go north on UT 92 for 5 miles, reaching a fee station for FR 114 just prior to the campground. You'll have to pay or use a pass to drive the road leading 0.1 mile to the campground. The campground is on the right (east) side of the sometimes steep, narrow, winding paved road. The Theater in the Pines Group Area is reached just prior to the campground, but on the left (west) side of the road.
About the campground: Maples and other trees add to the thick ground vegetation to make this a shady place to camp, though the sites are relatively small and the road is windy. Due to the length restriction, vans, small motor homes, and tent trailers are best. If you're in need of a group site, you'll find a spot for up to 150 tents just prior to entering the campground. Called Theater in the Pines, it's available by reservation only.

Nearby trails lead to a variety of places, including Mount Timpanogos—at 11,750 feet the highest point in the Mount Timpanogos Wilderness. A 9-mile trail takes off from the Aspen Grove Trailhead to climb about 4,900 vertical feet. It's a nice hike, with the view from the summit being one you won't soon forget.

68 Nunns Park

Location: About 3 miles north of Provo
GPS: N40 20.172'/W111 36.740'
Facilities: Fire pits, BBQ grills, picnic tables, drinking water, playground, and flush and vault toilets
Sites: 18 basic sites
Maximum RV length: 20 feet
Fee: $$ for basic sites
Maximum stay: 7 days
Elevation: 5,000 feet
Road conditions: Paved
Management: Utah County Parks, 2855 S. State St., Provo; (801) 370-8624; www.utahcounty
.gov/Parks/ParkDetails.asp?IDNO=1
Reservations: None
Activities: Mountain biking, hiking, fishing, and picnicking
Season: May through mid-October
Finding the campground: From the junction of UT 52 and US 189 in Provo, travel northwest on US 189 for 3.2 miles to the campground, which is on the left (north) side of the road. (After exiting the highway go left and under it to the campground.)
About the campground: Just off US 189, this pretty campground is shaded with box elders and other trees and offers the song of the Provo River, which flows alongside it. It's right next to the highway so expect highway noise as well. Bicyclists and hikers will find the Provo River Parkway a fun place to explore. It follows the Provo River from the campground down to Utah Lake State Park and up to Vivian Park. The river also offers anglers a place to wet a line and non-anglers a place to cool their feet.

69 Hope

Location: In the Uinta-Wasatch-Cache National Forest, about 7 miles northeast of Provo
GPS: N40 18.190'/W111 36.190'
Facilities: Fire pits, picnic tables, drinking water, and vault toilets
Sites: 24 basic sites and 2 double sites
Maximum RV length: 20 feet
Fee: $$ for basic sites; $$$$ for double sites
Maximum stay: 7 days
Elevation: 6,600 feet
Road conditions: Paved to the campground, then gravel
Management: Pleasant Grove Ranger District, 390 N. 100 East, Pleasant Grove; (801) 785-3563; www.fs.usda.gov/main/uwcnf/home
Reservations: Call (877) 444-6777 or TDD (877) 833-6777; www.recreation.gov
Activities: Mountain biking, hiking, and picnicking

Restrictions: Horses and ATVs not allowed

Season: May through October

Finding the campground: From the junction of UT 52 and US 189 in Provo, drive east on US 189 for 1.8 miles to Squaw Peak Road. Now travel south on Squaw Peak Road, a paved road that climbs and winds its way up the mountain for 4.5 miles to the campground turnoff, which is on the left (north). Follow it another 0.3 mile to the campground.

About the campground: Lush vegetation of box elder, maple, and oak makes for a shady campground best suited for small trailers, tent trailers, and tents. It's a spot where some come just to relax, while others use it as a base from which to explore the surrounding area. A bike ride along Squaw Peak Road begins here; see Gregg Bromka's *Mountain Biking Utah* for more information. Hikers will find the Rock Canyon and Squaw Peak Trails are nearby.

70 Rock Canyon

Location: In the Uinta-Wasatch-Cache National Forest, about 11 miles northeast of Provo

GPS: N40 16.205'/W111 35.138'

Facilities: Fire pits, picnic tables, drinking water, and vault toilets

Sites: 4 group sites (maximum varies from 45 to 90 people)

Maximum RV length: 20 feet

Fee: $$$$$ for group sites

Maximum stay: 7 days

Elevation: 6,900 feet

Road conditions: Dirt

Management: Pleasant Grove Ranger District, 390 N. 100 East, Pleasant Grove; (801) 785-3563; www.fs.usda.gov/main/uwcnf/home

Reservations: Call (877) 444-6777 or TDD (877) 833-6777; www.recreation.gov

Activities: Hiking, off-highway driving, mountain biking, and picnicking

Season: May through October

Finding the campground: From the junction of UT 52 and US 189 in Provo, drive east on US 189 for 1.8 miles to Squaw Peak Road. Now travel south on Squaw Peak Road, a paved road that climbs and winds its way up the mountain, then down into Rock Canyon. The road turns to gravel after 4.5 miles and isn't recommended for trailers or low-clearance vehicles. Travel another 4.3 miles to the campground, keeping right (west) when you come to a fork just prior to the campground.

About the campground: An abundance of trees and other vegetation shade this campground, which offers four group sites, all of which must be reserved. There are numerous four-wheel-drive roads in the area for mountain bikers and ATVers. Also, Rock Canyon Trail travels 6 miles from the campground to the mouth of Rock Canyon at the end of North Temple Drive in Provo.

71 Lakeshore: Utah Lake State Park

Location: About 3 miles west of Provo
GPS: N40 14.229'/W111 44.022'
Facilities: Fire pits, covered picnic tables, BBQ grills, ADA sites, partial hookups, flush toilets, showers, drinking water, dump station, boat launch ramps, boat docks, boat and watercraft rentals, and a visitor center
Sites: 32 partial-hookup sites (including 3 double sites)
Maximum RV length: Any
Fee: $$$ for partial-hookup sites; $$$$$ for partial-hookup double sites
Maximum stay: 14 days
Elevation: 4,500 feet
Road conditions: Paved
Management: Utah Lake State Park, 4400 W. Center, Provo; (801) 375-0731; www.stateparks .utah.gov/park/utah-lake-state-park
Reservations: In the Salt Lake area, call (801) 322-3770; elsewhere, (800) 322-3770; http:// utahstateparks.reserveamerica.com
Activities: Fishing, swimming, boating, ice skating, mountain biking, hiking, birding, and picnicking
Restrictions: Campground gate closed from 10 p.m. to 6 a.m.
Season: Year-round
Finding the campground: From exit 268B off I-15, travel west on Center Street (also known as UT 114 West) for 2.6 miles to the state park.
About the campground: Located along the east shore of Utah Lake, Utah's largest natural freshwater lake, this is a wonderful place to relax and play. The confluence of the Provo River and Utah Lake is found here, providing fabulous river and lakefront water play. Best of all, there are wonderful views of the Cedar Valley Mountains and the majestic Wasatch Range to gaze at while you enjoy a number of activities. These include swimming, fishing, waterskiing, sailing, canoeing, and kayaking, plus ice skating in winter. Bicyclists and hikers will find a 15-plus-mile path made of asphalt and hard-packed dirt and gravel that follows the Provo River from the state park to Vivian Park.

72 Willow Park

Location: About 3 miles west of Lehi
GPS: N40 23.488'/W111 53.857'
Facilities: Fire pits, picnic tables, BBQ grills, vault and flush toilets, drinking water, sand volleyball, playground, and a canoe launch
Sites: 41 individual sites within 13 group areas
Maximum RV length: Any
Fee: $$ for basic sites; $$$$$ for group sites
Maximum stay: 7 days (for self-contained units); 2 days (for those without self-contained units)
Elevation: 4,500 feet
Road conditions: Paved

Management: Utah County, 2855 S. State St., Provo; (801) 851-8600; www.utahcounty.gov/Parks/ParkDetails.asp?IDNO=11
Reservations: Call hosts Mike and Tina at (801) 420-6068 or Utah County at (801) 851-8640
Activities: Fishing, canoeing or kayaking, biking, hiking, birding, and picnicking
Restrictions: ATVs not allowed
Season: Year-round (water available mid-April through October)
Finding the campground: Traveling north on I-15, take exit 279 (Main Street) and go left (west) on Main Street. Drive 3.2 miles and turn right onto Willow Park Road; continue 0.3 mile, then make a left and enter the campground after another 0.1 mile.
About the campground: Trees and spacious sites fill this 50-plus-acre campground where the Jordan River flows nearby. Great for individuals and/or groups, the park was developed around a large group of old willow trees. There are thirteen group areas. If not reserved as a group, individuals can access forty-one individual sites within those group areas. The Jordan River Parkway, more than 15 miles in length, provides opportunities for walking, hiking, and biking.

73 Whiting

Location: In the Uinta-Wasatch-Cache National Forest, about 3 miles east of Mapleton
GPS: N40 07.907'/W111 31.728'
Facilities: Fire pits, picnic tables, drinking water, and vault toilets
Sites: 18 basic sites, 8 double sites, and 2 group sites (maximum 100 and 200 people respectively)
Maximum RV length: 35 feet
Fee: $$ for basic sites; $$$$ for double sites; $$$$$ for group sites
Maximum stay: 7 days
Elevation: 5,500 feet
Road conditions: Paved
Management: Spanish Fork Ranger District, 44 W. 400 North, Spanish Fork; (801) 798-3571; www.fs.usda.gov/main/uwcnf/home
Reservations: Call (877) 444-6777 or TDD (877) 833-6777; www.recreation.gov
Restrictions: OHVs/ATVs not allowed
Activities: Hiking, mountain biking, horseback riding, and picnicking
Season: April through September
Finding the campground: From the junction of Main Street and 400 North in Mapleton, follow the sign to the Whiting Campground via 400 North. You'll drive 2.7 miles east to the campground.
About the campground: Maple, box elder, and other types of vegetation shade this campground, which offers three horse camping units. In addition to two group sites, there's a stream and a hiking and horseback riding trail.

74 Jolley's Ranch

Location: About 6 miles east of Springville
GPS: N40 10.012' / W111 29.479'
Facilities: Fire pits, picnic tables, drinking water, partial hookups, and flush toilets
Sites: 57 partial-hookup sites
Maximum RV length: 50 feet
Fee: $$ for partial-hookup sites
Maximum stay: 7 days
Elevation: 5,100 feet
Road conditions: Paved to the campground, then gravel
Management: Springville City Parks Department, 443 S. 200 East, Springville; (801) 489-2700; www.springville.org/buildings-and-grounds/canyon-parks/jolleys-ranch-campground/
Reservations: Call (801) 489-2700
Activities: Fishing, mountain biking, and picnicking
Restrictions: ATVs, off-road motorcycles, and horses not allowed; also, smoking and alcohol consumption prohibited
Season: April through October
Finding the campground: From the junction of 400 South (UT 77) and US 89 (Main Street) in Springville, head east on 400 South. After 1.3 miles turn right onto Canyon Road (also known as Hobble Creek Road) and continue on the paved road for 4.7 miles to a fork. Now keep right (east) on Right Fork Hobble Creek, a paved road, for an additional 0.4 mile to the campground, which is on the south side of the highway.
About the campground: A city-owned establishment, this campground was voted Best RV Park in Utah Valley by *Daily Herald* readers. Hobble Creek meanders through the grassy, shaded park, with box elder, oak, and maple trees adding to the scene.

75 Cherry

Location: In the Uinta-Wasatch-Cache National Forest, about 7 miles east of Springville
GPS: N40 10.123' / W111 28.627'
Facilities: Fire pits, picnic tables, vault toilets, horseshoe pit, and volleyball court
Sites: 24 basic sites, 4 double sites, and 4 group sites (maximum varies from 50 to 75 people)
Maximum RV length: 35 feet
Fee: $$ for basic sites; $$$$ for double sites; $$$$$ for group sites
Maximum stay: 7 days
Elevation: 5,200 feet
Road conditions: Paved
Management: Spanish Fork Ranger District, 44 W. 400 North, Spanish Fork; (801) 798-3571; www.fs.usda.gov/main/uwcnf/home
Reservations: Call (877) 444-6777 or TDD (877) 833-6777; www.recreation.gov

Activities: Fishing, hiking, mountain biking, rock climbing, horseback riding, picnicking, and golfing at a local course
Season: May through October
Finding the campground: From the junction of 400 South (UT 77) and US 89 (Main Street) in Springville, head east on 400 South. After 1.3 miles turn right onto Canyon Road (also known as Hobble Creek Road) and continue on the paved road for 4.7 miles to a fork. Now keep right (east) on Right Fork Hobble Creek, a paved road, for an additional 1.4 miles to the campground, which is on the south side of the highway.
About the campground: Hobble Creek sings through this shady campground, with box elder, maple, and cottonwood making up the majority of the tree species. Hiking and horseback riding are popular here. The Left Fork Days Canyon Trail starts at the campground and leads 7 miles to Packard Canyon. Rock climbers will find several routes (5.11 to 5.12) on a limestone crag about 1.4 miles east of the campground entrance.

76 Balsam

Location: In the Uinta-Wasatch-Cache National Forest, about 13 miles east of Springville
GPS: N40 11.906' / W111 24.129'
Facilities: Fire pits, picnic tables, drinking water, and vault toilets
Sites: 24 basic sites, 1 triple site, and 1 group site (maximum 100 people)
Maximum RV length: 20 feet
Fee: $$ for basic sites; $$$$$ for triple and group sites
Maximum stay: 7 days
Elevation: 5,900 feet
Road conditions: Paved
Management: Spanish Fork Ranger District, 44 W. 400 North, Spanish Fork; (801) 798-3571; www.fs.usda.gov/main/uwcnf/home
Reservations: Call (877) 444-6777 or TDD (877) 833-6777; www.recreation.gov
Activities: Fishing, hiking, horseback riding, mountain biking, and picnicking
Season: May through October
Finding the campground: From the junction of 400 South (UT 77) and US 89 (Main Street) in Springville, head east on 400 South. After 1.3 miles turn right onto Canyon Road (also known as Hobble Creek Road) and continue on the paved road for 4.7 miles to a fork. Now keep right (east) on Right Fork Hobble Creek, a paved road, for an additional 6.7 miles to the campground, which is on the south side of the highway.
About the campground: As with the other campgrounds found in this area, Hobble Creek makes its appearance, but this time it shows up in a forest of conifers as well as cottonwood, box elder, and more. There are horseback riding and hiking trails in the nearby area.

77 Diamond

Location: In the Uinta-Wasatch-Cache National Forest, about 17 miles east of Spanish Fork
GPS: N40 04.365'/W111 25.842'
Facilities: Fire pits, picnic tables, drinking water, and flush toilets
Sites: 38 basic sites, 22 double sites, and 7 group sites (maximum varies from 25 to 125 people), including 1 walk-in group site
Maximum RV length: Any
Fee: $$ for basic sites; $$$$ for double sites; $$$$$ for group sites
Maximum stay: 7 days
Elevation: 5,200 feet
Road conditions: Paved
Management: Spanish Fork Ranger District, 44 W. 400 North, Spanish Fork; (801) 798-3571; www.fs.usda.gov/main/uwcnf/home
Reservations: Call (877) 444-6777 or TDD (877) 833-6777; www.recreation.gov
Activities: Fishing, hiking, mountain biking, and picnicking
Season: May through October
Finding the campground: From Spanish Fork drive southeast on US 6/89 for approximately 11 miles to Diamond Fork Canyon Road. Turn northeast onto the paved road and continue 5.8 miles to the campground.
About the campground: The Diamond Fork River and an abundance of deciduous trees make for a pleasant setting in this semi-open area. It's a popular place for fishing, hiking, and just plain relaxing. An interpretive nature trail winds through the campground. In addition, a nearby trail leads to popular Fifth Water Hot Springs, and the Monks Hollow Trail begins 5 miles from the campground. The seven group sites are located 2 to 3 miles farther down the road.

78 Spanish Fork River Park

Location: In the Uinta-Wasatch-Cache National Forest, about 17 miles southeast of Spanish Fork
GPS: N40 01.403'/W111 30.150'
Facilities: Fire pits, picnic tables (some covered), BBQ grills, 2 playgrounds, drinking water, and flush toilets
Sites: 9 basic sites and 2 group sites (maximum 120 people each)
Maximum RV length: Any
Fee: $$ for basic sites; $$$$$ for group sites
Maximum stay: 7 days
Elevation: 5,000 feet
Road conditions: Paved
Management: Utah County, 2855 S. State St., Provo; (801) 851-8600; www.utahcounty.gov/Parks/ParkDetails.asp?IDNO=7
Reservations: For group sites only, call Utah County at (801) 851-8640

Activities: Fishing, hiking, mountain biking, and picnicking
Restrictions: ATVs/OHVs, and alcoholic beverages not allowed
Season: Mid-April through mid-October
Finding the campground: From Spanish Fork drive southeast on US 6/89 for approximately 11 miles to the turnoff on the right for Spanish Fork River Park. A sign points the way. (The road may be named Thistle Slide Road on some maps.) Enter the park after 0.3 mile.
About the campground: Located at the confluence of the Diamond Fork and Spanish Fork Rivers, you'll find sites to the right and the left along the Spanish Fork. Cottonwoods and other deciduous trees shade some of the sites.

79 Maple Lake

Location: In the Uinta-Wasatch-Cache National Forest, approximately 8 miles southeast of Payson
GPS: N39 57.354'/W111 41.528'
Facilities: Vault toilet
Sites: 7 basic sites
Maximum RV length: 20 feet
Fee: $$ for basic sites
Maximum stay: 7 days
Elevation: 6,400 feet
Road conditions: Paved to the campground, then gravel
Management: Spanish Fork Ranger District, 44 W. 400 North, Spanish Fork; (801) 798-3571; www.fs.usda.gov/main/uwcnf/home
Reservations: None
Activities: Hiking, fishing, kayaking, and picnicking
Season: May through October
Finding the campground: From the junction of 100 North and 600 East in Payson, travel east on 600 East, following signs for the Mount Nebo Scenic Loop. After 6.6 miles you'll reach the campground turnoff, which is on the right (west); drive another 1.1 miles up a narrow, winding road to the campground.
About the campground: Thick vegetation surrounds Maple Lake, a small lake that's popular for fishing and best for tents, because there isn't room for much else. Though most sites lack a picnic table, you might find a table or two. Conifers, oaks, and maples shade the densely vegetated sites. Hikers can choose between two trails—the Shoreline Trail is 0.25 mile, while another trail leads 3 miles to Red Lake.

80 Maple Bench

Location: In the Uinta-Wasatch-Cache National Forest, approximately 7 miles southeast of Payson
GPS: N39 57.775'/W111 41.546'
Facilities: Fire pits, picnic tables, drinking water, and vault toilets

Sites: 10 basic sites
Maximum RV length: 20 feet
Fee: $$ for basic sites
Maximum stay: 7 days
Elevation: 5,900 feet
Road conditions: Paved to the campground, then gravel
Management: Spanish Fork Ranger District, 44 W. 400 North, Spanish Fork; (801) 798-3571; www.fs.usda.gov/main/uwcnf/home
Reservations: None
Activities: Hiking, fishing and kayaking at nearby Maple Lake, and picnicking
Season: May through October
Finding the campground: From the junction of 100 North and 600 East in Payson, travel east on 600 East, following signs for the Mount Nebo Scenic Loop. After 6.6 miles you'll reach the campground turnoff, which is on the right (west); drive another 0.3 mile to a fork and keep left to enter the campground. (The right fork leads 0.8 mile up a narrow, winding road to Maple Lake.)
About the campground: Turns are tight in this small campground, so you'd do best to bring nothing larger than a tent trailer or regular tent. Oaks and maples shade the small sites, which make a good base from which to explore the surrounding area.

81 Payson Lakes

Location: In the Uinta-Wasatch-Cache National Forest, approximately 13 miles southeast of Payson
GPS: N39 55.847'/W111 38.409'
Facilities: Fire pits, picnic tables, BBQ grills, ADA sites, drinking water, flush and vault toilets, and horse corrals
Sites: 98 basic sites, 10 double sites, and 3 group sites (maximum varies from 75 to 100 people)
Maximum RV length: 45 feet
Fee: $$ for basic sites; $$$$ for double sites; $$$$$ for group sites
Maximum stay: 7 days
Elevation: 8,000 feet
Road conditions: Paved
Management: Spanish Fork Ranger District, 44 W. 400 North, Spanish Fork; (801) 798-3571; www.fs.usda.gov/main/uwcnf/home
Reservations: Call (877) 444-6777 or TDD (877) 833-6777; www.recreation.gov
Activities: Hiking, horseback riding, fishing, kayaking and canoeing, swimming, and picnicking
Restrictions: ATVs/OHVs not allowed; powerboats prohibited in Payson Lakes
Season: May through October
Finding the campground: From the junction of 100 North and 600 East in Payson, travel east on 600 East, following signs for the Mount Nebo Scenic Loop. After 12.8 miles you'll reach the campground turnoff, which is on the right (west).
About the campground: Lush vegetation, including aspens and conifers, provides privacy for the sites found here at Big East Lake, one of three Payson Lakes. Fishing is a popular activity, as are rafting and boating, though powerboats are not allowed.

Boreal toads live throughout much of Utah.

Three group sites are available at Box Lake, another of the Payson Lakes, which also provides access for those interested in fishing. Hikers will find a trail around the lake and a trailhead across the road from the campground turnoff. It leads to Loafer Mountain and Santaquin Peak. See Dave Hall's *Hiking Utah* for more information.

82 Blackhawk

Location: In the Uinta-Wasatch-Cache National Forest, approximately 16 miles southeast of Payson
GPS: N39 53.846' / W111 37.805'
Facilities: Fire pits, picnic tables, BBQ grills, ADA sites, drinking water, flush toilets, dump station, hitching racks, horse corrals, and water troughs
Sites: 12 basic sites, 3 double sites, 21 group sites (maximum varies from 50 to 100 people), and 2 additional group sites equipped for horses (maximum 50 people each)
Maximum RV length: 40 feet
Fee: $$ for basic sites; $$$$ for double sites; $$$$$ for group sites
Maximum stay: 7 days

Elevation: 8,000 feet
Road conditions: Paved
Management: Spanish Fork Ranger District, 44 W. 400 North, Spanish Fork; (801) 798-3571; www.fs.usda.gov/main/uwcnf/home
Reservations: Call (877) 444-6777 or TDD (877) 833-6777; www.recreation.gov
Activities: Hiking, mountain biking, horseback riding, and picnicking
Restrictions: ATVs/OHVs not allowed
Season: June through October
Finding the campground: From the junction of 100 North and 600 East in Payson, travel east on 600 East, following signs for the Mount Nebo Scenic Loop. After 14.5 miles you'll reach the campground turnoff on the left (east). Travel another 1.6 miles to the campground.
About the campground: Open meadows merge with a mix of conifers and deciduous trees such as oaks, maples, and aspens, making this a delightful place to camp. It's a mecca for group sites, with Loops A, B, C, and most of D dedicated wholly to groups. There are single sites in Loop E, which is also the place for those with horses. A trailhead provides access to Blackhawk and Loafer Mountain. Payson Lake, a great place for kayaking and fishing, is 5 miles away.

83 Tinney Flat

Location: In the Uinta-Wasatch-Cache National Forest, approximately 7 miles southeast of Santaquin
GPS: N39 57.775'/W111 41.546'
Facilities: Fire pits, picnic tables, drinking water, and vault toilets
Sites: 11 basic sites, 2 double sites, and 3 group sites (maximum 50 people each)
Maximum RV length: 25 feet
Fee: $$ for basic sites; $$$$ for double sites; $$$$$ for group sites
Maximum stay: 7 days
Elevation: 7,000 feet
Road conditions: Paved
Management: Spanish Fork Ranger District, 44 W. 400 North, Spanish Fork; (801) 798-3571; www.fs.usda.gov/main/uwcnf/home
Reservations: Call (877) 444-6777 or TDD (877) 833-6777; www.recreation.gov
Activities: Fishing, rock climbing, hiking, and picnicking
Restrictions: No ATVs/OHVs allowed in campground
Season: May through September
Finding the campground: From exit 244 off I-15 in Santaquin, go southwest on Highland Drive, a frontage road. After 1.1 miles the road ends; make a left (southeast) onto Santaquin Canyon Road and drive another 5.7 miles to the campground. (*Note:* The road is narrow and winding and not recommended for large RVs or trailers.)
About the campground: Nestled in thick trees on the north slope of Mount Nebo, this campground can be quite busy. There's lots to do in the area, with access to three trails just up the road. There are also some bolted sport routes for rock climbers prior to reaching the campground.

84 Aspen Grove

Location: In the Uinta-Wasatch-Cache National Forest, about 39 miles southeast of Heber City
GPS: N40 07.264'/W111 02.196'
Facilities: Fire pits, picnic tables (some covered), ADA sites, one site with full hookups, drinking water, and flush toilets. There's also a boat ramp, a marina, ice, camping and fishing supplies, a boat slip, and boat rentals nearby.
Sites: 42 basic sites, 3 tents-only sites, 11 double sites, and 1 full-hookup site
Maximum RV length: 40 feet
Fee: $$ for basic and tents-only sites; $$$ for full-hookup site; $$$$ for double sites
Maximum stay: 7 days
Elevation: 7,800 feet
Road conditions: Paved
Management: Heber Ranger District, 2460 S. Hwy. 40, Heber City; (435) 654-0470; www.fs.usda.gov/main/uwcnf/home
Reservations: Call (877) 444-6777 or TDD (877) 833-6777; www.recreation.gov
Activities: Fishing, boating, photography, and picnicking
Restrictions: OHVs/ATVs and horses not allowed; campground requires a 2-day minimum stay on weekends and 3-day minimum stay on holiday weekends
Season: May through October
Finding the campground: From the junction of US 189 and US 40 in Heber City, drive southeast on US 40 for 32.9 miles, then go south at the sign for Aspen Grove and Soldier Creek Dam. Travel paved FR 090 for 5.2 miles, then make a left (south) onto FR 482 and drive another 0.5 mile to the campground entrance. At the point where you turn onto FR 482, you'll find Aspen Marina and a boat ramp on the right (north).
About the campground: Overlooking the southeast corner of 17,000-acre Strawberry Reservoir, this campground offers both shaded and open sites. Loop A is shaded with aspens and conifers, while Loop B is more open and provides a view of the lake.

Anglers should enjoy fishing the bountiful waters of Strawberry Reservoir; species include cutthroat and rainbow trout, as well as some kokanee salmon and brook trout. Sailing is popular, too, with predictable daily winds often gliding sailboats or sailboards across Strawberry Reservoir. Hardy water-skiers don wet suits when skiing across the cold waters found at this elevation.

85 Soldier Creek

Location: In the Uinta-Wasatch-Cache National Forest, about 34 miles southeast of Heber City
GPS: N40 09.288'/W111 03.475'
Facilities: Fire pits, picnic tables (most covered), drinking water, flush toilets, dump station (fee), boat ramp, and a marina with boat and automobile gas (including propane), boat rentals, boat slip rentals, deep moorage rentals, dry boat storage, fish cleaning station, and camping and fishing supplies
Sites: 155 basic sites, 10 double sites, and 1 group site (maximum 50 people)
Maximum RV length: Any

Fee: $$ for basic sites; $$$$ for double sites; $$$$$ for group site
Maximum stay: 7 days (long-term, month-to-month sites also available)
Elevation: 7,600 feet
Road conditions: Paved
Management: Heber Ranger District, 2460 S. Hwy. 40, Heber City; (435) 654-0470; www.fs.usda .gov/main/uwcnf/home
Reservations: Call (877) 444-6777 or TDD (877) 833-6777; www.recreation.gov
Activities: Fishing, boating, photography, and picnicking
Restrictions: OHVs not allowed; campground requires a 2-day minimum stay on weekends and 3-day minimum stay on holiday weekends
Season: May through October
Finding the campground: From the junction of US 189 and US 40 in Heber City, drive southeast on US 40 for 31.7 miles, then go south at the sign for Soldier Creek Recreation Complex. Travel the paved road for 2.5 miles to the campground.
About the campground: Four campground loops, all of which are open and offer wonderful views of the reservoir and surrounding mountains, overlook the southeast corner of 17,000-acre Strawberry Reservoir.

Anglers should enjoy fishing the bountiful waters of Strawberry Reservoir; species include cutthroat and rainbow trout, as well as some kokanee salmon and brook trout. Sailing is popular, too, with predictable daily winds often gliding sailboats or sailboards across Strawberry Reservoir. Hardy water-skiers don wet suits when skiing across the cold waters found at this elevation.

86 Strawberry Bay

Location: In the Uinta-Wasatch-Cache National Forest, about 26 miles southeast of Heber City
GPS: N40 11.276'/W111 11.001'
Facilities: Fire pits, picnic tables (some covered), drinking water, flush toilets, full hookups, dump station (fee), boat ramp, and a marina with boat and automobile gas (including propane), boat rentals, boat slip rentals, deep moorage rentals, dry boat storage, fish cleaning station, camping and fishing supplies, a cafe, and lodge.
Sites: 229 basic sites, 25 double sites, 27 full-hookup sites, and 7 group sites (maximum varies from 80 to 100 people)
Maximum RV length: Any
Fee: $$ for basic sites; $$$$ for double sites; $$$ for full-hookup sites; $$$$$ for group sites
Maximum stay: 7 days (long-term, month-to-month sites also available)
Elevation: 7,700 feet
Road conditions: Paved
Management: Heber Ranger District, 2460 S. Hwy. 40, Heber City; (435) 654-0470; www.fs.usda .gov/main/uwcnf/home
Reservations: Call (877) 444-6777 or TDD (877) 833-6777; www.recreation.gov
Activities: Fishing, boating, mountain biking, hiking, photography, and picnicking
Restrictions: OHVs not allowed; campground requires a 2-day minimum stay on weekends and 3-day minimum stay on holiday weekends.
Season: May through October

Finding the campground: From the junction of US 189 and US 40 in Heber City, drive southeast on US 40 for 22.4 miles, then go south at the sign for Strawberry Bay. There's a visitor center and a nature trail near the junction. Continue south on the paved road another 4 miles to the campground entrance, which is on the east side of the road.

About the campground: Eight campground loops and a large overflow serve up wonderful views of Strawberry Reservoir and the surrounding mountains. Sites are open, with wildflowers all around come summer. Most of the loops offer the same amenities, though Loop B does have full-hookup sites. There are also group sites at the 17,000-acre reservoir.

Anglers will find several species of fish at the reservoir, including cutthroat and rainbow trout, as well as kokanee salmon and brook trout. Other popular outdoor activities include sailing; predictable daily winds often glide sailboats or sailboards across Strawberry Reservoir. Hardy water-skiers need to wear wet suits because the water is cold at this elevation. Hikers and mountain bikers will be happy to find plenty of trails and roads to explore in the surrounding area.

87 Renegade Point

Location: In the Uinta-Wasatch-Cache National Forest, about 36 miles southeast of Heber City
GPS: N40 07.244'/W111 09.531'
Facilities: Fire pits, picnic tables, drinking water, and flush toilets. A marina, located just east of the campground, offers a small store with camping and fishing supplies, small-boat rentals, and boat slip rentals.
Sites: 61 basic sites and 5 double sites
Maximum RV length: 30 feet
Fee: $$ for basic sites; $$$$ for double sites
Maximum stay: 7 days (long-term, month-to-month sites also available)
Elevation: 7,600 feet
Road conditions: Paved
Management: Heber Ranger District, 2460 S. Hwy. 40, Heber City; (435) 654-0470; www.fs.usda .gov/main/uwcnf/home
Reservations: None
Activities: Fishing, boating, mountain biking, hiking, photography, and picnicking
Restrictions: OHVs not allowed; campground requires a 2-day minimum stay on weekends and 3-day minimum stay on holiday weekends
Season: May through October
Finding the campground: From the junction of US 189 and US 40 in Heber City, drive southeast on US 40 for 22.4 miles, then go south at the sign for Strawberry Bay. There's a visitor center and a nature trail near the junction. Continue south on the paved road another 13.8 miles to the campground entrance, which is on the south side of the road. Continue another 0.7 mile to a turnoff on the left (north) for the marina, which you'll reach in an additional 0.3 mile.
About the campground: Tucked away on the southwest end of 17,000-acre Strawberry Reservoir are two campground loops for folks wishing to camp here. Sites are open and offer nice views of the reservoir and mountains.

A marina is located just past the campground and provides a place for campers to launch or rent boats. Anglers will find several species of fish at the reservoir, including cutthroat and rainbow trout, as well as kokanee salmon and brook trout. Other popular outdoor activities include sailing; predictable daily winds often glide sailboats or sailboards across Strawberry Reservoir. Hardy water-skiers should wear wet suits, because the water is cold at this high-elevation lake. Hikers and mountain bikers will find plenty of trails and roads to explore in the surrounding area.

88 Lodgepole

Location: In the Uinta-Wasatch-Cache National Forest, about 16 miles southeast of Heber City
GPS: N40 18.669'/W111 15.485'
Facilities: Fire pits, picnic tables, drinking water, flush toilets, and dump station
Sites: 51 basic sites, 4 double sites, and 2 group sites (maximum 50 and 100 people respectively)
Maximum RV length: 40 feet
Fee: $$ for basic sites; $$$$ for double sites; $$$$$ for group sites
Maximum stay: 7 days
Elevation: 7,700 feet
Road conditions: Paved
Management: Heber-Kamas Ranger District, 2460 S. Hwy. 40, Heber City; (435) 654-0470; www .fs.usda.gov/main/uwcnf/home
Reservations: Call (877) 444-6777 or TDD (877) 833-6777; www.recreation.gov
Activities: Hiking, fishing, and picnicking
Season: May through September
Finding the campground: From the junction of US 189 and US 40 in Heber City, drive southeast on US 40 for 15.5 miles to the campground, which is on the south side of the road.
About the campground: Shady sites are common here, where aspens and a variety of conifers grow tall and stout. Hikers should check out Foreman Hollow Trail, located in Upper Daniels Canyon. It's a 3-mile loop with wonderful views of Strawberry Reservoir, Strawberry Peak, and Twin Peaks. Interpretive signs offer interesting facts about the wildlife and the vegetation. See Dave Hall's *Hiking Utah* for more information about other hikes in the area. If you like to fish, check out the rainbow, brown, and cutthroat trout in Daniels Creek.

89 Currant Creek

Location: In the Uinta-Wasatch-Cache National Forest, about 59 miles southeast of Heber City
GPS: N40 19.875'/W110 04.003'
Facilities: Fire pits, picnic tables, drinking water, flush toilets, dump station, boat ramp, fishing pier, and horse feeders in Loop C
Sites: 83 basic sites, 15 double sites, and 4 group sites (maximum varies from 25 to 40 people)
Maximum RV length: 40 feet

Fee: $$ for basic sites; $$$$ for double sites; $$$$$ for group sites
Maximum stay: 7 days
Elevation: 8,000 feet
Road conditions: Paved in the campground; gravel for the previous 19 miles
Management: Heber-Kamas Ranger District, 2460 S. Hwy. 40, Heber City; (435) 654-0470; www
.fs.usda.gov/main/uwcnf/home
Reservations: Call (877) 444-6777 or TDD (877) 833-6777; www.recreation.gov
Activities: Fishing, boating, hiking, horseback riding, mountain biking, and picnicking
Restrictions: ATVs/OHVs not allowed; campground requires a 2-day minimum stay on weekends
and 3-day minimum stay on holiday weekends
Season: June through September
Finding the campground: From the junction of US 189 and 40 in Heber City, drive southeast on
US 40 for 40.1 miles. At a sign for the Currant Creek Recreation Area, go north on gravel FR 471
for 17.4 miles, eventually curving around the north side of Currant Creek Reservoir. Here you'll
reach a fork; keep left (southwest) to the campground, which you will reach in another 1.6 miles.
The road is paved upon entering the campground.
About the campground: This campground is in a wonderful setting of aspens and conifers, with
the trees shading most of the sites. Located on the southwest shore of Currant Creek Reservoir,
several campground loops combine to offer more than 100 sites, with Loop C offering space for
horses as well. Here, in addition to a pretty setting, there are horse feeders.

In addition to horseback riding, there are plenty of opportunities for hiking and mountain bik-
ing. For those who want to walk in the campground, a 1-mile-long interpretive trail is both beauti-
ful and informative, and there's also a trail to a fishing pier, accessible to folks in wheelchairs.
Hopeful anglers may catch rainbow, brook, and cutthroat trout.

90 Hoop Lake

Location: In the Uinta-Wasatch-Cache National Forest, about 33 miles southeast of Mountain
View, Wyoming
GPS: N40 55.546' / W110 07.389'
Facilities: Fire pits, picnic tables, drinking water, and vault toilets
Sites: 44 basic sites
Maximum RV length: 25 feet
Fee: $$ for basic sites
Maximum stay: 14 days
Elevation: 9,000 feet
Road conditions: Dirt
Management: Evanston/Mountain View Ranger District, 321 Hwy. 414, Mountain View, WY 82939;
(307) 782-6555; www.fs.usda.gov/main/uwcnf/home
Reservations: None
Activities: Fishing, hiking, horseback riding, boating, wildlife watching, and picnicking
Season: June through October
Finding the campground: From Mountain View take WY 414 southeast for 23.6 miles, then take

gravel Uinta CR 264 south for 3.2 miles. A sign points the way to Hoop Lake and Hole-in-the-Rock. Upon reaching FR 078, a dirt road, continue south, then east, an additional 6.5 miles to the campground. (*Note:* The dirt road leading to the campground can be very slick when wet.)

About the campground: Fishing for both cutthroat and rainbow trout is popular in this high-mountain setting along the south shore of Hoop Lake Reservoir. Hikers and horseback riders will be happy to know that the place also offers access into the High Uinta Wilderness.

91 Stateline

Location: In the Uinta-Wasatch-Cache National Forest, about 22 miles south of Mountain View, Wyoming

GPS: N40 58.904'/W110 23.141'

Facilities: Fire pits, picnic tables, drinking water, vault toilets, boat ramp, and dump station

Sites: 41 basic sites

Maximum RV length: 30 feet

Fee: $$ for basic sites

Maximum stay: 14 days

Elevation: 9,200 feet

Road conditions: Gravel to the campground, then paved

Management: Evanston/Mountain View Ranger District, 321 Hwy. 414, Mountain View, WY 82939; (307) 782-6555; www.fs.usda.gov/main/uwcnf/home

Reservations: Call (877) 444-6777 or TDD (877) 833-6777; www.recreation.gov

Activities: Fishing, boating, hiking, mountain biking, wildlife watching, and picnicking

Season: June through October

Finding the campground: From the junction of WY 410 and WY 414 in Mountain View, drive south on paved WY 410 for 7 miles, then continue south on gravel Uinta CR 246 (which later becomes FR 072) for another 15.1 miles to the campground. There's a sign pointing the way to the Wasatch National Forest. Though FR 072 is gravel, it turns to pavement in front of the campground.

About the campground: Aspens and conifers shade this campground, which sits on the shore of Stateline Reservoir and offers summer wildflowers. It's a nice place for outdoor enthusiasts, with anglers hoping to catch rainbow and cutthroat trout, as well as kokanee salmon.

92 Bridger Lake

Location: In the Uinta-Wasatch-Cache National Forest, about 23 miles south of Mountain View, Wyoming

GPS: N40 58.016'/W110 23.287'

Facilities: Fire pits, picnic tables, drinking water, vault toilets, and a boat ramp

Sites: 28 basic sites and 2 double sites

Maximum RV length: 45 feet

Fee: $$ for basic sites; $$$$ for double sites

Maximum stay: 14 days
Elevation: 9,400 feet
Road conditions: Gravel
Management: Evanston/Mountain View Ranger District, 321 Hwy. 414, Mountain View, WY 82939; (307) 782-6555; www.fs.usda.gov/main/uwcnf/home
Reservations: Call (877) 444-6777 or TDD (877) 833-6777; www.recreation.gov
Activities: Fishing, boating, hiking, mountain biking, wildlife watching, and picnicking
Season: June through October
Finding the campground: From the junction of WY 410 and WY 414 in Mountain View, drive south on paved WY 410 for 7 miles, then continue south on gravel Uinta CR 246 (which later becomes FR 072) for another 15.7 miles to the signed turnoff on your left; now go east on FR 126 for 0.5 mile to the campground.
About the campground: Conifers shade this nice campground, and Bridger Lake provides a lovely backdrop for many of the sites. It's a good place for fishing or just plain relaxing and looking for deer and moose. It's also a great base from which to explore the surrounding area.

93 Marsh Lake

Location: In the Uinta-Wasatch-Cache National Forest, about 24 miles south of Mountain View, Wyoming
GPS: West Side: N40 57.124' / W110 23.897'
GPS: East Side: N40 57.093' / W110 23.715'
Facilities: Fire pits, picnic tables, drinking water, vault toilets, and a boat ramp
Sites: 40 basic sites and 6 double sites
Maximum RV length: 45 feet
Fee: $$ for basic sites; $$$$ for double sites
Maximum stay: 14 days
Elevation: 9,400 feet
Road conditions: Gravel
Management: Evanston/Mountain View Ranger District, 321 Hwy. 414, Mountain View, WY 82939; (307) 782-6555; www.fs.usda.gov/main/uwcnf/home
Reservations: Call (877) 444-6777 or TDD (877) 833-6777; www.recreation.gov
Activities: Fishing, boating, ATV riding, hiking, mountain biking, wildlife watching, and picnicking
Season: June through October
Finding the campground: From the junction of WY 410 and WY 414 in Mountain View, drive south on paved WY 410 for 7 miles, then continue south on gravel Uinta CR 246 (which later becomes FR 072) for another 17.3 miles to the campground.
About the campground: This lovely place is divided into two distinct sites—East and West Marsh Lake—both of which offer spaces with views of Marsh Lake. The east side is shaded by conifers, while the west is partially shaded with aspens and conifers. The China Trail begins at West Marsh Lake and is a nice place to hike.

94 China Meadows

Location: In the Uinta-Wasatch-Cache National Forest, about 26 miles south of Mountain View, Wyoming
GPS: N40 55.876'/W110 24.203'
Facilities: Fire pits, picnic tables, and vault toilets
Sites: 9 basic sites
Maximum RV length: 20 feet
Fee: $$ for basic sites
Maximum stay: 14 days
Elevation: 9,400 feet
Road conditions: Gravel
Management: Evanston/Mountain View Ranger District, 321 Hwy. 414, Mountain View, WY 82939; (307) 782-6555; www.fs.usda.gov/main/uwcnf/home
Reservations: None
Activities: Fishing, hiking, kayaking, mountain biking, horseback riding, wildlife watching, off-highway driving, and picnicking
Season: June through October
Finding the campground: From the junction of WY 410 and WY 414 in Mountain View, drive south on paved WY 410 for 7 miles, then continue south on gravel Uinta CR 246 (which later becomes FR 072) for another 18.7 miles to a turnoff on the left (south) to the China Meadows and Trailhead Campgrounds. Travel the dirt road 0.1 mile to the campground.
About the campground: This small campground offers small sites that overlook China Lake and are shaded by conifers. It's a fine place for fishing, relaxing, and going for a hike or mountain bike ride. Some folks also enjoy off-highway driving in the area.

95 Trailhead

Location: In the Uinta-Wasatch-Cache National Forest, about 26 miles south of Mountain View, Wyoming
GPS: N40 55.450'/W110 24.370'
Facilities: Fire pits, picnic tables, vault toilets, horse unloading ramp, horse corrals, and hitching posts
Sites: 11 basic sites, including 6 with horse corrals and hitching posts
Maximum RV length: 30 feet
Fee: $$ for basic sites
Maximum stay: 14 days
Elevation: 9,500 feet
Road conditions: Rough dirt
Management: Evanston/Mountain View Ranger District, 321 Hwy. 414, Mountain View, WY 82939; (307) 782-6555; www.fs.usda.gov/main/uwcnf/home
Reservations: None

Activities: Fishing, hiking, horseback riding, wildlife watching, and picnicking
Season: June through October
Finding the campground: From the junction of WY 410 and WY 414 in Mountain View, drive south on paved WY 410 for 7 miles, then continue south on gravel Uinta CR 246 (which later becomes FR 072) for another 18.7 miles to a turnoff on the left (south) to the China Meadows and Trailhead Campgrounds. Travel the rough dirt road 0.7 mile to the campground.
About the campground: A wonderful place for those with horses (and even those without), this campground offers shady conifers as well as horse corrals, a loading and unloading ramp, and hitching posts. The campground is a good place from which to enter the High Uintas Wilderness, with access to the Red Castle Lake area.

96 Little Lyman Lake

Location: In the Uinta-Wasatch-Cache National Forest, about 66 miles northeast of Kamas
GPS: N40 56.093'/W110 36.773'
Facilities: Fire pits, picnic tables, drinking water, and vault toilets
Sites: 10 basic sites
Maximum RV length: 16 feet
Fee: $$ for basic sites
Maximum stay: 14 days
Elevation: 9,200 feet
Road conditions: Dirt and gravel
Management: Evanston/Mountain View Ranger District, 321 Hwy. 414, Mountain View, WY 82939; (307) 782-6555; www.fs.usda.gov/main/uwcnf/home
Reservations: None
Activities: Fishing, off-highway driving, hiking, wildlife watching, and picnicking
Season: Mid-June through September
Finding the campground: From the junction of UT 32 and UT 150 in Kamas, go southeast then northeast on UT 150, a scenic toll road, for 48.6 miles to FR 058 (North Slope Road). Drive the maintained gravel road (before reaching the campground, it's rough and bumpy) for 16.7 miles, then turn north onto FR 070. A sign points the way to the campground, which you'll reach via another rough road in 0.4 mile.
About the campground: Small, shady sites among conifers overlook Lyman Lake, where the fishing is good. Nearby, hikers can explore West Fork Blacks Creek, which offers an excellent journey into the northwestern portion of the High Uintas Wilderness.

97 East Fork Bear River

Location: In the Uinta-Wasatch-Cache National Forest, about 48 miles northeast of Kamas
GPS: N40 54.721'/W110 49.766'
Facilities: Fire pits, picnic tables, drinking water, and vault toilets; dump station nearby at Lily Lake Dump Station
Sites: 7 basic sites
Maximum RV length: 20 feet
Fee: $$ for basic sites
Maximum stay: 14 days
Elevation: 8,400 feet
Road conditions: Paved to the campground, then gravel
Management: Evanston/Mountain View Ranger District, 321 Hwy. 414, Mountain View, WY 82939; (307) 782-6555; www.fs.usda.gov/main/uwcnf/home
Reservations: None
Activities: Fishing, off-highway driving, mountain biking, wildlife watching, and picnicking
Restrictions: ATVs and dirt bikes not allowed
Season: June through September
Finding the campground: From the junction of UT 32 and UT 150 in Kamas, go southeast then northeast on UT 150, a scenic toll road, for 48.4 miles to the campground, which is on the west side of the road. A steep road leads to the campground, which is not the place for large RVs. Tents, vans, and small motor homes are best. If you need to turn around, do so across from campsite 3.
About the campground: A small campground with lodgepole pines and aspens providing some shade, this spot is not suitable for large RVs. Situated along the Bear River, just below the East Fork confluence, this is a place for fishing and also a good base from which ATVers can enjoy the Wolverine ATV Trail, which is nearby. The trail is a 10-mile loop with impressive views. To reach the Lily Lake Dump Station, located between this campground and Stillwater Campground, turn left (east) onto FR 120 and go 0.5 mile to the dump station.

98 Bear River

Location: In the Uinta-Wasatch-Cache National Forest, about 48 miles northeast of Kamas
GPS: N40 54.674'/W110 49.833'
Facilities: Fire pits, picnic tables, drinking water, and vault toilets
Sites: 4 basic sites
Maximum RV length: 20 feet
Fee: $$ for basic sites
Maximum stay: 14 days
Elevation: 8,400 feet
Road conditions: Paved to the campground, then gravel
Management: Evanston/Mountain View Ranger District, 321 Hwy. 414, Mountain View, WY 82939; (307) 782-6555; www.fs.usda.gov/main/uwcnf/home

Reservations: None
Activities: Fishing, off-highway driving, mountain biking, wildlife watching, and picnicking
Restrictions: ATVs and dirt bikes not allowed
Season: June through September
Finding the campground: From the junction of UT 32 and UT 150 in Kamas, go southeast then northeast on UT 150, a scenic toll road, for 48.3 miles to the campground, which is on the west side of the road.
About the campground: A small place, with lodgepole pines and aspens providing some shade among a mere four semi-open sites, this campground is not suitable for large, or even moderate-size, RVs. I would recommend tents, vans, and small motor homes. It would also be a great spot for four sets of friends. Situated along the Bear River, upstream from the East Fork confluence, this is a good base from which to fish. ATVers can enjoy the nearby Wolverine ATV Trail, a 10-mile loop, with impressive views.

99 Christmas Meadows

Location: In the Uinta-Wasatch-Cache National Forest, about 50 miles northeast of Kamas
GPS: N40 49.504' / W110 48.121'
Facilities: Fire grates, picnic tables, drinking water, and vault toilets; dump station nearby at Lily Lake Dump Station
Sites: 11 basic sites
Maximum RV length: 20 feet
Fee: $$ for basic sites
Maximum stay: 14 days
Elevation: 8,900 feet
Road conditions: Gravel
Management: Evanston/Mountain View Ranger District, 321 Hwy. 414, Mountain View, WY 82939; (307) 782-6555; www.fs.usda.gov/main/uwcnf/home
Reservations: Call (877) 444-6777 or TDD (877) 833-6777; www.recreation.gov
Activities: Fishing, hiking, wildlife watching, and picnicking
Restrictions: ATVs, dirt bikes, and horses not allowed
Season: June through September
Finding the campground: From the junction of UT 32 and UT 150 in Kamas, go southeast then northeast on UT 150, a scenic toll road, for 45.9 miles to the junction of FR 057, which is on the east side of the road. A sign points the way to Christmas Meadows. Continue another 4.2 miles on gravel FR 057 to reach the campground. A trailhead is just beyond.
About the campground: A lovely semi-open setting of aspens and conifers provides more than enough shade; there's also a wonderful view up the Stillwater drainage of the Bear River to Spread Eagle and Amethyst Mountains. A trail offers three destinations: West Basin, with Kermsuh Lake; Middle Basin, with McPheters and Ryder Lakes; and Amethyst Basin, containing Amethyst and Ostler Lakes. See Dave Hall's *Hiking Utah* for additional information. Look for moose and other animal life as you hike, fish, or just plain relax at this splendid place. If you need a dump station, check out Lily Lake Dump Station, north of the Bear River Ranger Station, 0.5 mile east from the junction of UT 150 and FR 120.

100 Stillwater

Location: In the Uinta-Wasatch-Cache National Forest, about 46 miles northeast of Kamas
GPS: N40 52.266'/W110 50.001'
Facilities: Fire pits, picnic tables, drinking water, and vault toilets; dump station nearby at Lily Lake Dump Station
Sites: 19 basic sites, 1 double site, and 4 group sites (maximum varies from 25 to 50 people)
Maximum RV length: 35 feet
Fee: $$ for basic sites; $$$$ for double site; $$$$$ for group sites
Maximum stay: 14 days
Elevation: 8,500 feet
Road conditions: Paved to the campground, then gravel
Management: Evanston/Mountain View Ranger District, 321 Hwy. 414, Mountain View, WY 82939; (307) 782-6555; www.fs.usda.gov/main/uwcnf/home
Reservations: Call (877) 444-6777 or TDD (877) 833-6777; www.recreation.gov
Activities: Fishing, wildlife watching, and picnicking
Restrictions: ATVs, dirt bikes, and horses not allowed
Season: June through October
Finding the campground: From the junction of UT 32 and UT 150 in Kamas, go southeast then northeast on UT 150, a scenic toll road, for 45.6 miles to the campground, which is on the east side of the road.
About the campground: A lovely semi-open setting of aspens and lodgepole pines provides shade, while the Bear River sings and gives anglers the opportunity to fish for whitefish and both rainbow and cutthroat trout. For added appeal some sites rest on the bank along the river, near where the Stillwater Fork and Hayden Fork join the Bear. To reach the Lily Lake Dump Station, located north of the Bear River Ranger Station, turn right (east) onto FR 120 and go 0.5 mile to the dump station.

101 Hayden Fork

Location: In the Uinta-Wasatch-Cache National Forest, about 42 miles northeast of Kamas
GPS: N40 49.813'/W110 51.213'
Facilities: Fire pits, picnic tables, drinking water, and vault toilets; dump station nearby at Lily Lake Dump Station
Sites: 9 basic sites
Maximum RV length: 20 feet
Fee: $$ for basic sites
Maximum stay: 14 days
Elevation: 8,900 feet
Road conditions: Paved to the campground, then gravel
Management: Evanston/Mountain View Ranger District, 321 Hwy. 414, Mountain View, WY 82939; (307) 782-6555; www.fs.usda.gov/main/uwcnf/home
Reservations: None

Activities: Fishing, wildlife watching, and picnicking

Restrictions: ATVs and dirt bikes not allowed

Season: June through September

Finding the campground: From the junction of UT 32 and UT 150 in Kamas, go southeast then northeast on UT 150, a scenic toll road, for 42.4 miles to the campground, which is on the east side of the road.

About the campground: There are two sections to this small campground, with five sites gracing the banks of the Bear River and another four above on a small bluff. The hill is too steep for trailers, which should stay below. Typical vegetation shades all the sites here, where the fishing is fine and the animal life is plentiful. To reach the Lily Lake Dump Station, located north of the campground and north of Bear River Ranger Station, turn right (east) onto FR 120 and go 0.5 mile to the dump station.

102 Beaver View

Location: In the Uinta-Wasatch-Cache National Forest, about 42 miles northeast of Kamas

GPS: N40 49.488' / W110 51.779'

Facilities: Fire pits, picnic tables, drinking water, and vault toilets; dump station nearby at Lily Lake Dump Station

Sites: 18 basic sites

Maximum RV length: 22 feet

Fee: $$ for basic sites

Maximum stay: 14 days

Elevation: 9,000 feet

Road conditions: Paved to the campground, then gravel

Management: Evanston/Mountain View Ranger District, 321 Hwy. 414, Mountain View, WY 82939; (307) 782-6555; www.fs.usda.gov/main/uwcnf/home

Reservations: None

Activities: Fishing, wildlife watching, and picnicking

Restrictions: ATVs and dirt bikes not allowed

Season: June through September

Finding the campground: From the junction of UT 32 and UT 150 in Kamas, go southeast then northeast on UT 150, a scenic toll road, for 41.9 miles to the campground, which is on the east side of the road.

About the campground: Lodgepole pines and other typical mountain vegetation do their best to shade the sites here, a place where visitors have the chance to see a beaver pond and lodge and hopefully the cute critters themselves. Sites overlook the Hayden Fork Bear River and offer fine fishing and fun exploring. To reach the Lily Lake Dump Station, located north of the campground and north of Bear River Ranger Station, turn right (east) onto FR 120 and go 0.5 mile to the dump station.

103 Sulphur

Location: In the Uinta-Wasatch-Cache National Forest, about 39 miles northeast of Kamas
GPS: N40 47.277'/W110 53.111'
Facilities: Fire pits, picnic tables, drinking water, and vault toilets; dump station nearby at Lily Lake Dump Station
Sites: 15 basic sites, 6 double sites, and 1 group site (maximum 25 people)
Maximum RV length: 22 feet
Fee: $$ for basic sites; $$$$ for double sites; $$$$$ for group site
Maximum stay: 14 days
Elevation: 9,000 feet
Road conditions: Paved to the campground, then gravel
Management: Evanston/Mountain View Ranger District, 321 Hwy. 414, Mountain View, WY 82939; (307) 782-6555; www.fs.usda.gov/main/uwcnf/home
Reservations: Call (877) 444-6777 or TDD (877) 833-6777; www.recreation.gov
Activities: Fishing, wildlife watching, and picnicking
Restrictions: ATVs and dirt bikes not allowed
Season: June through October
Finding the campground: From the junction of UT 32 and UT 150 in Kamas, go southeast then northeast on UT 150, a scenic toll road, for 38.9 miles to the campground, which is on the east side of the road.
About the campground: Lodgepole pines and aspens grace this high-elevation campground, while meadows provide wildflowers and wide-open spaces. Sites are semi-open, so you shouldn't feel closed in. Nearby is the Hayden Fork Bear River, a good place for fishing and having fun. To reach the Lily Lake Dump Station, located north of the campground and north of Bear River Ranger Station, turn right (east) onto FR 120 and go 0.5 mile to the dump station.

104 Butterfly Lake

Location: In the Uinta-Wasatch-Cache National Forest, about 34 miles northeast of Kamas
GPS: N40 43.270'/W110 52.049'
Facilities: Fire grates, picnic tables, drinking water, and vault toilets
Sites: 20 basic sites
Maximum RV length: 25 feet
Fee: $$ for basic sites
Maximum stay: 7 days
Elevation: 10,300 feet
Road conditions: Paved to the campground, then gravel
Management: Heber-Kamas Ranger District, 2460 S. Hwy. 40, Heber City; (435) 654-0470; www.fs.usda.gov/main/uwcnf/home
Reservations: None

Butterfly Lake is a small, but beautiful high-elevation lake.

Activities: Fishing, kayaking and canoeing, hiking, horseback riding, wildlife watching, and picnicking

Restrictions: ATVs not allowed

Season: July through September

Finding the campground: From the junction of UT 32 and UT 150 in Kamas, go southeast then northeast on UT 150, a scenic toll road, for 34 miles to the campground, which is on the west side of the road.

About the campground: Lodgepole pines shade the somewhat small, sometimes uneven sites at this campground, which rests on the shore of Butterfly Lake. Nonmotorized boats are welcome. Campers come to fish, float, and just plain relax.

105 Mirror Lake

Location: In the Uinta-Wasatch-Cache National Forest, about 31 miles east of Kamas

GPS: N40 42.008' / W110 53.213'

Facilities: Fire pits, picnic tables, ADA sites, tent pads, stove stands, drinking water, vault toilets, boat ramp, and horse feeding stations

Sites: 70 basic sites, 7 double sites, and 1 triple site

Maximum RV length: 40 feet

Mirror Lake is the largest of the campgrounds on Mirror Lake Highway and one of the most popular, too.

Fee: $$ for basic sites; $$$$ for double sites; $$$$$ for triple site
Maximum stay: 7 days
Elevation: 10,100 feet
Road conditions: Paved to the campground, then gravel .
Management: Heber-Kamas Ranger District, 2460 S. Hwy. 40, Heber City; (435) 654-0470; www .fs.usda.gov/main/uwcnf/home
Reservations: Call (877) 444-6777 or TDD (877) 833-6777; www.recreation.gov
Activities: Fishing, boating, hiking, horseback riding, wildlife watching, and picnicking
Restrictions: ATVs not allowed
Season: July through September
Finding the campground: From the junction of UT 32 and UT 150 in Kamas, go southeast then northeast on UT 150, a scenic toll road, for 31.3 miles to the campground, which is on the east side of the road.
About the campground: Conifers shade the sites at this busy campground, with its lovely, often mirrored view of the nearby mountains. The largest campground on the Mirror Lake Highway, it's also a good place from which to access the Highline Trail. Rainbow and brook trout inhabit the lake's waters and delight anglers. Hikers will find the Shoreline Trail—a gentle 1.5-mile loop around the lake that's accessible to wheelchairs, with views of Bald Mountain and Hayden Peak. Boats can be launched by hand, though motorboats are not permitted.

106 Moosehorn

Location: In the Uinta-Wasatch-Cache National Forest, about 31 miles east of Kamas
GPS: N40 41.630'/W110 53.538'
Facilities: Fire pits, picnic tables, and vault toilets
Sites: 33 basic sites
Maximum RV length: 30 feet
Fee: $$ for basic sites
Maximum stay: 7 days
Elevation: 10,300 feet
Road conditions: Paved to the campground, then gravel
Management: Heber-Kamas Ranger District, 2460 S. Hwy. 40, Heber City; (435) 654-0470; www
.fs.usda.gov/main/uwcnf/home
Reservations: Call (877) 444-6777 or TDD (877) 833-6777; www.recreation.gov
Activities: Fishing, kayaking and canoeing, hiking, wildlife watching, and picnicking
Restrictions: ATVs not allowed
Season: July through September
Finding the campground: From the junction of UT 32 and UT 150 in Kamas, go southeast then
northeast on UT 150, a scenic toll road, for 30.6 miles to the campground, which is on the west
side of the road.
About the campground: Conifers shade the sites, some of which may be uneven, at this lovely
campground. Some of the sites overlook Moosehorn Lake, with a lovely peak in the background.
Nonmotorized boats are welcome.

If you want to hike, look for the Bald Mountain Trailhead at nearby Bald Mountain Pass. The
Bald Mountain Trail is a National Recreation Trail recognized for its outstanding scenery. It leads
2 miles and offers spectacular views of the High Uintas. Watch for mountain goats along the way.
There's also the Fehr Lake Trail, an easy hike that leads to Fehr, Shepard, and Hoover Lakes.

107 Lost Creek

Location: In the Uinta-Wasatch-Cache National Forest, about 27 miles east of Kamas
GPS: N40 40.862'/W110 56.070'
Facilities: Fire pits, picnic tables, drinking water, dump station, and vault toilets
Sites: 35 basic sites
Maximum RV length: 30 feet
Fee: $$ for basic sites
Maximum stay: 7 days
Elevation: 9,900 feet
Road conditions: Paved
Management: Heber-Kamas Ranger District, 2460 S. Hwy. 40, Heber City; (435) 654-0470; www
.fs.usda.gov/main/uwcnf/home
Reservations: Call (877) 444-6777 or TDD (877) 833-6777; www.recreation.gov

Activities: Fishing, kayaking and canoeing, wildlife watching, and picnicking
Restrictions: ATVs not allowed
Season: July through September
Finding the campground: From the junction of UT 32 and UT 150 in Kamas, go southeast then northeast on UT 150, a scenic toll road, for 26.7 miles to the campground, which is on the south side of the road.
About the campground: Some of the sites here overlook Lost Lake, a nice place for canoeing and kayaking. Nonmotorized boats are welcome. Conifers are interspersed with meadows, offering semi-open sites. Anglers may fish for rainbow trout in the lake.

108 Lilly Lake

Location: In the Uinta-Wasatch-Cache National Forest, about 27 miles east of Kamas
GPS: N40 40.842'/W110 56.319'
Facilities: Fire pits, picnic tables, drinking water, and vault toilets
Sites: 14 basic sites
Maximum RV length: 30 feet
Fee: $$ for basic sites
Maximum stay: 7 days
Elevation: 9,900 feet
Road conditions: Paved
Management: Heber-Kamas Ranger District, 2460 S. Hwy. 40, Heber City; (435) 654-0470; www .fs.usda.gov/main/uwcnf/home
Reservations: None
Activities: Fishing, kayaking and canoeing, wildlife watching, and picnicking
Restrictions: ATVs not allowed
Season: July through September
Finding the campground: From the junction of UT 32 and UT 150 in Kamas, go southeast then northeast on UT 150, a scenic toll road, for 26.5 miles to the campground, which is on the north side of the road.
About the campground: Lilly Lake is a nice place for canoeing and kayaking, with conifers providing shade for those who'd rather relax and enjoy the scenery. Nonmotorized boats are welcome.

109 Trial Lake

Location: In the Uinta-Wasatch-Cache National Forest, about 26 miles east of Kamas
GPS: N40 40.863'/W110 57.224'
Facilities: Fire grates, picnic tables, drinking water, and vault toilets
Sites: 60 basic sites
Maximum RV length: 35 feet
Fee: $$ for basic sites

Maximum stay: 7 days

Elevation: 9,800 feet

Road conditions: Paved

Management: Heber-Kamas Ranger District, 2460 S. Hwy. 40, Heber City; (435) 654-0470; www
.fs.usda.gov/main/uwcnf/home

Reservations: Call (877) 444-6777 or TDD (877) 833-6777; www.recreation.gov

Activities: Fishing, hiking, wildlife watching, and picnicking

Restrictions: Motorized boats and ATVs not allowed

Season: July through September

Finding the campground: From the junction of UT 32 and UT 150 in Kamas, go southeast then
northeast on UT 150, a scenic toll road, for 25.5 miles to the turnoff for the campground, which is
on the north side of the road. A sign points the way. Drive the paved road another 0.4 mile to the
campground.

About the campground: Conifers and meadows, along with mountains and beautiful Trial Lake,
join to make this a very nice place to camp. Some sites rest in the shady trees and do not provide
a view of the lake, while others are situated along the lakeshore, with varying amounts of shade.
Anglers can fish for rainbow trout, while hikers will find a trail leading to Three Divide Lakes, as well
as many others. See Dave Hall's *Hiking Utah* for additional information.

110 Cobblerest

Location: In the Uinta-Wasatch-Cache National Forest, about 19 miles southeast of Kamas

GPS: N40 35.679'/W110 58.520'

Facilities: Fire pits, picnic tables, and vault toilets

Sites: 18 basic sites

Maximum RV length: 20 feet

Fee: $$ for basic sites

Maximum stay: 7 days

Elevation: 8,300 feet

Road conditions: Paved

Management: Heber-Kamas Ranger District, 2460 S. Hwy. 40, Heber City; (435) 654-0470; www
.fs.usda.gov/main/uwcnf/home

Reservations: None

Activities: Fishing, hiking, wildlife watching, and picnicking

Restrictions: ATVs not allowed

Season: June through September

Finding the campground: From the junction of UT 32 and UT 150 in Kamas, go southeast on UT
150, a scenic toll road, for 19.1 miles to the campground, which is on the south side of the road.

About the campground: Pines and spruce serve to shade the sites found here, with the lovely
Provo River singing close by. Anglers may try for rainbow, cutthroat, brown, and brook trout.

111 Shady Dell

Location: In the Uinta-Wasatch-Cache National Forest, about 17 miles southeast of Kamas
GPS: N40 35.425'/W111 00.885'
Facilities: Fire pits, picnic tables, drinking water, and vault toilets
Sites: 19 basic sites and 1 double site
Maximum RV length: 25 feet
Fee: $$ for basic sites; $$$$ for double site
Maximum stay: 7 days
Elevation: 8,100 feet
Road conditions: Paved
Management: Heber-Kamas Ranger District, 2460 S. Hwy. 40, Heber City; (435) 654-0470; www .fs.usda.gov/main/uwcnf/home
Reservations: None
Activities: Fishing, hiking, wildlife watching, and picnicking
Restrictions: ATVs not allowed
Season: June through October
Finding the campground: From the junction of UT 32 and UT 150 in Kamas, go southeast on UT 150, a scenic toll road, for 16.9 miles to the campground, which is on the south side of the road.
About the campground: Conifers and aspens provide both shady and semi-open sites for those who visit this campground. It's a nice place from which to explore the area, or just relax and enjoy your surroundings. Anglers will find the bountiful Provo River nearby, with opportunities to catch rainbow, cutthroat, brown, and brook trout.

112 Soapstone

Location: In the Uinta-Wasatch-Cache National Forest, about 16 miles southeast of Kamas
GPS: N40 34.719'/W111 01.672'
Facilities: Fire pits, picnic tables, drinking water, and vault toilets; dump station nearby
Sites: 31 basic sites, 2 double sites, and 1 triple site
Maximum RV length: 40 feet
Fee: $$ for basic sites; $$$$ for double sites; $$$$$ for triple site
Maximum stay: 7 days
Elevation: 8,000 feet
Road conditions: Paved
Management: Heber-Kamas Ranger District, 2460 S. Hwy. 40, Heber City; (435) 654-0470; www .fs.usda.gov/main/uwcnf/home
Reservations: Call (877) 444-6777 or TDD (877) 833-6777; www.recreation.gov
Activities: Fishing, wildlife watching, and picnicking
Restrictions: ATVs not allowed
Season: June through October

Finding the campground: From the junction of UT 32 and UT 150 in Kamas, go southeast on UT 150, a scenic toll road, for 15.8 miles to the campground, which is on the south side of the road. (Find the sewage disposal station by driving 1.1 miles west of the campground via UT 150. A sign for Soapstone Basin points the way south 0.3 mile and then left, or east, to the dump.)

About the campground: Conifers and aspens provide both shady and semi-open sites for those who visit this campground. Anglers will find the bountiful Provo River nearby; bounties include rainbow, cutthroat, brown, and brook trout.

113 Pine Valley North

Location: In the Uinta-Wasatch-Cache National Forest, about 11 miles southeast of Kamas
GPS: N40 35.958'/W111 06.877'
Facilities: Fire pits, picnic tables, BBQ grills, stove stands, drinking water, and vault toilets
Sites: 3 group sites (maximum varies from 60 to 140 people)
Maximum RV length: 30 feet
Fee: $$$$$ for group sites
Maximum stay: 7 days
Elevation: 7,400 feet
Road conditions: Paved
Management: Heber-Kamas Ranger District, 2460 S. Hwy. 40, Heber City; (435) 654-0470; www .fs.usda.gov/main/uwcnf/home
Reservations: Call (877) 444-6777 or TDD (877) 833-6777; www.recreation.gov
Activities: Fishing, hiking, horseback riding, mountain biking, wildlife watching, and picnicking
Restrictions: ATVs not allowed
Season: June through September
Finding the campground: From the junction of UT 32 and UT 150 in Kamas, go southeast on UT 150, a scenic toll road, for 10.7 miles to its junction with FR 053, which is on the south side of the road. A sign points the way to the campground, which you'll reach via paved FR 053 in 0.1 mile. At this point go left (east) a short distance to the campground.

About the campground: Conifers and aspens and the nearby Provo River grace this campground, with the Scenic Byway Trail close at hand. Open to nonmotorized vehicles, including mountain bikes, horses, and foot travel, the trail extends for several miles.

114 Lower Provo River

Location: In the Uinta-Wasatch-Cache National Forest, about 11 miles southeast of Kamas
GPS: N40 35.593'/W111 07.086'
Facilities: Fire pits, picnic tables, and vault toilets
Sites: 10 basic sites
Maximum RV length: 30 feet
Fee: $$ for basic sites

Maximum stay: 7 days

Elevation: 7,450 feet

Road conditions: Gravel

Management: Heber-Kamas Ranger District, 2460 S. Hwy. 40, Heber City; (435) 654-0470; www .fs.usda.gov/main/uwcnf/home

Reservations: Call (877) 444-6777 or TDD (877) 833-6777; www.recreation.gov

Activities: Fishing, hiking, horseback riding, mountain biking, wildlife watching, and picnicking

Restrictions: ATVs not allowed

Season: June through September

Finding the campground: From the junction of UT 32 and UT 150 in Kamas, go southeast on UT 150, a scenic toll road, for 10.7 miles to its junction with FR 053, which is on the south side of the road. A sign points the way to the campground, which you'll reach via paved, then gravel, FR 053 in 0.6 mile. FR 053 ends at the campground.

About the campground: Conifers and the lovely Provo River grace this campground, with the Scenic Byway Trail close at hand. Open to nonmotorized vehicles, including mountain bikes, horses, and foot travel, the trail extends for several miles.

115 Shingle Creek

Location: In the Uinta-Wasatch-Cache National Forest, about 10 miles southeast of Kamas

GPS: N40 36.850'/W111 07.821'

Facilities: Fire pits, picnic tables, drinking water, and vault toilets

Sites: 33 basic sites

Maximum RV length: 25 feet

Fee: $$ for basic sites

Maximum stay: 7 days

Elevation: 7,400 feet

Road conditions: Paved to the campground, then gravel

Management: Heber-Kamas Ranger District, 2460 S. Hwy. 40, Heber City; (435) 654-0470; www .fs.usda.gov/main/uwcnf/home

Reservations: None

Activities: Fishing, off-highway driving, mountain biking, hiking, and picnicking

Season: May through October

Finding the campground: From the junction of UT 32 and UT 150 in Kamas, go southeast on UT 150, a scenic toll road, for 9.5 miles to the campground, which is on the south side of the highway.

About the campground: In recent years Shingle Creek Campground grew by one-third when it was combined with the adjacent Taylor Creek Campground to make one larger campground. Open to off-highway vehicles, this campground offers shady and semi-open sites. Aspens and conifers do the shade honors. Shingle Creek flows through the area, providing opportunities for anglers. The Shingle Creek Trailhead is 0.3 mile away. The trail is rated as moderate to difficult and leads to Shingle Lake, which is less than 6 miles away. Mountain bikers will want to ride the Beaver Creek Trail, which is part of the Taylor Fork ATV Trail System. See Gregg Bromka's *Mountain Biking Utah* for additional information.

116 Yellow Pine

Location: In the Uinta-Wasatch-Cache National Forest, about 7 miles southeast of Kamas
GPS: N40 37.794'/W111 10.469'
Facilities: Fire pits, picnic tables, tent pads, and vault toilets
Sites: 33 basic sites
Maximum RV length: 25 feet
Fee: $$ for basic sites
Maximum stay: 7 days
Elevation: 7,200 feet
Road conditions: Paved to the campground, then gravel
Management: Heber-Kamas Ranger District, 2460 S. Hwy. 40, Heber City; (435) 654-0470; www .fs.usda.gov/main/uwcnf/home
Reservations: None
Activities: Fishing, hiking, mountain biking, horseback riding, and picnicking
Restrictions: ATVs not allowed
Season: May through October
Finding the campground: From the junction of UT 32 and UT 150 in Kamas, go southeast on UT 150, a scenic toll road, for 6.8 miles to the campground, which is on the north side of the highway.
About the campground: Yellow Pine Creek flows near the campground, a place decorated in oaks and pines. Hikers and horseback riders will find the Yellow Pine Trailhead close by. The trail leads to Yellow Pine Lakes, about 4 miles away, and continues beyond. In addition, the Beaver Creek Trail is across the highway and is a good trail for mountain bikers of all levels. It's also part of the larger Taylor Fork–Cedar Hollow ATV Trail System, so be prepared for motorized vehicles. Another trail, the 8-mile Scenic Byway, is an easy interpretive trail and fun for everyone. If you need a group site, check out the nearby Ponderosa Group Area. The site holds 160 people maximum.

117 Mill Hollow

Location: In the Uinta-Wasatch-Cache National Forest, about 34 miles east of Heber City
GPS: N40 29.426'/W111 06.229'
Facilities: Fire pits, picnic tables, drinking water, and vault toilets
Sites: 28 basic sites
Maximum RV length: 40 feet
Fee: $$ for basic sites
Maximum stay: 7 days
Elevation: 8,800 feet
Road conditions: Gravel
Management: Heber-Kamas Ranger District, 2460 S. Hwy. 40, Heber City; (435) 654-0470; www .fs.usda.gov/main/uwcnf/home

Reservations: Call (877) 444-6777 or TDD (877) 833-6777; www.recreation.gov
Activities: Fishing, hiking, kayaking, bird watching, mountain biking, and picnicking
Restrictions: ATVs and motorboats not allowed; campground requires a 2-day minimum stay on weekends and 3-day minimum stay on holiday weekends
Season: June through October
Finding the campground: From the junction of US 40 and UT 32, about 6 miles north of Heber City, go north then east on UT 32 for 10.4 miles to its junction with UT 35. Keep straight at the junction, continuing east on UT 35, which is paved then becomes gravel, for 15.1 miles. At this point, turn right (south) onto FR 054; follow the gravel road 2.9 miles to the Mill Hollow Reservoir and Campground.
About the campground: It's no wonder that Mill Hollow is a favorite among campers—it sits along the shore of Mill Hollow Reservoir, where the trout fishing is fine. It's also a lovely place from which to take a hike. Look for the Mill Hollow Trail and the Lakeshore Trail before checking further. For other nearby hikes, check out *Hiking Utah*, Dave Hall's FalconGuides book, for more information. If mountain biking is more your thing, read about a nice loop in Gregg Bromka's *Mountain Biking Utah*.

Campsites are shady, with a forest of mostly conifers decorating the scene. Some of the sites overlook the reservoir, where floating, rafting, and kayaking are preferred.

118 Wolf Creek

Location: In the Uinta-Wasatch-Cache National Forest, about 36 miles east of Heber City
GPS: N40 19.875'/W110 04.003'
Facilities: Fire pits, picnic tables, drinking water, and vault toilets
Sites: 3 basic sites and 2 group sites (maximum 30 and 60 people respectively)
Maximum RV length: 25 feet (group sites accommodate large RVs)
Fee: $$ for basic sites; $$$$$ for group sites
Maximum stay: 7 days
Elevation: 9,400 feet
Road conditions: Gravel
Management: Heber-Kamas Ranger District, 2460 S. Hwy. 40, Heber City; (435) 654-0470; www.fs.usda.gov/main/uwcnf/home
Reservations: Call (877) 444-6777 or TDD (877) 833-6777; www.recreation.gov
Activities: Hiking, wildlife viewing, bird watching, and picnicking
Season: July through October
Finding the campground: From the junction of US 40 and UT 32, about 6 miles north of Heber City, go north then east on UT 32 for 10.4 miles to its junction with UT 35. Keep straight at the junction, continuing east on UT 35, which is paved then becomes gravel, for 19.7 miles to the campground.
About the campground: Set among conifers with plenty of shade, this is a place from which to explore the region. A hiking trail leads from the campground to the West Fork Duchesne River.

Dinosaurland

Dinosaurs once roamed the Utah travel region known as Dinosaurland. Today visitors roam as well, seeing evidence of that time and more, for this region is enhanced by more than just bones and fossils. Dinosaurland is a land of high mountains, bountiful lakes, trophy-class fishing, great mountain biking, superb hiking, serene float trips, wonderful opportunities for horseback riding, and grand vistas.

Comprising 8,424 square miles, Dinosaurland is located in northeastern Utah and bordered by the states of Wyoming and Colorado, as well as the Utah travel regions known as Mountainland, Castle Country, and Canyonlands. The area consists of three distinct geologic areas: from north to south, the Uinta Mountains, the Uinta Basin, and the East Tavaputs Plateau. Three counties—Daggett, Duchesne, and Uintah—call the region home.

The High Uintas, the highest mountain range in Utah, stand guard over the area, with Kings Peak, the highest point in Utah, a favorite goal for many backpackers. In addition, there's an abundance of things to do and see in the Flaming Gorge area, and at Dinosaur National Monument there are about 2,000 dinosaur bones to look and wonder at.

Fifty campgrounds, some of which are open year-round, make this an easy place to explore. You'll find sites everywhere, from the high alpine forest to the dry lowlands. There are three state park campgrounds, three Bureau of Land Management (BLM) campgrounds, fifteen national recreation area campgrounds, two national monument campgrounds, and twenty-seven national forest campgrounds.

The three state parks—Starvation, Steinaker, and Red Fleet—all offer water sports and fishing. Two of the BLM sites—Bridge Hollow and Indian Crossing—encourage the history buff to visit. Here, visitors can stop, just as Butch Cassidy and the Sundance Kid once did, at the John Jarvie Ranch. Now a historic site, the ranch is located on the Green River in Browns Park. The 35-acre site contains the Jarvies' first residence, an original stone house, and a two-room dugout. There is also a replica of the general store, originally built in 1881.

For the most part the national forest campgrounds promise shade and a multitude of activities, from hiking, backpacking, mountain biking, and horseback riding to fishing, boating, and swimming.

One national monument and one national recreation area exist in Dinosaurland. Dinosaur National Monument offers a wealth of dinosaur bones shown in relief on a 200-foot-long wall just waiting to be examined. North of the monument is the Flaming Gorge National Recreation Area, a popular place with boaters and anglers and those who want nothing more to do than relax and enjoy the stunning scenes

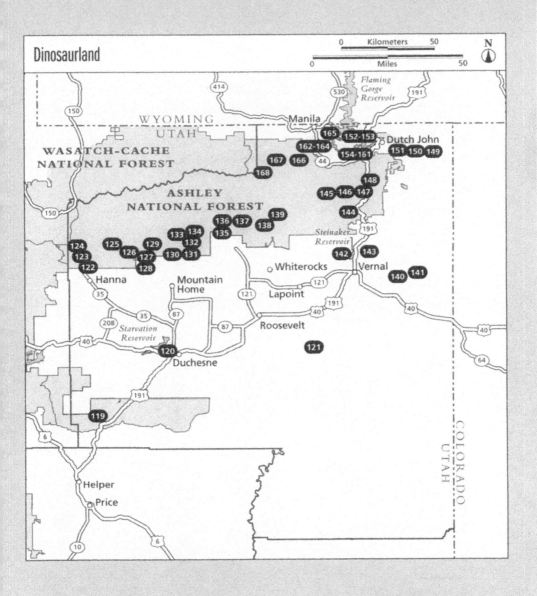

found there. Anglers are attracted by the world-record fish that have come from the 91-mile-long reservoir. Species include mackinaw (lake) trout, rainbow trout, small-mouth bass, and kokanee salmon.

Below the reservoir is the Green River, one of the finest tailwater fisheries in the world. It's a prime fly-fishing destination, offering ample populations of rainbow, brown, and cutthroat trout.

There are many scenic drives in the area, with the Sheep Creek Geologic Loop Tour a particularly impressive ride. Besides bighorn sheep you'll see dramatic geology that includes jagged rock spires and the dramatic Uinta Fault.

Wildlife is abundant in the region, with pronghorn, elk, deer, moose, and bighorn sheep sometimes visible. Near the water look for river otters, and be sure to watch for bald eagles come winter. In summer ospreys nest in the area, while marmots frequent grassy slopes. Numerous species of birds are common all year.

For more information contact the Dinosaurland Travel Region at 25 E. Main, Vernal; (435) 789-6932 or (800) 477-5558; http://utahtravelcenter.com/travelre gions/dinosaurland.htm.

		Total Sites	Group Sites	Hook-up Sites	Hookups	Max. RV Length	Dump Station	Toilets	Showers	Drinking Water	ADA Compliant	Fees	Reservations	Recreation
119	Avintaquin	25	1			20		V				$-$$	•	MH
120	Starvation State Park	71	1	61	WES	Any	•	F	•	•	•	$$-$$$$$$	•	FSBLOK
121	Pelican Lake	*				30		V				None		FBLK
122	Aspen	32	1			40		V		•		$-$$$	•	HMRF
123	Hades	16				20		V		•		$-$$	•	HMRF
124	Iron Mine	26	1			30		V		•		$-$$$	•	HMRF
125	Upper Stillwater	20	1			25		F		•		$-$$$	•	HMRBFKL
126	Yellowpine	29	2			20	•	F		•	•	$-$$$	•	HF
127	Miners Gulch	6	1			24		V				$-$$$$$	•	HF
128	Rock Creek Group Area	1	1			30		V				$$$$$	•	MHF
129	Moon Lake	56	2			40		F		•		$-$$$$$	•	HRF
130	Yellowstone Group	1	1			25		V		•		$$$		FO
131	Bridge	5				15		V		•		$		F
132	Reservoir	5				15		V		•		$		F
133	Riverview	19				20		V		•		$		FHR
134	Swift Creek	13				22		V		•		$		FHR
135	Uinta Canyon	25	1			22		V				$-$$$$$	•	HRF
136	Wandin	4				15		V				$		HRF

		Total Sites	Group Sites	Hook-up Sites	Hookups	Max. RV Length	Dump Station	Toilets	Showers	Drinking Water	ADA Compliant	Fees	Reservations	Recreation
137	Pole Creek Lake	19				25		V				$		F
138	Whiterocks	21				25		V		•		$		HOF
139	Paradise Park	15				25		V				$		FOHR
140	Split Mountain	4	4			30		F & V		•		$$$	•	FBLKH
141	Green River	83				Any		F		•	•	$$	•	FBHK
142	Steinaker State Park	32	1	16	WES	30	•	F		•	•	$$-$$$$$	•	FSBHKL
143	Red Fleet State Park	38		5	WES	25	•	F		•	•	$$-$$$	•	FSBHLK
144	Iron Springs	2	2			45		V		•		$$	•	MHO
145	Oaks Park	11				20		V				None		FBMHK
146	East Park	21				25		V		•		$		FBHMKL
147	Red Springs	13	1			32		V				$$-$$$$$	•	H
148	Lodgepole	35				45	•	F		•		$$	•	HM
149	Bridge Hollow	13				20		V		•		$		FMBK
150	Indian Crossing	21				20	•	V		•		$		FMBK
151	Dripping Springs	26	4			35		F & V		•	•	$$$-$$$$$	•	FBHM
152	Antelope Flat	50	4			40	•	F		•		$$-$$$$$	•	FBLSK
153	Mustang Ridge	74	1			40		F & V	•	•	•	$$$-$$$$$	•	FBSLK
154	Deer Run	19				35	•	F & V	•	•	•	$$$-$$$$$	•	FBSHMLK
155	Cedar Springs	24				35	•	V		•		$$$-$$$$$	•	FBSHMLK
156	Firefighters Memorial	94				Any	•	F		•	•	$$	•	HM
157	Greendale	10	2			30		V		•		$$-$$$$$	•	HM
158	Skull Creek	17				30		V		•		$$	•	MH
159	Greens Lake	21	1			35		V		•		$$-$$$$$	•	HMF
160	Canyon Rim	16				40		V		•		$$	•	HM
161	Red Canyon	8				20		V		•		$$	•	HM
162	Sheep Creek Bay	*				45		V				$		FBLK
163	Willows/Mann's	17				25/30		V				$		F
164	Carmel	15				35		V				$		F
165	Lucerne Valley	138	4	90	E	Any	•	F	•	•	•	$$$-$$$$$	•	FBSMLK
166	Deep Creek	17				30		V				$		FHMO
167	Browne Lake	24	4			40		V				$-$$$$$	•	FKRHM
168	Spirit Lake	24				30		V				$$		FBRHMK

Hookup: W = Water, E = Electric, S = Sewer   * = Dispersed Camping, no designated sites
Recreation: H = Hiking, C = Rock Climbing, M = Mountain Biking, S = Swimming, F = Fishing, B = Boating, L = Boat Launch, O = Off-highway Driving, R = Horseback Riding, K = Kayaking and Canoeing, G = Golf
Toilets: F = Flush, V = Vault, C = Chemical
Per-night campsite cost: $ = $10 or less $$ = $11 to $20 $$$ = $21 to 30 $$$$ = $31 to $40 $$$$$ = $41 and higher

119 Avintaquin

Location: In the Ashley National Forest, about 19 miles northeast of Helper
GPS: N39 52.968'/W110 46.537'
Facilities: Fire pits, picnic tables, and vault toilets
Sites: 24 basic sites and 1 group site (maximum 50 people)
Maximum RV length: 20 feet
Fee: $ for basic sites; $$ for group site
Maximum stay: 14 days
Elevation: 9,000 feet
Road conditions: Gravel
Management: Duchesne/Roosevelt Ranger District, 85 W. Main, PO Box 981, Duchesne, UT 84021; (435) 738-2482; www.fs.usda.gov/main/ashley/home
Reservations: Call (877) 444-6777 or TDD (877) 833-6777; www.recreation.gov
Activities: Mountain biking, hiking, picnicking, and wildlife watching
Restrictions: ATVs not allowed
Season: June through September
Finding the campground: From the junction of US 6 and US 191, about 3 miles north of Helper, go northeast on US 191 for 14.4 miles to the turnoff for Reservation Ridge Road (FR 147); it's on the left (west) side of the highway. The paved road turns to dirt in 0.2 mile; follow FR 147 a total of 1.2 miles from US 191.
About the campground: Conifers and aspens serve to shade these high-elevation sites located atop scenic Indian Canyon.

120 Starvation State Park

Location: About 4 miles northwest of Duchesne
GPS: N40 10.675'/W110 27.159'
Facilities: Fire pits, covered picnic tables, ADA sites, partial and full hookups, flush toilets, showers, drinking water, dump station, fish cleaning station, volleyball nets, horseshoe pits, boat ramp, and boat and watercraft rentals
Sites: 9 basic sites with water only, 56 partial-hookup sites, 5 full-hookup sites, 1 group site (maximum 75 people), 3 cabins, and 4 primitive campgrounds located around the lake
Maximum RV length: Any
Fee: $$ for basic sites; $$$ for partial-hookup and full-hookup sites; $$$$$ for group site and cabins
Maximum stay: 14 days
Elevation: 5,700 feet
Road conditions: Paved
Management: Starvation State Park, PO Box 584, Duchesne, UT 84021; (435) 738-2326; www.stateparks.utah.gov/park/starvation-state-park

Starvation State Park is a wonderful place to visit.

Reservations: In the Salt Lake area, call (801) 322-3770; elsewhere, (800) 322-3770; http://utahstateparks.reserveamerica.com

Activities: Fishing, swimming, boating, water activities, off-highway driving, and picnicking

Season: Year-round (if visiting in winter, call the ranger for more information)

Finding the campground: From Duchesne go west on US 40, then turn right (northwest) onto North UT 311 at the sign pointing the way to Starvation Reservoir. The fee station is 2.5 miles up the road.

About the campground: With 23 miles of shoreline, Starvation Reservoir is a popular place for water sports and fishing. Views of the Uinta Mountains add to the scene. There are two developed campgrounds: Mountain View and Beach. Beach is popular for tent camping. Mountain View is the newest campground and offers wonderful views. There are also three cabins for rent and a group area with grand views of the lake. Four primitive campgrounds—Knight Hollow, Juniper Point, Indian Bay, and Rabbit Gulch—are located around the reservoir.

This is one of Utah's best fisheries for walleye; other species include smallmouth bass and brown trout. Wildlife watching is popular too, with mule deer, prairie dogs, beavers, badgers, and rabbits living in the park. Coyotes, foxes, bobcats, and elk live in the area and are seen on occasion. Off-highway driving is allowed only in the Knight Hollow area designated open to OHV use.

121 Pelican Lake

Location: On BLM land, about 25 miles southwest of Vernal
GPS: N40 11.022'/W109 41.434'
Facilities: Fire pits, picnic tables, vault toilets, and a boat launch
Sites: Dispersed sites; 7 picnic tables and fire rings
Maximum RV length: 30 feet
Fee: None
Maximum stay: 14 days
Elevation: 4,800 feet
Road conditions: Maintained gravel
Management: Bureau of Land Management, Vernal Field Office, 170 S. 500 East, Vernal; (435) 781-4400; www.blm.gov/ut/st/en/fo/vernal.html
Reservations: None
Activities: Fishing, boating, bird watching in spring, and picnicking
Season: Year-round
Finding the campground: From Vernal, drive approximately 15 miles southwest on US 40/191, then go south on UT 88 for about 7 miles to a fork in the road. Going left leads to Ouray National Wildlife Refuge; drive right (west) on 5500 South, where there is a sign pointing the way to Pelican Lake. Travel 2.1 miles and make a left (south) onto 14500 East. Go another 1.5 miles to the junction of 7000 South. At this point continue straight (south) on 14500 East, which is gravel now. Some maps call this Pelican Lake Road. Continue another 2.3 miles to the camping area and boat launch.
About the campground: Located on the south shore of this natural lake in the Uinta Basin, this is a favorite with anglers, who vie for largemouth bass and bluegills. It's also a favorite with birders, who come to watch the large numbers of birds often seen here.

122 Aspen

Location: In the Ashley National Forest, about 9 miles northwest of Hanna
GPS: N40 29.742'/W110 50.697'
Facilities: Fire pits, picnic tables, drinking water, and vault toilets
Sites: 29 basic sites, 2 double sites, and 1 group site (maximum 32 people)
Maximum RV length: 40 feet
Fee: $ for basic sites; $$ for double sites; $$$ for group site
Maximum stay: 14 days
Elevation: 7,100 feet
Road conditions: Paved
Management: Duchesne/Roosevelt Ranger District, 85 W. Main, PO Box 981, Duchesne, UT 84021; (435) 738-2482; www.fs.usda.gov/main/ashley/home
Reservations: Call (877) 444-6777 or TDD (877) 833-6777; www.recreation.gov
Activities: Hiking, mountain biking, horseback riding, fishing, and picnicking
Season: Memorial Day through Labor Day

Finding the campground: From Hanna go northwest about 6 miles via paved UT 35, then turn right (north) onto the paved road paralleling the North Fork Duchesne River. You'll reach the campground after 2.7 miles.

About the campground: Located along the North Fork Duchesne River, aspens and spruce serve to shade this campground, though you'll find some semi-open sites if you desire.

123 Hades

Location: In the Ashley National Forest, about 12 miles northwest of Hanna
GPS: N40 32.039' / W110 52.314'
Facilities: Fire pits, picnic tables, drinking water, and vault toilets
Sites: 14 basic sites and 2 double sites
Maximum RV length: 20 feet
Fee: $ for basic sites; $$ for double sites
Maximum stay: 14 days
Elevation: 7,400 feet
Road conditions: Dirt
Management: Duchesne/Roosevelt Ranger District, 85 W. Main, PO Box 981, Duchesne, UT 84021; (435) 738-2482; www.fs.usda.gov/main/ashley/home
Reservations: Call (877) 444-6777 or TDD (877) 833-6777; www.recreation.gov
Activities: Hiking, mountain biking, horseback riding, fishing, and picnicking
Season: Memorial Day through Labor Day
Finding the campground: From Hanna go northwest about 6 miles via paved UT 35, then turn right (north) onto the paved road paralleling the North Fork Duchesne River. Reach the campground after approximately 6 miles. The pavement turns to gravel and dirt about 2 miles before the campground.
About the campground: This aspen- and conifer-blessed campground sits along the North Fork Duchesne River. Just north of the campground, hikers and horseback riders will find an access road leading to the Grand View Trailhead and eventually the High Uintas, a wonderful mountain range that stretches from west to east.

124 Iron Mine

Location: In the Ashley National Forest, about 14 miles northwest of Hanna
GPS: N40 33.296' / W110 53.289'
Facilities: Fire pits, picnic tables, drinking water, and vault toilets
Sites: 24 basic sites, 1 double site, and 1 group site (maximum 50 people)
Maximum RV length: 30 feet
Fee: $ for basic sites; $$ for double site; $$$ for group site
Maximum stay: 14 days
Elevation: 7,500 feet
Road conditions: Dirt

Management: Duchesne/Roosevelt Ranger District, 85 W. Main, PO Box 981, Duchesne, UT 84021; (435) 738-2482; www.fs.usda.gov/main/ashley/home
Reservations: Call (877) 444-6777 or TDD (877) 833-6777; www.recreation.gov
Activities: Hiking, mountain biking, horseback riding, fishing, and picnicking
Season: Memorial Day through Labor Day
Finding the campground: From Hanna go northwest about 6 miles via paved UT 35, then turn right (north) onto the paved road paralleling the North Fork Duchesne River. Reach the campground after driving another 7.6 miles. The pavement turns to gravel and dirt a few miles prior to the campground.
About the campground: Aspens and conifers serve to shade these sites, with access to mountain biking, hiking, and horseback riding trails. This is a place to explore to your heart's content.

125 Upper Stillwater

Location: In the Ashley National Forest, about 23 miles northwest of Mountain Home
GPS: N40 33.304'/W110 41.942'
Facilities: Fire pits, picnic tables, drinking water, flush toilets, and a boat ramp
Sites: 15 basic sites, 4 double sites, and 1 group site (maximum 32 people)
Maximum RV length: 25 feet
Fee: $ for basic sites; $$ for double sites; $$$ for group site
Maximum stay: 14 days
Elevation: 8,000 feet
Road conditions: Paved
Management: Duchesne/Roosevelt Ranger District, 85 W. Main, PO Box 981, Duchesne, UT 84021; (435) 738-2482; www.fs.usda.gov/main/ashley/home
Reservations: Call (877) 444-6777 or TDD (877) 833-6777; www.recreation.gov
Activities: Hiking, mountain biking, horseback riding, boating, fishing, and picnicking
Season: June through September
Finding the campground: From Mountain Home go west on Duchesne CR 95 (also known as 6750N) for 23.4 miles to the campground.
About the campground: Located just below Upper Stillwater Dam, the music of Rock Creek is available for all campers to hear. Hikers will find a trail leading to both the Yellowpine and Miners Gulch Campgrounds, which are down the canyon 4 and 5 miles, respectively. There's also a trail for hikers and horseback riders leading up Rock Creek and into the High Uintas Wilderness.

126 Yellowpine

Location: In the Ashley National Forest, about 19 miles northwest of Mountain Home
GPS: N40 32.132'/W110 38.250'
Facilities: Fire pits, picnic tables, tent pads, ADA sites, drinking water, flush toilets, and dump station

Sites: 23 basic sites, 4 double sites, and 2 group sites (maximum 32 people each)

Maximum RV length: 20 feet

Fee: $ for single sites; $$ for double sites; $$$ for group sites

Maximum stay: 14 days

Elevation: 7,600 feet

Road conditions: Paved

Management: Duchesne/Roosevelt Ranger District, 85 W. Main, PO Box 981, Duchesne, UT 84021; (435) 738-2482; www.fs.usda.gov/main/ashley/home

Reservations: Call (877) 444-6777 or TDD (877) 833-6777; www.recreation.gov

Activities: Hiking, fishing, and picnicking

Restrictions: ATVs not allowed

Season: June through September

Finding the campground: From Mountain Home go west on Duchesne CR 95 (also known as 6750N) for 19.3 miles to the campground.

About the campground: Sites are spread out among aspens, pines, and conifers, with Rock Creek flowing nearby. There's a trail leading from here on up to the Upper Stillwater Dam and Campground. In addition, you'll find a trail leading down the canyon to Miners Gulch. Hikers are bound to enjoy both trails.

127 Miners Gulch

Location: In the Ashley National Forest, about 18 miles northwest of Mountain Home

GPS: N40 32.029'/W110 37.412'

Facilities: Fire pits, picnic tables, and vault toilets

Sites: 5 basic sites that can make 1 big group site (maximum 40 people)

Maximum RV length: 24 feet

Fee: $$$$$ for entire campground; $ per site if not reserved

Maximum stay: 14 days

Elevation: 7,500 feet

Road conditions: Paved

Management: Duchesne/Roosevelt Ranger District, 85 W. Main, PO Box 981, Duchesne, UT 84021; (435) 738-2482; www.fs.usda.gov/main/ashley/home

Reservations: Call (877) 444-6777 or TDD (877) 833-6777; www.recreation.gov

Activities: Hiking, fishing, and picnicking

Restrictions: ATVs not allowed

Season: June through September

Finding the campground: From Mountain Home go west on Duchesne CR 95 (also known as 6750N) for 18.3 miles to the campground, which is on the right (north) side of the road.

About the campground: Situated on flat terrain, with lodgepole pines, ponderosa pines, and quaking aspens decorating the grounds, this is a group area that needs to be reserved. If not occupied, then sites can be rented individually. Anglers can look for cutthroat, brown, and rainbow trout in Rock Creek. Not too far away, hikers can take the Rock Creek Trail into the High Uintas Wilderness. Also, a pleasant trail leads from the campground to the Upper Stillwater Campground.

128 Rock Creek Group Area

Location: In the Ashley National Forest, about 18 miles northwest of Mountain Home
GPS: N40 31.791'/W110 36.692'
Facilities: Fire pits, picnic tables, BBQ grills, and vault toilets
Sites: 1 group site (maximum 75 people)
Maximum RV length: 30 feet
Fee: $$$$$ for group site
Maximum stay: 14 days
Elevation: 7,500 feet
Road conditions: Paved
Management: Duchesne/Roosevelt Ranger District, 85 W. Main, PO Box 981, Duchesne, UT 84021; (435) 738-2482; www.fs.usda.gov/main/ashley/home
Reservations: Call (877) 444-6777 or TDD (877) 833-6777; www.recreation.gov
Activities: Hiking, mountain biking, fishing, and picnicking
Restrictions: ATVs not allowed
Season: June through September
Finding the campground: From Mountain Home go west on Duchesne CR 95 (also known as 6750N) for 17.6 miles to the campground, which is on the left (south) side of the road.
About the campground: Situated on flat terrain, with lodgepole pines, ponderosa pines, and quaking aspens decorating the grounds, this is a group area that needs to be reserved. Anglers can look for cutthroat, brown, and rainbow trout in Rock Creek. Hikers can look for the Rock Creek Trail that leads into the High Uintas Wilderness. Also, a pleasant trail leads from the campground to the Upper Stillwater Campground.

129 Moon Lake

Location: In the Ashley National Forest, about 11 miles northwest of Mountain Home
GPS: N40 34.111'/W110 30.488'
Facilities: Fire pits, picnic tables, tent pads, drinking water, and flush toilets
Sites: 48 basic sites, 6 walk-in tent sites, and 2 group sites (maximum 75 people each)
Maximum RV length: 40 feet
Fee: $ for basic and walk-in tent sites; $$$$$ for group sites
Maximum stay: 14 days
Elevation: 8,100 feet
Road conditions: Paved
Management: Duchesne/Roosevelt Ranger District, 85 W. Main, PO Box 981, Duchesne, UT 84021; (435) 738-2482; www.fs.usda.gov/main/ashley/home
Reservations: Call (877) 444-6777 or TDD (877) 833-6777; www.recreation.gov
Activities: Hiking, horseback riding, fishing, and picnicking
Restrictions: ATVs and horses not allowed
Season: June through September

These boys are enjoying the mud at Moon Lake.

Finding the campground: From Mountain Home go north on 21000 West for 0.8 mile to a T inter-section, then make a right (east) onto 7500N. The road curves back to the north almost immedi-ately; continue approximately 15 miles to the campground.

About the campground: Newly renovated in 2012, this campground is located near Moon Lake, a beautiful lake with the High Uintas filling the background. This is a great spot from which to explore the area. While horses are not allowed in the campground, they are allowed on the nearby trails. Hikers and horseback riders will also find the trailheads for both Fish Creek and Lake Fork in the near vicinity. Among the tall pines there are also two group sites, which make this a nice spot for family reunions. Just across the road you'll find a store, cabins, and boat rentals.

130 Yellowstone Group

Location: In the Ashley National Forest, about 12 miles northeast of Mountain Home
GPS: N40 29.742'/W110 50.697'
Facilities: Fire pits, picnic tables, drinking water, and vault toilets
Sites: 1 group site (maximum 80 people)
Maximum RV length: 25 feet

Fee: $$$ for group site
Maximum stay: 14 days
Elevation: 7,700 feet
Road conditions: Gravel
Management: Duchesne/Roosevelt Ranger District, 85 W. Main, PO Box 981, Duchesne, UT 84021; (435) 738-2482; www.fs.usda.gov/main/ashley/home
Reservations: None
Activities: Fishing, off-highway driving, and picnicking
Season: June through September
Finding the campground: From Mountain Home go north on 21000 West for 0.8 mile to a T junction, then make a right (east) onto 7500N. The road curves back to the north almost immediately; continue another 4.4 miles to a road junction. Turn right (northeast); you're now traveling a gravel road to Yellowstone Canyon. You'll reach the campground after an additional 6.7 miles.
About the campground: Yellowstone Creek flows through this aspen- and conifer-graced campground. Anglers will find excellent fishing, while other campers will find nothing more—or less—than a great place to relax and enjoy their surroundings. ATVers should enjoy the Yellowstone ATV Trail, which is nearby.

131 Bridge

Location: In the Ashley National Forest, about 14 miles northeast of Mountain Home
GPS: N40 32.751'/W110 20.052'
Facilities: Fire pits, picnic tables, drinking water, and vault toilets
Sites: 5 basic sites
Maximum RV length: 15 feet
Fee: $ for basic sites
Maximum stay: 14 nights
Elevation: 7,700 feet
Road conditions: Gravel
Management: Duchesne/Roosevelt Ranger District, 85 W. Main, PO Box 981, Duchesne, UT 84021; (435) 738-2482; www.fs.usda.gov/main/ashley/home
Reservations: None
Activities: Fishing and picnicking
Season: Mid-May through mid-September
Finding the campground: From Mountain Home go north on 21000 West for 0.8 mile to a T junction, then make a right (east) onto 7500N. The road curves back to the north almost immediately; continue another 4.4 miles to a road junction. Turn right (northeast); you're now traveling a gravel road to Yellowstone Canyon. You'll reach the campground after an additional 8.4 miles.
About the campground: Set among aspens and conifers, with Yellowstone Creek singing nearby, this is a popular spot for anglers who fish the creek, and ATVers who ride the Yellowstone ATV Trail. Though trailers are allowed, there is a 15-foot limit. This is not really the best place for trailers; the campground is small and more suited for tents and tent trailers.

132 Reservoir

Location: In the Ashley National Forest, about 16 miles northeast of Mountain Home
GPS: N40 34.546'/W110 19.517'
Facilities: Fire pits, picnic tables, drinking water, and vault toilet
Sites: 5 basic sites
Maximum RV length: 15 feet
Fee: $ for basic sites
Maximum stay: 14 days
Elevation: 7,900 feet
Road conditions: Gravel
Management: Duchesne/Roosevelt Ranger District, 85 W. Main, PO Box 981, Duchesne, UT 84021; (435) 738-2482; www.fs.usda.gov/main/ashley/home
Reservations: None
Activities: Fishing and picnicking
Season: Mid-May through mid-September
Finding the campground: From Mountain Home go north on 21000 West for 0.8 mile to a T junction, then make a right (east) onto 7500N. The road curves back to the north almost immediately; continue another 4.4 miles to a road junction. Turn right (northeast); you're now traveling a gravel road to Yellowstone Canyon. You'll reach the campground after an additional 10.8 miles.
About the campground: Like the other campgrounds along this route, this one is more enchanting because of Yellowstone Creek, which flows nearby. In addition to the creek, there's a dam, with the upstream waters fun for playing and fishing. A fishing dock adds a nice touch. The campground is small and best for tents and tent trailers—aspens and conifers serve to partially shade the sites.

133 Riverview

Location: In the Ashley National Forest, about 17 miles northeast of Mountain Home
GPS: N40 35.405'/W111 20.174'
Facilities: Fire pits, picnic tables, drinking water, and vault toilets
Sites: 19 basic sites
Maximum RV length: 20 feet
Fee: $ for basic sites
Maximum stay: 14 days
Elevation: 8,000 feet
Road conditions: Gravel
Management: Duchesne/Roosevelt Ranger District, 85 W. Main, PO Box 981, Duchesne, UT 84021; (435) 738-2482; www.fs.usda.gov/main/ashley/home
Reservations: None
Activities: Fishing, hiking, horseback riding, and picnicking
Season: Mid-May through mid-September

Finding the campground: From Mountain Home go north on 21000 West for 0.8 mile to a T junction, then make a right (east) onto 7500N. The road curves back to the north almost immediately; continue another 4.4 miles to a road junction. Turn right (northeast); you're now traveling a gravel road to Yellowstone Canyon. You'll reach the campground after an additional 12 miles.

About the campground: Stretched out along the east bank of Yellowstone Creek, with aspens and conifers to shade all the sites, this is a favorite place for anglers and campers who just want to relax and have fun. It also provides close access to the trailhead at Swift Creek, which leads into the High Uintas Wilderness.

134 Swift Creek

Location: In the Ashley National Forest, about 18 miles northeast of Mountain Home
GPS: N40 36.056' / W110 20.882'
Facilities: Fire pits, picnic tables, drinking water, vault toilets, and a horse loading ramp
Sites: 13 basic sites
Maximum RV length: 22 feet
Fee: $ for basic sites
Maximum stay: 14 days
Elevation: 8,100 feet
Road conditions: Gravel
Management: Duchesne/Roosevelt Ranger District, 85 W. Main, PO Box 981, Duchesne, UT 84021; (435) 738-2482; www.fs.usda.gov/main/ashley/home
Reservations: None
Activities: Fishing, hiking, horseback riding, and picnicking
Season: June through September
Finding the campground: From Mountain Home go north on 21000 West for 0.8 mile to a T junction, then make a right (east) onto 7500N. The road curves back to the north almost immediately; continue another 4.4 miles to a road junction. Turn right (northeast); you're now traveling a gravel road to Yellowstone Canyon. You'll reach the campground after an additional 12.9 miles.

About the campground: Set among aspens and conifers, this campground is located at a trailhead leading into the High Uintas Wilderness. There's a horse loading ramp for those who want to ride into the wilderness, and nice campsites for those who'd like to day hike into the lovely region. A backpack trip is best, however. For more information, see Dave Hall's *Hiking Utah* by FalconGuides.

135 Uinta Canyon

Location: In the Ashley National Forest, about 25 miles northwest of Roosevelt
GPS: N40 37.347' / W110 08.585'
Facilities: Fire pits, picnic tables, and vault toilets
Sites: 24 basic sites and 1 nearby group site (maximum 150 people)
Maximum RV length: 22 feet

Fee: $ for basic sites; $$$$$ for group site
Maximum stay: 14 days
Elevation: 7,600 feet
Road conditions: Gravel
Management: Duchesne/Roosevelt Ranger District, 85 W. Main, PO Box 981, Duchesne, UT 84021; (435) 738-2482; www.fs.usda.gov/main/ashley/home
Reservations: For the Uinta River Group site, call (877) 444-6777 or TDD (877) 833-6777; www.recreation.gov
Activities: Hiking, horseback riding, fishing, and picnicking
Season: Mid-May through mid-September
Finding the campground: From the junction of US 40/191 and UT 121 in Roosevelt, travel north on UT 121. There are signs for Uinta Canyon. UT 121 heads east after 10.1 miles, but you should stay straight (north) on 2000 West. After another 8.4 miles you'll reach a fork; keep right to Uinta Canyon. (A left would take you to Yellowstone Canyon.) Drive an additional 4 miles to another fork; go right again, continuing to follow signs for Uinta Canyon. After another 2.2 miles the road turns to gravel; the campground is 0.7 mile beyond.
About the campground: Conifers serve to shade the sites here along the Uinta River. Looking for a trail to hike? When camped at Uinta Canyon, there's a nearby trail that provides hikers and horseback riders access into the lovely High Uintas Wilderness. Anglers fish for rainbow, cutthroat, brown, and brook trout.

136 Wandin

Location: In the Ashley National Forest, about 27 miles northwest of Roosevelt
GPS: N40 37.843'/W110 09.133'
Facilities: Fire pits, picnic tables, and vault toilet
Sites: 4 basic sites
Maximum RV length: 15 feet
Fee: $ for basic sites
Maximum stay: 14 days
Elevation: 7,800 feet
Road conditions: Gravel
Management: Duchesne/Roosevelt Ranger District, 85 W. Main, PO Box 981, Duchesne, UT 84021; (435) 738-2482; www.fs.usda.gov/main/ashley/home
Reservations: None
Activities: Hiking, horseback riding, fishing, and picnicking
Season: Mid-May through September
Finding the campground: From the junction of US 40/191 and UT 121 in Roosevelt, travel north on UT 121. There are signs for Uinta Canyon. UT 121 heads east after 10.1 miles, but you should stay straight (north) on 2000 West. After another 8.4 miles you'll reach a fork; keep right to Uinta Canyon. (A left would take you to Yellowstone Canyon.) Drive an additional 4 miles to another fork; go right again, continuing to follow signs for Uinta Canyon. After another 2.2 miles the road turns to gravel; the campground is 2.1 miles beyond.

About the campground: Conifers and aspens partially shade this small campground, which is used by tenters and those with small trailers. It's located along the Uinta River, and there's also the must-see Smokey Spring just up the road. A nearby trail leads horseback riders and hikers into the lovely High Uintas Wilderness. If you enjoy fishing, expect to find rainbow, cutthroat, brown, and brook trout.

137 Pole Creek Lake

Location: In the Ashley National Forest, about 34 miles north of Roosevelt
GPS: N40 40.740'/W110 03.423'
Facilities: Fire pits, picnic tables, and vault toilets
Sites: 19 basic sites
Maximum RV length: 25 feet
Fee: $ for basic sites
Maximum stay: 14 days
Elevation: 10,000 feet
Road conditions: Gravel
Management: Duchesne/Roosevelt Ranger District, 85 W. Main, PO Box 981, Duchesne, UT 84021; (435) 738-2482; www.fs.usda.gov/main/ashley/home
Reservations: None
Activities: Fishing and picnicking
Season: June through early September
Finding the campground: From the junction of US 40/191 and UT 121 in Roosevelt, travel north on UT 121. There are signs for Uinta Canyon. UT 121 heads east after 10.1 miles, but you should stay straight (north) on 2000 West. After another 8.4 miles you'll reach a fork; keep right to Uinta Canyon. (A left would take you to Yellowstone Canyon.) Drive an additional 4 miles to another fork; go right again and, after crossing a bridge over the river, stay right on the Elkhorn Loop, which is gravel. The road is rough and narrow for the first few miles. You'll reach a fork after 3.6 miles; keep straight (north). Continue an additional 8 miles to the northeast to the campground.
About the campground: Conifers shade this high-elevation campground, with Pole Creek Lake adding to the southern vista. It's a nice place for fishing and relaxing and exploring to your heart's content.

138 Whiterocks

Location: In the Ashley National Forest, about 14 miles north of Whiterocks
GPS: N40 37.231'/W109 56.501'
Facilities: Fire pits, picnic tables, drinking water, and vault toilets
Sites: 21 basic sites
Maximum RV length: 25 feet
Fee: $ for basic sites

Maximum stay: 14 days
Elevation: 7,400 feet
Road conditions: Gravel
Management: Vernal Ranger District, 355 N. Vernal Ave., Vernal; (435) 789-1181; www.fs.usda
.gov/main/ashley/home
Reservations: None
Activities: Hiking, ATVing, fishing, and picnicking
Season: May through September
Finding the campground: From the Elkhorn Guard Station, which is a few miles north of White-
rocks (Whiterocks is approximately 18 miles northeast of Roosevelt), go south for 1 mile on a
paved road, then east on a paved road for another 2.3 miles. Now turn north onto the gravel road
for 6.5 miles; a sign points the way to the campground.
About the campground: Spruce, conifers, and aspens serve to shade this campground, with the
Whiterocks River singing nearby. It's a nice place for fishing, relaxing, and just plain enjoying the
sights and sounds of the forest.

139 Paradise Park

Location: In the Ashley National Forest, 25 miles northwest of Lapoint
GPS: N40 39.914'/W109 54.801'
Facilities: Fire pits, picnic tables, and vault toilets
Sites: 15 basic sites
Maximum RV length: 25 feet
Fee: $ for basic sites
Maximum stay: 14 days
Elevation: 10,800 feet
Road conditions: Gravel
Management: Vernal Ranger District, 355 N. Vernal Ave., Vernal; (435) 789-1181; www.fs.usda
.gov/main/ashley/home
Reservations: None
Activities: Fishing, ATVing, hiking, horseback riding, and picnicking
Season: June through September
Finding the campground: From Lapoint and the UT 121 and 11500 East junction, on the east
side of town, go north on paved 11500 East. A sign points the way to Paradise. You'll reach a fork
after 6.9 miles; keep left (northwest) to reach Paradise Reservoir. This road is known as Mosby
Canyon Road. After another 8.5 miles the road turns to dirt. Drive an additional 9.6 miles, climbing
to the campground entrance and continuing beyond to reach the reservoir.
About the campground: Located in a high-mountain setting, there's an overflow camping area in
addition to the main campground. There's also a trailhead leading into the High Uintas Wilderness,
so this is a great place for hikers and horseback riders. It's popular among anglers too, because
there are fish (rainbow and brook trout) to be had in Paradise Park Reservoir. ATVs can access the
areas north and east of Paradise Park.

The scenic overlook at Split Mountain Campground offers spectacular views.

140 Split Mountain: Dinosaur National Monument

Location: About 22 miles east of Vernal
GPS: N40 26.656' / W109 15.197'
Facilities: Fire pits, picnic tables, flush and vault toilets, drinking water, and boat launch
Sites: 4 group sites (maximum 25 people each)
Maximum RV length: 30 feet
Fee: $$$ for group sites (no fee in winter when water is not available)
Maximum stay: 14 days
Elevation: 4,800 feet
Road conditions: Paved
Management: Dinosaur National Monument, Quarry Visitor Center, Box 128, Jensen, UT 84035; (435) 781-7700; www.nps.gov/dino/index.htm
Reservations: Call (877) 444-6777 or TDD (877) 833-6777; www.recreation.gov
Activities: Fishing, boating, hiking, photography, and picnicking
Season: Year-round

Finding the campground: From Vernal head south then east on US 40 for about 12 miles, then go north on UT 149 for 6 miles to the entrance station and visitor center. Continue 2.6 miles to the campground turnoff, which is on the left (north) side of the road. You'll reach the campground in another 1.1 miles.

About the campground: Situated among cottonwoods, with the Green River meandering nearby and Split Mountain jutting straight into the heavens, this is a beautiful place to stay. There are four group sites, all of which are located near a day-use area that's a popular put-in point for rafters. Hikers will want to check out two trails that lead to and from the campground.

For many campers the best thing about staying here is the chance to see dinosaur bones, and lots of them. Don't miss the Dinosaur Quarry; it's open every day of the year except for Thanksgiving, Christmas, and New Year's.

The campground is open year-round, though the water is shut off from fall through spring. During this time the campground is open to all visitors on a first-come, first-served basis.

141 Green River: Dinosaur National Monument

Location: About 23 miles east of Vernal
GPS: N40 25.345'/W109 14.683'
Facilities: Fire pits, picnic tables, ADA site, flush toilets, and drinking water
Sites: 83 basic sites
Maximum RV length: Any
Fee: $$ for basic sites
Maximum stay: 14 days
Elevation: 4,800 feet
Road conditions: Paved
Management: Dinosaur National Monument, Quarry Visitor Center, Box 128, Jensen, UT 84035; (435) 781-7700; www.nps.gov/dino/index.htm
Reservations: Call (877) 444-6777 or TDD (877) 833-6777; www.recreation.gov
Activities: Fishing, boating, hiking, photography, and picnicking
Season: Mid-April through early-October. (When this campground is closed, nearby Split Mountain is open as a first-come, first-served campground.)
Finding the campground: From Vernal head south then east on US 40 for about 12 miles, then go north on UT 149 for 6 miles to the entrance station and visitor center. Continue, now traveling east, then south, 4.1 miles to the campground turnoff, which is on the left (east) side of the road. You'll reach the campground in another 0.4 mile.
About the campground: Huge cottonwoods decorate these partially open sites, with the Green River wandering along the campground border. A hiking trail leads 1.8 miles from this campground to the one at Split Mountain, another beautiful area with yet another trail to hike.

Of course, you won't want to miss seeing dinosaur bones—and lots of them. Be sure to tour the Dinosaur Quarry; it's open every day of the year except for Thanksgiving, Christmas, and New Year's.

142 Steinaker State Park

Location: About 7 miles north of Vernal
GPS: N40 31.121'/W109 32.558'
Facilities: Fire pits, full and electric hookups, ADA sites, picnic tables (some covered), flush toilets, drinking water, dump station, boat launch, and fish cleaning station
Sites: 15 basic sites, 8 full-hookup sites, 8 electric-hookup sites, 1 group site (maximum 50 people), and 1 cabin
Maximum RV length: 30 feet
Fee: $$ for basic sites; $$$ for electric-hookup and full-hookup sites; $$$$$ for group site and cabin
Maximum stay: 14 days
Elevation: 5,500 feet
Road conditions: Paved
Management: Steinaker State Park, 4335 N. Hwy. 191, Vernal; (435) 789-4432; www.stateparks .utah.gov/park/steinaker-state-park
Reservations: In the Salt Lake area, call (801) 322-3770; elsewhere, (800) 322-3770; http:// utahstateparks.reserveamerica.com
Activities: Fishing, swimming, boating, waterskiing, wildlife watching, hiking, and picnicking
Restrictions: Dogs not allowed on the beach; campground gate closed from 10 p.m. to 6 a.m.
Season: Year-round
Finding the campground: From Vernal, and the junction of US 40 and US 191, go north on US 191 for 5.6 miles, then turn left (west) at the signed junction. Continue another 1.8 miles on the paved road to the campground.
About the campground: With sites overlooking Steinaker Reservoir and cottonwoods and junipers to partially shade them, this campground is certainly an extra-nice place to stay. Visitors come to this desert oasis to fish, enjoy various water sports, and sometimes to set up a base camp from which to explore the surrounding area.

When it's full, Steinaker Reservoir covers 780 surface acres and is up to 130 feet deep. Water temperatures reach 70°F in July, making the park a water recreation paradise. It's also one of Utah's prime fisheries, with rainbow trout, largemouth bass, and an occasional brown trout. Many wildlife species live in the park, including mule deer, rabbits, porcupines, and birds such as golden eagles and ospreys. Elk make rare appearances.

143 Red Fleet State Park

Location: About 12 miles northeast of Vernal
GPS: N40 35.109'/W109 26.616'
Facilities: Fire pits, covered picnic tables, full hookups, ADA sites, flush toilets, drinking water, dump station, boat launch, canoe and kayak rentals, and fish cleaning station
Sites: 24 basic sites, 5 full-hookup sites, and 9 tents-only sites
Maximum RV length: 25 feet

Dilophosaurus tracks can be spotted at Red Fleet State Park.

Fee: $$ for basic and tents-only sites; $$$ for full-hookup sites
Maximum stay: 14 days
Elevation: 5,700 feet
Road conditions: Paved
Management: Red Fleet State Park, 8750 N. Hwy. 191, Vernal; (435) 789-4432; www.stateparks.utah.gov/park/red-fleet-state-park
Reservations: In the Salt Lake area, call (801) 322-3770; elsewhere, (800) 322-3770; http://utahstateparks.reserveamerica.com
Activities: Fishing, swimming, boating, hiking, wildlife watching, and picnicking
Restrictions: Campground gate closed from 10 p.m. to 6 a.m.
Season: Year-round
Finding the campground: From Vernal and the junction of US 40 and US 191, go north on US 191 for 10.2 miles, then turn right (east) at the signed junction. Continue another 1.9 miles on the paved road to the campground.
About the campground: Even though campers park side by side, with two parking spaces allotted for each site, it's still a popular place to camp. Hillside sites seem to stand guard over 650-acre Red Fleet Reservoir, named for the three large Navajo sandstone outcrops that jut up from the water like a fleet of ships. Known by local boaters as Little Lake Powell, this oasis offers spectacular sandstone cliffs and secluded sandy beaches to visitors who enjoy water-oriented activities. Anglers target rainbow and brown trout, bluegills, and bass, while other visitors go waterskiing and swimming. Swimmers should use caution; the water may be extremely deep just offshore.

In addition to present-day animal life, you can see dinosaur tracks made 190 to 200 million years ago. Preserved in rock, the tracks are on the shore immediately across the reservoir from the boat ramp. You can kayak across to the tracks, or you can hike in from the north via a 1.5-mile one-way trail.

144 Iron Springs

Location: In the Ashley National Forest, about 24 miles north of Vernal
GPS: N40 42.144'/W109 33.362'
Facilities: Fire pits, picnic tables, drinking water, and vault toilets
Sites: 2 group sites (maximum 50 people each)
Maximum RV length: 45 feet
Fee: $$ for group sites
Maximum stay: 14 days
Elevation: 8,700 feet
Road conditions: Gravel
Management: Vernal Ranger District, 355 N. Vernal Ave., Vernal; (435) 789-1181; www.fs.usda.gov/main/ashley/home
Reservations: Call (877) 444-6777 or TDD (877) 833-6777; www.recreation.gov
Activities: Mountain biking, ATVing, hiking, and picnicking
Season: June through September
Finding the campground: From Vernal go north on US 191 for about 19 miles to a paved road heading northwest. This is FR 018 (also known as the Red Cloud Loop). Drive 3.3 miles to another

junction; continue left (west) on FR 018, which is now gravel, for 1.4 miles to the campground.
About the campground: Open by reservation only, this campground is set amid conifers and aspens but overlooks a vast meadow. Two group sites serve a maximum of fifty people each. It's a nice base from which to go mountain biking and ATVing. There are hiking trails nearby. The East Park Loop, a 32-mile ride, is a particular favorite, touring some of the highlights of this lovely region.

145 Oaks Park

Location: In the Ashley National Forest, about 32 miles northwest of Vernal
GPS: N40 44.564'/W109 37.442'
Facilities: Fire pits, picnic tables, and vault toilets
Sites: 11 basic sites
Maximum RV length: 20 feet
Fee: None
Maximum stay: 14 days
Elevation: 9,200 feet
Road conditions: Dirt
Management: Vernal Ranger District, 355 N. Vernal Ave., Vernal; (435) 789-1181; www.fs.usda .gov/main/ashley/home
Reservations: None
Activities: Fishing, boating, mountain biking, hiking, and picnicking
Season: June through mid-September
Finding the campground: From Vernal go north on US 191 for about 19 miles to a paved road heading northwest. This is FR 018 (also known as the Red Cloud Loop). Drive it for 3.3 miles to another junction; continue left (west) on FR 018, which is now gravel, for 8.8 miles to the signed campground turnoff. Now go right (northeast) for another 0.9 mile to the campground.
About the campground: Located in a previously logged area, these sites near Oaks Park Reservoir are partially shaded by surviving conifers. You'll find plenty of dirt roads for mountain biking or walking, while anglers vie for rainbow trout. Mountain bikers should check out the East Park Loop mountain bike ride. It's about 32 miles long and passes near the campground. A hiking trail leads south from the campground to Big Brush Creek Cave. Contact the forest service if you want to do some caving.

146 East Park

Location: In the Ashley National Forest, about 28 miles northwest of Vernal
GPS: N40 46.858'/W109 33.190'
Facilities: Fire pits, picnic tables, drinking water, vault toilets, and a gravel boat ramp
Sites: 21 basic sites
Maximum RV length: 25 feet
Fee: $ for basic sites
Maximum stay: 14 days

Elevation: 9,000 feet

Road conditions: Paved to the campground, then gravel

Management: Vernal Ranger District, 355 N. Vernal Ave., Vernal; (435) 789-1181; www.fs.usda .gov/main/ashley/home

Reservations: None

Activities: Fishing, boating, hiking, mountain biking, and picnicking

Season: June through mid-September

Finding the campground: From Vernal go north on US 191 for about 19 miles to a paved road heading northwest. This is FR 018 (also known as the Red Cloud Loop). Drive it for 3.3 miles, then stay straight on FR 020 (FR 018 takes off to the west) for a total of 8.4 miles to the signed campground turnoff. Turn right (east) onto the gravel road for an additional 0.7 mile to the campground.

About the campground: Situated in a previously logged area, this partially shaded campground overlooks East Park Reservoir. Conifers add to the scene. There's a gravel boat ramp for boaters, and this is a fine place for mountain biking as well. The East Park Loop, a 32-mile bike ride, passes through here. Anglers have the opportunity to catch rainbow and brook trout.

147 Red Springs

Location: In the Ashley National Forest, about 30 miles north of Vernal

GPS: N40 48.492'/W109 28.060'

Facilities: Fire pits, picnic tables, tent pads, and vault toilets (dump station at nearby Lodgepole Campground)

Sites: 13 basic sites that can be reserved as 1 big group site (maximum 100 people)

Maximum RV length: 32 feet

Fee: $$ for basic sites; $$$$$ for group site

Maximum stay: 14 days

Elevation: 8,100 feet

Road conditions: Paved

Management: Flaming Gorge Ranger District, 25 W. Hwy. 43, PO Box 279, Manila, UT 84046; (435) 784-3445; www.fs.usda.gov/main/ashley/home

Reservations: To reserve the entire campground as one group site, call (877) 444-6777 or TDD (877) 833-6777; www.recreation.gov

Activities: Hiking and picnicking

Season: Mid-May through mid-September

Finding the campground: From Vernal go north on US 191 for about 30 miles to the campground, which is on the left (west) side of the road.

About the campground: Aspens and conifers offer a shady place to camp. There's not much else to do in the campground but relax and enjoy, though it makes a good stopover en route to your next destination.

148 Lodgepole

Location: In the Ashley National Forest, about 31 miles north of Vernal
GPS: N40 48.816'/W109 27.941'
Facilities: Fire pits, picnic tables, drinking water, flush toilets, and dump station
Sites: 35 basic sites
Maximum RV length: 45 feet
Fee: $$ for basic sites
Maximum stay: 14 days
Elevation: 8,100 feet
Road conditions: Paved
Management: Flaming Gorge Ranger District, 25 W. Hwy. 43, PO Box 279, Manila, UT 84046; (435) 784-3445; www.fs.usda.gov/main/ashley/home
Reservations: Call (877) 444-6777 or TDD (877) 833-6777; www.recreation.gov
Activities: Picnicking, wildlife watching, hiking, mountain biking
Season: Mid-May through mid-September
Finding the campground: From Vernal go north on US 191 for about 30.5 miles to the campground, which is on the right (east) side of the road.
About the campground: Semi-open, with aspens and lodgepole pines calling the place home, this is a nice campground with shade and plenty of opportunities to hike or mountain bike or do nothing more than relax and enjoy. If that's not enough, you can explore Flaming Gorge National Recreation Area; it's close by.

149 Bridge Hollow

Location: In Browns Park, about 31 miles east of Dutch John
GPS: N40 53.939'/W109 10.284'
Facilities: Fire pits, picnic tables, drinking water, and vault toilets
Sites: 13 basic sites
Maximum RV length: 20 feet
Fee: $ for basic sites
Maximum stay: 14 days
Elevation: 5,500 feet
Road conditions: Gravel
Management: Bureau of Land Management, Vernal Field Office, 170 S. 500 East, Vernal; (435) 781-4400; www.blm.gov/ut/st/en/fo/vernal.html
Reservations: None
Activities: Fishing, rafting, mountain biking, photography, and picnicking
Season: Year-round; water turned off from October through April
Finding the campground: From Dutch John go west then north on US 191. Soon after crossing into Wyoming, turn right (east) onto Wyoming CR 700. The turnoff is 8.9 miles from Dutch John and is signed. The road is both paved and gravel along the way. After 11 miles you'll reach a

fork; go right (southeast) to Browns Park. Drive another 9.1 miles (at one point descending a 14 percent grade) to the turnoff for both the Indian Crossing and Bridge Hollow Campgrounds. You'll reach Bridge Hollow after 1.5 miles.

About the campground: The Green River flows near this campground, and huge junipers and cottonwoods shade most of it. The site is a short walk from the John Jarvie Historic Ranch. Self-guided grounds tours are always available; the ranch is open for guided tours on specific days from 10 a.m. to 4:30 p.m. Call (435) 885-3307 to arrange a tour.

There are some original structures, each more than a hundred years old, at the ranch. You'll see a stone house, a two-room dugout, a blacksmith shop, a corral, and a replica of the original general store, which was built in 1881. It's furnished with numerous artifacts from the Jarvie period. In addition, there's a cemetery and a museum.

150 Indian Crossing

Location: In Browns Park, about 31 miles east of Dutch John
GPS: N40 53.932' / W109 11.005'
Facilities: Fire pits, picnic tables (most covered), drinking water, dump station, vault toilets, and a raft ramp
Sites: 21 basic sites
Maximum RV length: 20 feet
Fee: $ for basic sites
Maximum stay: 14 days
Elevation: 5,500 feet
Road conditions: Gravel
Management: Bureau of Land Management, Vernal Field Office, 170 S. 500 East, Vernal; (435) 781-4400; www.blm.gov/ut/st/en/fo/vernal.html
Reservations: None
Activities: Fishing, rafting, mountain biking, photography, and picnicking
Season: Year-round; water turned off from October through April
Finding the campground: From Dutch John go west then north on US 191. Soon after crossing into Wyoming, turn right (east) onto Wyoming CR 700. The turnoff is 8.9 miles from Dutch John and is signed. The road is both paved and gravel along the way. After 11 miles you'll reach a fork; go right (southeast) to Browns Park. Drive another 9.1 miles (at one point descending a 14 percent grade) to the turnoff for both the Indian Crossing and Bridge Hollow Campgrounds. You'll reach Indian Crossing after 2.1 miles.

About the campground: Situated above the lovely Green River, the campground is a short walk from the Jarvie Historic Ranch. Self-guided grounds tours are always available; the ranch is open for guided tours on specific days from 10 a.m. to 4:30 p.m. Call (435) 885-3307 to arrange a tour.

Blessed with sagebrush and other desert vegetation, and with riparian growth along the river, this is a good place from which to observe wildlife. Deer frequent the campground, as do many kinds of birds, including hummingbirds. It's also a place from which some folks begin rafting.

Though the campground can accommodate large RVs, the road leading to the campground is recommended for smaller RVs, mostly because of the steep 14 percent grade. You'll have to determine whether or not you want to drive down there.

151 Dripping Springs: Flaming Gorge National Recreation Area

Location: In the Flaming Gorge National Recreation Area, about 2 miles southeast of Dutch John
GPS: N40 55.367'/W109 21.409'
Facilities: Fire pits, covered picnic tables, ADA sites, drinking water, and flush and vault toilets
Sites: 21 basic sites, 1 double site, and 4 group sites (maximum 60 people each)
Maximum RV length: 35 feet
Fee: $$$ for basic sites; $$$$ for double site; $$$$$ for group sites
Maximum stay: 16 days
Elevation: 6,100 feet
Road conditions: Paved
Management: Flaming Gorge Ranger District, 25 W. Hwy. 43, PO Box 279, Manila, UT 84046; (435) 784-3445; www.fs.usda.gov/main/ashley/home
Reservations: Call (877) 444-6777 or TDD (877) 833-6777; www.recreation.gov
Activities: Fishing, rafting, hiking, mountain biking, and picnicking
Season: Year-round
Finding the campground: From Dutch John drive east then southeast on the first paved road (FR 075, also called Little Hole Road) for about 3 miles to the campground.
About the campground: Situated on flat terrain in an area burned in the Mustang Wildfire in July 2002, this campground offers no shade. However, there are covered picnic tables, so that helps. Folks come to fish, hike, bike, and raft.

Little Hole Boat Ramp on the Green River is about 3 miles east of the campground. Rafters use the area, while others hike 7 miles from the Little Hole Trailhead at the boat ramp to the other end of the trail, Flaming Gorge Dam.

152 Antelope Flat: Flaming Gorge National Recreation Area

Location: In the Flaming Gorge National Recreation Area, about 10 miles northwest of Dutch John
GPS: N40 57.859'/W109 33.231'
Facilities: Fire pits, picnic tables (some covered), BBQ grills, drinking water, flush toilets, dump station, fish cleaning station, and boat ramp
Sites: 46 basic sites and 4 group sites (maximum varies from 50 to 80 people)
Maximum RV length: 40 feet
Fee: $$ for basic sites; $$$$$ for group sites
Maximum stay: 16 days
Elevation: 6,200 feet
Road conditions: Paved
Management: Flaming Gorge Ranger District, 25 W. Hwy. 43, PO Box 279, Manila, UT 84046; (435) 784-3445; www.fs.usda.gov/main/ashley/home

Reservations: Call (877) 444-6777 or TDD (877) 833-6777; www.recreation.gov
Activities: Fishing, boating, swimming, wildlife watching, photography, and picnicking
Season: Mid-May through early September
Finding the campground: From Dutch John go northwest on US 191 for 4.6 miles. At the signed junction go west on gravel FR 145 to the campground; you'll reach it in another 4.9 miles.
About the campground: Antelope Flat is located on sagebrush flats overlooking the reservoir. Vegetation is mainly sage, with some small deciduous trees such as poplar, cottonwood, and so on.

In addition to nice views of the 91-mile-long reservoir, there's also the opportunity to fish for rainbow trout, kokanee salmon, smallmouth bass, and lake trout or mackinaw. This is also a good place from which to observe pronghorn, North America's fastest land mammal. (***Note:*** Strong winds can develop on this part of the reservoir without warning.)

153 Mustang Ridge: Flaming Gorge National Recreation Area

Location: In the Flaming Gorge National Recreation Area, about 4 miles west of Dutch John
GPS: N40 55.635' / W109 26.623'
Facilities: Fire pits, picnic tables, ADA sites, drinking water, flush and vault toilets, and showers; boat launch and swimming beach nearby
Sites: 73 basic sites and 1 group site (maximum 50 people)
Maximum RV length: 40 feet
Fee: $$$ for basic sites; $$$$$ for group site
Maximum stay: 16 days
Elevation: 6,200 feet
Road conditions: Paved
Management: Flaming Gorge Ranger District, 25 W. Hwy. 43, PO Box 279, Manila, UT 84046; (435) 784-3445; www.fs.usda.gov/main/ashley/home
Reservations: Call (877) 444-6777 or TDD (877) 833-6777; www.recreation.gov
Activities: Fishing, boating, swimming, wildlife watching, photography, and picnicking
Season: Mid-May through early September
Finding the campground: From Dutch John go northwest on US 191 for 1.9 miles. At the signed junction go south on paved FR 184 for another 1.9 miles to the campground.
About the campground: A thick forest of juniper and pinyon pine, with some sagebrush thrown in, makes this a moderately shady place to camp. There are some more-open sites that offer nice views of the reservoir. Non-campers can come into the campground and take a shower for a fee.

The area is close to a boat ramp and boat trailer parking, as well as an undeveloped swimming area. Flaming Gorge Reservoir is 91 miles long and covers 42,000 acres. It's a premier trophy lake trout region, and you can expect to find rainbow trout, kokanee salmon, and smallmouth bass, too.

In addition to the group site at the campground, a more remote group site is also available. Check out Dutch John Draw Group Site. The turnoff to the site is 0.3 mile south of Dutch John, and the site is down by the lake.

154 Deer Run: Flaming Gorge National Recreation Area

Location: In the Flaming Gorge National Recreation Area, about 5 miles southwest of Dutch John
GPS: N40 54.439'/W109 26.585'
Facilities: Fire pits, picnic tables, ADA sites, drinking water, flush and vault toilets, and showers; dump station, boat ramp, marina, bar and grill, and fish cleaning station nearby
Sites: 16 basic sites and 3 double sites
Maximum RV length: 35 feet
Fee: $$$ for basic sites; $$$$$ for double sites
Maximum stay: 16 days
Elevation: 6,200 feet
Road conditions: Paved
Management: Flaming Gorge Ranger District, 25 W. Hwy. 43, PO Box 279, Manila, UT 84046; (435) 784-3445; www.fs.usda.gov/main/ashley/home
Reservations: Call (877) 444-6777 or TDD (877) 833-6777; www.recreation.gov
Activities: Fishing, boating, swimming, hiking, mountain biking, wildlife watching, photography, and picnicking
Season: April through early September
Finding the campground: From Dutch John go southwest on US 191 for 4.2 miles, then turn right (north) onto paved FR 183, also called Cedar Springs Road. A sign points the way to the Cedar Springs Recreation Complex. Continue 0.2 mile to the campground turnoff, which is on the west side of the road.
About the campground: Rolling terrain with tall pinyon pine and juniper trees is offered at this campground. Moderate amounts of shade are found. Non-campers can come into the campground and shower for a fee.

There's plenty to do in the area. A nearby marina offers boat rentals, groceries, gas, mooring, and guided fishing excursions, while there are hiking and mountain biking trails a short distance away. If you're looking for a group site, check out Arch Dam Group Site, 1.8 miles south of Dutch John and 2.4 miles north of the Cedar Springs Recreation Area.

155 Cedar Springs: Flaming Gorge National Recreation Area

Location: In the Flaming Gorge National Recreation Area, about 5 miles southwest of Dutch John
GPS: N40 54.519'/W109 26.837'
Facilities: Fire pits, picnic tables, drinking water, and vault toilets; dump station, fish cleaning station, boat ramp, and marina nearby
Sites: 20 basic sites and 4 double sites
Maximum RV length: 35 feet
Fee: $$$ for basic sites; $$$$$ for double sites
Maximum stay: 16 days

Elevation: 6,100 feet

Road conditions: Paved

Management: Flaming Gorge Ranger District, 25 W. Hwy. 43, PO Box 279, Manila, UT 84046; (435) 784-3445; www.fs.usda.gov/main/ashley/home

Reservations: Call (877) 444-6777 or TDD (877) 833-6777; www.recreation.gov

Activities: Fishing, boating, swimming, hiking, mountain biking, wildlife watching, photography, and picnicking

Season: May through early September

Finding the campground: From Dutch John go southwest on US 191 for 4.2 miles, then make a right (north) onto paved FR 183, also called Cedar Springs Road. A sign points the way to the Cedar Springs Recreation Complex. Continue 0.4 mile to the campground turnoff, which is on the west side of the road.

About the campground: Located between the Deer Run Campground and the marina—which offers boat rentals, groceries, gas, mooring, and guided fishing—this campground is set on rolling terrain, with pinyon pine, juniper, and sagebrush serving to decorate the place.

Area activities abound. In addition to touring the dam, you'll find wonderful opportunities for fishing, mountain biking, hiking, and just plain relaxing at the 91-mile-long reservoir.

156 Firefighters Memorial: Flaming Gorge National Recreation Area

Location: In the Flaming Gorge National Recreation Area, about 6 miles southwest of Dutch John

GPS: N40 53.475'/W109 27.395'

Facilities: Fire pits, picnic tables, ADA sites, some tent pads, drinking water, flush toilets, and dump station

Sites: 94 basic sites

Maximum RV length: Any

Fee: $$ for basic sites

Maximum stay: 16 days

Elevation: 6,800 feet

Road conditions: Paved

Management: Flaming Gorge Ranger District, 25 W. Hwy. 43, PO Box 279, Manila, UT 84046; (435) 784-3445; www.fs.usda.gov/main/ashley/home

Reservations: Call (877) 444-6777 or TDD (877) 833-6777; www.recreation.gov

Activities: Hiking, mountain biking, and picnicking

Season: Mid-May through early September

Finding the campground: From Dutch John go southwest on US 191 for 6.2 miles to the campground turnoff, which is on the left (east) side of the road.

About the campground: This campground, blessed with a mix of stately ponderosa pines and sage, is named for the memorial that shares a place on its grounds. A short walk leads from a two-car parking area near sites 18 and 19 to a simple memorial, dedicated to three firefighters who died in the late 1970s.

Mike Vining takes in the view while mountain biking the Bear Canyon–Bootleg Trail.

Across the highway you'll find the Bear Canyon–Bootleg Trail for hiking and biking, while just down the road there's the Flaming Gorge Lodge, with a motel, cafe, store, service station, and raft rentals.

157 Greendale: Flaming Gorge National Recreation Area

Location: In the Flaming Gorge National Recreation Area, about 7 miles southwest of Dutch John
GPS: N40 52.958'/W109 27.555'
Facilities: Fire pits, picnic tables, drinking water, and vault toilets
Sites: 8 basic sites and 2 group sites (located across the road; maximum 40 people each)
Maximum RV length: 30 feet
Fee: $$ for basic sites; $$$$$ for group sites
Maximum stay: 16 days
Elevation: 7,000 feet
Road conditions: Paved

Management: Flaming Gorge Ranger District, 25 W. Hwy. 43, PO Box 279, Manila, UT 84046; (435) 784-3445; www.fs.usda.gov/main/ashley/home
Reservations: Call (877) 444-6777 or TDD (877) 833-6777; www.recreation.gov
Activities: Hiking, mountain biking, and picnicking
Season: May through early September
Finding the campground: From Dutch John go southwest on US 191 for 6.9 miles to the campground turnoff, which is on the right (west) side of the road.
About the campground: A small, ponderosa pine–blessed campground, this is a nice place for those who don't want to camp with crowds. If you're looking for a group site, check out the campground across the road; it offers two group areas with lots of room.

The campground is within walking distance of the Bear Canyon–Bootleg Trail, a nice trail for hikers and bikers. It's also close to the Flaming Gorge Lodge, which offers a motel, cafe, store, service station, and raft rentals.

158 Skull Creek: Flaming Gorge National Recreation Area

Location: In the Flaming Gorge National Recreation Area, about 12 miles southwest of Dutch John
GPS: N40 51.787'/W109 31.695'
Facilities: Fire pits, picnic tables, drinking water, and vault toilets
Sites: 17 basic sites
Maximum RV length: 30 feet
Fee: $$ for basic sites
Maximum stay: 16 days
Elevation: 7,500 feet
Road conditions: Paved
Management: Flaming Gorge Ranger District, 25 W. Hwy. 43, PO Box 279, Manila, UT 84046; (435) 784-3445; www.fs.usda.gov/main/ashley/home
Reservations: Call (877) 444-6777 or TDD (877) 833-6777; www.recreation.gov
Activities: Hiking, mountain biking, and picnicking
Season: Mid-May through early September
Finding the campground: From Dutch John go southwest on US 191 for 8.8 miles to its junction with UT 44. Now drive northwest on UT 44 for another 2.7 miles to the campground turnoff, which is on the north (right) side of the road.
About the campground: Aspens, ponderosa pines, and a variety of other conifers decorate this semi-open setting. The Canyon Rim Trail leads from this campground to three other campgrounds— Greendale, Greens Lake, and Canyon Rim. It's open to hikers and bicyclists. Quiet hikers may see moose, elk, or other animal life.

159 Greens Lake: Flaming Gorge National Recreation Area

Location: In the Flaming Gorge National Recreation Area, about 13 miles southwest of Dutch John
GPS: N40 52.402'/W109 32.168'
Facilities: Fire pits, picnic tables, some BBQ grills, drinking water, and vault toilets
Sites: 20 basic sites and 1 group site (maximum 40 people)
Maximum RV length: 35 feet
Fee: $$ for basic sites; $$$$$ for group site
Maximum stay: 16 days
Elevation: 7,400 feet
Road conditions: Paved
Management: Flaming Gorge Ranger District, 25 W. Hwy. 43, PO Box 279, Manila, UT 84046; (435) 784-3445; www.fs.usda.gov/main/ashley/home
Reservations: Call (877) 444-6777 or TDD (877) 833-6777; www.recreation.gov
Activities: Hiking, mountain biking, fishing, and picnicking
Season: Mid-May through early September
Finding the campground: From Dutch John go southwest on US 191 for 8.8 miles to its junction with UT 44. Now drive northwest on UT 44 for another 3.5 miles to its junction with FR 95, also called Red Canyon Road. A sign points the way north to the Red Canyon Recreation Complex. You'll reach the campground turnoff after traveling another 0.5 mile; turn east and proceed yet another 0.5 mile via FR 371 to the campground.
About the campground: Lovely ponderosa pines and aspens decorate this semi-open setting, where there is plenty of shade. Greens Lake is located at the edge of the campground near the Red Canyon Lodge, where you'll find cabins, a restaurant, horseback rides, a children's fishing pond, fishing supplies, and gas.

The Canyon Rim Trail leads from this campground to three others—Skull Creek, Greendale, and Canyon Rim. It's open to hikers and bicyclists. Quiet visitors may see wildlife, including moose and elk.

160 Canyon Rim: Flaming Gorge National Recreation Area

Location: In the Flaming Gorge National Recreation Area, about 14 miles southwest of Dutch John
GPS: N40 53.072'/W109 32.916'
Facilities: Fire pits, picnic tables, stove stands, drinking water, and vault toilets
Sites: 7 basic sites and 9 tents-only sites
Maximum RV length: 40 feet
Fee: $$ for basic and tents-only sites

Maximum stay: 16 days

Elevation: 7,400 feet

Road conditions: Paved

Management: Flaming Gorge Ranger District, 25 W. Hwy 43, PO Box 279, Manila, UT 84046; (435) 784-3445; www.fs.usda.gov/main/ashley/home

Reservations: Call (877) 444-6777 or TDD (877) 833-6777; www.recreation.gov

Activities: Hiking, mountain biking, photography, and picnicking

Season: Mid-May through early September

Finding the campground: From Dutch John go southwest on US 191 for 8.8 miles to its junction with UT 44. Now drive northwest on UT 44 for another 3.5 miles to its junction with FR 95, also called Red Canyon Road. A sign points the way north to the Red Canyon Recreation Complex. Drive FR 95 for an additional 1.6 miles to the campground, which is on the right via FR 373.

About the campground: Aspens, ponderosa pines, and a variety of mountain vegetation offer scattered shade in this semi-open setting. The campground is close to the Red Canyon Visitor Center and the spectacular Red Canyon Overlook. From the overlook you can gaze down on the reservoir 1,369 feet below. In addition, the Canyon Rim Trail leads from this campground to three others—Skull Creek, Greendale, and Greens Lake—and is open to hikers and bicyclists.

The Red Canyon Lodge is nearby, offering a restaurant, cabins, groceries, horseback rides, fishing supplies, and a children's fishing pond.

161 Red Canyon: Flaming Gorge National Recreation Area

Location: In the Flaming Gorge National Recreation Area, about 15 miles southwest of Dutch John

GPS: N40 53.414'/W109 33.595'

Facilities: Fire pits, picnic tables, drinking water, and vault toilets

Sites: 8 basic sites

Maximum RV length: 20 feet

Fee: $$ for basic sites

Maximum stay: 16 days

Elevation: 7,400 feet

Road conditions: Paved

Management: Flaming Gorge Ranger District, 25 W. Hwy. 43, PO Box 279, Manila, UT 84046; (435) 784-3445; www.fs.usda.gov/main/ashley/home

Reservations: Call (877) 444-6777 or TDD (877) 833-6777; www.recreation.gov

Activities: Hiking, mountain biking, photography, and picnicking

Season: Mid-May through mid-September

Finding the campground: From Dutch John go southwest on US 191 for 8.8 miles to its junction with UT 44. Now drive northwest on UT 44 for another 3.5 miles to its junction with FR 95, also called Red Canyon Road. A sign points the way north to the Red Canyon Recreation Complex. Drive FR 95 for another 2.4 miles to the campground.

About the campground: Ponderosa pines and junipers provide shade in this campground, which

One of the best views of Flaming Gorge is at Red Canyon.

was once a picnic area. The semi-open sites are within easy walking distance of the Red Canyon Visitor Center, which offers a wheelchair-accessible hiking trail and overlook. The campground is also close to the Red Canyon Lodge, which offers cabins, a restaurant, gas, horseback rides, canoe rentals, and fishing.

162 Sheep Creek Bay: Flaming Gorge National Recreation Area

Location: In the Flaming Gorge National Recreation Area, about 8 miles south of Manila
GPS: N40 55.273' / W109 40.497'
Facilities: Picnic tables and vault toilets
Sites: Dispersed
Maximum RV length: 45 feet
Fee: $ for dispersed sites
Maximum stay: 16 days
Elevation: 6,000 feet
Road conditions: Paved

Management: Flaming Gorge Ranger District, 25 W. Hwy. 43, PO Box 279, Manila, UT 84046; (435) 784-3445; www.fs.usda.gov/main/ashley/home
Reservations: None
Activities: Boating, fishing, and picnicking
Restrictions: No tents allowed
Season: May through early September
Finding the campground: From Manila drive south on UT 44 for about 7.5 miles to a sign for Sheep Creek Bay. Make a left and drive another 0.9 mile to the campground and a boat launch.
About the campground: Located in the far end of the parking lot for the boat launch, this campground is near the boat launch for quick access to Flaming Gorge Reservoir. You're also close to Sheep Creek Canyon Geological Area, where you can take a scenic drive to see rock formations, lovely canyon cliffs, and perhaps bighorn sheep.

163 Willows/Mann's: Flaming Gorge National Recreation Area

Location: In the Flaming Gorge National Recreation Area, about 7 miles south of Manila
GPS: N40 55.561'/W109 42.911' (Willows)
GPS: N40 55.412'/W109 42.518' (Mann's)
Facilities: Fire pits, picnic tables, and vault toilets
Sites: 17 basic sites (9 sites at Willows and 8 sites at Mann's)
Maximum RV length: 25 feet (Willows) and 30 feet (Mann's)
Fee: $ for basic sites
Maximum stay: 16 days
Elevation: 7,200 feet
Road conditions: Paved to the campground, then gravel
Management: Flaming Gorge Ranger District, 25 W. Hwy. 43, PO Box 279, Manila, UT 84046; (435) 784-3445; www.fs.usda.gov/main/ashley/home
Reservations: None
Activities: Fishing and picnicking
Season: April through September
Finding the campground: From Manila drive south on UT 44 for about 6 or 7 miles to the campgrounds, which are located 0.4 mile apart.
About the campground: I combined these two campgrounds because they are very near one another, with both located in beautiful Sheep Creek Valley. Fishing in Sheep Creek is a popular activity at these two campgrounds, but fishing is prohibited here between August 15 and the last Saturday in November to protect spawning kokanee salmon. Willows has partially shaded sites with cottonwoods, spruce, and willows along the creek. At Mann's there are few trees and almost no shade.

164 Carmel: Flaming Gorge National Recreation Area

Location: In the Flaming Gorge National Recreation Area, about 7 miles south of Manila
GPS: N40 55.863'/W109 43.939'
Facilities: Fire pits, picnic tables, and vault toilets
Sites: 15 basic sites
Maximum RV length: 35 feet
Fee: $ for basic sites
Maximum stay: 16 days
Elevation: 6,200 feet
Road conditions: Paved to the campground, then gravel
Management: Flaming Gorge Ranger District, 25 W. Hwy. 43, PO Box 279, Manila, UT 84046; (435) 784-3445; www.fs.usda.gov/main/ashley/home
Reservations: None
Activities: Fishing and picnicking
Season: May through early September
Finding the campground: From Manila and the junction of UT 44 and UT 43, drive south on UT 44 for 5.8 miles to its junction with FR 218, also called Sheep Creek Geological Loop. Go west on FR 218 for 0.8 mile to the campground.
About the campground: Cottonwoods and conifers shade these sites, some of which are semi-open, all of which provide close access to the Flaming Gorge National Recreation Area and the rest of Sheep Rock Geological Loop, a must-see. Drive or bike the scenic road and watch for wildlife, including bighorn sheep. In addition, anglers may want to try their luck at trout fishing along Sheep Creek, although fishing isn't allowed between August 15 and the last Saturday in November to protect spawning kokanee salmon.

165 Lucerne Valley: Flaming Gorge National Recreation Area

Location: In the Flaming Gorge National Recreation Area, about 8 miles east of Manila
GPS: N40 59.206'/W109 35.571'
Facilities: Fire pits, picnic tables (some covered), ADA sites, stove stands (at some sites), BBQ grills (at some sites), electric hookups, drinking water, showers, flush toilets, dump station, and a marina with a boat ramp, fish cleaning station, grocery store, boat rentals, and dry storage area
Sites: 44 basic sites, 90 electric-hookup sites, and 4 group sites (maximum 80 people each)
Maximum RV length: Any
Fee: $$$ for basic and electric-hookup sites; $$$$$ for group sites
Maximum stay: 16 days
Elevation: 6,100 feet
Road conditions: Paved

Mike Vining looks for wildlife at Lucerne Campground.

Management: Flaming Gorge Ranger District, 25 W. Hwy. 43, PO Box 279, Manila, UT 84046; (435) 784-3445; www.fs.usda.gov/main/ashley/home

Reservations: Call (877) 444-6777 or TDD (877) 833-6777; www.recreation.gov

Activities: Fishing, boating, swimming, mountain biking, wildlife watching, and picnicking

Restrictions: ATVs and off-road motorcycles not allowed

Season: May through early September

Finding the campground: From Manila and the junction of UT 44 and UT 43, drive east then northeast on UT 43 for 2.8 miles, where you'll cross into Wyoming. Continue on what is now WY 530 for another 1.1 miles. Turn right (southeast) onto FR 146 (Lucerne Valley Road); a sign points the way to the Lucerne Valley Complex and Marina. Continue into Utah, driving an additional 3.9 miles to the campground.

About the campground: Cottonwoods only partially shade this open area, with its lovely view of the reservoir. Pronghorn hang out in the campground and ospreys often nest in the park, making this a great place for wildlife watching.

If you'd rather save a few dollars, try camping at the primitive site known as State Line Cove. It's located about 1 mile prior to Lucerne Valley. The cost is less, but the only amenities are vault toilets.

166 Deep Creek

Location: In the Ashley National Forest, about 21 miles south of Manila
GPS: N40 51.302'/W109 43.775'
Facilities: Fire pits, picnic tables, vault toilets; no trash service (pack it out)
Sites: 17 basic sites
Maximum RV length: 30 feet
Fee: $ for basic sites
Maximum stay: 14 days
Elevation: 7,600 feet
Road conditions: Gravel
Management: Flaming Gorge Ranger District, 25 W. Hwy. 43, PO Box 279, Manila, UT 84046; (435) 784-3445; www.fs.usda.gov/main/ashley/home
Reservations: None
Activities: Fishing, hiking, mountain biking, off-highway driving, and picnicking
Season: Mid-May through early September
Finding the campground: From Manila drive south on UT 44 for about 17 miles to its junction with FR 539. A sign points the way to the campground. Drive west on FR 539 for 3.8 miles to the campground.
About the campground: Deep Creek flows near this campground, which provides both shady and semi-open sites. Conifers serve to shade the sites. Nearby Elk Park offers some nice hiking and mountain biking trails, including one strenuous trip that is nearly 20 miles round-trip. The trail passes this campground, as well as the one at Browne Lake. See Gregg Bromka's *Mountain Biking Utah*, or contact the forest service, for additional information.

167 Browne Lake

Location: In the Ashley National Forest, about 22 miles southwest of Manila
GPS: N40 51.621'/W109 49.043'
Facilities: Fire pits, picnic tables, and vault toilets
Sites: 20 basic sites and 4 group sites (maximum 40 people each)
Maximum RV length: 40 feet
Fee: $ for basic sites; $$$$ for group sites
Maximum stay: 14 days
Elevation: 8,400 feet
Road conditions: Narrow gravel road; can get rough and slick when wet
Management: Flaming Gorge Ranger District, 25 W. Hwy. 43, PO Box 279, Manila, UT 84046; (435) 784-3445; www.fs.usda.gov/main/ashley/home
Reservations: For group sites only, call (877) 444-6777 or TDD (877) 833-6777; www .recreation.gov
Activities: Fishing, nonmotorized boating, horseback riding, hiking, mountain biking, and picnicking
Season: Mid-May through early September

Finding the campground: From Manila and the junction of UT 44 and UT 43, drive south on UT 44 for 5.8 miles to its junction with FR 218, also called Sheep Creek Geological Loop. Go west, then south, on FR 218. The road is mostly paved, but it does have sections of gravel. After 10 miles you'll reach the junction of FR 221 and make a right (west); after another 4.8 miles turn left (southeast) at the sign and continue 1.8 miles to the campground.

About the campground: Situated near Browne Lake, on the north side of the Uinta Mountains, the campground offers views of Leidy Peak and other fine places. Trailheads abound in the area, leading to such places as Elk Park, Weyman Park, Anson Lake, Spirit Lake, and Leidy Peak. Some of them allow mountain bikes, but all were designed for hikers and horseback riders. On a historical note, you may want to check out the Ute Mountain Fire Lookout Tower at 8,834 feet; it's open seasonally to the public.

168 Spirit Lake

Location: In the Ashley National Forest, about 33 miles southwest of Manila
GPS: N40 50.217' / W110 00.046'
Facilities: Fire pits, picnic tables, and vault toilets; no garbage service (pack it out). Nearby, Spirit Lodge offers cabins, meals, showers, groceries, rowboat and canoe rentals, and horse rentals.
Sites: 24 basic sites
Maximum RV length: 30 feet
Fee: $$ for basic sites
Maximum stay: 14 days
Elevation: 10,200 feet
Road conditions: Dirt
Management: Flaming Gorge Ranger District, 25 W. Hwy. 43, PO Box 279, Manila, UT 84046; (435) 784-3445; www.fs.usda.gov/main/ashley/home
Reservations: None
Activities: Fishing, boating, horseback riding, hiking, mountain biking, and picnicking
Restrictions: Only electric boat motors allowed
Season: June through early September
Finding the campground: From Manila and the junction of UT 44 and UT 43, drive south on UT 44 for 5.8 miles to its junction with FR 218, also called Sheep Creek Geological Loop. Go west, then south, on FR 218. The road is mostly paved, but it does have sections of gravel. After 10 miles you'll reach the junction of FR 221 and make a right (west); after another 10.8 miles you'll reach a junction. Turn south onto FR 1 and drive another 6.4 miles to the campground.

About the campground: This campground is set near a lovely high alpine lake. There are several trailheads in the area, with many alpine lakes being just a half-day hike from the campground. Look for a 3-mile round-trip trail that begins between the campground and Spirit Lodge. It ascends moderately to Tamarack Lake, with a side trail leading to Jessen Lake.

Panoramaland

Panoramaland is a vast and varied place, with everything from barren deserts to towering forested mountains, high alpine tundra, an array of rock monoliths, wide valleys, and perhaps a human-made lake or two.

Located in central Utah in the geologic regions known as the Great Basin and Rocky Mountain Province, this is the second largest of Utah's nine travel regions. Comprising a whopping 17,043 square miles, Panoramaland consists of five counties—Juab, Millard, Sanpete, Sevier, and Piute. The region is bordered by the state of Nevada to the west, and by the state travel regions known as Color Country to the south, Canyonlands and Castle Country to the east, and Mountainland and Great Salt Lake Country to the north.

Thirty-eight campgrounds offer base sites from which to explore everything from Mount Nebo—at 11,928 feet the highest point in the region—to the white-sand dunes of the Little Sahara Recreation Area, a favorite with campers who thrill to off-highway driving. Mountains are abundant in this land, with most of the public campgrounds found in the Fishlake and Manti–La Sal National Forests. In addition, there are two in the Uinta–Wasatch–Cache National Forest and one in the Dixie National Forest. The remaining campgrounds are managed by various agencies, including the Bureau of Land Management, the National Park Service, and Utah state parks.

There are five state parks in the region, each one a sharp contrast to the others. Fremont Indian State Park offers the Castle Rock Campground in addition to a treasure trove of rock art and archaeological sites. Visitors to this wonderful park discover the riches of Clear Creek Canyon. Indoor activities include a video program that introduces visitors to the Fremont Indians. Outside are interpretive trails, one accessible to wheelchairs, that lead to various pictographs and petroglyphs.

In contrast, Yuba State Park provides an unlimited array of water activities, including swimming, sailing, Jet Skiing, waterskiing, and a whole lot more. Yuba State Park boasted a first in the Utah state parks system: It was the first to offer a boat access–only campground, called Eagle View Campground. The campground is now accessible by motor vehicle as well, and each site offers a covered picnic table, stove stand, BBQ grill, fire pit, tent pads, and solar lighting.

The area's other state parks are Piute, Otter Creek, and Palisade. Though their settings vary, all three offer warm waters that draw swimmers as well as water-skiers, Jet Skiers, and those with nothing more than boating on their minds.

An assortment of forest campgrounds make this a fun place to visit. Look for an abundance of sites along the shores of Fish Lake, where anglers fish to their hearts'

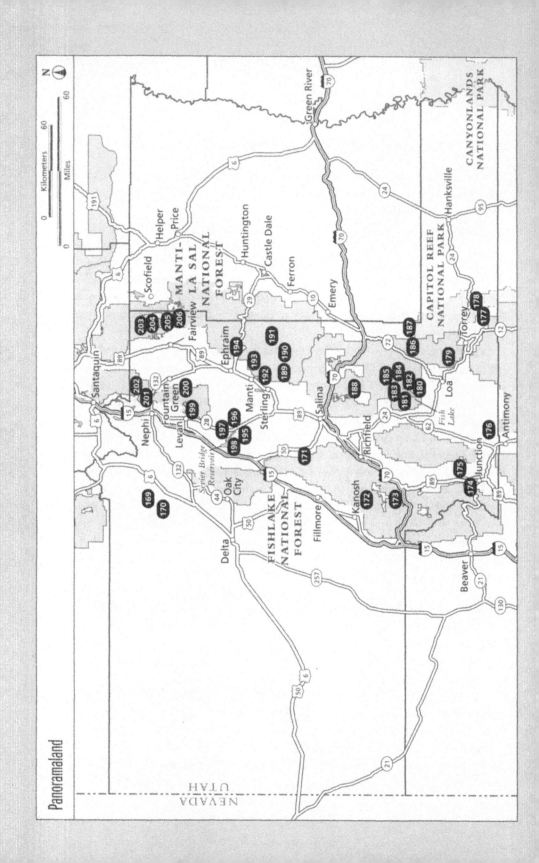

content, photographers while away the hours making images, and campers come to just relax. At 2,500 acres Fish Lake is Utah's largest natural mountain lake. It's especially beautiful in the fall when aspens turn golden and the air is crisp. The lake is famous for its 20- to 40-pound mackinaw (lake) trout. At Maple Canyon folks hike and climb on conglomerate, an amazing mix of rock that is a great climbing surface.

Some campgrounds are found at or near Skyline Drive, a magnificent 100-mile byway that follows the crest of the Wasatch Plateau. Winding through desert and mountains, several other scenic highways are must-travels, including UT 12, UT 24, and UT 28.

Capitol Reef is the only national park in the region. Here, magnificent scenery and fascinating history combine to make this one of the country's most unusual national parks. It's also a wonderful place for rock climbers. The park is open year-round and is a must-see for all who come to this wonderful area.

For more information contact Panoramaland Travel Region, 4 S. Main, PO Box 71, Nephi, UT 84648; (435) 623-5203 or (800) 748-4361; http://utahtravelcenter .com/travelregions/panoramaland.htm.

		Total Sites	Group Sites	Hook-up Sites	Hookups	Max. RV Length	Dump Station	Toilets	Showers	Drinking Water	ADA Compliant	Fees	Reservations	Recreation
169	White Sands	100				40		F & V		•		$$		O
170	Oasis	115				40	•	F & V		•		$$		O
171	Maple Grove	23	3			30		V		•		$$-$$$$$	•	FH
172	Adelaide	9	1			30		F & V		•		$$-$$$$$	•	FO
173	Castle Rock	31	1			30		F & C		•	•	$$-$$$$$	•	HM
174	City Creek	5				24		V		•		None		FRHO
175	Piute State Park	*				Any		V				$		FBLSM
176	Otter Creek State Park	54	1			45	•	F	•	•		$$-$$$$$	•	FBLO
177	Singletree	33	2			40		F & V		•		$-$$$$	•	H
178	Fruita	72	1			Any	•	F & V		•	•	$-$$$$$	•	HMR
179	Sunglow	9	2			30		F		•		$-$$$	•	HM
180	Doctor Creek	32	2			50	•	F		•	•	$$-$$$$$	•	FBSMHK
181	Mackinaw	67	4			45		F	•	•		$$-$$$$	•	FBSMHK
182	Bowery Creek	43				40		F		•	•	$$-$$$$$	•	FBSMHK
183	Frying Pan	12	1			45		F		•		$$-$$$$$	•	MH

Hookup: W = Water, E = Electric, S = Sewer   * = Dispersed Camping, no designated sites
Recreation: H = Hiking, C = Rock Climbing, M = Mountain Biking, S = Swimming, F = Fishing, B = Boating, L = Boat Launch,
O = Off-highway Driving, R = Horseback Riding, K = Kayaking and Canoeing, G = Golf
Toilets: F = Flush, V = Vault, C = Chemical
Per-night campsite cost: $ = $10 or less $$ = $11 to $20 $$$ = $21 to 30 $$$$ = $31 to $40 $$$$$ = $41 and higher

		Total Sites	Group Sites	Hook-up Sites	Hookups	Max. RV Length	Dump Station	Toilets	Showers	Drinking Water	ADA Compliant	Fees	Reservations	Recreation
184	Paiute Recreation Area	48				Any		V		•		$		MHF
185	Tasha Equestrian	11	1			Any		F		•		$-$$$	•	R
186	Elkhorn	7	1			22/70		V		•		0-$$$	•	HROM
187	Cathedral Valley	6				None		V				None		H
188	Gooseberry (Salina)	14	1			30		V		•		$-$$	•	FO
189	Twin Lake	22	1			30		V				$-$$$	•	HMO
190	Twelve Mile Flat	17	2			30		V				$-$$$$	•	HMO
191	Ferron Reservoir	30	1			20/45		V		•		$-$$$$	•	FBLHMK
192	Palisade State Park	79	5	28	WES	Any	•	F	•	•	•	$$-$$$$$	•	SFGHMKBL
193	Manti Community	10	1			30		V		•		$-$$$$	•	FKMO
194	Lake Hill	11	2			30		V		•		$-$$$$	•	FHM
195	Painted Rocks	42	1	38	WE	40	•	V		•		$-$$$$$	•	FMOBLKS
196	Eagle View	20				20		V				$-$$	•	FMOBSLK
197	North and West Beach	*				Any	•	V				$		FMOBSLK
198	Oasis	29	1	11	WE	Any	•	F	•	•	•	$$-$$$$$	•	FMOBSLK
199	Chicken Creek	9	1			25		V				None		F
200	Maple Canyon	13	1			30		V				$-$$$$	•	CMH
201	Ponderosa	23				45		V		•		$$	•	FH
202	Bear Canyon	9	3			30		F &V				$$-$$$$$	•	FHR
203	Gooseberry Reservoir	16				40		V				$	•	FKMO
204	Gooseberry	9	1			30		V		•		$-$$	•	FKOM
205	Flat Canyon	13	1			30		V				$-$$	•	F
206	Lake Canyon Recreation Area	52	5			Any		V				$-$$$$$	•	FO

Hookup: W = Water, E = Electric, S = Sewer   * = Dispersed Camping, no designated sites

Recreation: H = Hiking, C = Rock Climbing, M = Mountain Biking, S = Swimming, F = Fishing, B = Boating, L = Boat Launch, O = Off-highway Driving, R = Horseback Riding, K = Kayaking and Canoeing, G = Golf

Toilets: F = Flush, V = Vault, C = Chemical

Per-night campsite cost: $ = $10 or less $$ = $11 to $20 $$$ = $21 to 30 $$$$ = $31 to $40 $$$$$ = $41 and higher

169 White Sands: Little Sahara Recreation Area

Location: In the Little Sahara Recreation Area, about 40 miles northeast of Delta
GPS: N39 44.740'/W112 18.915'
Facilities: Fire pits, picnic tables, drinking water, and flush and vault toilets
Sites: 100 basic sites
Maximum RV length: 40 feet
Fee: $$ for basic sites
Maximum stay: 14 days
Elevation: 5,300 feet
Road conditions: Paved to the campground, then hard-packed sand
Management: Bureau of Land Management, Fillmore Field Office, 95 E. 500 North, Fillmore; (435) 743-3100; www.blm.gov/ut/st/en/fo/fillmore.html
Reservations: None
Activities: Off-highway driving, playing on the sand dunes, photography, and picnicking
Season: Year-round; water shut off in winter, but available at the Willard R. Fullmer Visitor Center
Finding the campground: From Delta drive US 6 northeast for about 32 miles to Jericho Junction and turn left (west) at the sign pointing the way to the Little Sahara Recreation Area. Take the paved road 4.4 miles to another paved road and turn left (southwest). In another 1.7 miles you'll reach the visitor center. Follow more signs an additional 2.1 miles to the campground.
About the campground: Located in the sand and juniper trees of one of Utah's largest dune fields, this is a popular place for off-highway driving. Be sure to use a whip flag and stay on constructed roads and trails. There's also a fenced-in sand play area for kids.
   If you have a large group, check out the Jericho and Sand Mountain areas.

170 Oasis: Little Sahara Recreation Area

Location: In the Little Sahara Recreation Area, about 43 miles northeast of Delta
GPS: N39 41.347'/W112 21.277'
Facilities: Fire pits, picnic tables, drinking water, dump station, and flush and vault toilets
Sites: 115 basic sites
Maximum RV length: 40 feet
Fee: $$ for basic sites
Maximum stay: 14 days
Elevation: 5,000 feet
Road conditions: Paved
Management: Bureau of Land Management, Fillmore Field Office, 95 E. 500 North, Fillmore; (435) 743-3100; www.blm.gov/ut/st/en/fo/fillmore.html
Reservations: None
Activities: Off-highway driving, playing on the sand dunes, photography, and picnicking
Season: Year-round; water shut off in winter, but available at the Willard R. Fullmer Visitor Center
Finding the campground: From Delta drive US 6 northeast for about 32 miles to Jericho Junction

and turn left (west) at the sign pointing the way to the Little Sahara Recreation Area. Take the paved road 4.4 miles to another paved road and turn left (southwest). In another 1.7 miles you'll reach the visitor center. Follow more signs an additional 5.2 miles to the campground.

About the campground: Located in the sand and juniper trees of the Little Sahara Recreation Area, one of Utah's largest dune fields, this campground is popular with the ATV and motorcycle crowd. Be sure to use a whip flag and stay on constructed roads and trails.

If you have a large group, check out the Jericho and Sand Mountain areas.

171 Maple Grove

Location: In the Fishlake National Forest, approximately 16 miles northwest of Salina
GPS: N39 01.116'/W112 05.326'
Facilities: Fire pits, picnic tables, drinking water, and vault toilets; no trash service (pack it out)
Sites: 20 basic sites and 3 group sites (maximum varies from 56 to 100 people)
Maximum RV length: 30 feet
Fee: $$ for basic sites; $$$$$ for group sites
Maximum stay: 14 days
Elevation: 6,400 feet
Road conditions: Paved
Management: Fillmore Ranger District, 390 S. Main, Fillmore, UT 84631; (435) 743-5721; www .fs.usda.gov/main/fishlake/home
Reservations: For group sites only, call (877) 444-6777 or TDD (877) 833-6777; www .recreation.gov
Activities: Fishing, hiking, and picnicking
Restrictions: ATVs not allowed
Season: Mid-May through mid-September
Finding the campground: From the junction of US 50 and US 89 in downtown Salina, go west on US 50, eventually heading northwest. After 12.6 miles turn left (west) at the signed, paved road. Drive another 3.7 miles to the campground.
About the campground: If you like trees, and lots of them, then this is the place for you. Shaded by dense groves of box elders, maples, conifers, and even a few oaks and junipers, these canopied sites lie along a creek that offers fishing for rainbow trout. Hikers will find the 3.2-mile Rock Canyon Trail nearby.

172 Adelaide

Location: In the Fishlake National Forest, approximately 5 miles southeast of Kanosh
GPS: N38 45.245'/W112 21.916'
Facilities: Fire pits, picnic tables, drinking water, and flush and vault toilets; no garbage service (pack it out)
Sites: 8 tent sites and 1 group site (maximum 48 people)
Maximum RV length: 30 feet

Fee: $$ for tent sites; $$$$$ for group site
Maximum stay: 14 days
Elevation: 5,500 feet
Road conditions: Gravel
Management: Fillmore Ranger District, 390 S. Main, Fillmore, UT 84631; (435) 743-5721; www
.fs.usda.gov/main/fishlake/home
Reservations: For the group site only, call (877) 444-6777 or TDD (877) 833-6777; www
.recreation.gov
Activities: Fishing, OHV riding, and picnicking
Restrictions: Live music or sound systems not allowed
Season: Late May through September
Finding the campground: From Main Street and 300 South (FR 106) in Kanosh, drive southeast
for 5 miles to the campground.
About the campground: Located along Corn Creek in a posted flash-flood area, this is a place
to avoid during big thunderstorms. Box elders, cottonwoods, and maples shade the grassy sites
found here, with plenty of room to fish, read a book, or just plain relax.

173 Castle Rock: Fremont Indian State Park

Location: About 24 miles southwest of Richfield
GPS: N38 33.393'/W112 21.326'
Facilities: Fire pits, picnic tables, ADA sites, chemical and flush toilets, and drinking water
Sites: 24 basic sites, 6 double sites, and 1 group site (maximum 100 people)
Maximum RV length: 30 feet
Fee: $$ for basic sites; $$$ for double sites; $$$$$ for group site
Maximum stay: 14 days
Elevation: 6,500 feet
Road conditions: Maintained gravel
Management: Fremont Indian State Park, 11550 W. Clear Creek Canyon Rd., Sevier; (435) 527-
4631; http://stateparks.utah.gov/park/fremont-indian-state-park-and-museum
Reservations: In the Salt Lake area, call (801) 322-3770; elsewhere, (800) 322-3770; http://
utahstateparks.reserveamerica.com
Activities: Hiking, mountain biking, picnicking, and photography. Three trails provide access to the
260-mile Paiute ATV Trail.
Season: April through November
Finding the campground: From Richfield travel southwest on I-70 for about 23 miles, getting off
at exit 17. The visitor center and museum are about 1 mile to the right (east). Reach the camp-
ground by heading south, crossing over the interstate, and driving FR 478 for 1.3 miles. Signs
point the way to both places.
About the campground: Campsites are situated among junipers and oaks, with Joe Lott Creek
singing nearby. The campground snuggles up to an amazing medley of mud towers, a conglomera-
tion of volcanic ash from 17-million-year-old explosions in the Tushar Mountains area.

The campground is also near the museum at Fremont Indian State Park. Here you'll learn
all about Clear Creek Canyon's treasury of rock art and archaeological sites. A video program

introduces you to the Fremont Indians. In addition, twelve interpretive trails, one accessible to wheelchairs, lead you to various pictographs and petroglyphs.

The state park offers a wide assortment of special activities, many related to learning about the Indians who once lived here. Contact the state park for further information.

174 City Creek

Location: In the Fishlake National Forest, about 5.5 miles northwest of Junction
GPS: N38 16.184' / W112 18.676'
Facilities: Fire pits, picnic tables, drinking water, and vault toilets
Sites: 5 basic sites that can make 1 big group site
Maximum RV length: 24 feet
Fee: None
Maximum stay: 14 days
Elevation: 7,600 feet
Road conditions: Paved and gravel
Management: Beaver Ranger District, 575 S. Main St., Beaver; (435) 438-2436; www.fs.usda .gov/main/fishlake/home
Reservations: None
Activities: Fishing, horseback riding, hiking, ATV riding, and picnicking
Restrictions: ATVs allowed in the campground, but only on designated routes
Season: May through October
Finding the campground: From Junction travel northwest on UT 153, which is paved for about 5 miles then turns to maintained gravel. You'll reach the campground in 5.5 miles.
About the campground: City Creek flows near this campground set among cottonwood, ponderosa pine, pinyon pine, and juniper trees; it makes a nice base for anglers, hikers, and horseback riders. There are hiking opportunities on both the North and South Forks of City Creek. Anglers can expect fish up to 9 inches in length. Wild rainbow trout are the most common species; the South Fork offers the greatest success rate.

175 Piute State Park

Location: About 6 miles north of Junction
GPS: N38 19.233' / W112 11.899'
Facilities: Fire pits, picnic tables, vault toilets, boat launch, and dock
Sites: Dispersed
Maximum RV length: Any
Fee: $ for dispersed sites
Maximum stay: 14 days
Elevation: 5,900 feet
Road conditions: Maintained gravel

Management: Piute State Park, c/o Otter Creek State Park, PO Box 43, Antimony, UT 84712-0043; (435) 624-3268; www.stateparks.utah.gov/parks/piute
Reservations: None
Activities: Fishing, boating, swimming, waterskiing, rockhounding, mountain biking, and picnicking
Season: Year-round
Finding the campground: From Junction travel north on US 89 for 6.2 miles to signed Piute State Park. A wide, gravel road leads right (east) for 0.5 mile to its end at the reservoir.
About the campground: Piute Reservoir, one of Utah's largest artificial lakes at 3,300 acres, is the setting for this state park. It offers primitive camping with a couple of toilets, a few picnic tables, a boat ramp, a dock, and little more in the way of amenities. Still, the primitive conditions may be just fine for those who enjoy fishing for trout, boating, water sports, rockhounding, or riding the local dirt roads on a mountain bike.

176 Otter Creek State Park

Location: About 60 miles south of Richfield
GPS: N38 10.002'/W112 01.081'
Facilities: Fire pits, picnic tables, tent pads, some BBQ grills, some windscreens, drinking water, flush toilets, showers, fish cleaning station, boat launch, loading docks, and sewage disposal station
Sites: 46 basic sites, 7 tents-only sites, and 1 group site (maximum 100 people)
Maximum RV length: 45 feet
Fee: $$ for basic and tents-only sites; $$$$$ for group site
Maximum stay: 14 days
Elevation: 6,300 feet
Road conditions: Paved
Management: Otter Creek State Park, PO Box 43, Antimony, UT 84712-0043; (435) 624-3268; www.stateparks.utah.gov/parks/otter-creek
Reservations: In the Salt Lake area, call (801) 322-3770; elsewhere, (800) 322-3770; http://utahstateparks.reserveamerica.com
Activities: Fishing, boating, waterskiing, bird watching, off-highway driving, picnicking, ice skating, and ice fishing
Restrictions: Campground gate closed from 10 p.m. to 6 a.m.
Season: Year-round
Finding the campground: From the old mining town of Antimony, travel north for about 4 miles on UT 22.
About the campground: Located on the south end of Otter Creek Reservoir, the campground and surrounding area are good places to look for both resident and migratory birdlife, including ospreys, bald eagles, ducks, geese, and swans. The reservoir offers some of the state's finest year-round rainbow trout fishing; cutthroat and brown trout also swim in these waters. The lake's record is a 16-pound, 7-ounce brown trout.

Hookups are nonexistent, but there are wooden windscreens and shade trees for privacy.

Three ATV trails originate in the park, including the popular Paiute ATV Trail, which is a 260-mile loop over three mountain ranges and through rugged canyons and deserts.

RV on BLM land with Otter Creek Campground in background.

177 **Singletree**

Location: In the Dixie National Forest (though managed by Fishlake National Forest), approximately 12 miles southeast of Torrey
GPS: N38 09.681' / W111 20.036'
Facilities: Fire pits, picnic tables, drinking water, vault and flush toilets, volleyball area, and horseshoe area. Wireless internet is available for a fee ($).
Sites: 27 basic sites, 4 double sites, and 2 group sites (maximum 50 people each)
Maximum RV length: 40 feet
Fee: $ for basic sites; $$$ for double sites; $$$$ for group sites
Maximum stay: 14 days
Elevation: 8,200 feet
Road conditions: Paved
Management: Fremont River Ranger District, 138 S. Main St., Loa; (435) 836-2800; www.fs.usda .gov/main/fishlake/home
Reservations: Call (877) 444-6777 or TDD (877) 833-6777; www.recreation.gov
Activities: Hiking and picnicking

Restrictions: ATVs not allowed

Season: Mid-May through early September

Finding the campground: From Torrey, drive south on UT 12 for 11.7 miles. You'll see the campground and turnoff on your left (east).

About the campground: Embraced by ponderosa pines and aspens, with Singletree Creek singing its way through the center of the campground, this is a great spot for relaxing. There's also a nice view east to the Henry Mountains from the east edge of the campground. The Singletree Falls Trail leads 1 mile from the campground to the waterfall.

178 Fruita: Capitol Reef National Park

Location: About 1 mile south of the national park visitor center

GPS: N38 16.935'/W111 14.801'

Facilities: Fire pits, picnic tables, ADA sites, drinking water, flush and vault toilets, dump station

Sites: 71 basic sites and 1 group site (maximum 40 people)

Maximum RV length: Any

Fee: $ for basic sites; $$$$$ for group site

Maximum stay: 14 days for basic sites April 1 to November 30 (30-day limit December to March 31); 5 days for group site

Elevation: 5,500 feet

Road conditions: Paved

Management: Capitol Reef National Park, HC 70 Box 15, Torrey, UT 84775; (435) 425-3791; www.nps.gov/care/index.htm

Reservations: Reserve the group site by faxing your request to (435) 425-3026 or mailing your reservation to Capitol Reef at the above Torrey address.

Activities: Hiking, mountain biking, rock climbing, picnicking, scenic driving, and photography

Season: Year-round (group site open April 1 through October 20, except for Tuesday and Wednesday when it is closed for groundskeeping purposes)

Finding the campground: From the visitor center, about 11 miles east of Torrey off UT 24, go south about 1 mile to the campground.

About the campground: An oasis in the desert, the campground is blanketed with grass and lovely trees that provide shade come summer. Nearby you'll find Fruita's historic orchards, harvested for almost a century. The legacy lives on, for the National Park Service preserves the orchards, replacing old trees with historical varieties. Fruit is available throughout most of the summer and fall. You may eat as much fruit as you wish in an orchard open for public harvest—you must purchase it at a self-pay station. A scale for weighing fruit and plastic bags are provided.

When you're done gorging on fruit, you'll find a multitude of trails to explore and a lovely scenic drive; rock climbing is popular as well. (*Note:* If you're climbing, you must use colored chalk; white chalk is not permitted.)

Hickman Natural Bridge is a popular hiking destination in Capitol Reef State Park.

179 **Sunglow**

Location: In the Fishlake National Forest, about 1 mile east of Bicknell and 7 miles west of Torrey
GPS: N38 20.510'/W111 31.229'
Facilities: Fire pits, picnic tables, drinking water, and flush toilets
Sites: 7 basic sites and 2 group sites (maximum 20 people each)
Maximum RV length: 30 feet
Fee: $ for basic sites; $$$ for group sites
Maximum stay: 14 days
Elevation: 7,200 feet
Road conditions: Gravel
Management: Fremont River Ranger District, 138 S. Main St., Loa; (435) 836-2800; www.fs.usda
.gov/main/fishlake/home
Reservations: For group sites only, call (877) 444-6777 or TDD (877) 833-6777; www
.recreation.gov
Activities: Hiking, mountain biking, and picnicking
Restrictions: ATVs not allowed
Season: April through October

Finding the campground: From the center of the small town of Bicknell, drive east on UT 24 for about 1 mile. Turn left (north) onto a paved road (there's a sign for Sunglow) and drive 1 mile before the road turns to gravel. Continue another 0.1 mile to the campground.

About the campground: The campground has the feel of being out in the boonies, yet it is close to the small town of Bicknell. Partially surrounded by red rock and tucked away in a box canyon of sorts, this site is decorated with juniper and cottonwood trees. A small creek flows through the campground. Although there are no designated trails, you'll see trails throughout the area for hiking and mountain biking.

180 Doctor Creek: Fish Lake Recreation Area

Location: In the Fishlake National Forest, about 20 miles northwest of Loa
GPS: N38 31.728'/W111 44.400'
Facilities: Fire pits, picnic tables, ADA sites, some BBQ grills, some tent pads, drinking water, flush toilets, and dump station
Sites: 30 basic sites and 2 group sites (maximum 150 people each)
Maximum RV length: 50 feet
Fee: $$ for basic sites; $$$$$ for group sites
Maximum stay: 10 days
Elevation: 8,800 feet
Road conditions: Paved
Management: Fremont River Ranger District, 138 S. Main St., Loa; (435) 836-2800; www.fs.usda .gov/main/fishlake/home
Reservations: Call (877) 444-6777 or TDD (877) 833-6777; www.recreation.gov
Activities: Fishing, boating, scuba diving, swimming, mountain biking, hiking, wildlife watching, photography, and picnicking
Restrictions: ATVs not allowed; ATV riding not allowed in Fish Lake Basin
Season: Memorial Day through Labor Day
Finding the campground: From Loa travel northwest on UT 24 for 12.9 miles to its junction with UT 25. Make a right (northeast) onto paved UT 25 and drive 7.2 miles to a turnoff on the right (southeast) for the campground. Pass the sewage disposal station and continue 0.3 mile to the fee station.

About the campground: Located near the southern shore of Fish Lake at Mallard Bay, this beautiful campground is set among aspens and cottonwoods. There's plenty to do in the area, with many hiking and mountain biking trails nearby, including one along the lakeshore. There are also three resorts in the area; they offer showers, self-service laundries, limited groceries, dining facilities, boat rentals, and boat ramps.

Fish Lake in early May

181 Mackinaw: Fish Lake Recreation Area

Location: In the Fishlake National Forest, approximately 22 miles northwest of Loa
GPS: N38 33.126' / W111 43.165' (southernmost entrance)
Facilities: Fire pits, picnic tables, drinking water, flush toilets, and showers
Sites: 63 basic sites and 4 group sites (maximum 20 people each)
Maximum RV length: 45 feet
Fee: $$ for basic sites; $$$$ for group sites
Maximum stay: 10 days
Elevation: 8,900 feet
Road conditions: Paved
Management: Fremont River Ranger District, 138 S. Main St., Loa; (435) 836-2800; www.fs.usda
.gov/main/fishlake/home
Reservations: Call (877) 444-6777 or TDD (877) 833-6777; www.recreation.gov
Activities: Fishing, boating, scuba diving, swimming, mountain biking, hiking, wildlife watching,
photography, and picnicking
Restrictions: ATVs not allowed in campground; ATV riding not allowed in Fish Lake Basin
Season: Memorial Day through Labor Day
Finding the campground: From Loa travel northwest on UT 24 for 12.9 miles to its junction with
UT 25. Make a right (northeast) onto paved UT 25 and drive 9.1 miles to a turnoff on the left

(north) for the campground. There are two more entrances 0.2 and 0.4 mile farther down the road.
About the campground: There are three entrances to this wonderful campground set amid a beautiful grove of aspens. Located across the highway from the west shore of Fish Lake, there's a multitude of things to do in the area. For example, hiking and mountain biking trails abound; there's even a trail that parallels the lakeshore. In addition, there are three resorts in the area that offer boat rentals and boat ramps, showers, self-service laundries, limited groceries, and dining facilities.

182 Bowery Creek: Fish Lake Recreation Area

Location: In the Fishlake National Forest, about 23 miles northwest of Loa
GPS: N38 33.569' / W111 42.607'
Facilities: Fire pits, picnic tables, ADA sites, drinking water, and flush toilets
Sites: 33 basic sites, 7 double sites, and 3 triple sites
Maximum RV length: 40 feet
Fee: $$ for basic sites; $$$ for double sites, $$$$$ for triple sites
Maximum stay: 10 days
Elevation: 8,900 feet
Road conditions: Paved
Management: Fremont River Ranger District, 138 S. Main St., Loa; (435) 836-2800; www.fs.usda .gov/main/fishlake/home
Reservations: Call (877) 444-6777 or TDD (877) 833-6777; www.recreation.gov
Activities: Fishing, boating, scuba diving, swimming, mountain biking, hiking, wildlife watching, photography, and picnicking
Restrictions: ATVs not allowed; ATV riding not allowed in Fish Lake Basin
Season: Memorial Day through Labor Day
Finding the campground: From Loa travel northwest on UT 24 for 12.9 miles to its junction with UT 25. Make a right (northeast) onto paved UT 25 and drive 9.9 miles to the campground turnoff on the left (north).
About the campground: Located among aspens and pines, the campground rests across the highway from the west shore of Fish Lake. There are many activities to enjoy in the region. For instance, hiking and mountain biking trails abound; there's even one that parallels the lakeshore and follows part of the Old Spanish Trail. Three nearby resorts offer boat rentals and boat ramps, showers, self-service laundries, limited groceries, and dining facilities.

183 Frying Pan: Fish Lake Recreation Area

Location: In the Fishlake National Forest, approximately 28 miles northwest of Loa
GPS: N38 36.495' / W111 40.768'
Facilities: Fire pits, picnic tables, some BBQ grills, drinking water, and flush toilets
Sites: 11 basic sites and 1 group site (maximum 100 people)
Maximum RV length: 45 feet
Fee: $$ for basic sites; $$$$$ for group site

Maximum stay: 10 days
Elevation: 9,000 feet
Road conditions: Paved
Management: Fremont River Ranger District, 138 S. Main St., Loa; (435) 836-2800; www.fs.usda
.gov/main/fishlake/home
Reservations: Call (877) 444-6777 or TDD (877) 833-6777; www.recreation.gov
Activities: Mountain biking, hiking, wildlife watching, photography, and picnicking
Restrictions: ATVs not allowed; ATV riding not allowed in Fish Lake Basin
Season: Memorial Day through Labor Day
Finding the campground: From Loa travel northwest on UT 24 for 12.9 miles to its junction with
UT 25. Make a right (northeast) onto paved UT 25 and drive 14.9 miles to the campground turnoff
on the left (north).
About the campground: Located among aspens and pines, the campground is tucked away on
the north side of the road. There are many activities to enjoy in the area; hiking and mountain bik-
ing are especially popular. You can even enjoy fishing at nearby Fish Lake and Johnson Reservoir.
In addition, three resorts offer boat rentals and boat ramps, showers, self-service laundries, limited
groceries, and dining facilities. There are also Sunday church services at Fish Lake Lodge.

184 Paiute Recreation Area

Location: In the Fishlake National Forest, about 24 miles north of Loa
GPS: N38 37.102'/W111 39.115'
Facilities: Some fire pits, some picnic tables, drinking water, and vault toilets
Sites: 48 basic sites
Maximum RV length: Any
Fee: $ for basic sites
Maximum stay: 60 days
Elevation: 8,900 feet
Road conditions: Paved
Management: Fremont River Ranger District, 138 S. Main St., Loa; (435) 836-2800; www.fs.usda
.gov/main/fishlake/home
Reservations: None
Activities: Mountain biking, hiking, and fishing
Restrictions: ATVs not allowed in Fish Lake Basin
Season: May through October
Finding the campground: From Loa travel north-northeast on paved UT 72 for about 10 miles.
Upon reaching the junction, turn left (northwest) onto Fremont River Road and continue 13.6
miles to the campground.
About the campground: Sometimes known as the Piute (yes, sometimes it is spelled Piute and
sometimes Paiute) Parking Campground, this 48-site area is in the open, with close access to
fishing at Johnson Reservoir. The sites are set up parking-lot style, with paved slabs a plus for this
RV-friendly park. Still, it's an inexpensive place to set up a base camp for fishing, mountain biking,
and hiking. See Gregg Bromka's FalconGuides book *Mountain Biking Utah* for more mountain
biking information.

185 Tasha Equestrian

Location: In the Fishlake National Forest, about 25 miles north of Loa
GPS: N38 37.238'/W111 39.775'
Facilities: Fire pits, picnic tables, drinking water, flush toilets, hitching racks and rails, horse camp facility, horse corrals, horse loading ramp, horse trail, and equestrian area
Sites: 10 basic sites and 1 group site (maximum 25 people)
Maximum RV length: Any
Fee: $ for basic sites, $$$ for group site
Maximum stay: 14 days
Elevation: 9,000 feet
Road conditions: Dirt
Management: Fremont River Ranger District, 138 S. Main St., Loa; (435) 836-2800; www.fs.usda .gov/main/fishlake/home
Reservations: Call (877) 444-6777 or TDD (877) 833-6777; www.recreation.gov
Activities: Horseback riding
Restrictions: Not allowed: persons without horses; ATVs; ATV riding in Fish Lake Basin
Season: Mid-May through mid-October
Finding the campground: From Loa travel north-northeast on paved UT 72 for about 10 miles. Upon reaching the junction, turn left (northwest) onto Fremont River Road and continue 14.2 miles to the campground turnoff, which is on the right (north) side of the road. Follow the dirt road 0.7 mile to the campground.
About the campground: Managed by the forest service, this campground is cleaned and maintained by the Central Utah Backcountry Horsemen under an adoption agreement. The association also helps maintain some trails. It's a horses-only kind of place, so if you don't have a horse you won't be staying here. People without horses are not allowed! It's an excellent base for those with horses, with many nearby trails leading up Tasha Canyon and Mytoge Mountain. The campground is tucked away amid pines and aspens. There are several sets of corrals throughout the campground. Each site has a tie rack for horses, as well as the usual amenities.

186 Elkhorn

Location: In the Fishlake National Forest, about 20 miles northeast of Loa
GPS: N38 27.826'/W111 27.416'
Facilities: Fire pits, picnic tables, drinking water, and vault toilets
Sites: 6 basic sites and 1 group site (maximum 75 people)
Maximum RV length: 22 feet for basic sites; 70 feet for group site
Fee: None for basic sites; $$$ for group site
Maximum stay: 14 days
Elevation: 9,800 feet
Road conditions: Dirt
Management: Fremont River Ranger District, 138 S. Main St., Loa; (435) 836-2800; www.fs.usda .gov/main/fishlake/home

Reservations: For the group site only, call (877) 444-6777 or TDD (877) 833-6777; www .recreation.gov

Activities: Hiking, horseback riding, ATV riding, and mountain biking

Season: Mid-June through September

Finding the campground: From Loa travel north-northeast on paved UT 72 for about 12 miles. At this point make a right (east) onto FR 206, which is gravel. A sign says it's 8 miles to the campground. As you continue, the road narrows to one lane with turnouts; its surface is dirt with a sprinkling of gravel. Stay on FR 206, driving 4.6 miles to a fork; continue on FR 206 to the campground in less than 4 miles. (*Note:* The road has sharp turns and rises 1,650 feet in elevation.)

About the campground: Set in a forest of spruce, fir, and aspen, this small, isolated campground makes a good base from which to explore a number of nearby hiking, biking, and horseback trails.

187 Cathedral Valley: Capitol Reef National Park

Location: About 39 miles north of the national park visitor center

GPS: N38 28.415' / W111 21.939'

Facilities: Fire pits, picnic tables, and vault toilets

Sites: 6 basic sites

Maximum RV length: RVs not recommended due to poor road conditions

Fee: None

Maximum stay: 14 days

Elevation: 7,000 feet

Road conditions: Dirt and sand; high-clearance or four-wheel-drive vehicles are recommended and often required. Road conditions change due to rain or snow; check with the visitor center for current conditions.

Management: Capitol Reef National Park, HC 70 Box 15, Torrey, UT 84775; (435) 425-3791; www.nps.gov/care/index.htm

Reservations: None

Activities: Hiking, picnicking, and photography

Season: Year-round

Finding the campground: From the visitor center, about 11 miles east of Torrey, continue east on UT 24 for another 11.7 miles. Make a left at the small sign onto River Ford Road (also known as Hartnet Road), a dirt road, to a fork at 25.4 miles. Straight (west) would lead to Thousand Lake Mountain; keep right (north) for 0.3 mile to the campground, which is on the left (west). If you'd rather not ford the river, continue east on UT 24 for an additional 6.7 miles to Caineville Wash Road; follow it about 29 miles to the campground.

About the campground: Spacious sites sit among a partially open forest of pinyon pine and juniper on the flanks of Thousand Lake Mountain. From here there are views of the mountain as well as into the eastern reaches of Capitol Reef. This primitive, bring-your-own-water campground is suitable for tenters.

Hikers with map and compass in hand can explore to their hearts' content, while photographers will find an endless array of images to make.

188 Gooseberry (Salina)

Location: In the Fishlake National Forest, about 16 miles southeast of Salina
GPS: N38 48.416'/W111 41.195'
Facilities: Fire pits, picnic tables, drinking water, and vault toilets
Sites: 13 basic sites and 1 group site (maximum 40 people)
Maximum RV length: 30 feet
Fee: $ for basic sites; $$ for group site
Maximum stay: 14 days
Elevation: 7,800 feet
Road conditions: Dirt
Management: Richfield Ranger District, 115 E. 900 North, Richfield; (435) 896-9233; www
.fs.usda.gov/main/fishlake/home
Reservations: For the group site only, call (877) 444-6777 or TDD (877) 833-6777; www
.recreation.gov
Activities: Fishing, ATV riding, and picnicking
Restrictions: ATVs allowed only to access the adjacent trail system
Season: April through November
Finding the campground: From Salina head east on I-70 for about 7 miles to Gooseberry Road,
exit 61. Head south on Gooseberry Road, which is paved for about 6 miles then turns to a one-
lane dirt road with turnouts. You'll reach the campground, which is on your right, after another 3.3
miles of dirt road.
About the campground: A pretty setting with aspens all around, there's a group site as well as
single sites. The host told us that some folks try their luck fishing in Gooseberry Creek. He claims
the fish are small but "good tasting."

189 Twin Lake

Location: In the Manti–La Sal National Forest, approximately 7.5 miles east of Mayfield
GPS: N39 07.252'/W111 36.080'
Facilities: Fire pits, picnic tables, vault toilets; no garbage service (pack it out)
Sites: 21 basic sites and 1 group site (maximum 40 people)
Maximum RV length: 30 feet
Fee: $ for basic sites; $$$ for group site
Maximum stay: 14 days
Elevation: 7,300 feet
Road conditions: Gravel
Management: Sanpete Ranger District, 540 N. Main St., Ephraim; (435) 283-4151; www.fs.usda
.gov/main/mantilasal/home
Reservations: Call (877) 444-6777 or TDD (877) 833-6777; www.recreation.gov
Activities: Hiking, mountain biking, OHV riding, and picnicking
Restrictions: Horses not allowed; OHV riding not allowed except for entering and exiting
Season: June through October

Finding the campground: From the junction of Main Street and Canyon Road in downtown Mayfield, head east on paved Canyon Road. After 1.7 miles the road becomes gravel. After another 1.8 miles the road becomes FR 022. Reach the entrance to the campground on the left after another 4 miles.

About the campground: Located in Twelve Mile Canyon, in a thick forest with lots of shade, sites 1 to 19 plus the group site are on the west side of FR 022, while sites 20 and 21 are on the east side of the road near an ATV staging area. There are many ATV trails including the ATV Learners Loop. Campers may see boreal toads and rattlesnakes.

190 Twelve Mile Flat

Location: In the Manti–La Sal National Forest, approximately 19 miles east of Mayfield
GPS: N39 07.393'/W111 29.219'
Facilities: Fire pits, picnic tables, vault toilets; no garbage service (pack it out)
Sites: 15 basic sites and 2 group sites (maximum 50 people each)
Maximum RV length: 30 feet
Fee: $ for basic sites; $$$$ for group sites
Maximum stay: 14 days
Elevation: 10,000 feet
Road conditions: Gravel
Management: Sanpete Ranger District, 540 N. Main St., Ephraim; (435) 283-4151; www.fs.usda .gov/main/mantilasal/home
Reservations: Call (877) 444-6777 or TDD (877) 833-6777; www.recreation.gov
Activities: Hiking, mountain biking, OHV riding, photography, and picnicking
Restrictions: Horses not allowed; OHV riding not allowed except for entering and exiting
Season: June through October
Finding the campground: From the junction of Main Street and Canyon Road in downtown Mayfield, head east on paved Canyon Road. After 1.7 miles the road becomes gravel; later the road name changes to FR 022. Continue approximately 17 miles to the campground.
About the campground: Located beneath the shadow of Mount Baldy, campers will find a wildflower-filled meadow surrounded by spruce and pines. There are many ATV trails in the area, including Skyline Drive, which passes just above the campground.

191 Ferron Reservoir

Location: In the Manti–La Sal National Forest, about 26 miles west of Ferron
GPS: N39 08.729'/W111 26.944' (northeast campground)
GPS: N39 08.302'/W111 27.123' (south shore campground)
GPS: N39 08.550'/W111 27.492' (west shore campground)
Facilities: Fire pits, boat launch (for small craft only), picnic tables, drinking water, and vault toilets; no garbage service (pack it out)
Sites: 29 basic sites and 1 group site (maximum 50 people)

Maximum RV length: 20 feet (northeast and south shore campgrounds); 45 feet (west shore)
Fee: $ for basic sites; $$$$ for group site
Maximum stay: 14 days
Elevation: 9,500 feet
Road conditions: Gravel
Management: Ferron Ranger District, 115 W. Canyon Rd., PO Box 310, Ferron, UT 84523; (435) 384-2372; www.fs.usda.gov/main/mantilasal/home
Reservations: Call (877) 444-6777 or TDD (877) 833-6777; www.recreation.gov
Activities: Fishing, boating, hiking, mountain biking, and picnicking
Season: June through October
Finding the campground: From the junction of UT 10 and Canyon Road in downtown Ferron, head west on paved Canyon Road. Signs for Millstate State Park and Ferron Reservoir point the way. Travel 4.3 miles before the road turns to gravel; later the road is signed FR 022. Continue another 21.7 miles (sometimes encountering steep grades on the one-lane road with turnouts) to Ferron Reservoir and a fork. You'll find the northeast campground if you make a right (north) onto FR 049 and travel 0.3 mile, then make a left (west) onto FR 2072. Back on the main road, find the south shore campground on the south end of the lake after 0.2 mile. The west shore campground is another 0.5 mile to the west on the west side of the lake.
About the campground: This campground is managed in three sections; one (with six non-reservable primitive sites without water) is on the northeast side of the lake. The south shore campground also offers six sites, plus there is water. The largest campground is on the west shore and offers seventeen sites and one group site.

Conifers and some aspens shade most of the sites, many of which overlook lovely Ferron Reservoir. Near the west shore section you'll find a 0.5 mile long nature trail. Mountain bikers will find plenty of roads and trails for biking. For more information see the FalconGuides book *Mountain Biking Utah*, by Gregg Bromka.

192 Palisade State Park

Location: About 2 miles northeast of Sterling
GPS: N39 12.145'/W111 39.937'
Facilities: BBQ grills, picnic tables (covered at Wakara), ADA sites, tent pads (at Wakara), drinking water, flush toilets, showers, dump station, full-hookup sites (at Wakara; some full-hookups at Sanpitch), boat launch and docks, canoe and paddleboat rentals, golf course and clubhouse, and playground
Sites: 23 basic sites, 20 double sites, 28 full-hookup sites, 3 walk-in tent sites, 5 group sites (maximum varies from 30 to 75 people), and 6 cabins
Maximum RV length: Any
Fee: $$ for basic and walk-in tent sites; $$$$ for double sites; $$$ for full-hookup sites; $$$$$ for group sites and cabins
Maximum stay: 14 days
Elevation: 5,800 feet
Road conditions: Paved
Management: Palisade State Park, PO Box 650070, Sterling, UT 84665; (435) 835-7275; www.stateparks.utah.gov/park/palisade-state-park

Kids play on the beach at Arapeen Campground.

Reservations: In the Salt Lake area, call (801) 322-3770; elsewhere, (800) 322-3770; http://utahstateparks.reserveamerica.com
Activities: Mountain biking, hiking, boating (nonmotorized), swimming, fishing, golfing, ice fishing and ice skating (in winter), and picnicking
Season: Year-round
Finding the campground: From the north end of Sterling, turn right (east) off US 89 onto paved Palisades Road. A sign points the way. You'll reach the park entrance station after 1.6 miles.
About the campground: Landscaped with grass and a variety of deciduous trees, this state park offers four campground units spread out along the north, east, and south ends of Palisade Lake. Along the lake the northernmost section is known as Arapeen, the eastern side is called Pioneer, and the south section is named Sanpitch. Just above the lakeshore you'll find the newest campground, Wakara, with full hookups, tent pads, and covered picnic tables; there are also six cabins for rent.

In summer folks come to this lovely area to swim, go boating, do some fishing, indulge in some golfing, or just plain relax. In winter visitors come to skate on the frozen lake or to drop a line into a hole in the lake to do some ice fishing.

193 Manti Community

Location: In the Manti–La Sal National Forest, approximately 6 miles east of Manti
GPS: N39 15.286'/W111 32.439'
Facilities: Fire pits, picnic tables, drinking water, and vault toilets; no garbage service (pack it out)
Sites: 9 basic sites and 1 group site (maximum 30 people)
Maximum RV length: 30 feet
Fee: $ for basic sites; $$$$ for group site
Maximum stay: 14 days
Elevation: 7,500 feet
Road conditions: Gravel
Management: Sanpete Ranger District, 540 N. Main St., Ephraim; (435) 283-4151; www.fs.usda.gov/main/mantilasal/home
Reservations: Call (877) 444-6777 or TDD (877) 833-6777; www.recreation.gov
Activities: Fishing, canoeing and kayaking, mountain biking, OHV riding, and picnicking
Season: June through October
Finding the campground: From Fifth South and Main in Manti, head east on paved Fifth South. After 0.8 mile the road turns to gravel and later dirt; it can be very bumpy. The road also turns into FR 045 as you continue. You'll reach the campground, which is on your right, in another 5.2 miles.
About the campground: Set amid a forest of aspen, juniper, spruce, and other pines, this campground offers more than just woods. It's adjacent to Yearns Reservoir, a small man-made lake, and the chance to fish for cutthroat trout.

A hiking and OHV trail is found at the Patton Trailhead, about 3 miles prior to the campground. There are many dirt roads and trails for mountain bikes as well.

194 Lake Hill

Location: In the Manti–La Sal National Forest, about 8 miles east of Ephraim
GPS: N39 19.659'/W111 29.916'
Facilities: Fire pits, picnic tables, drinking water, and vault toilets; no trash service (pack it out)
Sites: 9 basic sites and 2 group sites (maximum 30 and 75 people, respectively)
Maximum RV length: 30 feet
Fee: $ for basic sites; $$$$ for group sites
Maximum stay: 14 days
Elevation: 8,400 feet
Road conditions: Gravel
Management: Sanpete Ranger District, 540 N. Main St., Ephraim; (435) 283-4151; www.fs.usda.gov/main/mantilasal/home
Reservations: Call (877) 444-6777 or TDD (877) 833-6777; www.recreation.gov
Activities: Fishing, hiking, mountain biking, and picnicking
Restrictions: OHVs and livestock not allowed
Season: June through October

Finding the campground: From the junction of Main and 400 South on the south end of Ephraim, travel east on 400 South for 0.4 mile, then turn right (south) onto 300 East. Signs for Ephraim Canyon point the way at both junctions. Road 400 South curves east after a short distance and becomes Canyon Road. The paved road turns to gravel after 2.2 miles. Continue another 5.2 miles to the campground entrance, which is on your right; travel an additional 0.3 mile to the fee station.

About the campground: Aspens and conifers shade the sites in this campground, which offers fishing at Lake Hill Reservoir. It's stocked with fish on a yearly basis. Hikers will find several trails in the area, and mountain bikers will find pathways for riding.

195 Painted Rocks: Yuba State Park

Location: About 25 miles south of Nephi
GPS: N39 21.216' / W111 56.428'
Facilities: Fire pits, covered picnic tables, stove stands, partial hookups, tent pads, drinking water, vault toilets, dump station, and boat ramp
Sites: 38 partial-hookup sites, 3 tents-only sites, and 1 group site (maximum 150 people)
Maximum RV length: 40 feet
Fee: $ for tents-only sites; $$ for partial-hookup sites; $$$$$ for group site
Maximum stay: 14 days
Elevation: 5,000 feet
Road conditions: Paved
Management: Yuba State Park, PO Box 159, Levan, UT 84639-0159; (435) 758-2611; www .stateparks.utah.gov/parks/yuba
Reservations: In the Salt Lake area, call (801) 322-3770; elsewhere, (800) 322-3770; http:// utahstateparks.reserveamerica.com
Activities: Fishing, mountain biking, off-highway driving (in designated areas), boating, sailing, swimming, photography, and picnicking
Restrictions: Campground gate closed from 10 p.m. to 6 a.m.
Season: Year-round
Finding the campground: From Nephi, head south on paved UT 28 for about 10 miles to Levan; from there continue south another 14 miles or so via UT 28 to a sign that says "Full Hookups," pointing the way to Yuba Reservoir. The road is paved. After 0.3 mile there's a fork; go left another 0.4 mile to Painted Rocks. (Going right on the gravel road leads to Eagle View Campground.)
About the campground: Painted Rocks is a lovely campground with views of the reservoir. There are some cottonwoods dotting the campground, but the trees don't provide much in the way of shade. The 22-mile-long Yuba Reservoir (originally called Sevier Bridge Reservoir) is a popular spot for those with fishing or boating on their minds. The water boasts a whopping 70°F tempera-ture in summer, making this a great place for activities such as waterskiing, boating, sailboarding, sailing, and swimming. Ancient rock art is also a draw, with the art at Painted Rocks accessible by boat only.

Anglers can enjoy year-round fishing—species include walleye, yellow perch, channel catfish, and northern pike. Other activities include mountain biking (there are many dirt roads to ride), rockhounding, and off-highway vehicle riding in designated areas just outside the park.

Beach sites at Eagle View Campground welcome campers.

196 Eagle View: Yuba State Park

Location: About 27 miles south of Nephi
GPS: N39 22.646'/W111 57.759'
Facilities: Fire pits, covered picnic tables, stove stands, tent pads, vault toilets, solar lighting, and boat docks for sites 1 and 2
Sites: 5 basic sites and 15 double sites
Maximum RV length: 20 feet
Fee: $ for basic sites; $$ for double sites
Maximum stay: 14 days
Elevation: 5,000 feet
Road conditions: Dirt and sand; passenger cars not recommended—4WD is best
Management: Yuba State Park, PO Box 159, Levan, UT 84639-0159; (435) 758-2611; www .stateparks.utah.gov/parks/yuba
Reservations: In the Salt Lake area, call (801) 322-3770; elsewhere, (800) 322-3770; http:// utahstateparks.reserveamerica.com
Activities: Fishing, mountain biking, off-highway driving (in designated areas), boating, sailing, swimming, photography, and picnicking
Season: Year-round
Finding the campground: From Nephi head south on paved UT 28 for about 10 miles to Levan;

from there continue south another 14 miles or so via UT 28 to a sign that says "Full Hookups," pointing the way to Yuba Reservoir. The road is paved. After 0.3 mile there's a fork; go right (northwest) on the gravel road to Eagle View Campground. (Left takes you to Painted Rocks Campground.) Follow the gravel road, which eventually turns to dirt, for another 2.3 miles to another sign pointing the way 0.1 mile to the fee station. (**Note:** The road is not maintained in winter.)

About the campground: At one time Eagle View Campground was a boats-only kind of place. In fact, there was no access via road. Now it is available for everyone, but I recommend leaving sites 1 and 2 for those with boats. Located near the beach, there is limited parking and absolutely no room to turn around. Best of all, there are boat docks for the lucky ones who arrive via boat. The rest of the campground is spread out over an expansive area with slopes covered in sage, Utah juniper, and pinyon pine. There are nice views of the lake, but the campground is best for tents, pickup trucks, vans, and very small motor homes. The 22-mile-long Yuba Reservoir (originally called Sevier Bridge Reservoir) is a popular spot for those with fishing or boating on their minds. The water boasts a whopping 70°F temperature in summer, making this a great place for activities such as waterskiing, boating, sailboarding, sailing, and swimming.

Anglers can enjoy year-round fishing—species include walleye, yellow perch, channel catfish, and northern pike.

197 North and West Beach: Yuba State Park

Location: About 25 miles southwest of Nephi
GPS: N39 24.457' / W112 01.663'
Facilities: Fire pits, picnic tables, vault toilets, and dump station (at nearby Oasis Campground)
Sites: Dispersed sites on North and West beaches
Maximum RV length: Any
Fee: $ for dispersed sites
Maximum stay: 14 days
Elevation: 5,000 feet
Road conditions: Gravel
Management: Yuba State Park, PO Box 159, Levan, UT 84639-0159; (435) 758-2611; www .stateparks.utah.gov/parks/yuba
Reservations: None
Activities: Fishing, mountain biking, off-highway driving (in designated areas), boating, sailing, swimming, photography, and picnicking
Restrictions: Campground gate closed from 10 a.m. to 6 p.m.
Season: Year-round
Finding the campground: Drive I-15 south from Nephi for about 23 miles, getting off at exit 202. Continue south on the signed, paved road toward Yuba Lake; after about 2 miles turn left (east) onto a gravel road named Temple Road on maps. It leads 0.1 mile to the entrance station, which is on your right (south).
About the campground: There are wonderful views from North and West beaches. Located on the shores of Yuba Reservoir (originally called Sevier Bridge Reservoir), this is a fine place to indulge in water activities such as waterskiing, boating, sailboarding, sailing, and swimming. The water warms to a whopping 70°F in summer.

Views are expansive from West Beach Campground at Yuba State Park.

Anglers can enjoy year-round fishing—species include walleye, yellow perch, channel catfish, and northern pike. Other activities include mountain biking (there are many dirt roads to ride), rockhounding, and off-highway vehicle riding in designated areas just outside the park.

198 Oasis: Yuba State Park

Location: About 27 miles southwest of Nephi
GPS: N39 22.612' / W112 01.674'
Facilities: Fire pits, covered picnic tables, ADA site, partial hookups, tent pads, BBQ grills, drinking water, showers, dump station, flush toilets, boat ramp, and a store with supplies, food, and ATV and boat rentals
Sites: 15 basic sites, 11 partial-hookup sites, 2 tents-only sites, 1 group site (maximum 75 people), and 2 cabins
Maximum RV length: Any
Fee: $$ for basic, partial-hookup, and tents-only sites; $$$$$ for group site and cabins
Maximum stay: 14 days
Elevation: 5,000 feet
Road conditions: Paved
Management: Yuba State Park, PO Box 159, Levan, UT 84639-0159; (435) 758-2611; www .stateparks.utah.gov/parks/yuba

Reservations: In the Salt Lake area, call (801) 322-3770; elsewhere, (800) 322-3770; http://utahstateparks.reserveamerica.com

Activities: Fishing, mountain biking, off-highway driving (in designated areas), boating, sailing, swimming, photography, and picnicking

Restrictions: Campground gate closed from 10 p.m. to 6 a.m.

Season: Year-round

Finding the campground: Drive I-15 south from Nephi for about 23 miles, getting off at exit 202. Continue south on the signed, paved road to Yuba Lake; you'll reach the entrance station on your left after another 4 miles.

About the campground: A sprinkling of deciduous trees, including cottonwoods, and a grand view across the 22-mile-long lake to Mount Nebo, the highest point in the Wasatch Range, make this a pleasant spot to camp. Located on the western shore of Yuba Reservoir (originally called Sevier Bridge Reservoir), this is a fine place to indulge in water activities such as waterskiing, boating, sailboarding, sailing, and swimming. The water warms to a whopping 70°F in summer.

Anglers can enjoy year-round fishing—species include walleye, yellow perch, channel catfish, and northern pike. Other activities include mountain biking (there are many dirt roads to ride), rockhounding, and off-highway vehicle riding in designated areas just outside the park.

199 Chicken Creek

Location: In the Manti–La Sal National Forest, about 6 miles southeast of Levan

GPS: N39 31.874'/W111 46.463'

Facilities: Fire pits, picnic tables, and vault toilets; no trash service (pack it out)

Sites: 8 basic sites and 1 group site (maximum 50 people)

Maximum RV length: 25 feet

Fee: None

Maximum stay: 14 days

Elevation: 6,200 feet

Road conditions: Gravel

Management: Sanpete Ranger District, 540 N. Main St., Ephraim; (435) 283-4151; www.fs.usda.gov/main/mantilasal/home

Reservations: None

Activities: Fishing and picnicking

Restrictions: Horses not allowed

Season: May through October

Finding the campground: From the small town of Levan, go east on paved First South Street. There's a sign for the paved street, but not for the campground. After 1.5 miles you'll reach a fork; go right (southeast) onto gravel Chicken Creek Canyon Road (also known as FR 101) for an additional 4.5 miles.

About the campground: Marmots inhabit this campground, which is decorated with junipers, oaks, maples, and conifers. Chicken Creek flows alongside the camp, offering anglers an opportunity to fish and others a place to just plain sit and relax. A group site holds 20 to 50 people and is 0.2 mile up the road from the main campground.

200 Maple Canyon

Location: In the Manti–La Sal National Forest, approximately 10 miles southwest of Fountain Green
GPS: N39 33.355'/W111 41.174'
Facilities: Fire pits, picnic tables, and vault toilets
Sites: 9 basic sites, 3 walk-in tent sites, and 1 group site (maximum 40 people)
Maximum RV length: 30 feet
Fee: $ for basic and walk-in tent sites; $$$$ for group site
Maximum stay: 14 days
Elevation: 6,800 feet
Road conditions: Dirt
Management: Sanpete Ranger District, 540 N. Main St., Ephraim; (435) 283-4151; www.fs.usda.gov/main/mantilasal/home
Reservations: Call (877) 444-6777 or TDD (877) 833-6777; www.recreation.gov
Activities: Rock climbing, mountain biking, hiking, bird watching, photography, and picnicking
Season: May through October
Finding the campground: From Fountain Green (about 14 miles southeast of Nephi), head west on 400 South. A sign reading "Maple Canyon" points the way. After 0.5 mile the paved road curves south and becomes West Side Road. Continue another 5.5 miles and make a right (west) onto Freedom Road. After an additional 0.5 mile, the road curves north and later west; it turns into a gravel one-lane with turnouts. You'll reach the campground in another 3 miles.
About the campground: Located in a narrow canyon on the eastern flank of the San Pitch Mountains—a small range—this campground is shaded by a thick grove of maple trees. Sites are not very long, so vans or tents are best.

The area is a popular spot for rock climbers, with more than 160 climbs ranging from an easy 5.4 to a very difficult 5.13c. It's also a place for engaging in some hikes; be sure to check out the one that leads to an arch. In spring look for nesting birds along the trail.

201 Ponderosa

Location: In the Uinta-Wasatch-Cache National Forest, approximately 9 miles northeast of Nephi
GPS: N39 46.119'/W111 42.840'
Facilities: Fire pits, picnic tables, drinking water, and vault toilets
Sites: 23 basic sites
Maximum RV length: 45 feet
Fee: $$ for basic sites
Maximum stay: 7 days
Elevation: 6,200 feet
Road conditions: Paved
Management: Spanish Fork Ranger District, 44 W. 400 North, Spanish Fork; (801) 798-3571; www.fs.usda.gov/main/uwcnf/home
Reservations: Call (877) 444-6777 or TDD (877) 833-6777; www.recreation.gov
Activities: Fishing, hiking, and picnicking

Restrictions: ATVs and horses not allowed
Season: May through early September
Finding the campground: From the junction of UT 132 and I-15 in Nephi, drive east on UT 132 for 4.9 miles. Turn left (north) at the signed Mount Nebo Scenic Loop (FR 048), a paved road; continue 3.4 miles to a fork. Go left (northwest) up the paved road leading to Bear Canyon. After 0.5 mile you'll see the campground entrance on your left.
About the campground: Salt Creek sings through the campground, providing music to campers' ears and the opportunity to fish for trout. Ponderosa pines provide shade; in fact, the place was named for the pines that were planted here in 1914.

Hikers should note the trailhead for Andrews Ridge, which is another 0.7 mile up the road. An 8-mile trail leads from there to the top of Mount Nebo—at 11,928 feet the highest point in the Wasatch Range.

202 Bear Canyon

Location: In the Uinta-Wasatch-Cache National Forest, about 11 miles northeast of Nephi
GPS: N39 47.223'/W111 43.797'
Facilities: Fire pits, picnic tables, flush and vault toilets, non-potable water, and baseball fields
Sites: 6 basic sites and 3 group sites (maximum varies from 50 to 75 people)
Maximum RV length: 30 feet
Fee: $$ for basic sites; $$$$$ for group sites
Maximum stay: 7 days
Elevation: 6,800 feet
Road conditions: Paved
Management: Spanish Fork Ranger District, 44 W. 400 North, Spanish Fork; (801) 798-3571; www.fs.usda.gov/main/uwcnf/home
Reservations: For group sites only, call (877) 444-6777 or TDD (877) 833-6777; www.recreation.gov
Activities: Fishing, hiking, horseback riding, and picnicking
Restrictions: ATVs not allowed
Season: May through September
Finding the campground: From the junction of UT 132 and I-15 in Nephi, drive east on UT 132 for 4.9 miles. Turn left (north) at the signed Mount Nebo Scenic Loop (FR 048), a paved road; continue 3.4 miles to a fork. Go left (northwest) up the paved road leading to Bear Canyon. After 2.1 miles you'll reach the end of the narrow road at the campground.
About the campground: Salt Creek flows through this campground, a great spot for hikers. A mix of lofty conifers and deciduous trees shades many of the sites.

Hikers will find the Bear Canyon Trailhead at the bridge. It's a 3-mile hike from here to Nebo Loop Road 015. If you'd rather be on top of things, it's just 0.9 mile back to the Andrews Ridge Trailhead. From here an 8-mile trail leads to the top of Mount Nebo—at 11,928 feet the highest point in the Wasatch Range.

Gooseberry Reservoir Campground is viewed from the lake.

203 Gooseberry Reservoir

Location: In the Manti–La Sal National Forest, about 11 miles northeast of Fairview
GPS: N39 42.622'/W111 17.652'
Facilities: Fire pits, picnic tables, and vault toilets; no garbage service (pack it out)
Sites: 16 basic sites
Maximum RV length: 40 feet
Fee: $ for basic sites
Maximum stay: 14 days
Elevation: 8,400 feet
Road conditions: Gravel
Management: Ferron Ranger District, 115 W. Canyon Rd., PO Box 310, Ferron, UT 84523; (435) 384-2372; www.fs.usda.gov/main/mantilasal/home
Reservations: Call (877) 444-6777 or TDD (877) 833-6777; www.recreation.gov
Activities: Fishing, canoeing and kayaking, off-highway driving, mountain biking, and picnicking
Season: Late May through October

Finding the campground: From the junction of US 89 and UT 31 in Fairview, head northeast on UT 31, a paved road that climbs an 8 percent grade. After 8.4 miles you'll reach the junction with UT 264 to Scofield. Turn left (east) onto UT 264, then curve immediately around to the north. You'll reach a large parking area with vault toilets and a sign for Skyline Drive—a 100-mile-long Scenic Byway that follows the crest of the Wasatch Plateau—after 0.2 mile. The road forks just after the parking area and soon turns to gravel. Go right (northeast) on FR 124. (Left goes to US 6 in 28 miles via Skyline Road North.) After 1.1 miles reach the junction to FR 224. A sign points the way to Gooseberry Campground—but don't turn here. Instead, notice the sign pointing to Gooseberry Reservoir. It not only leads to the reservoir, but the Gooseberry Reservoir Campground, too; continue straight (north) to reach the campground in another 1.5 miles.

About the campground: Set on the shore of Gooseberry Reservoir, kayakers and canoers can just walk a few steps to put in and enjoy! While some sites are located along the water's edge, all sites have views of the lake. The lake is a popular place for ATVers and mountain bike riders as well as those who enjoy fishing. The 90-acre lake is stocked with rainbow trout and wild cutthroats. Although water isn't available at the campground, you can find it just up the road where you came from. Pass the junction to Gooseberry Campground, and you'll see it on the right 0.2 mile toward the reservoir.

204 Gooseberry

Location: In the Manti–La Sal National Forest, about 10 miles northeast of Fairview
GPS: N39 41.266'/W111 17.942'
Facilities: Fire pits, picnic tables, drinking water, and vault toilets
Sites: 8 basic sites and 1 group site (maximum 40 people)
Maximum RV length: 30 feet
Fee: $ for basic sites; $$ for group site
Maximum stay: 14 days
Elevation: 8,600 feet
Road conditions: Gravel
Management: Ferron Ranger District, 115 W. Canyon Rd., PO Box 310, Ferron, UT 84523; (435) 384-2372; www.fs.usda.gov/main/mantilasal/home
Reservations: For the group site only, call (877) 444-6777 or TDD (877) 833-6777; www.recreation.gov
Activities: Fishing, canoeing and kayaking, off-highway driving, mountain biking, and picnicking
Restrictions: Horses not allowed
Season: Late May through October
Finding the campground: From the junction of US 89 and UT 31 in Fairview, head northeast on UT 31, a paved road that climbs an 8 percent grade. After 8.4 miles you'll reach the junction with UT 264 to Scofield. Turn left (east) onto UT 264, then curve immediately around to the north. You'll reach a large parking area with vault toilets and a sign for Skyline Drive—a 100-mile-long Scenic Byway that follows the crest of the Wasatch Plateau—after 0.2 mile. The road forks just after the

parking area and soon turns to gravel. Go right (northeast) on FR 124. (Left goes to US 6 in 28 miles via Skyline Road North.) After 1.1 miles go right on FR 224. A sign points the way to Gooseberry Campground. (There's another sign pointing to Gooseberry Reservoir in 1.5 miles. It not only leads to the reservoir, but the Gooseberry Reservoir Campground, too.) Enter the Gooseberry Campground in another 0.5 mile.

About the campground: Set in a grove of aspens and conifers, this campground offers some sites with a nice view of Gooseberry Lake. There are several dirt roads to explore, by either ATV or mountain bike. One of the roads leads to the 90-acre lake where anglers vie for stocked rainbow trout and wild cutthroats. Wildlife watchers should keep an eye out for abundant animal life, including the usually elusive badger.

205 Flat Canyon

Location: In the Manti-La Sal National Forest, approximately 13 miles east of Fairview
GPS: N39 38.830'/W111 15.586'
Facilities: Fire pits, picnic tables, BBQ grills, and vault toilets
Sites: 12 basic sites and 1 group site (maximum 50 people)
Maximum RV length: 30 feet
Fee: $ for basic sites; $$ for group site
Maximum stay: 14 days
Elevation: 8,800 feet
Road conditions: Paved
Management: Ferron Ranger District, 115 W. Canyon Rd., PO Box 310, Ferron, UT 84523; (435) 384-2372; www.fs.usda.gov/main/mantilasal/home
Reservations: Call (877) 444-6777 or TDD (877) 833-6777; www.recreation.gov
Activities: Fishing and picnicking
Season: Mid-June through early September
Finding the campground: From the junction of US 89 and UT 31 in Fairview, head northeast on UT 31, a paved road that climbs an 8 percent grade. After 8.4 miles you'll reach the junction with UT 264 to Scofield. Turn left (east) onto paved UT 264, then curve immediately around to the north. You'll reach a large parking area with vault toilets and a sign for Skyline Drive—a 100-mile-long Scenic Byway that follows the crest of the Wasatch Plateau—after 0.2 mile. Continue driving UT 264 another 4.2 miles to the campground, which is on your right (south).
About the campground: Partially shaded by pines, this small campground has a group site that overlooks Boulger Reservoir, a fine place for fishing. If you drive, it's just over a mile away; if you walk the unmaintained trail, it's just 0.5 mile. Other nearby fishing spots include Electric Lake and Beaver Dam Reservoir, both about 2 miles distant.

206 Lake Canyon Recreation Area

Location: In the Manti–La Sal National Forest, approximately 18 miles southeast of Fairview
GPS: N39 34.915'/W111 15.087'
Facilities: Fire pits, picnic tables, and vault toilets; no garbage service (pack it out)
Sites: 47 double sites and 5 group sites (maximum varies from 30 to 150 people)
Maximum RV length: Any
Fee: $ for double sites; $$ to $$$$$ for group sites
Maximum stay: 14 days
Elevation: 8,900 feet
Road conditions: Paved to the campground, then gravel
Management: Ferron Ranger District, 115 W. Canyon Rd., PO Box 310, Ferron, UT 84523; (435) 384-2372; www.fs.usda.gov/main/mantilasal/home
Reservations: For group sites and 4 of the double sites, call (877) 444-6777 or TDD (877) 833-6777; www.recreation.gov
Activities: Fishing, ATVing, and picnicking
Restrictions: ATVs on designated trails only
Season: June through October
Finding the campground: From the junction of US 89 and UT 31 in Fairview, head northeast on UT 31, a paved road that climbs an 8 percent grade. Also called Energy Loop, UT 31 is a beautiful drive that tops out on the Wasatch Plateau. After 8.4 miles you'll reach the junction with UT 264 to Scofield. Continue driving UT 31 for just under another 10 miles to the campground turnoff, which is on your right (south). Millers Flat Road (FR 014) is just past the Mammoth Discovery Stop. A sign points the way to Joes Valley Reservoir. Just past the gate FR 014 turns to gravel, and you enter the very spread out campground.
About the campground: Located between the Huntington and Cleveland Reservoirs, this expansive campground is a mecca for ATVers and those who enjoy fishing. It's also a nice place to relax and enjoy life among the aspens, conifers, sagebrush plains—and wildlife too. Look for deer and boreal toads, and in the summer enjoy wildflower-filled meadows.

Castle Country

Barren, bleak, and unoccupied are probably the words most often used to describe what is known as Castle Country, but the place is much more than that to those who spend time exploring its lovely realms. Travel around the region and you'll find a world of towering sandstone walls and monoliths, strange formations—some of which do indeed look like castles—and a whole lot more. In addition, there are quiet oases of cottonwoods and water that attract a variety of animal life; tall forests and open meadows where you can find moose and solitude; and places where ancient drawings and etchings lure visitors from all around. In addition to being what I'd rather call remote and unencumbered, Castle Country embraces part of the Manti–La Sal National Forest, where cool, lush, high-elevation refuges provide places for folks to come and fish, ride their OHVs, hike, ride horseback, photograph vistas that beg to be captured on film, or just sit and enjoy the shade and scenery.

One of Utah's nine travel regions, Castle Country is located pretty much in the heart of the state, with just a little push to the east. Bordered by four state travel regions—Dinosaurland, Mountainland, Panoramaland, and Canyonlands—it encompasses all of Emery and Carbon Counties for a total of 5,915 square miles. Composed of five distinct geologic areas—the Wasatch Plateau, the San Rafael Swell, the East Tavaputs Plateau, the San Rafael Desert, and the Mancos Shale Lowlands—its fifteen campgrounds are found in a potpourri of settings. Sites range from the cool realms of the national forest, to the water-blessed likes of several state parks, to the strange pillars and knobs of Goblin Valley State Park, and to the amazing sandstone pillars and walls of the San Rafael Swell.

Fortunately, there's a campground at the San Rafael Swell. Located along the San Rafael River and close to hundreds of climbs (you can see some of the routes from there), the place is a marvelous geologic wonder. Though there are moderate routes for climbers, the majority of climbs are for the more experienced. The San Rafael Swell is also a popular place to view prehistoric rock art—the Buckhorn Wash Pictograph Panel is a must-see. It's believed to have been created about 2,000 years ago by members of the Barrier Canyon Culture. Distinctive features of this culture's rock art include life-size anthropomorphic figures that lack arms and legs. Broad shoulders, tapered trunks, and bug eyes are also characteristic. In addition, you'll see rays, crowns, and dots above the figures' heads, with many of the figures accompanied by birds, insects, snakes, and dogs.

At the very southern edge of Castle Country you'll find Goblin Valley State Park, with its unique sandstone formations and numerous claims to fame: The state park has been featured in various films, including *City Slickers II*.

The northwest corner of the region offers the most campgrounds, with the state park system contributing two lake-blessed sites. Visitors to Huntington and Scofield have the opportunity to fish, engage in various water sports, and so on.

There's no doubt that Castle Country offers a wide variety of activities to enjoy and wonderful places to see on a year-round basis. Though some of the campgrounds are closed in winter, the areas can still be visited and enjoyed by those with a desire to engage in winter sports.

For more information contact the Castle Country Travel Region, 90 N. 100 East, PO Box 1037, Price, UT 84501; (435) 637-3009 or (800) 842-0789; fax (435) 637-7010; www.utahtravelcenter.com/travelregions/castlecountry.htm.

		Total Sites	Group Sites	Hook-up Sites	Hookups	Max. RV Length	Dump Station	Toilets	Showers	Drinking Water	ADA Compliant	Fees	Reservations	Recreation
207	Madsen Bay	37	1	36	WE	35	•	F		•	•	$$-$$$$$	•	FBSHLK
208	Mountain View	33				20	•	F	•	•		$$	•	FBSHLK
209	Fish Creek	7				None		V				$		FHM
210	Price Canyon	18				35		V		•		$		H
211	Old Folks Flat	9	5			30		F		•		$-$$$$$	•	FH
212	Forks of Huntington	6	1			25		V		•		$-$$$$	•	FH
213	Bear Creek	29				25		F & V		•		$	•	F
214	Huntington State Park	25		5	WES	35	•	F	•	•	•	$$-$$$	•	FSBHLK
215	Indian Creek	7	7			40		V		•	•	$$$-$$$$$	•	KMOHF
216	Potters Pond	19	1			35		V				$-$$$$$	•	KMOFHR
217	Joes Valley	50	1			40		V		•		$-$$$$$	•	FBLHMK
218	Millsite State Park	20		10	WE	45	•	F	•	•	•	$$-$$$	•	FSBHLKMG
219	San Rafael Bridge	23				35		V				$		HCM
220	Green River State Park	42	2	34	E	45	•	F	•	•		$$-$$$$$	•	FKGLB
221	Goblin Valley State Park	35	1			40	•	F	•	•	•	$$-$$$$$	•	HM

Hookup: W = Water, E = Electric, S = Sewer
Recreation: H = Hiking, C = Rock Climbing, M = Mountain Biking, S = Swimming, F = Fishing, B = Boating, L = Boat Launch, O = Off-highway Driving, R = Horseback Riding, K = Kayaking and Canoeing, G = Golf
Toilets: F = Flush, V = Vault, C = Chemical
Per-night campsite cost: $ = $10 or less $$ = $11 to $20 $$$ = $21 to 30 $$$$ = $31 to $40 $$$$$ = $41 and higher

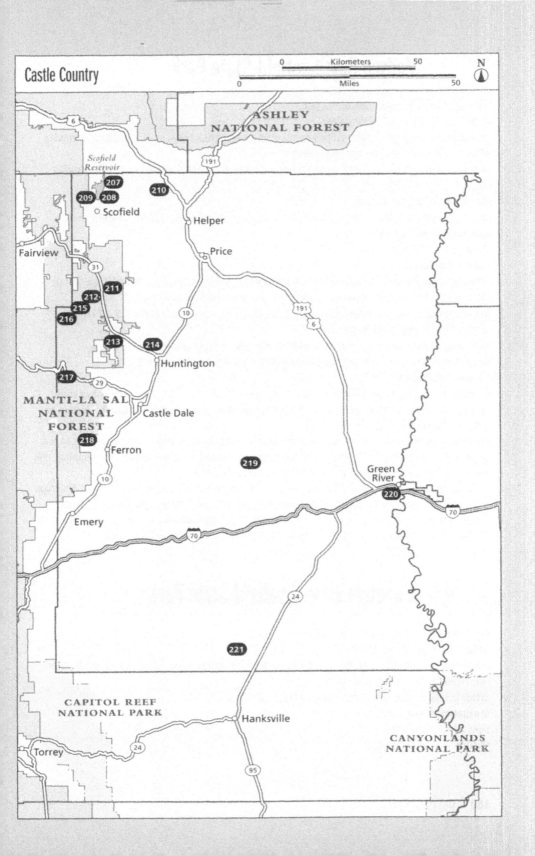

Castle Country

Kilometers 0 — 50
Miles 0 — 50

N

ASHLEY
NATIONAL FOREST

Scofield Reservoir

207
209 208
○ Scofield

210

Helper

Price

Fairview

31

211
212
215
216
213 214

Huntington

217
29

MANTI-LA SAL
NATIONAL
FOREST

Castle Dale

218
Ferron

10

Emery

219

Green River

220

70

70

24

221

CAPITOL REEF
NATIONAL PARK

Hanksville

Torrey
24

95

CANYONLANDS
NATIONAL PARK

207 Madsen Bay: Scofield State Park

Location: About 7 miles north of Scofield
GPS: N39 48.949'/W111 08.198'
Facilities: Fire pits, picnic tables, flush toilets, ADA sites, partial hookups, dump station, drinking water, fish cleaning station, and boat ramp
Sites: 34 partial-hookup sites, 2 partial-hookup double sites, and 1 group site (maximum 50 people)
Maximum RV length: 35 feet
Fee: $$ for partial-hookup sites, $$$ for partial-hookup double sites; $$$$$ for group site
Maximum stay: 14 days
Elevation: 7,600 feet
Road conditions: Paved
Management: Scofield State Park, PO Box 166, Price, UT 84501; (435) 448-9449 (summer); (435) 687-2491 (winter); www.stateparks.utah.gov/park/scofield-state-park
Reservations: In the Salt Lake area, call (801) 322-3770; elsewhere, (800) 322-3770; http://utahstateparks.reserveamerica.com
Activities: Fishing, boating, swimming, waterskiing, hiking, photography, and picnicking
Restrictions: OHVs not allowed; campground gate closed from 10 p.m. to 6 a.m.
Season: May through October
Finding the campground: From the junction of US 6 and UT 96, about 17 miles northwest of Helper, head west and then south on UT 96 for 8.9 miles to the campground turnoff, which is on the west side of the road.
About the campground: One of two campgrounds at Scofield State Park, Madsen Bay sits in the open on the north shore of Scofield Lake and offers the largest sites. A forested tent-camping area and a wildlife interpretive area are located a short distance away.

Located in the Manti–La Sal Mountains of the Wasatch Plateau, 2,800-acre Scofield Reservoir is an excellent place for boating and is known for its year-round fishing potential. One of Utah's prime fisheries, the cool waters are ideal for rainbow and cutthroat trout as well as crawfish. Below Scofield Dam a footbridge leads to hiking and fishing areas along Lower Fish Creek.

208 Mountain View: Scofield State Park

Location: About 6 miles north of Scofield
GPS: N39 47.455'/W111 07.935'
Facilities: Fire pits, picnic tables, tent pads, flush toilets, showers, dump station, drinking water, fish cleaning station and boat ramp
Sites: 33 basic sites, including 6 sites best for tents
Maximum RV length: 20 feet
Fee: $$ for basic sites
Maximum stay: 14 days

Elevation: 7,700 feet
Road conditions: Paved
Management: Scofield State Park, PO Box 166, Price, UT 84501; (435) 448-9449 (summer); (435) 687-2491 (winter); www.stateparks.utah.gov/park/scofield-state-park
Reservations: In the Salt Lake area, call (801) 322-3770; elsewhere, (800) 322-3770; http://utahstateparks.reserveamerica.com
Activities: Fishing, boating, swimming, waterskiing, hiking, photography, and picnicking
Restrictions: OHVs not allowed; campground gate closed from 10 p.m. to 6 a.m.
Season: May through October
Finding the campground: From the junction of US 6 and UT 96, about 17 miles northwest of Helper, head west and then south on UT 96 for 10.5 miles to the campground turnoff, which is on the west side of the road.
About the campground: The smaller of the two campgrounds at Scofield State Park, Mountain View's campers rest parking-lot-style next to their neighbors. The small sites are partially shaded with aspens and conifers, and there's a boat ramp nearby. The plus to this campground is that it offers a shower, whereas the other one, Madsen Bay, does not.

Located in the Manti–La Sal Mountains of the Wasatch Plateau, 2,800-acre Scofield Reservoir is an excellent place for boating and is known for its year-round fishing potential. One of Utah's prime fisheries, the cool waters are ideal for rainbow and cutthroat trout as well as crawfish. Below Scofield Dam, a footbridge leads to hiking and fishing areas along Lower Fish Creek.

209 Fish Creek

Location: In the Manti–La Sal National Forest, about 5 miles northwest of Scofield
GPS: N39 46.481'/W111 12.120'
Facilities: Fire pits, picnic tables, and vault toilet; no trash service (pack it out)
Sites: 7 basic sites (best for tents)
Maximum RV length: None
Fee: $ for basic sites
Maximum stay: 14 days
Elevation: 7,700 feet
Road conditions: Dirt
Management: Ferron-Price Ranger Districts, 599 W. Price River Dr., Price; (435) 637-2817; www.fs.usda.gov/main/mantilasal/home
Reservations: None
Activities: Fishing, hiking, mountain biking, photography, and picnicking
Season: June through September
Finding the campground: From the small town of Scofield, go north on an unsigned paved road that follows along the east shore of Scofield Lake. You'll travel for 3.5 miles before the road turns to dirt. After another 0.2 mile you'll reach a fork to the Fish Creek Trailhead; it's on the left (west). Drive the road—which can be impassable when it's wet, and impassable to passenger cars at any time of year—for another 1.7 miles until it ends at the campground and the trailhead.

About the campground: Though primitive, this spot makes a nice place for tent campers set on exploring the gentle realms of the Fish Creek drainage via the Fish Creek National Recreation Trail. It's also a wonderful place for anglers set on catching trout.

Aspens and conifers decorate the periphery of the campground, which is in a mostly open setting and provides good views of Fish Creek. Look for animal life while you are here. Bears live in the area, so be sure to keep a clean camp; there are also opportunities to observe moose, elk, mule deer, mountain lions, beavers, and a whole lot more.

210 Price Canyon

Location: About 13 miles northwest of Helper
GPS: N39 45.615' / W110 54.960'
Facilities: Fire pits, picnic tables, drinking water, and vault toilets
Sites: 18 basic sites
Maximum RV length: 35 feet
Fee: $ for basic sites
Maximum stay: 14 days
Elevation: 7,800 feet
Road conditions: Paved to the campground, then gravel
Management: Bureau of Land Management, Price Field Office, 125 S. 600 West, Price; (435) 636-3600; www.blm.gov/ut/st/en/fo/price.html
Reservations: None
Activities: Hiking and picnicking
Season: June through October
Finding the campground: From the junction of US 191 and US 6, about 3 miles north of Helper, drive northwest on US 6 for 6.7 miles to the Price Canyon Recreation Area turnoff, which is on the south side of the road. Travel this paved, winding, steep, and narrow road for 3.2 miles to a T junction. You'll find day-use sites to your right and overnight campsites to your left; the road is gravel at this point.
About the campground: Situated among oaks and pines, this is a nice, high-elevation campground with views of nearby mountains and canyons. There's an even better view from a 1-mile-long trail to a nearby butte. The Bristlecone Ridge Trail climbs past oak, mahogany, and both ponderosa and bristlecone pine trees, gaining more than 600 feet in its quest for the summit.

211 Old Folks Flat

Location: In the Manti–La Sal National Forest, about 21 miles northwest of Huntington
GPS: N39 32.307' / W111 09.602'
Facilities: Fire pits, picnic tables, drinking water, and flush toilets
Sites: 4 basic sites and 5 group sites (maximum varies from 20 to 60 people)
Maximum RV length: 30 feet
Fee: $ for basic sites; $$$ to $$$$$ for group sites

Maximum stay: 14 days
Elevation: 8,000 feet
Road conditions: Paved to the campground, then dirt
Management: Ferron Ranger District, 115 W. Canyon Rd., PO Box 310, Ferron, UT 84523; (435) 384-2372; www.fs.usda.gov/main/mantilasal/home
Reservations: Call (877) 444-6777 or TDD (877) 833-6777; www.recreation.gov
Activities: Fishing, hiking, and picnicking
Restrictions: ATVs/OHVs and horses not allowed
Season: Mid-May through early September
Finding the campground: From the junction of UT 10 and UT 31 in Huntington, travel northwest on paved UT 31 for 20.5 miles to the campground, which is on your right.
About the campground: Set among aspens and spruce, this small campground caters to those wanting group sites. A nature trail leads into the canyon, and the fishing in Huntington Creek is good for rainbow, cutthroat, and brown trout.
Note: The Seeley Fire of 2012 closed the campground in 2013 for an indeterminate period. Although the campground wasn't burned, the area suffered from post-fire flooding. Also, there are two group campgrounds—Chute and Bridges—north of Old Folks Flat. They may or may not reopen in the coming years. Call to check its status.

212 Forks of Huntington

Location: In the Manti–La Sal National Forest, approximately 18 miles northwest of Huntington
GPS: N39 30.078'/W111 09.569'
Facilities: Fire pits, picnic tables, drinking water, and vault toilets; no garbage service (pack it out)
Sites: 5 basic sites and 1 group site (maximum 50 people)
Maximum RV length: 25 feet
Fee: $ for basic sites; $$$$ for group site
Maximum stay: 14 days
Elevation: 7,700 feet
Road conditions: Paved to the campground, then dirt
Management: Ferron Ranger District, 115 W. Canyon Rd., PO Box 310, Ferron, UT 84523; (435) 384-2372; www.fs.usda.gov/main/mantilasal/home
Reservations: For the group site only, call (877) 444-6777 or TDD (877) 833-6777; www .recreation.gov
Activities: Fishing, hiking, and picnicking
Season: June through October
Finding the campground: From the junction of UT 10 and UT 31 in Huntington, travel northwest on paved UT 31 for 17.7 miles to the campground, which is on your left.
About the campground: Sites are located along the rushing waters of Left Fork Huntington Creek. Fir and spruce serve to shade the small sites, accessible to only the smallest of RVs. Anglers can vie for trout, while hikers can check out the Left Fork of Huntington Creek National Recreation Trail. The trail is 4.5 miles long and gains about 650 feet en route to the confluence of Scad Valley Creek. See *Hiking Utah* by Dave Hall for more information.

Note: The Seeley Fire of 2012 closed the campground in 2013 for an indeterminate time. Although the campground wasn't burned, the area suffered from post-fire flooding. Also, there is one group campground—Little Bear—south of Forks of Huntington. It may or may not reopen in the coming years. Call for status.

213 Bear Creek

Location: About 9 miles northwest of Huntington
GPS: N39 23.571'/W111 05.953'
Facilities: Fire pits, picnic tables, drinking water, and flush and vault toilets
Sites: 29 basic sites
Maximum RV length: 25 feet
Fee: $ for basic sites
Maximum stay: 14 days
Elevation: 6,600 feet
Road conditions: Paved to the campground, then dirt
Management: Emery County Recreation Department, PO Box 531, Castle Dale, UT 84513; (435) 381-2108; www.emerycounty.com/rec/campground.htm
Reservations: Reserve online at www.emerycounty.com/rec/campground.htm
Activities: Fishing, volleyball, and picnicking
Restrictions: ATVs and motorcycles not allowed
Season: May through September
Finding the campground: From the junction of UT 10 and UT 31 in Huntington, travel northwest on paved UT 31 for 8.7 miles to the campground, which is on your left.
About the campground: Cottonwoods and other deciduous trees shade the campsites at this county park. There's a nice picnic area with green grass and a volleyball court, too. Bear Creek flows only 30 feet from the campground and offers the chance to hook rainbow or brook trout. On a special note, beware, there is no turnaround if you head down the road signed "Dead End."

214 Huntington State Park

Location: About 2 miles north of Huntington
GPS: N39 20.837'/W110 56.585'
Facilities: Fire pits, picnic tables, ADA site, partial and full hookups, flush toilets, showers, drinking water, dump station, boat ramp, and boat docks
Sites: 20 basic sites, 2 partial-hookup sites, and 3 full-hookup sites
Maximum RV length: 35 feet
Fee: $$ for basic and partial-hookup sites; $$$ for full-hookup sites
Maximum stay: 14 days
Elevation: 5,800 feet
Road conditions: Paved

Water activities are popular at Huntington State Park.

Management: Huntington State Park, PO Box 1343, Huntington, UT 84528; (435) 687-2491; www.stateparks.utah.gov/park/huntington-state-park

Reservations: In the Salt Lake area, call (801) 322-3770; elsewhere, (800) 322-3770; http://utahstateparks.reserveamerica.com

Activities: Fishing, swimming, boating, birding, hiking, and picnicking

Restrictions: Campground gate closed from 10 p.m. to 6 a.m.

Season: Mid-April through mid October (camping allowed in the day-use parking area during winter)

Finding the campground: From the junction of UT 10 and UT 31 in Huntington, travel north on UT 10 for 1.7 miles to its junction with Mohrland Road on the left (west). Drive west/northwest on paved Mohrland Road for 0.3 mile to the entrance station on your left (southwest).

About the campground: Green grass and shade trees blanket the north shore of Huntington Reservoir, one of Utah's finest warm-water fisheries. Anglers can hook largemouth bass and bluegills. Crawdad fishing is especially popular with children.

Migrating birds will delight birders, while the boat ramp provides access for all types of watercraft. The warm water makes the reservoir a popular place for waterskiing and swimming. Service roads around the reservoir offer 2 miles of hiking and jogging trails. OHVs are not allowed to unload in the park; there are areas just outside the park, however, where they are permitted.

RVers with newer RVs with slide-outs should note that the pull-through sites here are too narrow; be sure to request a back-in site if you have a slide-out.

215 Indian Creek

Location: In the Manti–La Sal National Forest, about 25 miles northwest of Castle Dale
GPS: N39 26.514'/W111 14.257'
Facilities: Fire pits, picnic tables, ADA site, drinking water, and vault toilets; no trash service (pack it out)
Sites: 7 group sites (maximum varies from 50 to 70 people)
Maximum RV length: 40 feet
Fee: $$$ to $$$$$ for group sites
Maximum stay: 14 days
Elevation: 8,700 feet
Road conditions: Dirt
Management: Ferron Ranger District, 115 W. Canyon Rd., PO Box 310, Ferron, UT 84523; (435) 384-2372; www.fs.usda.gov/main/mantilasal/home
Reservations: Call (877) 444-6777 or TDD (877) 833-6777; www.recreation.gov
Activities: Canoeing, mountain biking, OHV riding (trails nearby) hiking, fishing, and picnicking
Restrictions: Horses and OHVs not allowed
Season: Memorial Day through October
Finding the campground: From the junction of UT 10 and UT 29, about 2 miles north of Castle Dale, head northwest on paved UT 29 for 11.7 miles to a junction. Turn right (north) onto Cottonwood Canyon Road (also known as FR 040). The paved road turns to gravel in a few miles. It is 13 miles from UT 29 to the campground.
About the campground: Blessed with aspens, this high-elevation site caters to groups. Seven group sites can handle anywhere from thirty to seventy people. Reservations can be made for sites; when not reserved they are first-come, first-served. Nearby Potters Pond offers great canoeing and rainbow trout fishing. The expansive Arapeen OHV Trail System is close by and offers more than 350 miles of designated, well-maintained trails for off-road vehicles.

216 Potters Pond

Location: In the Manti–La Sal National Forest, about 30 miles southeast of Fairview
GPS: N39 27.017'/W111 16.129'
Facilities: Fire pits, picnic tables, stove stands, and vault toilets; hitching rails at some sites; no trash service (pack it out)
Sites: 3 basic sites, 11 double sites, 4 equestrian sites, and 1 group site (maximum 50 people)
Maximum RV length: 35 feet
Fee: $ for basic sites; $$ for double sites; $$ to $$$ for equestrian sites; $$$$$ for group site
Maximum stay: 14 days
Elevation: 8,900 feet
Road conditions: Dirt
Management: Ferron Ranger District, 115 W. Canyon Rd., PO Box 310, Ferron, UT 84523; (435) 384-2372; www.fs.usda.gov/main/mantilasal/home
Reservations: Call (877) 444-6777 or TDD (877) 833-6777; www.recreation.gov

Activities: Kayaking, mountain biking, OHV riding, fishing, hiking, horseback riding, and picnicking
Season: June through October
Finding the campground: From the junction of US 89 and UT 31 in Fairview, head northeast on UT 31, a paved road that climbs an 8 percent grade. Also called Energy Loop, UT 31 is a beautiful drive that tops out on the Wasatch Plateau. After 8.4 miles you'll reach the junction with UT 264 to Scofield. Continue driving UT 31 for just under another 10 miles to the turnoff for the Lake Canyon Recreation Area campground, which is on your right (south). Millers Flat Road (FR 014) is just past the Mammoth Discovery Stop. A sign points the way to Joes Valley Reservoir. Just past the gate the paved road turns to gravel and you enter the Lake Canyon Recreation Area. Continue driving through it, traveling south 11 miles to the Potters Pond Campground turnoff. From FR 014 turn right (west) onto FR 271 and drive the gravel road 0.8 mile to the fee station.
About the campground: Located in a high-mountain valley, there are two Potters Ponds, popular for fishing for rainbow trout. There are many pines around the spacious campground, as well as grasses and summer wildflowers. Mountain bikers and ATV riders will enjoy the expansive Arapeen OHV Trail System, which includes more than 350 miles of designated, well-maintained trails.

217 Joes Valley

Location: In the Manti–La Sal National Forest, approximately 22 miles northwest of Castle Dale
GPS: N39 17.805'/W111 17.845'
Facilities: Fire pits, picnic tables, ADA sites, drinking water, and vault toilets; boat ramp, fish cleaning station, and marina nearby. The marina offers watercraft, ATV, and bike rentals, supplies, a cafe, and fishing tackle.
Sites: 34 basic sites, 15 double sites, and 1 group site (maximum 100 people)
Maximum RV length: 40 feet
Fee: $ for basic sites; $$ for double sites; $$$$$ for group site
Maximum stay: 14 days
Elevation: 7,200 feet
Road conditions: Paved
Management: Ferron Ranger District, 115 W. Canyon Rd., PO Box 310, Ferron, UT 84523; (435) 384-2372; www.fs.usda.gov/main/mantilasal/home
Reservations: Call (877) 444-6777 or TDD (877) 833-6777; www.recreation.gov
Activities: Fishing, waterskiing, boating, hiking, mountain biking, and picnicking
Restrictions: Horses not allowed
Season: May through October
Finding the campground: From the junction of UT 10 and UT 57, about 2 miles south of Castle Dale, drive northwest on paved UT 57 for 6.7 miles to its junction with UT 29. Now turn left (west) onto UT 29 for an additional 14.8 miles to the end of UT 29. Turn left (south) onto FR 170 and drive 0.1 mile to FR 137, where you will make another left (east) and enter the campground.
About the campground: Situated on a bluff overlooking Joes Valley Reservoir and nearly surrounded by mountains, this campground is decorated with juniper, pinyon pine, and ponderosa pine trees. The lake offers anglers the chance to hook rainbow and cutthroat trout, and gives water enthusiasts the opportunity to enjoy a multitude of water sports. A group site is located near the reservoir, about 1 mile to the northeast.

218 Millsite State Park

Location: About 4 miles west of Ferron
GPS: N39 05.476' / W111 11.606'
Facilities: Fire pits, picnic tables, ADA site, partial hookups, flush toilets, showers, drinking water, dump station, boat ramp, boat docks, and adjacent golf course
Sites: 10 basic sites and 10 partial-hookup sites
Maximum RV length: 45 feet
Fee: $$ for basic sites; $$$ for partial-hookup sites
Maximum stay: 14 days
Elevation: 6,200 feet
Road conditions: Paved
Management: Millsite State Park, c/o Huntington State Park, PO Box 1343, Huntington, UT 84528; (435) 384-2552; www.stateparks.utah.gov/parks/millsite
Reservations: In the Salt Lake area, call (801) 322-3770; elsewhere, (800) 322-3770; http://utahstateparks.reserveamerica.com
Activities: Fishing, swimming, boating, hiking, and picnicking; golfing and unlimited mountain biking opportunities nearby
Restrictions: Campground gate closed from 10 p.m. to 6 a.m.
Season: Year-round
Finding the campground: From the junction of UT 10 and Canyon Road in downtown Ferron, head west on paved Canyon Road. Signs for the state park and Ferron Reservoir point the way. Travel 4.3 miles to the campground entrance, which is on your right (north).
About the campground: Located on the southwest shore of Millsite Reservoir, a 435-acre jewel with majestic cliffs towering 2,000 feet above, campsites are shaded by a smattering of poplar trees and landscaped lawns. However, a large natural section contains native plants with a nature trail interpreting the vegetation.

Water activities are popular, with visitors indulging in swimming, sailing, Jet Skiing, and waterskiing. Anglers fish from a boat or the shoreline, netting cutthroat and rainbow trout. OHVs are not allowed in the park, but there are many areas nearby in which to travel off road. Golfers will find Ferron City's challenging nine-hole golf course adjacent to the park. Wildlife is abundant, especially in winter, when you can enjoy ice fishing and possibly see deer, elk, and moose.

219 San Rafael Bridge

Location: In the San Rafael Swell, about 49 miles northwest of Green River
GPS: N39 04.758' / W110 40.028'
Facilities: Fire pits, tent pads, picnic tables, and vault toilets
Sites: 17 basic sites and 6 equestrian sites
Maximum RV length: 35 feet
Fee: $ for basic and equestrian sites
Maximum stay: 14 days
Elevation: 5,100 feet

Road conditions: Gravel
Management: Bureau of Land Management, Price Field Office, 125 S. 600 West, Price; (435) 636-3600; www.blm.gov/ut/st/en/fo/price.html
Reservations: None
Activities: Hiking, rock climbing, mountain biking, photography, and picnicking
Season: Year-round
Finding the campground: From Green River drive I-70 west for approximately 29 miles, getting off at ranch exit 131. A sign points the way to Buckhorn Draw, the Buckhorn Wash Pictograph Panel, and the Wedge Overlook. The gravel road immediately curves around to the east and parallels the interstate for a few miles before heading north; it may be impassable during wet weather. After 18.9 miles you'll reach the southern campground. Continue a few hundred yards and you'll cross a bridge over the San Rafael River that leads to the northern campground and points beyond.
About the campground: Located on both the south and north sides of the river, this is a nice spot with tent pads and plenty of room, though you'll want to beware of biting flies in early summer. The campground on the south end offers twelve sites; the north side campground has five sites as well as six equestrian sites.

The San Rafael Swell is an excellent place for hiking (with map and compass in hand), mountain biking, or rock climbing. There are many climbs here, ranging from moderate to very difficult, and from traditional climbs to sport routes.

A must-see is the Buckhorn Wash Pictograph Panel, which is about 5 miles across the bridge and up Buckhorn Wash. The pictographs, fine art created by the Barrier Canyon Culture, are believed to have been made 2,000 or more years ago. Distinctive features of this culture's rock art include life-size anthropomorphic figures lacking arms or legs. These figures have broad shoulders, tapered trunks, and bug eyes. There are dots, rays, and crowns above their heads, with many of the figures accompanied by birds, insects, snakes, and dogs.

220 Green River State Park

Location: About 0.5 mile south of Green River
GPS: N38 59.385'/W110 09.265'
Facilities: Fire pits, picnic tables, tent pads, electric hookups, drinking water, flush toilets, showers, dump station, and boat launch
Sites: 6 basic sites, 34 electric-hookup sites, 2 group sites (maximum 30 and 50 people, respectively), and 1 cabin
Maximum RV length: 45 feet
Fee: $$ for basic sites; $$$ for electric-hookup sites; $$$$$ for group sites and cabin
Maximum stay: 14 days
Elevation: 4,100 feet
Road conditions: Paved
Management: Green River State Park, PO Box 637, Green River, UT 84525; (435) 564-3633; www.stateparks.utah.gov/park/green-river-state-park
Reservations: In the Salt Lake area, call (801) 322-3770; elsewhere, (800) 322-3770; http://utahstateparks.reserveamerica.com
Activities: Fishing, rafting, kayaking, wildlife watching, golfing, and picnicking

Restrictions: Campground gate closed from 10 p.m. to 6 a.m.

Season: Year-round

Finding the campground: From the junction of Main Street and Green River Boulevard in Green River, head south on paved Green River Boulevard for 0.4 mile; make a left (east) at the signed entrance.

About the campground: Shaded by stately cottonwoods and lush Russian olive trees, this campground is a haven for those interested in watching wildlife (look for owls, egrets, beavers, and much more), rafting the Green River, playing a little golf, or using the site as a base camp to explore other nearby areas. The campground is a favorite embarkation point for river trips through Labyrinth and Stillwater Canyons. In addition, a nine-hole golf course is challenging and fun for all levels of golfers.

221 Goblin Valley State Park

Location: About 31 miles north of Hanksville

GPS: N38 34.675'/W110 42.440'

Facilities: Fire pits, covered picnic tables with two-sided shelters, ADA site, tent pads, flush toilets, showers, dump station, and drinking water

Sites: 24 basic sites, 10 walk-in tent sites, 1 group site (maximum 35 people), and 2 yurts

Maximum RV length: 40 feet

Fee: $$ for basic and walk-in tent sites; $$$$$ for group site and yurts

Maximum stay: 14 days

Elevation: 5,000 feet

Road conditions: Paved

Management: Goblin Valley State Park, c/o Green River State Park, PO Box 637, Green River, UT 84525; (435) 275-4584; www.stateparks.utah.gov/park/goblin-valley-state-park

Reservations: In the Salt Lake area, call (801) 322-3770; elsewhere, (800) 322-3770; http://utahstateparks.reserveamerica.com

Activities: Hiking, mountain biking, photography, and picnicking

Restrictions: Campground gate closed from 10 p.m. to 6 a.m.

Season: Year-round

Finding the campground: From the junction of UT 24 and 95 in Hanksville, drive north on UT 24 for 19.3 miles. Now turn left (west) where a sign points the way to Goblin Valley. This paved road is sometimes called Goblin Valley Road (also known as Temple Mountain Road). Continue for 5.2 miles, then make another left (south) at another sign for Goblin Valley. Proceed on the paved road for 6.4 miles to the campground entrance station.

About the campground: Goblins and unique rock formations and sculptures complement the scene at this wonderful campground. Goblin Valley is a fantasyland of eroded sandstone formations, some of which look like mushrooms while others suggest mischievous folklore goblins. While mountain biking is permitted only on the roadways and not on park trails, there are plenty of nearby roads to explore. In addition, there are 5 miles of marked trails here, as well as self-discovery hiking throughout the Valley of Goblins.

If you want to explore a wonderful slot canyon, drive 8.8 miles to the Wild Horse Canyon Trailhead; a hike up Wild Horse Canyon and down Bell Canyon makes a great 8-mile loop.

Gorgeous scenery from Goblin Valley State Park.

Color Country

Color Country is, well, full of color! It's a vast and varied place, where rainbow hues tend to be commonplace, and campers come to share in the glory.

Located in southwestern Utah, Color Country snuggles up to Arizona and Nevada to the south and west, respectively, while the state travel regions known as Panoramaland and Canyonlands sit to the north and east. One of the state's nine travel regions, Color Country encompasses a mix of five distinct counties—Beaver, Iron, Washington, Garfield, and Kane—for a total of 17,370 square miles. The largest of the state's travel regions, the place is composed of a wonderful world of national parks, national monuments, national recreation areas, state parks, national forests, and other public lands. Fortunately, sixty-three public campgrounds provide a place to camp while exploring its realms.

The region stretches across two distinct geologic areas: the Great Basin and Colorado Plateau. Here you'll find tall mountains, shimmering lakes, sandstone cliffs, lofty plateaus, and deep, often narrow canyons. With this sort of geology, travelers can expect to wind up and down many a roadway. Sure, there are lots of straight and fairly level roads, but you'll find just as many—or perhaps even more—with 15-mile-per-hour turns and signs prompting drivers to use low gears instead of their brakes. No doubt there may even come a time when you are poking up a 14 percent grade or two.

Zion National Park is probably the most visited place in this area, and while it's definitely worth a visit, it isn't the only place worthy of your time. Perhaps it's just the place everyone thinks they should see when they pass through southwest Utah. In addition to Zion, however, is one of Utah's finest national parks, Bryce Canyon. Here you'll find a fairyland of fun, a potpourri offering a remarkable display of fascinating orange, red, and pink hoodoos, and a whole lot more.

In addition to the national parks, campers have access (though in summer only) to the likes of Cedar Breaks National Monument; year-round (though it's often cold in winter) you can enjoy the great expanse of one of Utah's most beautiful national monuments, Grand Staircase–Escalante. Visitors to this big (1.7 million acres), awesome place can see time in the making as they marvel at "stairsteps" leading from one geologic formation to the next.

Utah offers a number of wonderful state parks, many of them with campgrounds to make exploring just that much easier. In Snow Canyon, a place usually devoid of snow, mountain bikers bike, climbers climb, and hikers hike to their hearts' content, while at Quail Creek boaters fish and enjoy a variety of water sports. Sand Hollow, Utah's newest state park, is also a must-visit and offers much in the way of activities

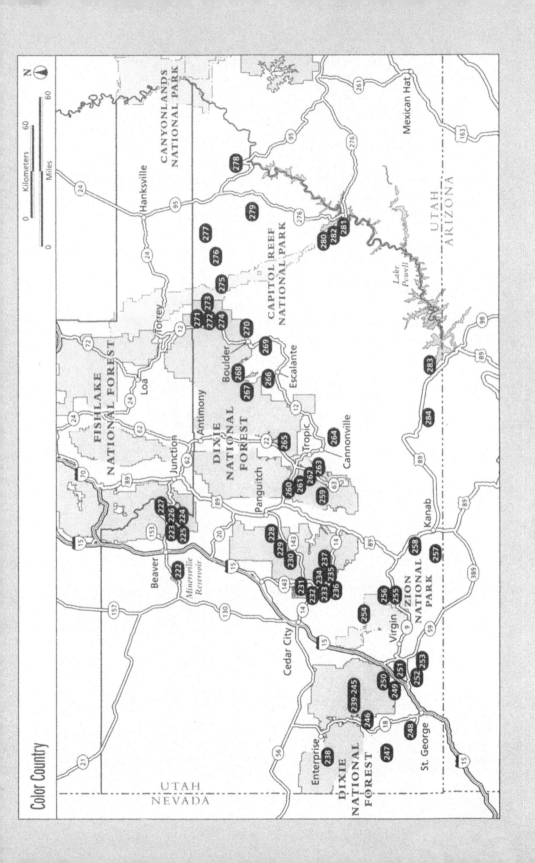

Color Country

for those who enjoy boating, fishing, and ATVing. Utah's state parks definitely offer something for just about everyone.

The southeast corner of Color Country is the setting of the Glen Canyon National Recreation Area, home to Lake Powell and the world's largest natural bridge. Spanning 275 feet across and standing 290 feet high, Rainbow Bridge is accessed by a strenuous backpack trip or an easy boat ride.

The national forests offer plenty to see and do as well. Here you'll find camping throughout the Dixie National Forest: four distinct segments of forest offering a multitude of campgrounds and opportunities to enjoy the outdoors. In addition, you'll enjoy a small portion of the Fishlake National Forest in the northwest corner of the region.

Exploring is fun year-round in Color Country, though you will find the mountain campgrounds closed in winter. Of course, during winter you can always camp at one of the low-elevation campgrounds and explore high.

For more information on things to see and do in Color Country, contact the Color Country Travel Council, 906 N. 1400 West, PO Box 1550, St. George, UT 84771; (800) 233-8824; www.utahtravelcenter.com/travelregions/colorcountry.htm.

		Total Sites	Group Sites	Hook-up Sites	Hookups	Max. RV Length	Dump Station	Toilets	Showers	Drinking Water	ADA Compliant	Fees	Reservations	Recreation
222	Minersville Reservoir Park	29		20	E	30	•	F	•	•		$-$$	•	SBLFK
223	Little Cottonwood	14				40		F		•	•	$$	•	F
224	Kents Lake	30				Any		F & V		•		$$-$$$	•	FSK
225	Anderson Meadow	10				30		V		•		$$-$$$		FSHK
226	Little Reservoir	10	2			40		V		•	•	$$-$$$$$		FHMK
227	Mahogany Cove	7				24		V		•		$-$$$$$	•	HM
228	White Bridge	28				35	•	F & V		•		$$-$$$	•	FHMO
229	Panguitch Lake North	50	3			40	•	F		•		$$-$$$$$	•	FBLSMH
230	Panguitch Lake South	18				None		F		•		$$		HMFBLSK
231	Point Supreme	28				40		F		•	•	$$	•	H
232	Cedar Canyon	18	1			25		V		•		$$-$$$$$	•	HM
233	Deer Haven Organizational Camp	11	1			24		F & V		•		$-$$$$$	•	HM
234	Spruces	29				24		F		•		$$-$$$		FSBLHMK
235	Navajo Lake	27				24	•	F		•		$$-$$$		FBLSHMK
236	Te-Ah	43	1			40	•	F & V		•		$$-$$$$	•	FHBLK
237	Duck Creek	98	4			45	•	F & V		•	•	$$-$$$$$	•	FHM
238	Honeycomb Rocks	21				24		V		•		$		FSBHMLK

#		Total Sites	Group Sites	Hook-up Sites	Hookups	Max. RV Length	Dump Station	Toilets	Showers	Drinking Water	ADA Compliant	Fees	Reservations	Recreation
239	Equestrian	19				45		V		•	•	$$-$$$	•	RHFM
240	Yellow Pine	8				45		V		•	•	$$-$$$	•	HFM
241	Dean Gardner	27				45		V		•	•	$$-$$$	•	HFM
242	Crackfoot	23				45		V		•	•	$$-$$$	•	HFM
243	Effie Beckstrom Groups	2	2			30		V		•	•	$$$$$	•	HFM
244	Ebenezer Bryce	19				20		V		•		$$-$$$		HFM
245	Mitt Moody	6				None		V		•		$$-$$$		HFM
246	Baker Dam	19				25		V				$		FHML
247	Gunlock State Park	6				Any		V				$$		BLSFMK
248	Snow Canyon State Park	31	2	14	WE	40	•	F	•	•		$$-$$$$$	•	HCMR
249	Red Cliffs Recreation Site	12				25		V		•		$		HM
250	Oak Grove	9	1			20		V				$		HR
251	Quail Creek State Park	22				35		F		•		$$	•	FSBLK
252	Westside	50		50	WES	Any	•	F	•	•	•	$$$	•	FSBLKMO
253	Sandpit	30	5	6	WE	Any	•	F	•	•		$$-$$$$$	•	FSBLOMK
254	Lava Point	6				19		V				None		H
255	South	127				Any	•	F		•	•	$$		HCM
256	Watchman	189	7	95	E	40	•	F		•	•	$$	•	HCM
257	Coral Pink Sand Dunes State Park	23	1			40		F	•	•		$$-$$$$$	•	OH
258	Ponderosa Grove	9				24		V				$		O
259	Kings Creek	39	2			45/35	•	F & V		•		$$-$$$$$	•	HFSMBLKO
260	Red Canyon	37				Any	•	F	•	•		$$-$$$		HMR
261	Coyote Hollow Equestrian	4				Any		V				$		HMRO
262	Sunset	101	1			45	•	F	•	•	•	$$-$$$$$	•	H
263	North	102				Any	•	F	•	•		$$	•	H
264	Kodachrome Basin State Park	35	2	10	WES	45	•	F	•	•	•	$$-$$$$$	•	HRM
265	Pine Lake	38	5			45		V		•	•	$$-$$$$$	•	HFMLKO
266	Escalante Petrified Forest State Park	23	1	8	WE	50	•	F	•	•	•	$$-$$$$$	•	FBLSHK

Hookup: W = Water, E = Electric, S = Sewer

Recreation: H = Hiking, C = Rock Climbing, M = Mountain Biking, S = Swimming, F = Fishing, B = Boating, L = Boat Launch, O = Off-highway Driving, R = Horseback Riding, K = Kayaking and Canoeing, G = Golf

Toilets: F = Flush, V = Vault, C = Chemical

Per-night campsite cost: $ = $10 or less $$ = $11 to $20 $$$ = $21 to 30 $$$$ = $31 to $40 $$$$$ = $41 and higher

		Total Sites	Group Sites	Hook-up Sites	Hookups	Max. RV Length	Dump Station	Toilets	Showers	Drinking Water	ADA Compliant	Fees	Reservations	Recreation
267	Posey Lake	22	1			25		V		•		$-$$$$	•	FBLHK
268	Blue Spruce	6				18		V		•		$-$$		F
269	Calf Creek	14				25		F & V		•		$		FH
270	Deer Creek	7				None		V				$		FH
271	Upper Pleasant Creek	12				25		V		•		$		HMF
272	Lower Pleasant Creek	5				20		V		•		$		HMF
273	Lower Bowns	5	1			30		V			•	$-$$$$	•	FMO
274	Oak Creek	9				20		V		•		$-$$		FMH
275	Cedar Mesa	5				None		V				None		H
276	McMillan Springs	10				None		V		•		$		HM
277	Lonesome Beaver	5				None		V		•		$		HM
278	Dirty Devil River	*				Any		V				$-$$		FBKS
279	Starr Springs	12				20		V		•		$		H
280	Stanton Creek	*				Any		V				$-$$		FBLSK
281	Bullfrog	78				Any	•	F		•	•	$$		FBLKS
282	Bullfrog RV	24		24	WES	Any		F	•	•		$$$$$	•	FBLSK
283	Lone Rock	*				Any	•	V	•	•		$		BSFK
284	White House	5				None		V				$		H

Hookup: W = Water, E = Electric, S = Sewer   * = Dispersed Camping, no designated sites
Recreation: H = Hiking, C = Rock Climbing, M = Mountain Biking, S = Swimming, F = Fishing, B = Boating, L = Boat Launch,
O = Off-highway Driving, R = Horseback Riding, K = Kayaking and Canoeing, G = Golf
Toilets: F = Flush, V = Vault, C = Chemical
Per-night campsite cost: $ = $10 or less $$ = $11 to $20 $$$ = $21 to 30 $$$$ = $31 to $40 $$$$$ = $41 and higher

222 Minersville Reservoir Park

Location: About 11 miles southwest of Beaver
GPS: N38 13.072'/W112 49.596'
Facilities: Fire pits, picnic tables, flush toilets, showers, electric hookups, dump station, fish cleaning station, drinking water, boat launch, and a large overflow area for primitive camping
Sites: 9 tent sites and 20 electric-hookup sites
Maximum RV length: 30 feet
Fee: $ for tent sites; $$ for electric-hookup sites
Maximum stay: 14 days
Elevation: 5,500 feet
Road conditions: Paved
Management: Minersville Reservoir Park/Beaver County Campground, 1651 W. 2630 South, Beaver; (435) 438-5472; http://beaver.utah.gov/facilities/Facility/Details/2
Reservations: Call (435) 438-5472; http://beaver.utah.gov/index.aspx?NID=360
Activities: Swimming, boating, water sports, fishing, bird watching, photography, and picnicking
Season: Year-round
Finding the campground: From Beaver travel west and then southwest on UT 21 for 11.2 miles.
About the campground: Located between the Tushar and Mineral Mountains and surrounded by sagebrush and wild grass, with cottonwoods and willows growing near the water, Minersville Reservoir encompasses 1,130 acres. It's a wonderful place to swim, water-ski, kayak, and canoe. The reservoir is also one of Utah's prime fisheries, with the highlights being rainbow and cutthroat trout, as well as smallmouth bass.

The campground is a nice spot from which to enjoy all the above activities. It also makes a good base for day trips into the nearby mountains. If you opt for a trailer space, you'll sit parking-lot-style next to your neighbor. The sites are nice, but too close together for some folks; tent spaces along the lakeshore offer a lot more room.

223 Little Cottonwood

Location: In the Fishlake National Forest, about 7 miles east of Beaver
GPS: N38 15.312'/W112 32.478'
Facilities: Fire pits, picnic tables, ADA sites, flush toilets, drinking water, paved path to the river for wheelchair access
Sites: 14 basic sites
Maximum RV length: 40 feet
Fee: $$ for basic sites
Maximum stay: 14 days
Elevation: 6,500 feet
Road conditions: Paved
Management: Beaver Ranger District, 575 S. Main St., Beaver; (435) 438-2436; www.fs.usda.gov/main/fishlake/home

Reservations: Call (877) 444-6777 or TDD (877) 833-6777; www.recreation.gov
Activities: Fishing and picnicking
Restrictions: ATVs and horses not allowed
Season: Mid-May through mid-September
Finding the campground: From Beaver travel east on UT 153 (200 North Street) through Beaver Canyon and on to the Little Cottonwood Campground, which is on your right, just off the highway. You'll reach it after driving 6.8 miles.
About the campground: Situated on the banks of Beaver Creek, with pines and cottonwoods all around, the campground is a pleasant place to stay come summer. Fishing is popular here; a paved path makes it possible for those in wheelchairs to enjoy angling as well.

224 Kents Lake

Location: In the Fishlake National Forest, about 15 miles southeast of Beaver
GPS: N38 14.254'/W112 27.516'
Facilities: Fire pits, picnic tables, vault and flush toilets, and drinking water
Sites: 28 basic sites and 2 double sites
Maximum RV length: Any
Fee: $$ for basic sites; $$$ for double sites
Maximum stay: 14 days
Elevation: 8,800 feet
Road conditions: Maintained gravel
Management: Beaver Ranger District, 575 S. Main St., Beaver; (435) 438-2436; www.fs.usda .gov/main/fishlake/home
Reservations: Call (877) 444-6777 or TDD (877) 833-6777; www.recreation.gov
Activities: Fishing, swimming, boating (nonmotorized), and picnicking
Restrictions: Horses and ATVs are not allowed
Season: Mid-May through mid-September
Finding the campground: From Beaver travel east on UT 153 (200 North Street) for 10.2 miles to FR 137. Turn right (southeast) onto the gravel road and drive about 5 miles to the campground.
About the campground: Situated in a lush forest of aspen and fir and set amid spectacular mountain scenery, this campground promises good trout fishing at Kents Lake. A cool refuge come summer, it's a wonderful place to just sit and relax.

225 Anderson Meadow

Location: In the Fishlake National Forest, about 15 miles southeast of Beaver
GPS: N38 12.551'/W112 25.853'
Facilities: Fire pits, picnic tables, vault toilets, and drinking water
Sites: 8 basic sites and 2 double sites
Maximum RV length: 30 feet

Fee: $$ for basic sites; $$$ for double sites
Maximum stay: 14 days
Elevation: 9,400 feet
Road conditions: Maintained gravel
Management: Beaver Ranger District, 575 S. Main St., Beaver; (435) 438-2436; www.fs.usda
.gov/main/fishlake/home
Reservations: None
Activities: Fishing, swimming, kayaking and canoeing, hiking, and picnicking
Restrictions: Horses and ATVs not allowed
Season: June through mid-September
Finding the campground: From Beaver travel east on UT 153 (200 North Street) for 10.2 miles
to FR 137. Turn right (southeast) onto the gravel road and drive another 8 miles or so to the
campground.
About the campground: Nestled in a mix of Engelmann spruce, aspen, and fir, the campground
overlooks Anderson Meadow Reservoir. The lake is within walking distance of the campground. A
potpourri of beautiful scenery, the reservoir offers trout fishing. Swimming is also a must-do if you
can stand the frigid waters. If you'd rather stay on dry land, check out one of the nearby popular
trails.

226 Little Reservoir

Location: In the Fishlake National Forest, about 11 miles east of Beaver
GPS: N38 15.593'/W112 29.302'
Facilities: Fire pits, picnic tables, ADA site, vault toilets, and drinking water
Sites: 8 basic sites and 2 group sites (no limit)
Maximum RV length: 40 feet
Fee: $$ for basic sites; $$ to $$$$$ for group sites
Maximum stay: 14 days
Elevation: 7,300 feet
Road conditions: Maintained gravel
Management: Beaver Ranger District, 575 S. Main St., Beaver; (435) 438-2436; www.fs.usda
.gov/main/fishlake/home
Reservations: None
Activities: Fishing, hiking, mountain biking, boating (nonmotorized), bird watching, and picnicking
Season: May through September
Finding the campground: From Beaver travel east on UT 153 (200 North Street) for 10.2 miles
to FR 137. Turn right (southeast) and drive the maintained gravel road less than 1 mile to the
campground.
About the campground: Set amid spectacular mountain scenery, the campground is tucked away
in a ponderosa pine forest mixed with pinyon, juniper, and scrub oak. About half the sites are
shaded. A paved trail leads to a small, 4-acre lake where good fishing allows anglers to while away
the hours or days. Hiking and bird watching are also popular.

227 Mahogany Cove

Location: In the Fishlake National Forest, about 12 miles east of Beaver
GPS: N38 16.121'/W112 29.176'
Facilities: Fire pits, picnic tables, vault toilets, and drinking water
Sites: 7 basic sites that can make 1 big group site (maximum 75 people)
Maximum RV length: 24 feet
Fee: $ for basic sites; $$$$$ for entire campground
Maximum stay: 14 days
Elevation: 7,500 feet
Road conditions: Paved
Management: Beaver Ranger District, 575 S. Main St., Beaver; (435) 438-2436; www.fs.usda
.gov/main/fishlake/home
Reservations: Call (877) 444-6777 or TDD (877) 833-6777; www.recreation.gov
Activities: Hiking, mountain biking, and picnicking
Season: May through September
Finding the campground: From Beaver travel east on UT 153 (200 North Street) through Beaver
Canyon and on up to the Mahogany Cove Campground, which is right off the highway. You'll reach
it after driving 11.4 miles.
About the campground: This campground can be reserved as a whole, but if it's not reserved
individuals can use the seven basic sites. Set on a high bench overlooking Beaver Canyon, the
campground offers plenty of its namesake—mountain mahogany. There's also ponderosa pine, juniper, Gambel oak, and cottonwood trees in the area. The views from this spot are nice. In fact, the
campground's only downfall is its close proximity to the road. You won't find any trailheads leading
from the campground, but you'll have access to some trails nearby. Explore to your heart's content.
Mountain bikers should check out Gregg Bromka's *Mountain Biking Utah*, by FalconGuides, for a
nearby ride.

228 White Bridge

Location: In the Dixie National Forest, about 12 miles southwest of Panguitch
GPS: N37 44.744'/W112 35.226'
Facilities: Fire pits, picnic tables, drinking water, vault and flush toilets, and dump station
Sites: 27 basic sites and 1 double site
Maximum RV length: 35 feet
Fee: $$ for basic sites; $$$ for double site
Maximum stay: 14 days
Elevation: 7,900 feet
Road conditions: Paved
Management: Cedar City Ranger District, 1789 N. Wedgewood Ln., Cedar City; (435) 865-3200;
www.fs.usda.gov/main/dixie/home

Reservations: Call (877) 444-6777 or TDD (877) 833-6777; www.recreation.gov
Activities: Fishing, hiking, mountain biking, off-road driving, and picnicking
Restrictions: OHVs/ATVs not allowed
Season: Mid-May through September
Finding the campground: From the junction of UT 143 and US 89 in Panguitch, travel southwest on UT 143 for 12.5 miles to the campground.
About the campground: This pleasant campground is just across a white bridge that spans Panguitch Creek. Campers can fish and wade in the creek. Junipers and cottonwoods provide campground shade. The forest service boasts of hiking and mountain biking opportunities adjacent to the campground. The Panguitch Lake ATV Trail System offers more than 100 miles of trails and can be accessed nearby. (*Note:* You must trailer your ATV to and from the trailhead to the campground.) If you're itching to swim or boat, you can always travel to Panguitch Lake, about 5 miles southwest of the campground.

229 Panguitch Lake North

Location: In the Dixie National Forest, about 19 miles southwest of Panguitch
GPS: N37 42.088'/W112 39.363'
Facilities: Fire pits, picnic tables, boat ramp, drinking water, flush toilets, and dump station
Sites: 39 basic sites, 8 double sites, and 3 group sites (maximum varies from 24 to 35 people)
Maximum RV length: 40 feet
Fee: $$ for basic sites; $$$ for double sites; $$$$$ for group sites
Maximum stay: 14 days
Elevation: 8,400 feet
Road conditions: Paved
Management: Cedar City Ranger District, 1789 N. Wedgewood Ln., Cedar City; (435) 865-3200; www.fs.usda.gov/main/dixie/home
Reservations: Call (877) 444-6777 or TDD (877) 833-6777; www.recreation.gov
Activities: Fishing, boating, swimming, mountain biking, hiking, and picnicking
Restrictions: OHVs/ATVs not allowed
Season: Late May through September
Finding the campground: From the junction of UT 143 and US 89 in Panguitch, travel southwest on UT 143 for 18.7 miles to the campground.
About the campground: Set among ponderosa pines, some of the sites at this spacious campground have a view of Panguitch Lake. The campground is on the southwest end of the 1,250-acre reservoir, which is especially popular for fishing. Rainbow trout are particularly outstanding, though German brown trout can also be caught in the lake and downstream in Panguitch Creek. Access to the lake is via UT 143. There are also excellent opportunities for hiking and mountain biking.

230 Panguitch Lake South

Location: In the Dixie National Forest, about 19 miles southwest of Panguitch
GPS: N37 42.035'/W112 39.314'
Facilities: Fire pits, picnic tables, boat launch, drinking water, and flush toilets
Sites: 18 tent sites
Maximum RV length: None (best for tents, camper vans, and truck campers)
Fee: $$ for tent sites
Maximum stay: 14 days
Elevation: 8,400 feet
Road conditions: Paved to the campground, then dirt
Management: Cedar City Ranger District, 1789 N. Wedgewood Ln., Cedar City; (435) 865-3200; www.fs.usda.gov/main/dixie/home
Reservations: None
Activities: Hiking, mountain biking, and picnicking; fishing, boating, and swimming at nearby Panguitch Lake
Restrictions: OHVs/ATVs not allowed
Season: Late May through September
Finding the campground: From the junction of UT 143 and US 89 in Panguitch, travel southwest on UT 143 for 18.7 miles to the campground.
About the campground: Set among ponderosa pines, these small sites are suitable for tents; trailers are not recommended. The campground is about 0.5 mile from Panguitch Lake, which is especially popular for fishing. Rainbow trout are outstanding, though German brown trout can also be caught in the lake and downstream in Panguitch Creek. Mountain biking and hiking opportunities abound in the area.

231 Point Supreme: Cedar Breaks National Monument

Location: About 1.5 miles north of the south entrance
GPS: N37 36.670'/W112 49.885'
Facilities: Fire pits, picnic tables, ADA sites, drinking water, and flush toilets
Sites: 26 basic sites and 2 tents-only sites
Maximum RV length: 40 feet
Fee: $$ for basic and tents-only sites
Maximum stay: 14 days
Elevation: 10,350 feet
Road conditions: Paved
Management: Cedar Breaks National Monument, 2390 W. Hwy. 56, Ste. 11, Cedar City; (435) 586-9451; www.nps.gov/cebr/index.htm
Reservations: Call (877) 444-6777 or TDD (877) 833-6777; www.recreation.gov
Activities: Hiking, photography, and picnicking
Season: Mid-June through mid-September

Cedar Breaks Amphitheater is a great place to hike near Point Supreme.

Finding the campground: From the south entrance of the monument, off UT 14, go north about 1.5 miles on a paved road.

About the campground: A great base from which to explore Cedar Breaks National Monument, this campground is located just east of the visitor center. Here, staff offer nature walks, geology talks, and campfire programs.

There are two easy hikes near the rim; in addition, you'll find a 5-mile-long scenic drive past four breathtaking overlooks. The season is short here; visit while you can.

232 Cedar Canyon

Location: In the Dixie National Forest, about 13 miles southeast of Cedar City
GPS: N37 35.505' / W112 54.267'
Facilities: Fire pits, picnic tables, drinking water, and vault toilets
Sites: 13 basic sites, 4 double sites, and 1 group site (maximum 35 people)
Maximum RV length: 25 feet
Fee: $$ for basic sites; $$$ for double sites; $$$$$ for group site
Maximum stay: 14 days
Elevation: 8,400 feet

Road conditions: Paved
Management: Cedar City Ranger District, 1789 N. Wedgewood Ln., Cedar City; (435) 865-3200; www.fs.usda.gov/main/dixie/home
Reservations: Call (877) 444-6777 or TDD (877) 833-6777; www.recreation.gov
Activities: Hiking, mountain biking, and picnicking
Restrictions: OHVs/ATVs not allowed
Season: Late May through September
Finding the campground: From the junction of UT 14 and UT 130 in downtown Cedar City, travel southeast on UT 14 for 12.3 miles. The campground is on the left (north) side of the highway.
About the campground: The Cedar Canyon Campground is located in a beautiful canyon by the same name. Campsites snuggle up to Crow Creek, while aspen, fir, and spruce trees add to the scene. If you want to see bristlecone pine trees, you can drive or bike about 5 miles southeast on UT 14 to a trailhead on the south side of the road. The Bristlecone Pine Trail is an easy 0.5-mile loop and is wheelchair accessible. Some of the pines are 300 to 500 years old. From the trail there are excellent views of the North Fork of the Virgin River and the northern areas of Zion National Park.

233 Deer Haven Organizational Camp

Location: In the Dixie National Forest, about 17 miles southeast of Cedar City
GPS: N37 34.408'/W112 54.530'
Facilities: Fire pits, picnic tables, drinking water, and flush and vault toilets; no trash service (pack it out)
Sites: 10 walk-in tent sites and 1 group site (maximum 200 people)
Maximum RV length: 24 feet
Fee: $ for tent sites; $$$$$ for group site
Maximum stay: 14 days
Elevation: 9,000 feet
Road conditions: Dirt
Management: Cedar City Ranger District, 1789 N. Wedgewood Ln., Cedar City; (435) 865-3200; www.fs.usda.gov/main/dixie/home
Reservations: Call (877) 444-6777 or TDD (877) 833-6777; www.recreation.gov
Activities: Hiking, mountain biking, and picnicking
Restrictions: OHVs/ATVs not allowed
Season: June through early September
Finding the campground: From the junction of UT 14 and UT 130 in downtown Cedar City, travel southeast on UT 14 for about 15 miles to FR 052 (also known as Webster Flat Road). Turn right (south) and continue approximately 3 more miles on the dirt road to the campground.
About the campground: Set in aspen trees at the base of Black Mountain, this campground is designed and constructed to accommodate group organizations. The entire campground may be reserved for large groups. Mountain biking and hiking opportunities abound in the area. Hikers will find an access trail to the Virgin River Rim Trail, a 32-mile journey along the rim between Strawberry Point and Woods Ranch, which is about 2 miles from the campground. It provides wonderful views of the Virgin River basin and Zion National Park.

234 Spruces

Location: In the Dixie National Forest, about 28 miles southeast of Cedar City
GPS: N37 31.095'/W112 46.456'
Facilities: Fire pits, picnic tables, tent pads, drinking water, and flush toilets; commercial boat rentals and launching at nearby Behmer Lodge and Landing (between Spruces and Navajo Lake Campgrounds) and Navajo Lake Lodge (at the west end of the lake)
Sites: 24 basic sites, 3 walk-in tent sites, and 2 double sites
Maximum RV length: 24 feet
Fee: $$ for basic and tent sites; $$$ for double sites
Maximum stay: 14 days
Elevation: 9,200 feet
Road conditions: Paved
Management: Cedar City Ranger District, 1789 N. Wedgewood Ln., Cedar City; (435) 865-3200; www.fs.usda.gov/main/dixie/home
Reservations: None
Activities: Fishing, swimming, boating, hiking, mountain biking, and picnicking
Restrictions: OHVs/ATVs not allowed
Season: Late May through early September
Finding the campground: From the junction of UT 14 and UT 130 in downtown Cedar City, travel southeast on UT 14 for 25.6 miles to FR 053 (Navajo Lake Road). Turn right (south) and follow the paved road approximately 1.5 miles to the campground, the first of three located along the road.
About the campground: Situated along the south shore of 3.5-mile-long Navajo Lake, the campground straddles Navajo Lake Road and is embraced by aspen, spruce, and fir trees. Anglers vie for rainbow trout as well as eastern brook and brown trout. Mountain bikers find plenty to do, while hikers have access to the 32-mile-long Virgin River Rim Trail. Hike this trail and you'll have wonderful views of Zion National Park and the Virgin River basin.

235 Navajo Lake

Location: In the Dixie National Forest, about 29 miles southeast of Cedar City
GPS: N37 31.263'/W112 47.358'
Facilities: Fire pits, picnic tables, tent pads, drinking water, flush toilets, dump station (located 2 miles west), and boat ramp; commercial boat rentals and launching at nearby Behmer Lodge and Landing (between the Spruces and Navajo Lake Campgrounds) and Navajo Lake Lodge (at the west end of the lake)
Sites: 12 basic sites, 11 walk-in tent sites, and 4 double sites
Maximum RV length: 24 feet
Fee: $$ for basic and walk-in tent sites; $$$ for double sites
Maximum stay: 14 days
Elevation: 9,200 feet
Road conditions: Paved

Management: Cedar City Ranger District, 1789 N. Wedgewood Ln., Cedar City; (435) 865-3200; www.fs.usda.gov/main/dixie/home

Reservations: None

Activities: Fishing, boating, swimming, hiking, mountain biking, and picnicking

Restrictions: OHVs/ATVs not allowed

Season: Late May through September

Finding the campground: From the junction of UT 14 and UT 130 in downtown Cedar City, travel southeast on UT 14 for 25.6 miles to FR 053 (Navajo Lake Road). Turn right (south) and follow the paved road for about 3.5 miles to the second of three public campgrounds.

About the campground: Situated along the south shore of 3.5-mile-long Navajo Lake, the campground straddles Navajo Lake Road and is embraced by aspen, spruce, and fir trees. Here, anglers vie for rainbow trout as well as eastern brook and brown trout. Mountain bikers ride to their hearts' content, and hikers find an access trail to the Virgin River Rim Trail. This trail spans about 32 miles and provides wonderful views of the Virgin River basin and Zion National Park.

236 Te-Ah

Location: In the Dixie National Forest, about 30 miles southeast of Cedar City

GPS: N37 31.981'/W112 49.111'

Facilities: Fire pits, picnic tables, drinking water, flush and vault toilets, and dump station; commercial boat rentals and launching available at nearby Behmer Lodge and Landing (between the Spruces and Navajo Lake Campgrounds) and Navajo Lake Lodge (at the west end of the lake).

Sites: 42 basic sites and 1 group site (maximum 24 people)

Maximum RV length: 40 feet

Fee: $$ for basic sites, $$$$ for group site

Maximum stay: 14 days

Elevation: 9,200 feet

Road conditions: Paved

Management: Cedar City Ranger District, 1789 N. Wedgewood Ln., Cedar City; (435) 865-3200; www.fs.usda.gov/main/dixie/home

Reservations: Call (877) 444-6777 or TDD (877) 833-6777; www.recreation.gov

Activities: Fishing, hiking, boating, and picnicking

Restrictions: OHVs/ATVs not allowed

Season: Late May through early September

Finding the campground: From the junction of UT 14 and UT 130 in downtown Cedar City, travel southeast on UT 14 for 25.6 miles to FR 053 (Navajo Lake Road). Turn right (south) and follow the paved road for about 4.5 miles to the last of three public campgrounds.

About the campground: Unlike the two campgrounds you passed en route to Te-Ah, this site is situated about 1.5 miles from Navajo Lake. Still, it's a popular spot for anglers with trout on their minds. It's also an excellent place from which to observe wild turkeys and deer.

237 Duck Creek

Location: In the Dixie National Forest, about 28 miles southeast of Cedar City
GPS: N37 31.135' / W112 41.924'
Facilities: Fire pits, picnic tables, ADA sites, drinking water, flush and vault toilets, dump station, and ATV corral for all OHV parking
Sites: 84 basic sites, 7 double sites, 3 triple sites, and 4 group sites (maximum varies from 50 to 150 people)
Maximum RV length: 45 feet
Fee: $$ for basic sites; $$$ for double sites; $$$$$ for triple and group sites
Maximum stay: 14 days
Elevation: 8,600 feet
Road conditions: Paved
Management: Cedar City Ranger District, 1789 N. Wedgewood Ln., Cedar City; (435) 865-3200; www.fs.usda.gov/main/dixie/home
Reservations: Call (877) 444-6777 or TDD (877) 833-6777; www.recreation.gov
Activities: Fishing, hiking, mountain biking, and picnicking
Restrictions: OHVs/ATVs not allowed
Season: Mid-May through September
Finding the campground: From the junction of UT 14 and UT 130 in downtown Cedar City, travel southeast on UT 14 for 28 miles. You'll see the campground on the north side of the road; a ranger station/visitor center sits on the south side.
About the campground: Fishing is popular both in the adjacent creek and in Duck Lake. Visit and you'll know exactly how the lake got its name: Ducks seem to enjoy the place as much as human visitors.

There are several hiking trails in the vicinity. The longest trail is the Lost Hunter Trail, a 3-mile loop with some nice views of the area. You're bound to enjoy the Singing Pines Interpretive Trail, which is just across the street, east of the ranger station/visitor center. Be sure to pick up an information sheet for the easy, 0.5-mile loop; this trail introduces the trees through songs. The Old Ranger Interpretive Trail does a similar thing—only this time you'll learn about the forest from the eyes of an old ranger. This trail is the shortest of the three, a 0.3-mile loop through an aspen, Douglas fir, and ponderosa pine forest.

238 Honeycomb Rocks

Location: In the Dixie National Forest, about 12 miles southwest of Enterprise and 53 miles southwest of Cedar City
GPS: N37 31.086' / W113 51.483'
Facilities: Fire pits, covered picnic tables, tent pads, vault toilets, drinking water, and nearby boat ramp; no trash service (pack it out)
Sites: 21 basic sites
Maximum RV length: 24 feet

Fee: $ for basic sites
Maximum stay: 14 days
Elevation: 5,700 feet
Road conditions: Paved
Management: Pine Valley Ranger District, 196 E. Tabernacle, Ste. 40, St. George; (435) 652-3100; www.fs.usda.gov/main/dixie/home
Reservations: None
Activities: Fishing, swimming, boating, hiking, mountain biking, picnicking, and photography
Restrictions: OHVs/ATVs not allowed
Season: May through September
Finding the campground: From Enterprise go west on paved UT 219. After 7.1 miles turn left (south) onto an unnamed paved road. A sign points the way to the campground and Enterprise Reservoirs. After another 5.6 miles you'll find the campground, which is just across the road from the upper reservoir.
About the campground: There are plenty of activities at this scenic campground, where sites are nestled into an unusual series of welded tuff formations. Part of the Ox Valley Tuff Formation of the late Miocene—which means they're about 12 to 15 million years old—the porous volcanic rocks do look a bit like honeycombs; thus their name. The rest of the country is wide open, a place where sage and grass are predominant. An occasional pine or oak adds to the scene.

Rainbow trout thrive in both the lower and upper reservoirs. The larger of the two is Upper Enterprise Reservoir, where you'll find a paved boat ramp. It's also the closest water source to the campground.

239 Equestrian: Pine Valley Recreation Area

Location: In the Dixie National Forest, about 23 miles southeast of Enterprise
GPS: N37 22.815'/W113 28.992'
Facilities: Fire pits, stove stands, picnic tables, ADA sites, tent pads, vault toilets, drinking water, hitching posts, and corrals. (There's also a dump station on the north side of FR 035, 4.5 miles east of UT 18.)
Sites: 9 basic sites, 6 double sites, and 4 tents-only sites
Maximum RV length: 45 feet
Fee: $$ for basic and tents-only sites; $$$ for double sites
Maximum stay: 14 days
Elevation: 6,700 feet
Road conditions: Paved
Management: Pine Valley Ranger District, 196 E. Tabernacle, Ste. 40, St. George; (435) 652-3100; www.fs.usda.gov/main/dixie/home
Reservations: Call (877) 444-6777 or TDD (877) 833-6777; www.recreation.gov
Activities: Horseback riding, hiking, mountain biking, fishing, and picnicking
Restrictions: OHVs/ATVs not allowed
Season: Mid-May through September

Finding the campground: From Enterprise drive south on UT 18 for 13.6 miles, then turn left (east) onto paved Pine Valley Highway (FR 035). Drive another 9.7 miles, passing through the small community of Pine Valley, en route to the Pine Valley Recreation Area entrance station. Just 0.2 mile after entering the recreation area, you'll see the campground turnoff on the right (south).

About the campground: The campground is set among pines and firs, and offers a nice place for horse owners to camp with their four-legged friends. Two sites are reserved until 6 p.m. for campers with horses; otherwise you don't have to have a horse to camp here. In addition, there's the opportunity to fish for rainbow and brook trout at Pine Valley Reservoir, which is about 0.7 mile farther up the road. You can also fish in the Santa Clara River, which flows nearby.

Whether you want to hike or ride horses, there are plenty of nearby trails that allow access into the Pine Valley Mountain Wilderness, a region rich in pine, aspen, fir, and spruce. The granite spire known as Signal Peak stands more than 10,000 feet in elevation and is the highest point in the wilderness.

240 Yellow Pine: Pine Valley Recreation Area

Location: In the Dixie National Forest, about 23 miles southeast of Enterprise
GPS: N37 22.763'/W113 28.806'
Facilities: Fire pits, picnic tables, ADA sites, stove stands, tent pads, vault toilets, and drinking water. (There's also a dump station on the north side of FR 035, 4.5 miles east of UT 18.)
Sites: 7 basic sites and 1 double site
Maximum RV length: 45 feet
Fee: $$ for basic sites; $$$ for double site
Maximum stay: 14 days
Elevation: 6,700 feet
Road conditions: Paved
Management: Pine Valley Ranger District, 196 E. Tabernacle, Ste. 40, St. George; (435) 652-3100; www.fs.usda.gov/main/dixie/home
Reservations: Call (877) 444-6777 or TDD (877) 833-6777; www.recreation.gov
Activities: Hiking, fishing, mountain biking, and picnicking
Restrictions: OHVs/ATVs not allowed
Season: Mid-May through September
Finding the campground: From Enterprise drive south on UT 18 for 13.6 miles, then turn left (east) onto paved Pine Valley Highway (FR 035). Drive another 9.7 miles, passing through the small community of Pine Valley, en route to the Pine Valley Recreation Area entrance station. Nearly 0.5 mile after entering the recreation area, you'll see the campground turnoff on the left (east).
About the campground: Set among pines and firs, this small, but popular, campground must be reserved. It's a nice place for just relaxing and enjoying the cool realms of the forest. In addition, there's the opportunity to fish for rainbow and brook trout at nearby Pine Valley Reservoir. There's also fishing upstream and downstream in the Santa Clara River.

An abundance of nearby trails allow access into the Pine Valley Mountain Wilderness, a region rich in pine, aspen, fir, and spruce. The granite spire known as Signal Peak stands more than 10,000 feet in elevation and is the highest point in the wilderness.

241 Dean Gardner: Pine Valley Recreation Area

Location: In the Dixie National Forest, about 24 miles southeast of Enterprise
GPS: N37 22.646'/W113 28.604'
Facilities: Fire pits, picnic tables, stove stands, ADA sites, tent pads, vault toilets, and drinking water. (There's also a dump station on the north side of FR 035, 4.5 miles east of UT 18.)
Sites: 25 basic sites and 2 double sites
Maximum RV length: 45 feet
Fee: $$ for basic sites; $$$ for double sites
Maximum stay: 14 days
Elevation: 6,700 feet
Road conditions: Paved
Management: Pine Valley Ranger District, 196 E. Tabernacle, Ste. 40, St. George; (435) 652-3100; www.fs.usda.gov/main/dixie/home
Reservations: Call (877) 444-6777 or TDD (877) 833-6777; www.recreation.gov
Activities: Hiking, fishing, mountain biking, and picnicking
Restrictions: OHVs/ATVs not allowed
Season: Mid-May through September
Finding the campground: From Enterprise drive south on UT 18 for 13.6 miles, then turn left (east) onto paved Pine Valley Highway (FR 035). Drive another 9.7 miles, passing through the small community of Pine Valley, en route to the Pine Valley Recreation Area entrance station. Drive another 0.8 mile and you'll see the campground turnoff on the left (north).
About the campground: The campground, newly constructed in 2012, is set among lofty ponderosa pines and offers a nice place for simply relaxing and enjoying the cool realms of the forest. In addition, there's the opportunity to fish for rainbow and brook trout at Pine Valley Reservoir, which is close by. In fact, Dean Gardner is the closest campground to the reservoir; thus it is extremely popular. There's also fishing upstream and downstream in the Santa Clara River.

An abundance of nearby trails allow access into the Pine Valley Mountain Wilderness, a region rich in pine, aspen, fir, and spruce. Signal Peak, a granite spire, stands more than 10,000 feet in elevation and is the highest point in the wilderness.

242 Crackfoot: Pine Valley Recreation Area

Location: In the Dixie National Forest, about 24 miles southeast of Enterprise
GPS: N37 22.422'/W113 27.989'
Facilities: Fire pits, picnic tables, stove stands, ADA sites, tent pads, vault toilets, and drinking water. (There's also a dump station on the north side of FR 035, 4.5 miles east of UT 18.)
Sites: 16 basic sites, 2 double sites, and 5 tents-only sites
Maximum RV length: 45 feet
Fee: $$ for basic and tents-only sites; $$$ for double sites
Maximum stay: 14 days

Elevation: 6,900 feet

Road conditions: Paved

Management: Pine Valley Ranger District, 196 E. Tabernacle, Ste. 40, St. George; (435) 652-3100; www.fs.usda.gov/main/dixie/home

Reservations: Call (877) 444-6777 or TDD (877) 833-6777; www.recreation.gov

Activities: Hiking, fishing, mountain biking, and picnicking

Restrictions: OHVs/ATVs not allowed

Season: Mid-May through September

Finding the campground: From Enterprise drive south on UT 18 for 13.6 miles, then turn left (east) onto paved Pine Valley Highway (FR 035). Drive another 9.7 miles, passing through the small community of Pine Valley, en route to the Pine Valley Recreation Area entrance station. Drive another 1.3 miles and you'll see the entrance to Crackfoot on the right (south).

About the campground: This new campground, constructed in 2012, offers campsites shaded by lofty ponderosa pines and is a nice place to relax and enjoy the cool realms of the forest. In addition, there's the opportunity to fish for rainbow and brook trout at Pine Valley Reservoir, as well as opportunities to fish the Santa Clara River.

An abundance of nearby trails allow access into the Pine Valley Mountain Wilderness, a region rich in pine, aspen, fir, and spruce. The granite spire known as Signal Peak stands more than 10,000 feet in elevation and is the highest point in the wilderness.

243 Effie Beckstrom Groups West and East: Pine Valley Recreation Area

Location: In the Dixie National Forest, about 24 miles southeast of Enterprise

GPS: N37 22.507' / W113 27.974'

Facilities: Fire pits, covered picnic tables, stove stands, ADA sites, tent pads, vault toilets, drinking water, horseshoe pits, and volleyball. (There's also a dump station on the north side of FR 035, 4.5 miles east of UT 18.)

Sites: 2 group sites (maximum 80 people each)

Maximum RV length: 30 feet

Fee: $$$$$ for group sites

Maximum stay: 14 days

Elevation: 6,900 feet

Road conditions: Paved

Management: Pine Valley Ranger District, 196 E. Tabernacle, Ste. 40, St. George; (435) 652-3100; www.fs.usda.gov/main/dixie/home

Reservations: Call (877) 444-6777 or TDD (877) 833-6777; www.recreation.gov

Activities: Hiking, fishing, mountain biking, and picnicking

Restrictions: OHVs/ATVs not allowed

Season: Mid-May through September

Finding the campground: From Enterprise drive south on UT 18 for 13.6 miles, then turn left (east) onto paved Pine Valley Highway (FR 035). Drive another 9.7 miles, passing through the small community of Pine Valley, en route to the Pine Valley Recreation Area entrance station. Drive another 1.4 miles and you'll see the entrance to both group sites on the left (north).

About the campground: The campground is set among pines and firs, and offers a nice place for simply relaxing and enjoying the cool realms of the forest. In addition, there's the opportunity to fish for rainbow and brook trout at nearby Pine Valley Reservoir. There's also fishing upstream and downstream in the Santa Clara River.

An abundance of nearby trails allow access into the Pine Valley Mountain Wilderness, a region rich in pine, aspen, fir, and spruce. Signal Peak, a granite spire, stands more than 10,000 feet in elevation and is the highest point in the wilderness.

244 Ebenezer Bryce: Pine Valley Recreation Area

Location: In the Dixie National Forest, about 24 miles southeast of Enterprise
GPS: N37 22.492' / W113 27.729'
Facilities: Fire pits, picnic tables, stove stands, tent pads, vault toilets, and drinking water. (There's also a dump station on the north side of FR 035, 4.5 miles east of UT 18.)
Sites: 17 basic sites and 2 double sites
Maximum RV length: 20 feet (not suitable for trailers; best for small motor homes, tents, and vans)
Fee: $$ for basic sites; $$$ for double sites
Maximum stay: 14 days
Elevation: 6,900 feet
Road conditions: Paved
Management: Pine Valley Ranger District, 196 E. Tabernacle, Ste. 40, St. George; (435) 652-3100; www.fs.usda.gov/main/dixie/home
Reservations: None
Activities: Hiking, fishing, mountain biking, and picnicking
Restrictions: OHVs/ATVs not allowed
Season: Mid-May through September
Finding the campground: From Enterprise drive south on UT 18 for 13.6 miles, then turn left (east) onto paved Pine Valley Highway (FR 035). Drive another 9.7 miles, passing through the small community of Pine Valley, en route to the Pine Valley Recreation Area entrance station. As you pass the entrance station, keep to the left as you drive another 1.7 miles to the campground on the right (west).

About the campground: The 2012 renovated campground was previously known as Blue Springs. Set among pines and firs, it offers a nice place for simply relaxing and enjoying the cool realms of the forest. In addition, there's the opportunity to fish for rainbow and brook trout at nearby Pine Valley Reservoir. There's also fishing in the Santa Clara River.

An abundance of nearby trails allow access into the Pine Valley Mountain Wilderness, a region rich in pine, aspen, fir, and spruce. Signal Peak, a granite spire, stands more than 10,000 feet in elevation and is the highest point in the wilderness.

245 Mitt Moody: Pine Valley Recreation Area

Location: In the Dixie National Forest, about 24 miles southeast of Enterprise
GPS: N37 22.516'/W113 27.320'
Facilities: Fire pits, picnic tables, stove stands, tent pads, vault toilets, and drinking water.
Sites: 6 walk-in tent sites, including 1 double site
Maximum RV length: None
Fee: $$ for walk-in tent sites; $$$ for double site
Maximum stay: 14 days
Elevation: 6,900 feet
Road conditions: Paved
Management: Pine Valley Ranger District, 196 E. Tabernacle, Ste. 40, St. George; (435) 652-3100; www.fs.usda.gov/main/dixie/home
Reservations: None
Activities: Hiking, fishing, mountain biking, and picnicking
Restrictions: OHVs/ATVs not allowed
Season: Mid-May through September
Finding the campground: From Enterprise drive south on UT 18 for 13.6 miles, then turn left (east) onto paved Pine Valley Highway (FR 035). Drive another 9.7 miles, passing through the small community of Pine Valley, en route to the Pine Valley Recreation Area entrance station. As you pass the entrance station, keep to the left as you drive another 1.9 miles to the end of the road and the campground.
About the campground: Sites at Mitt Moody are tucked away in the hillside that overlooks a nearby stream. The trailhead for the Pine Valley Canal Trail and the Santa Clara River Trail begin from this loop. In addition to hiking and biking, there's the opportunity to fish for rainbow and brook trout at nearby Pine Valley Reservoir and the Santa Clara River.

An abundance of nearby trails allow access into the Pine Valley Mountain Wilderness, a region rich in pine, aspen, fir, and spruce. Signal Peak, a granite spire, stands more than 10,000 feet in elevation and is the highest point in the wilderness.

246 Baker Dam

Location: On the west side of the Pine Valley Mountains, about 25 miles north of St. George
GPS: N37 22.665'/W113 38.589'
Facilities: Fire pits, picnic tables, vault toilets, and boat launch
Sites: 19 basic sites
Maximum RV length: 25 feet
Fee: $ for basic sites
Maximum stay: 14 days
Elevation: 5,000 feet
Road conditions: Paved to the campground, then gravel

Management: Bureau of Land Management, St. George Field Office, 345 E. Riverside Dr., St. George; (435) 688-3200; www.blm.gov/ut/st/en/fo/st__george.html [Note: 2 underscores]
Reservations: None
Activities: Fishing, hiking, mountain biking, and picnicking
Season: April through December
Finding the campground: From I-15 in St. George, travel northwest on UT 18. Just past mile marker 24, turn right (east) onto a wide, paved road. A sign points the way to Baker Dam Reservoir; you'll reach the campground in about 0.5 mile.
About the campground: Utah juniper trees decorate this lovely campground, while the nearby Pine Valley Mountains provide a picturesque backdrop. You can roam to your heart's content if you have a good map and compass, or opt for the short, but maintained, 0.2-mile trail.

Most people come here to relax and fish. One camp host claims that 14-pound cutthroat trout have been hooked here at the 50-acre reservoir. Other species include rainbow, brook, and German brown trout.

247 Gunlock State Park

Location: About 20 miles northwest of St. George
GPS: N37 15.299'/W113 46.253'
Facilities: Picnic tables, fire pits, BBQ grills, vault toilets, and boat ramp (April–October)
Sites: 6 basic sites
Maximum RV length: Any
Fee: $$ for basic sites
Maximum stay: 14 days
Elevation: 3,600 feet
Road conditions: Paved to the campground, then dirt
Management: Gunlock State Park, c/o Sand Hollow State Park, 4405 W. 3600 South, Hurricane; (435) 680-0715; www.stateparks.utah.gov/parks/gunlock
Reservations: None
Activities: Boating, water sports, swimming, fishing, mountain biking, and picnicking
Season: Year-round
Finding the campground: From I-15 in St. George, travel north on UT 18 about 3 miles to its junction with UT 8 (Sunset Boulevard). Go left (west) on UT 8 for 5 miles. At this point UT 8 heads north; keep straight, now driving Old Highway 91. Go an additional 6 miles to a fork and stay right (north) for another 5.8 miles to the state park entrance.
About the campground: This primitive campground hugs the east shore of 266-acre Gunlock Reservoir, which is quite popular. Boating and other water sports are favorites; fishing for quality largemouth bass, channel catfish, and bluegills is also a high priority for many visitors. Though the boat ramp is closed in the winter, kayakers can launch from the campground whenever the water is ice-free. Near the dam you'll find a parking area and a paved boat ramp. There's a red-sand beach across the lake. Reach it by boat or by walking across the dam. On a historical note, the road leading to Gunlock Lake is part of the Old Spanish Trail, which once stretched from Santa Fe, New Mexico, to Los Angeles, California.

Beautiful reflection of Gunlock Reservoir

248 Snow Canyon State Park

Location: About 11 miles northwest of St. George
GPS: N37 12.222'/W113 38.460'
Facilities: Fire pits, picnic tables (some covered), BBQ grills, flush toilets, showers, partial hook-ups, dump station, and drinking water
Sites: 15 basic sites, 14 partial-hookup sites, and 2 group sites (maximum 35 and 55 people respectively)
Maximum RV length: 40 feet
Fee: $$ for basic and partial-hookup sites; $$$$$ for group sites
Maximum stay: 14 days (5-day limit February through May and September through November)
Elevation: 3,300 feet
Road conditions: Paved
Management: Snow Canyon State Park, 1002 Snow Canyon Dr., Ivins; (435) 628-2255; www .stateparks.utah.gov/parks/snow-canyon
Reservations: In the Salt Lake area, call (801) 322-3770; elsewhere, (800) 322-3770; http:// utahstateparks.reserveamerica.com
Activities: Hiking, rock climbing, mountain biking, horseback riding, picnicking, and photography
Restrictions: Campground gate closed from 10 p.m. to 6 a.m.
Season: Year-round

Petrified dunes area, Snow Canyon State Park

Finding the campground: From I-15 in St. George, travel north on UT 18 about 11 miles to the paved park road, which drops into the canyon. You'll reach the campground and entrance station in less than 3 miles.

About the campground: Set in Snow Canyon, a land of Navajo sandstone boasting shades of pink, red, and yellow, capped by black lava rock, the campground offers some shaded sites. If you camp sans hookups, you'll enjoy wide sites and privacy; opt for hookups and you'll sit parking-lot-style next to your neighbor. (**Note:** Use of slide-outs and awnings are not guaranteed at these sites. Reservations are not required, but they are advised.)

Activities are abundant, with a volleyball court in the campground. There are also more than 16 miles of hiking trails in the 7,400-acre state park, over a hundred rock climbing routes, and a 5-mile-long bike trail. More than 5 miles of horseback riding trails exist in the 5-mile-long canyon, too. Cacti bloom in the spring; wildlife watching can be enjoyed all year, though summers are very hot.

249 Red Cliffs Recreation Site

Location: On the south end of the Pine Valley Mountains, about 15 miles northeast of St. George
GPS: N37 13.373' / W113 24.233'
Facilities: Fire pits, covered picnic tables, BBQ grills, vault toilets, and drinking water
Sites: 12 basic sites
Maximum RV length: 25 feet

Fee: $ for basic sites
Maximum stay: 14 days
Elevation: 3,200 feet
Road conditions: Paved, with 2 narrow, 1-lane tunnels
Management: Bureau of Land Management, St. George Field Office, 345 E. Riverside Dr., St. George; (435) 688-3200; www.blm.gov/ut/st/en/fo/st__george.html [Note: 2 underscores]
Reservations: None
Activities: HIking, mountain biking, picnicking, and photography
Restrictions: Tunnels are restricted to vehicles less than 11 feet, 6 inches high and no wider than 12 feet. Visitors with long RVs should beware of steep dips and sharp curves.
Season: Year-round
Finding the campground: From I-15 and Leeds exits 22 and 23 (use exit 22 if you're northbound, exit 23 if you're southbound), about 15 miles northeast of St. George, go south on the frontage road for 2 to 3 miles to the signed Red Cliffs turnoff. Go right (west) and through two tunnels, crossing Quail Creek en route to the campground fee station, another 1.5 miles away.
About the campground: The campground at the Red Cliffs Recreation Site guards the mouth of one of many Utah redrock canyons. Cottonwood trees shade most of the campsites, and several trails lead to very different places. One leads to some nearby dinosaur tracks; another a mere 0.8 mile to a lookout point; another travels across fairly open country to an Ancestral Puebloan archaeological site; and the longest leads a mile up Quail Creek, more if you're up to exploring on your own.

Red Cliffs is a busy place, so you shouldn't expect to have it to yourself. The hike up Quail Creek is especially popular, but there are good reasons for its popularity. Several deep pools offer the chance to cool off, while a slot canyon offers slickrock, alcoves, grottoes, and pictographs.

250 Oak Grove

Location: In the Dixie National Forest, approximately 19 miles northeast of St. George
GPS: N37 19.008'/W113 27.182'
Facilities: Fire pits, picnic tables, and vault toilets
Sites: 8 basic sites and 1 group site (maximum 15 people)
Maximum RV length: 20 feet (trailers not recommended)
Fee: $ for basic sites and group site
Maximum stay: 14 days
Elevation: 6,500 feet
Road conditions: One lane with turnouts, maintained dirt; not recommended for trailers
Management: Pine Valley Ranger District, 196 E. Tabernacle, Ste. 40, St. George; (435) 652-3100; www.fs.usda.gov/main/dixie/home
Reservations: None
Activities: Hiking, horseback riding, and picnicking
Season: Memorial Day through Labor Day
Finding the campground: From I-15 and Leeds exits 22 and 23 (use exit 22 if you're northbound, exit 23 if you're southbound), about 15 miles northeast of St. George, go northwest on Silver Reef Road. The road is paved for a while, then turns to gravel and then dirt. Along the 9-mile route you'll pass by dispersed sites 1 through 13. The sites are free, offer no amenities, and have a 16-day

limit. After traveling 4.4 miles, you'll see the Children's Forest of the Kiln on the right. There's room to park and a walking trail as well. The campground is located at the end of the road.

About the campground: Situated in a forest of ponderosa pine, spruce, Gambel oak, and shrub live oak, this small campground provides a cool refuge come summer. Leeds Creek offers trout fishing, though dense shrubs make access difficult.

Hiking is none too easy, but it is available. The Oak Grove Trail begins at the campground and climbs a steady, steep grade through the beautiful Pine Valley Mountain Wilderness. A sign says the trail leads 3 miles to the Summit Trail, though it seems more like 4 miles to most people. Regardless of its length, it climbs just over 3,000 feet to the trail junction.

251 Quail Creek State Park

Location: About 12 miles northeast of St. George
GPS: N37 11.423'/W113 23.557'
Facilities: Fire pits, covered picnic tables, flush toilets, drinking water, fish cleaning station, and 2 boat ramps
Sites: 22 basic sites
Maximum RV length: 35 feet
Fee: $$ for basic sites
Maximum stay: 14 days
Elevation: 3,300 feet
Road conditions: Paved
Management: Quail Creek State Park, 472 N. 5300 West, Hurricane; (435) 879-2378; www .stateparks.utah.gov/park/quail-creek-state-park
Reservations: In the Salt Lake area, call (801) 322-3770; elsewhere, (800) 322-3770; http:// utahstateparks.reserveamerica.com
Activities: Fishing, swimming, waterskiing, Jet Skiing, sailboarding, boating, and picnicking
Restrictions: Campground gate is closed from 9 p.m. to 7 a.m. Quail Creek enforces a 40-boat limit on the reservoir. Boat ramp access times vary from season to season. Check with the state park for more information. Also, in order to prevent the spread of quagga mussels, all boats outside of Utah, including float tubes, must be officially decontaminated at nearby Sand Hollow State Park before launching at Quail Creek.
Season: Year-round
Finding the campground: From the south (St. George area), drive northeast on I-15 for about 8 miles to UT 9. Turn right (east) onto UT 9 for 2.6 miles to the park entrance via UT 318. You'll reach the campground and entrance station in 1.8 miles. If you're coming from the north, exit I-15 at Leeds exit 23 (about 15 miles northeast of St. George) and follow the frontage road south for 3.4 miles, then turn left and continue for about 1.5 miles.
About the campground: Excellent year-round camping can be had in this part of sunny, southwest Utah. In fact, during summer Quail Creek Reservoir boasts the warmest water in the state. It is an especially nice place to camp if you enjoy waterskiing, boating, swimming, or fishing for largemouth bass, catfish, bluegills, and rainbow trout.

252 Westside: Sand Hollow State Park

Location: About 17 miles northeast of St. George
GPS: N37 07.094'/W113 23.314'
Facilities: Fire pits, covered picnic tables, ADA sites, BBQ grills, full hookups, dump station, flush toilets, showers, drinking water, fish cleaning station, and boat ramp
Sites: 50 full-hookup sites
Maximum RV length: Any
Fee: $$$ for full-hookup sites
Maximum stay: 14 days
Elevation: 3,000 feet
Road conditions: Paved
Management: Sand Hollow State Park, 3351 S. Sand Hollow Rd.; (435) 680-0715; http://state parks.utah.gov/parks/sand-hollow
Reservations: In the Salt Lake area, call (801) 322-3770; elsewhere, (800) 322-3770; http:// utahstateparks.reserveamerica.com
Activities: Fishing, swimming, waterskiing, Jet Skiing, sailboarding, boating, OHV riding, mountain biking, and picnicking
Restrictions: Campground gate is closed from 10 p.m. to 6 a.m. Quagga mussels, an invasive species, have been found in Sand Hollow Reservoir. If your boat, trailer, or any gear has been in Sand Hollow Reservoir within the last 30 days, you are legally required to decontaminate equipment before going to another body of water. Decontamination is free of charge. OHVs are not allowed to be ridden in or from the Westside Campground.
Season: Year-round
Finding the campground: From the south (St. George area), drive northeast on I-15 for about 8 miles to UT 9. Turn right (east) onto UT 9 for 4.9 miles and make a right (south) onto Sand Hollow Road. Drive another 4 miles and make a left (east) to the park entrance.
About the campground: Utah's newest state park, and one of its most popular, provides for excellent year-round camping in this part of sunny, southwest Utah. Westside Campground is located on the northwest side of Sand Hollow Reservoir. Some of the sites have wonderful views of nearby mountains and the reservoir. Sand Hollow is a great place for water activities, and offers more than 6,000 acres of OHV riding at Sand Mountain. In addition to two developed campgrounds, campers can also camp in primitive areas for a fee.

253 Sandpit: Sand Hollow State Park

Location: About 17 miles northeast of St. George
GPS: N37 07.094'/W113 23.314'
Facilities: Fire pits, picnic tables, BBQ grills, partial hookups, dump station, flush toilets, showers, and drinking water; fish cleaning station and boat ramp nearby
Sites: 19 basic sites, 6 partial-hookup sites, and 5 group sites (maximum 100 people each)
Maximum RV length: Any

Fee: $$ for basic sites; $$$ for partial-hookup sites; $$$$$ for group sites
Maximum stay: 14 days
Elevation: 3,000 feet
Road conditions: Paved to the campground, then gravel
Management: Sand Hollow State Park, 3351 S. Sand Hollow Rd.; (435) 680-0715; http://state parks.utah.gov/parks/sand-hollow
Reservations: In the Salt Lake area, call (801) 322-3770; elsewhere, (800) 322-3770; http://utahstateparks.reserveamerica.com
Activities: Fishing, swimming, waterskiing, Jet Skiing, sailboarding, boating, OHV riding, mountain biking, and picnicking
Restrictions: Campground gate is closed from 10 p.m. to 6 a.m. Quagga mussels, an invasive species, have been found in Sand Hollow Reservoir. If your boat, trailer, or any gear has been in Sand Hollow Reservoir within the last 30 days, you are legally required to decontaminate equipment before going to another body of water. Decontamination is free of charge.
Season: Year-round
Finding the campground: From the south (St. George area), drive northeast on I-15 for about 8 miles to UT 9. Turn right (east) onto UT 9 for 4.9 miles and make a right (south) onto Sand Hollow Road. Drive another 4 miles and make a left (east) to the park entrance.
About the campground: Excellent year-round camping can be had in this part of sunny, southwest Utah. Sandpit Campground is located on the south end of Sand Hollow Reservoir with close access to Sand Mountain. OHV riding is permitted from the campground. Some of the sites have wonderful views of mountains and the reservoir. Sand Hollow is a great place for water activities, and offers more than 6,000 acres of OHV riding at Sand Mountain. In addition to two developed campgrounds, campers can also camp in primitive areas for a fee.

254 Lava Point: Zion National Park

Location: North-central Zion National Park, about 20 miles north of Virgin
GPS: N37 23.007'/W113 01.969'
Facilities: Fire pits, picnic tables, and vault toilets; no trash service (pack it out)
Sites: 6 basic sites (best for tents, vans, and truck campers)
Maximum RV length: 19 feet (vehicles longer than 19 feet not permitted on the road to the campground)
Fee: None
Maximum stay: 14 days
Elevation: 7,890 feet
Road conditions: One-and-a-half-lane, gravel. (During spring and fall, weather conditions can change rapidly. Check www.nps.gov/zion/planyourvisit/roadconditions.htm for road conditions.)
Management: Zion National Park, Springdale, UT 84767-1099; (435) 772-3256; www.nps.gov/zion/index.htm
Reservations: None
Activities: Hiking, picnicking, and photography

Restrictions: Generators are prohibited. Also, travel in Zion Canyon via Zion Canyon Scenic Drive is by free shuttle bus only from late March to early November; check with headquarters for exact dates.

Season: June through October

Finding the campground: From UT 9 in Virgin, drive north on Kolob Reservoir Road (called Kolob Terrace Road on park maps). The road is paved and climbs dramatically for wonderful views of Zion National Park and surrounding areas. After 20.2 miles turn right (east) where a sign points the way to the Lava Point Campground. Drive the dirt road less than 2 miles to the campground.

About the campground: Surrounded by aspens, ponderosa pines, Gambel oaks, and white firs, the Lava Point Campground sits at just under 7,900 feet in elevation. For a magnificent view of the park and beyond, you can walk to the Lava Point Fire Lookout a few hundred yards to the east. Signs help identify Cedar Breaks National Monument to the north and Pink Cliffs to the northeast; if you look east, you'll see Zion Canyon Narrows. And if that isn't enough, gaze southeast and see the Sentinel and other grand features of Zion Canyon, and look south into Arizona. Nearby hiking trails lead to various points. In addition, you can fish at Kolob Reservoir, a high-country lake reached by driving another 3.5 miles north past the Lava Point turnoff via Kolob Reservoir Road.

255 South: Zion National Park

Location: Just north of the south entrance
GPS: N37 12.228'/W112 59.046'
Facilities: Fire pits, picnic tables, ADA sites, flush toilets, dump station, utility sinks, and drinking water
Sites: 127 basic sites
Maximum RV length: Any (maximum height clearance 13 feet, 1 inch)
Fee: $$ for basic sites
Maximum stay: 14 days March through mid-November; 30 days the rest of the year
Elevation: 4,100 feet
Road conditions: Paved
Management: Zion National Park, Springdale, UT 84767-1099; (435) 772-3256; www.nps.gov/zion/index.htm
Reservations: None
Activities: Hiking, rock climbing, mountain biking, photography, and picnicking
Restrictions: If you enter the park from the west, you'll have no problems negotiating UT 9. Enter from the east, however, traveling what is also called Zion–Mt. Carmel Highway, and you'll have to travel through two narrow tunnels. The shorter is 530 feet long; the longer is 5,600 feet. Vehicles over 13 feet high, single vehicles over 40 feet long, combined vehicles over 50 feet long, and pedestrians and bicyclists are prohibited. Vehicles over 7 feet, 10 inches wide and/or 11 feet, 4 inches high must travel through the tunnel with one-way traffic; a fee is charged; check for travel times. Also, travel in Zion Canyon via Zion Canyon Scenic Drive is by free shuttle bus only from late March to early November; check with headquarters for exact dates.
Season: Early March through early November

Finding the campground: The campground is located off UT 9, just north of the south entrance station, about 2 miles north of Springdale.

About the campground: South Campground is the smaller of the two campgrounds located near the south entrance. Located along the North Fork Virgin River, campsites are shaded compliments of netleaf hackberries and Fremont cottonwoods. The campground fills by early to midafternoon during the peak spring-through-fall season, so you should arrive early if you hope to camp here.

Activities abound in Zion National Park. Some folks come to sit by the river and read a book, some to hike a short trail, others to hoist a heavy backpack and head for Zion's backcountry. Still others come to climb one of Zion's monoliths. While most of the big-wall climbs are in the difficult range—5.10 and above—there's a wonderful 5.8 climb on the northwest side of Mount Spry. Check with the backcountry office for more information.

256 Watchman: Zion National Park

Location: At the south entrance station
GPS: N37 11.112'/W112 59.173'
Facilities: Fire pits, picnic tables, ADA sites, electric hookups, tent pads, flush toilets, dump station, utility sinks, and drinking water
Sites: 69 basic sites (best for tents or combined vehicle length of 19 feet), 89 electric-hookup sites, 6 electric-hookup sites for RVs only, 18 walk-in tent sites, and 7 group sites (maximum varies from 9 to 40 people)
Maximum RV length: 40 feet (maximum height clearance 13 feet, 1 inch)
Fee: $$ for basic, walk-in tent, and electric-hookup sites; $ per person per night for group sites
Maximum stay: 14 days March through mid-November; 30 days the rest of the year; 7 days for group sites
Elevation: 3,900 feet
Road conditions: Paved
Management: Zion National Park, Springdale, UT 84767-1099; (435) 772-3256; www.nps.gov/zion/index.htm
Reservations: Call (877) 444-6777 or TDD (877) 833-6777; www.recreation.gov
Activities: Hiking, rock climbing, mountain biking, picnicking, and photography
Restrictions: If you enter the park from the west, you'll have no problems negotiating UT 9. Enter from the east, however, traveling what is also called Zion–Mt. Carmel Highway, and you'll have to travel through two narrow tunnels. The shorter is 530 feet long; the longer is 5,600 feet. Vehicles over 13 feet high, single vehicles over 40 feet long, combined vehicles over 50 feet long, and pedestrians and bicyclists are prohibited. Vehicles over 7 feet, 10 inches wide and/or 11 feet, 4 inches high must travel through the tunnel with one-way traffic; a fee is charged; check for travel times. Also, travel in Zion Canyon via Zion Canyon Scenic Drive is by free shuttle bus only from late March to early November; check with headquarters for exact dates.
Season: Year-round
Finding the campground: The campground is located off UT 9, at the entrance station, about 1 mile north of Springdale.

The Watchman is visible from the bridge over the Virgin River.

About the campground: Named for The Watchman, a famous rock formation that stretches 6,545 feet into the heavens, this campground is situated on a bench above the North Fork Virgin River. Hackberry, ash, and cottonwood trees serve to shade campers. The campground fills by early to midafternoon during the peak spring-through-fall season, so you should make plans to arrive early if you want to camp here.

Hiking, climbing, and photography opportunities abound. A popular hike begins at the Grotto Picnic Area and ascends some steep switchbacks before traveling through the magnificent realms of Refrigerator Canyon. It then ascends a series of short switchbacks—called Walter's Wiggles—to Scott Lookout. From there you'll have to decide whether or not to ascend the steep, 500-foot-high, knife-edged sandstone rib to Angel's Landing. Steps, human-made depressions cut into the rock, and thick chains may help calm the nerves of those afraid of heights. Children and hikers who are seriously afraid of heights should stay below. Atop Angel's Landing, about 1,500 feet above the valley floor, you'll thrill to close-up views of the likes of the Great White Throne and Zion Canyon.

257 Coral Pink Sand Dunes State Park

Location: About 22 miles west of Kanab
GPS: N37 02.212' / W112 43.875'
Facilities: Fire pits, picnic tables, drinking water, showers, flush toilets, and dump station

Sites: 19 basic sites, 3 double sites, and 1 group site (maximum 50 people)
Maximum RV length: 40 feet
Fee: $$ for basic sites; $$$$ for double sites; $$$$$ for group site
Maximum stay: 14 days
Elevation: 6,000 feet
Road conditions: Paved
Management: Coral Pink Sand Dunes State Park, PO Box 95, Kanab, UT 84741-0095; (435) 648-2800; www.stateparks.utah.gov/parks/coral-pink
Reservations: In the Salt Lake area, call (801) 322-3770; elsewhere, (800) 322-3770; http://utahstateparks.reserveamerica.com
Activities: Off-highway driving, hiking, photography, and picnicking
Restrictions: ATV flags mandatory
Season: Year-round
Finding the campground: From Kanab drive north on US 89 for 8.2 miles, then turn left (west) onto signed Hancock Road, which is paved. Drive 9.3 miles to its end at another paved road. A sign points left (southwest) to the state park, which you'll reach in another 4.2 miles. The park is on the left (east) side of the road.
About the campground: This is a great place for those with OHVs, which are especially popular with weekend folks. Weekdays find most people happy to hike and photograph the dunes. A short boardwalk trail allows access via wheelchair.

258 Ponderosa Grove

Location: About 15 miles northwest of Kanab
GPS: N37 05.297' / W112 40.307'
Facilities: Fire pits, picnic tables, BBQ grills, and vault toilets
Sites: 9 basic sites
Maximum RV length: 24 feet
Fee: $ for basic sites
Maximum stay: 14 days
Elevation: 6,300 feet
Road conditions: Paved to the campground, then gravel
Management: Bureau of Land Management, Kanab Field Office, 669 S. Hwy. 89A, Kanab; (435) 644-1200; www.blm.gov/ut/st/en.html
Reservations: None
Activities: Off-highway driving and picnicking
Restrictions: ATVs not allowed
Season: Year-round
Finding the campground: From Kanab drive north on US 89 for 8.2 miles, then turn left (west) onto signed Hancock Road, which is paved. Drive 7.3 miles to the campground turnoff, which is on the right side of the road.
About the campground: This is a popular place for those with OHVs, though you are not allowed to ride ATVs in the campground. The campground, in a lovely setting of Utah junipers and ponderosa pines, provides access to Coral Pink Sand Dunes State Park, just 4 miles southwest.

259 Kings Creek

Location: In the Dixie National Forest, approximately 26 miles southeast of Panguitch
GPS: N37 36.526'/W112 15.491'
Facilities: Fire pits, picnic tables, tent pads, flush and vault toilets, dump station, and drinking water; boat ramp nearby at Tropic Reservoir; horseshoe pit and volleyball court in group area; no garbage service (pack it out)
Sites: 37 basic sites and 2 group sites (maximum 50 and 100 people respectively)
Maximum RV length: 45 feet for basic sites; 35 feet for group site
Fee: $$ for basic sites; $$$$ to $$$$$ for group sites
Maximum stay: 14 days
Elevation: 8,000 feet
Road conditions: Maintained gravel to the campground, then paved
Management: Powell Ranger District, 225 E. Center, Panguitch; (435) 676-9300; www.fs.usda.gov/main/dixie/home
Reservations: For group sites only, call (877) 444-6777 or TDD (877) 833-6777; www.recreation.gov
Activities: Hiking, fishing, boating, swimming, mountain biking, access to the Fremont ATV Trail, and picnicking
Season: Mid-May through September
Finding the campground: From the junction of UT 12 and US 89, about 7 miles south of Panguitch, travel east on UT 12 for 10.8 miles. At this point head south on gravel FR 087 (also known as East Fork of the Sevier Road) for another 7 miles to FR 572. Make a right (west) onto gravel FR 572, passing Tropic Reservoir and reaching the campground in less than 1 mile.
About the campground: A ponderosa pine forest blankets the west shore of Tropic Reservoir, where the campground is located, making this a nice spot for boating, trout fishing, swimming, hiking, off-highway driving, or just plain relaxing. Nearby, the East Fork of the Sevier River offers fishing opportunities for brook, cutthroat, brown, and rainbow trout.

Several hiking trails of varying difficulty begin at the campground. Mountain bikers may want to check out *Mountain Biking Utah*; Gregg Bromka's book describes a ride from the campground. ATVers should sample the Fremont ATV Trail. This popular ATV trail, which is about 60 miles long, starts near the campground and ends in Circleville, connecting with other ATV trails—East Fork, the Great Western Trail, and Casto Canyon—along the way.

260 Red Canyon: Red Canyon Recreation Area

Location: In the Dixie National Forest, about 11 miles southeast of Panguitch
GPS: N37 44.641'/W112 18.637'
Facilities: Fire pits, picnic tables, BBQ grills, showers (fee), flush toilets, dump station, and drinking water; also free Wi-Fi in Loop A, campsite 5
Sites: 33 basic sites and 4 double sites
Maximum RV length: Any
Fee: $$ for basic sites; $$$ for double sites

Maximum stay: 14 days
Elevation: 7,200 feet
Road conditions: Paved
Management: Powell Ranger District, PO Box 80, Panguitch, UT 84759; (435) 676-9300; www .fs.usda.gov/main/dixie/home
Reservations: None
Activities: Hiking, mountain biking, horseback riding, and picnicking
Season: Early May through late September
Finding the campground: From the junction of UT 12 and US 89, about 7 miles south of Panguitch, travel east on scenic UT 12 for 3.8 miles. The campground is on the right (south) side of the highway.
About the campground: Situated in a mini Bryce Canyon–like setting, with its own collection of hoodoos and spires, Red Canyon is a nice place to camp if you don't mind being next to the highway.

There are 16 miles of hiking trails in the area, 34 miles of mountain biking trails, and 8 miles of paved riding and hiking trails. One of the most popular trails takes off from the visitor center, located just west of the campground. The Pink Ledges Trail loops about 0.5 mile, with signs to identify the most common trees and plants.

261 Coyote Hollow Equestrian

Location: In the Dixie National Forest, about 15 miles southeast of Panguitch
GPS: N37 42.887' / W112 16.275'
Facilities: Fire pits, picnic tables, BBQ grills, vault toilets, hitching rails, and non-potable water for horses
Sites: 4 basic sites
Maximum RV length: Any
Fee: $ for basic sites
Maximum stay: 14 days
Elevation: 7,800 feet
Road conditions: Gravel
Management: Powell Ranger District, PO Box 80, Panguitch, UT 84759; (435) 676-9300; www .fs.usda.gov/main/dixie/home
Reservations: None
Activities: Hiking, mountain biking, horseback riding, off-road vehicle riding, and picnicking
Season: Year-round
Finding the campground: From the junction of UT 12 and US 89, about 7 miles south of Panguitch, travel east on scenic UT 12 for 7.5 miles. There are no signs pointing the way to the campground, but you will see a large staging area for the Fremont ATV Trail on the right (south) side of the road. Turn here and drive FR 113, a gravel road, southwest for 1 mile to the campground.
About the campground: Situated in a lovely ponderosa pine forest on the beautiful Pausaugunt Plateau, this campground offers large sites for those both with and without horses. The campground provides easy access to Thunder Mountain, a popular trail for hiking, biking, and horseback riding. At nearby Red Canyon there are 16 miles of hiking trails in the area, 34 miles of mountain biking trails, and 8 miles of paved riding and hiking trails.

262 Sunset: Bryce Canyon National Park

Location: South of the entrance station
GPS: N37 37.373'/W112 10.366'
Facilities: Fire pits, picnic tables, ADA sites, drinking water, and flush toilets; in summer a dump station (fee) near the North Campground, showers (fee) near the general store, and a free shuttle system
Sites: 48 RV sites, 52 tent sites, and 1 group site (maximum 30 people)
Maximum RV length: RV and trailer combinations over 45 feet discouraged, but not prohibited
Fee: $$ for RV and tent sites; $$$$$ for group site
Maximum stay: 14 days
Elevation: 8,000 feet
Road conditions: Paved
Management: Bryce Canyon National Park, PO Box 640201, Bryce Canyon, UT 84764; (435) 834-5322; www.nps.gov/brca
Reservations: Call (877) 444-6777 or TDD (877) 833-6777; www.recreation.gov
Activities: Hiking, picnicking, and photography
Restrictions: Trailers are not allowed beyond Sunset Campground. Campers should leave their trailers at their campsite. Motor homes and trailers are not permitted to park in spaces designated for buses.
Season: Mid-May through mid-October
Finding the campground: The campground entrance is just over 1 mile south of the entrance station and visitor center, on the west side of the road.
About the campground: Open during the busy days of summer, this campground is near Sunset Point. It provides access to one of the most beautiful places in all the world—Bryce Canyon. An amazing array of hoodoos and other unique formations makes this canyon, which is really an amphitheater, a great place for hiking. There are approximately 50 miles of trails here. If you don't enjoy hiking, you can explore the park by automobile. To do so, drive the 18-mile park road along Plateau Rim to Yovimpa and Rainbow Points. Thirteen pullouts offer views you won't soon forget.

263 North: Bryce Canyon National Park

Location: At the north end of the park
GPS: N37 38.239'/W112 10.148'
Facilities: Fire pits, picnic tables, drinking water, and flush toilets; in summer a dump station (fee), showers (fee) near the general store, and a free shuttle system
Sites: 52 RV sites and 50 tent sites
Maximum RV length: Any
Fee: $$ for RV and tent sites
Maximum stay: 14 days
Elevation: 7,800 feet
Road conditions: Paved

Even with roots exposed, this limber pine grows at Sunrise Point, Bryce Canyon National Park.

Management: Bryce Canyon National Park, PO Box 640201, Bryce Canyon, UT 84764; (435) 834-5322; www.nps.gov/brca

Reservations: Call (877) 444-6777 or TDD (877) 833-6777; www.recreation.gov

Activities: Hiking, picnicking, and photography

Restrictions: Trailers are not permitted beyond Sunset Campground. Campers should leave their trailers at their campsite. Motor homes and trailers are not permitted to park in spaces designated for buses.

Season: Year-round.

Finding the campground: The campground entrance is just south of the entrance station and visitor center, on the east side of the road.

About the campground: Open all year, this campground provides access to one of the most beautiful places in all the world—Bryce Canyon. Its amazing array of hoodoos and other unique formations makes this a great place for hiking and exploring; about 50 miles of trails are found here. If you prefer you can explore by automobile, driving the 18-mile park road along the Plateau Rim to Yovimpa and Rainbow Points. Thirteen pullouts offer views you won't soon forget.

264 Kodachrome Basin State Park

Location: Approximately 9 miles south of Cannonville
GPS: N37 30.882'/W111 59.311'
Facilities: Fire pits, picnic tables, ADA sites, full hookups, drinking water, flush toilets, showers, and dump station. Red Stone Cabins, located in the center of the park, offers information, film, food, ice, and supplies. You can also arrange for guided horseback rides: Phone (435) 679-8536 for additional information.
Sites: 23 basic sites, 10 full-hookup sites, and 2 group campsites (maximum 35 people each)
Maximum RV length: 45 feet
Fee: $$ for basic sites; $$$ for full-hookup sites; $$$$$ for group sites
Maximum stay: 14 days
Elevation: 5,800 feet
Road conditions: Paved
Management: Kodachrome Basin State Park, PO Box 180069, Cannonville, UT 84718-0069; (435) 679-8562; http://stateparks.utah.gov/parks/kodachrome
Reservations: In the Salt Lake area, call (801) 322-3770; elsewhere, (800) 322-3770; http://utahstateparks.reserveamerica.com
Activities: Hiking, horseback riding, mountain biking, photography, and picnicking
Restrictions: Campground gate closed from 10 p.m. to 6 a.m; limited generator use (2 hours maximum)
Season: Year-round
Finding the campground: From UT 12 in Cannonville, head south on the paved road known as Cottonwood Canyon Road. Signs point the way to Kodachrome Basin. You'll reach the entrance station after 7.7 miles. Travel another 1 mile to the campground.
About the campground: This is one of Utah's nicest state parks, where campsites are partially surrounded by unique red- and white-tinged rock formations. It should be no surprise that the National Geographic Society conceived the name of this place, which practically begs to be photographed.

There are plenty of hiking trails to keep you occupied. All have their own attractions. Of particular interest is the nature trail, a paved, wheelchair-accessible path where visitors learn about the native vegetation and geology.

265 Pine Lake

Location: In the Dixie National Forest, about 17 miles northeast of Bryce Canyon National Park
GPS: N37 44.736'/W111 57.150'
Facilities: Fire pits, picnic tables, ADA site, tent pads, vault toilets, drinking water, gravel boat ramp, and OHV unloading ramp; no trash service (pack it out)
Sites: 33 basic sites and 5 group sites (maximum varies from 30 to 100 people)
Maximum RV length: 45 feet

Fee: $$ for basic sites; $$$$$ for group sites
Maximum stay: 14 days
Elevation: 8,300 feet
Road conditions: Maintained gravel
Management: Escalante Ranger District, 755 W. Center, Escalante; (435) 826-5499; www
.fs.usda.gov/main/dixie/home
Reservations: Call (877) 444-6777 or TDD (877) 833-6777; www.recreation.gov
Activities: Hiking, fishing, kayaking and canoeing, mountain biking, off-highway driving, and
picnicking
Restrictions: OHVs/ATVs not allowed
Season: Late May through mid-September
Finding the campground: From the junction of UT 12, UT 63, and John Valley Road (a sign says
this is Route 1660), drive northeast on John Valley Road for 10.7 miles. At this point there's a sign
pointing the way to the campground; make a right (east) onto FR 132, which is maintained gravel.
Follow it, driving an additional 6 miles or so to the campground.
About the campground: Located on the east side of Pine Lake, the campground is in a lovely
setting of ponderosa pine trees. Fishing, kayaking, and canoeing are popular here. It's also a great
place to hike, mountain bike, or ride ATVs. FR 132, a jeep road, leads to 10,188-foot Powell Point
Overlook for a grand view of Bryce Canyon National Park.

266 Escalante Petrified Forest State Park

Location: About 1 mile west of Escalante
GPS: N37 47.208'/W111 37.852'
Facilities: Fire pits, covered picnic tables, partial hookups, ADA sites, drinking water, boat ramp,
canoe rentals, gift shop, dump station, showers, and flush toilets
Sites: 14 basic sites, 8 partial-hookup sites, and 1 group site (maximum 50 people)
Maximum RV length: 50 feet
Fee: $$ for basic and partial-hookup sites; $$$$$ for group campsite
Maximum stay: 14 days
Elevation: 6,000 feet
Road conditions: Paved
Management: Escalante Petrified Forest State Park, 710 N. Reservoir Rd., Escalante; (435) 826-
4466; www.stateparks.utah.gov/parks/escalante
Reservations: In the Salt Lake area, call (801) 322-3770; elsewhere, (800) 322-3770; http://
utahstateparks.reserveamerica.com
Activities: Fishing, boating, swimming, water sports, hiking, and picnicking
Restrictions: Campground gate closed from 10 p.m. to 6 a.m.
Season: Year-round
Finding the campground: From Escalante, travel west on scenic UT 12 for about 1.5 miles. You'll
see the park entrance on the right (north) side of the road; continue 0.7 mile to the fee station/
visitor center.

About the campground: If you like petrified wood, chukars calling, and a lake nearby, then you'll like this Utah state park. Wide Hollow Reservoir, 130 acres in size, offers fishing as well as kayaking, canoeing, and the like. Two interpretive trails allow hikers to learn all about the colorful petrified wood and dinosaur bones found in this park; hike the trails here and you'll quickly learn where it got that name. Collecting is not permitted in the park and should be discouraged elsewhere.

267 Posey Lake

Location: In the Dixie National Forest, approximately 16 miles northwest of Escalante
GPS: N37 56.173'/W111 41.631'
Facilities: Fire pits, picnic tables, bear-proof boxes, drinking water, boat ramp, fish cleaning station, and vault toilets; no trash service (pack it out)
Sites: 21 basic sites and 1 group site (maximum 35 people)
Maximum RV length: 25 feet
Fee: $ for basic sites; $$$$ for group site
Maximum stay: 14 days
Elevation: 8,600 feet
Road conditions: Maintained gravel
Management: Escalante Ranger District, 755 W. Center, Escalante; (435) 826-5499; www .fs.usda.gov/main/dixie/home
Reservations: Call (877) 444-6777 or TDD (877) 833-6777; www.recreation.gov
Activities: Fishing, boating, hiking, and picnicking
Restrictions: ATVs not allowed
Season: Late May through early September
Finding the campground: From Escalante travel east on UT 12 for about 1 mile to the turnoff for Hells Backbone Road (called 300 East here, and later FR 153), which is on the left (north). You'll travel on paved road for the first 3.5 miles, then maintained gravel. After another 10 miles you'll reach a fork in the road; FR 153 continues to the right (north), while FR 154 heads left (west). Keep left on FR 154, and you'll reach Posey Lake after 1.8 miles.
About the campground: The south shore of Posey Lake is the setting for this small campground, with ponderosa pine and aspen trees all around. Anglers vie for both rainbow and brook trout, while hikers, mountain bikers, and horseback riders can travel 1 mile and 385 feet up (2 miles round-trip) to the Posey Lake Lookout, a historic landmark. Access to the nice view is via a trailhead across from campsite 14. Another trail, the Posey Lake Spur Trail, is 1.2 miles long and begins in the campground near the boat dock on the south side of the lake; it ends at John Allen Bottom on the Great Western Trail.

268 Blue Spruce

Location: In the Dixie National Forest, about 20 miles north of Escalante
GPS: N37 58.382' / W111 39.105'
Facilities: Fire pits, picnic tables, drinking water, and vault toilets; no trash service (pack it out)
Sites: 5 basic sites and 1 double site
Maximum RV length: 18 feet
Fee: $ for basic sites; $$ for double site
Maximum stay: 14 days
Elevation: 8,000 feet
Road conditions: Maintained gravel, then dirt
Management: Escalante Ranger District, 755 W. Center, Escalante; (435) 826-5499; www
.fs.usda.gov/main/dixie/home
Reservations: None
Activities: Fishing in a nearby stream and picnicking
Restrictions: ATVs not allowed
Season: Year-round, weather permitting
Finding the campground: From Escalante travel east on UT 12 for about 1 mile to the turnoff for Hells Backbone Road (called 300 East here, and later FR 153), which is on the left (north). You'll travel on paved road for the first 3.5 miles, then maintained gravel. After another 10 miles you'll reach a fork in the road; FR 153 continues to the right (north), while FR 154 heads left (west). Keep right on FR 153, and you'll reach the campground turnoff in 4.6 miles. The turnoff is to the left (north) on FR 145, a narrow dirt and gravel road. Travel 0.5 mile to the campground. (**Note:** This is a tents-only kind of place; sites are small and trailer turnaround space is nonexistent.)
About the campground: As its name implies, this campground is set among blue spruce, with some aspen and ponderosa pine trees as well. You can use the site as a base from which to explore several nearby trails; anglers can fish for trout in a nearby stream.

Just west of the campground, look for the Blue Springs Trail; it's 1.5 miles long. Other nearby trails include the Box Trail, about 0.5 mile southwest, along with the Jubilee Trail, Auger Hole Trail, and West Fork Trail.

269 Calf Creek: Grand Staircase–Escalante National Monument

Location: About 16 miles northeast of Escalante
GPS: N37 47.492' / W111 24.862'
Facilities: Fire pits, picnic tables, drinking water, and vault and flush toilets
Sites: 14 basic sites
Maximum RV length: 25 feet
Fee: $ for basic sites

The trail to the enchanting Lower Calf Creek Falls starts at Calf Creek Campground.

Maximum stay: 14 days
Elevation: 5,400 feet
Road conditions: Paved
Management: Bureau of Land Management, Escalante Field Station, PO Box 225, 755 W. Main St., Escalante, UT 84726; (435) 826-5600; www.blm.gov/ut/st/en/fo/grand_staircase -escalante.html
Reservations: None
Activities: Fishing, hiking, and picnicking
Season: Year-round
Finding the campground: From Escalante travel southeast then northeast on scenic UT 12 for about 16 miles. A sign points the way to the campground entrance, which is on the left (west) side of the road; go 0.2 mile to the entrance.
About the campground: If you have a vehicle less than 25 feet long, you'll be able to indulge in the cottonwoods and oaks of this scenic campground, located in the much larger Grand Staircase– Escalante National Monument. Tucked into a canyon along Calf Creek, anglers can wet a line while hikers enjoy the trail to Lower Calf Creek Falls. It's an interpretive trail, so with guide in hand you can learn all about the native vegetation, see amazing pictographs and Indian ruins, and know that the gorgeous falls are 126 feet high.

270 Deer Creek: Grand Staircase–Escalante National Monument

Location: About 6 miles southeast of Boulder
GPS: N37 51.286' / W111 21.315'
Facilities: Fire pits, picnic tables, and vault toilets; no garbage service (pack it out)
Sites: 7 basic sites
Maximum RV length: RVs not recommended due to numerous sharp curves and no trailer turn-around
Fee: $ for basic sites
Maximum stay: 14 days
Elevation: 5,800 feet
Road conditions: Paved to the campground, then dirt
Management: Bureau of Land Management, Escalante Field Station, PO Box 225, 755 W. Main St., Escalante, UT 84726; (435) 826-5600; www.blm.gov/ut/st/en/fo/grand_staircase -escalante.html
Reservations: None
Activities: Fishing, hiking, and picnicking
Season: Year-round
Finding the campground: At the south end of Boulder, go east on Boulder-Bullfrog Scenic Road (also known as the Burr Trail). Though this portion of the road is paved, it is not recommended for trailer traffic due to numerous sharp curves. You'll reach the campground after 6.3 miles. (**Note:** A trailer turnaround is nonexistent.)
About the campground: Located in the grand expanse of Grand Staircase–Escalante National Monument, these small sites are set along Deer Creek, where there is fishing. A trailhead is just across the road; it leads south through Deer Creek Canyon.

271 Upper Pleasant Creek

Location: In the Dixie National Forest (though managed by Fishlake National Forest), approximately 17 miles southeast of Torrey
GPS: N38 06.126' / W111 20.218'
Facilities: Fire pits, picnic tables, drinking water, and vault toilets
Sites: 12 basic sites
Maximum RV length: 25 feet
Fee: $ for basic sites
Maximum stay: 14 days
Elevation: 8,700 feet
Road conditions: Paved

Management: Fremont River Ranger District, 138 S. Main St., Loa; (435) 836-2800; www.fs.usda.gov/main/fishlake/home
Reservations: None
Activities: Hiking, mountain biking, fishing, and picnicking
Restrictions: ATVs not allowed
Season: Mid-May through early September
Finding the campground: From Torrey drive south on scenic UT 12 for 16.8 miles. You'll see the campground and turnoff on the left (east) side of the road.
About the campground: The upper portion of two side-by-side campgrounds (known as Upper and Lower Pleasant Creek), this campground is set in a forest of ponderosa pine. There's fishing at Pleasant Creek, as well as access to many trails nearby. Hikers should check out the Pleasant Creek Trailhead, which includes access to the Great Western Divide Trail. It's off UT 12, 0.4 mile to the north.

272 Lower Pleasant Creek

Location: In the Dixie National Forest (though managed by Fishlake National Forest), about 17 miles southeast of Torrey
GPS: N38 06.039' / W111 20.236'
Facilities: Fire pits, picnic tables, drinking water, and vault toilets
Sites: 5 basic sites
Maximum RV length: 20 feet
Fee: $ for basic sites
Maximum stay: 14 days
Elevation: 8,700 feet
Road conditions: Paved
Management: Fremont River Ranger District, 138 S. Main St., Loa; (435) 836-2800; www.fs.usda.gov/main/fishlake/home
Reservations: None
Activities: Hiking, mountain biking, fishing, and picnicking
Restrictions: ATVs not allowed
Season: Mid-May through early September
Finding the campground: From Torrey drive south on scenic UT 12 for 16.9 miles. You'll see the campground and turnoff on the left (east) side of the road.
About the campground: The lower portion of two side-by-side campgrounds (known as Upper and Lower Pleasant Creek), this campground is set in a forest of ponderosa pine. Trailer turnaround is tight here—if your vehicle is longer than 20 feet, you should check out the Upper Pleasant Creek Campground. There's fishing at Pleasant Creek, as well as access to many trails nearby. Check out the Pleasant Creek Trailhead, which includes access to the Great Western Divide Trail; it's off UT 12, 0.5 mile to the north.

273 Lower Bowns

Location: In the Dixie National Forest (though managed by Fishlake National Forest), about 21 miles southeast of Torrey
GPS: N38 06.039'/W111 20.236'
Facilities: Fire pits, picnic tables, stove stands, ADA sites, and vault toilets; no trash service (pack it out)
Sites: 4 basic sites and 1 group site (maximum 50 people)
Maximum RV length: 30 feet
Fee: $ for basic sites; $$$$ for group site
Maximum stay: 14 days
Elevation: 7,400 feet
Road conditions: Gravel
Management: Fremont River Ranger District, 138 S. Main St., Loa; (435) 836-2800; www.fs.usda .gov/main/fishlake/home
Reservations: Call (877) 444-6777 or TDD (877) 833-6777; www.recreation.gov
Activities: Fishing, mountain biking, off-road riding, bird watching, and picnicking
Season: Late May through late September
Finding the campground: From Torrey drive south on scenic UT 12 for 17 miles to a turnoff for Lower Bowns Reservoir. Make a left (east) onto FR 186, a narrow dirt road that can be impassable in wet weather. Reach the reservoir in 3.8 miles.
About the campground: Sites are dispersed, shaded by pinyon pines, and embraced by the sagebrush found around the reservoir. The fishing for rainbow (and occasionally cutthroat) trout can be good; bird watching is fun, too. ATVers will enjoy riding the Rosebud ATV Trail, which is nearby. In addition, a bike ride is described in FalconGuides' *Mountain Biking Utah*, by Gregg Bromka.

274 Oak Creek

Location: In the Dixie National Forest (though managed by the Fishlake National Forest), approximately 18 miles south of Torrey
GPS: N38 05.370'/W111 20.503'
Facilities: Fire pits, picnic tables, drinking water, and vault toilets
Sites: 8 basic sites and 1 double site
Maximum RV length: 20 feet
Fee: $ for basic sites; $$ for double site
Maximum stay: 14 days
Elevation: 8,800 feet
Road conditions: Paved
Management: Fremont River Ranger District, 138 S. Main St., Loa; (435) 836-2800; www.fs.usda .gov/main/fishlake/home
Reservations: None
Activities: Fishing, mountain biking, hiking, and picnicking
Season: Mid-May through mid-September

Finding the campground: From Torrey drive south on scenic UT 12 for 18 miles; turn left (east) at the campground sign and travel 0.1 mile to the campground.

About the campground: Small RVs (there's a 20-foot maximum here) should note that there's little room to turn around at the end of this campground, which is set in a forest of ponderosa pine, spruce, and aspen. Oak Creek provides music nearby. Hikers and bikers looking for a trail needn't look far; the High Ranger Trailhead is just across the street.

275 Cedar Mesa: Capitol Reef National Park

Location: About 30 miles southeast of the visitor center
GPS: N38 04.433'/W111 04.960'
Facilities: Fire pits, picnic tables, and vault toilet
Sites: 5 basic sites (best for tents and truck campers)
Maximum RV length: RVs not recommended due to poor road conditions
Fee: None
Maximum stay: 14 days
Elevation: 5,400 feet
Road conditions: Dirt and sand; usually passable to passenger vehicles, but high-clearance vehicles are recommended. Road conditions change due to rain or snow and sometimes require a four-wheel-drive vehicle; check at the visitor center for current conditions.
Management: Capitol Reef National Park, HC 70 Box 15, Torrey, UT 84775; (435) 425-3791; www.nps.gov/care/index.htm
Reservations: None
Activities: Hiking, photography, and picnicking
Season: Year-round
Finding the campground: From the visitor center, about 11 miles east of Torrey, continue east on UT 24 for 8.9 miles. Make a right, driving Notom-Bullfrog Road (it's paved at first, then turns to dirt and sand) for 21.1 miles. At this point go right (west) on a short spur road leading to the campground.
About the campground: Excellent views of Red Canyon and the wide mesas east of Waterfold Mesa are yours from broad Cedar Mesa, where the campground is located. Tucked away in a forest of juniper trees, the campground provides access to Red Canyon. Travel both by trail and cross-country to the canyon and a huge amphitheater, which is partially surrounded by lofty cliffs of reddish-orange Wingate sandstone.

276 McMillan Springs

Location: In the Henry Mountains, about 53 miles southwest of Hanksville
GPS: N38 04.327'/W110 50.893'
Facilities: Fire pits, picnic tables, drinking water (water may or may not be potable; check with the managing agency for current conditions), and vault toilets
Sites: 10 basic sites (best for tents and truck campers)

Maximum RV length: RVs not recommended due to poor roads
Fee: $ for basic sites
Maximum stay: 14 days
Elevation: 8,400 feet
Road conditions: One lane, dirt; high-clearance vehicles recommended
Management: Bureau of Land Management, Henry Mountains Field Station, 380 S. 100 West, Hanksville; (435) 542-3461; www.blm.gov/ut/st/en/fo/richfield/recreation_/henry_mountains .html
Reservations: None
Activities: Hiking, mountain biking, and picnicking
Season: May through November
Finding the campground: From the junction of UT 24 and Notom-Bullfrog Road, about 28 miles west of Hanksville, head south on paved Notom-Bullfrog Road, which later turns to dirt and sand. Drive it about 8 miles to Sandy Ranch; head left (east) on a dirt road. A sign may point the way to McMillan Springs. Continue approximately 17 miles to the campground, merging onto Bull Creek Pass National Backcountry Byway a couple of miles prior to the campground. When you reach the byway, head left (northeast).
About the campground: McMillan Springs is a scenic campground set in a forest of lofty ponderosa pine trees. A local herd of bison hangs out in the area, making this a popular spot for wildlife watching. The Henry Mountains are home to one of the few free-roaming herds of bison in the continental United States. Transplanted from Yellowstone National Park in 1941, the original herd of 18 now tops out at about 300 animals. Lucky visitors may also see mule deer, pronghorn, bighorn sheep, elk, and mountain lions.

Though you can reach the campground by traveling to the Lonesome Beaver Campground and continuing another 10 miles or so, you'd have to wait until July to do this, because the 10,485-foot Bull Creek Pass is often closed by snow until then. Use the above route via Notom-Bullfrog Road when snow prevails.

277 Lonesome Beaver

Location: In the Henry Mountains, about 21 miles southwest of Hanksville
GPS: N38 06.578'/W110 46.685'
Facilities: Fire pits, picnic tables, drinking water, and vault toilets
Sites: 5 basic sites (best for tents and truck campers)
Maximum RV length: RVs not recommended due to poor road conditions
Fee: $ for basic sites
Maximum stay: 14 days
Elevation: 8,300 feet
Road conditions: One lane, dirt, winding with steep grades; high-clearance vehicles recommended
Management: Bureau of Land Management, Henry Mountains Field Station, 380 S. 100 West, Hanksville; (435) 542-3461; www.blm.gov/ut/st/en/fo/richfield/recreation_/henry_mountains .html

Reservations: None
Activities: Hiking, mountain biking, and picnicking
Season: May through October
Finding the campground: From the junction of UT 24 and Henry Mountain Access Road (100 East) in Hanksville, head south on Henry Mountain Access Road. The road is paved for 0.4 mile, then turns to maintained gravel, and eventually deteriorates to a one-lane dirt road. As you climb in elevation, the road becomes winding and very steep. Trailers are not recommended; no doubt drivers would have trouble making some of the tight turns. Reach the campground after a total of 21.3 miles. You'll see the Dandelion Flat Picnic Area about 0.4 mile prior to the campground.
About the campground: There's lots of shade in this campground, with aspen, spruce, and pine trees all around. Bull Creek does a little singing near the camp, which is best suited for tenters.

This is a nice base for a classic Utah bike ride. A grueling, 20-mile loop is described in Gregg Bromka's book *Mountain Biking Utah*. You can also hike to the top of Mount Ellen from several areas, including Bull Creek Pass, about 4 miles farther. (*Note:* The pass is at 10,485 feet and usually only open from early June through late October.

278 Dirty Devil River: Glen Canyon National Recreation Area

Location: About 44 miles southeast of Hanksville
GPS: N37 54.722'/W110 23.902'
Facilities: Vault toilets
Sites: Dispersed
Maximum RV length: Any
Fee: $ per person; $$ maximum per vehicle
Maximum stay: 14 days
Elevation: 3,800 feet
Road conditions: One lane, dirt
Management: Glen Canyon National Recreation Area, PO Box 1507, Page, AZ 86040-1507; (928) 608-6200; www.nps.gov/glca/index.htm
Reservations: None
Activities: Fishing, boating, water sports, swimming, picnicking, and photography
Season: Year-round
Finding the campground: From Hanksville travel south then southeast on UT 95 for 43.8 miles.
About the campground: Several areas of dispersed, shadeless sites are found along the sandstone-blessed shores of the Dirty Devil River. There are magnificent views of the surrounding area, as well as the chance to indulge in the water sport of your choice. Also, anglers may want to fish while photographers make lasting images of the place.

279 Starr Springs

Location: In the Henry Mountains, approximately 47 miles south of Hanksville
GPS: N37 50.942'/W110 39.801'
Facilities: Fire pits, BBQ grills, picnic tables, drinking water, and vault toilets
Sites: 12 basic sites (best for tents, truck campers, and camper vans)
Maximum RV length: 20 feet
Fee: $ for basic sites
Maximum stay: 14 days
Elevation: 6,200 feet
Road conditions: Maintained gravel (one lane upon entering the campground)
Management: Bureau of Land Management, Henry Mountains Field Station, 380 S. 100 West, Hanksville; (435) 542-3461; www.blm.gov/ut/st/en/fo/richfield/recreation_/henry_mountains .html
Reservations: None
Activities: Hiking and picnicking
Season: April through October
Finding the campground: From the junction of UT 95 and UT 24 in Hanksville, head south on UT 95 for 25.8 miles. At this point continue right (south) on paved UT 276 toward Bullfrog. Drive another 16.9 miles to the turnoff for Starr Springs Recreation Site and turn right (northwest) on the well-maintained gravel road for 3.9 miles to the campground.
About the campground: Situated in a forest of oak and juniper at the base of Mount Hillers, the campground provides access to the Panorama Knoll Nature Trail, which is across from the fee station and picnic area. A short loop trail gives hikers access to a viewpoint. On another note, about 0.5 mile prior to reaching the campground, there are old ranch ruins for visitors to see and photograph, though you shouldn't pass beyond the fenced enclosure.

280 Stanton Creek: Glen Canyon National Recreation Area

Location: About 2 miles southeast of the north entrance station near Bullfrog
GPS: N37 30.529'/W110 41.985'
Facilities: Boat launch and vault toilets
Sites: Dispersed
Maximum RV length: Any
Fee: $ per person; $$ maximum per vehicle
Maximum stay: 14 days
Elevation: 3,800 feet
Road conditions: One lane, dirt
Management: Glen Canyon National Recreation Area, PO Box 1507, Page, AZ 86040; (520) 608-6200; www.nps.gov/glca/index.htm
Reservations: None

Stanton Creek Campground

Activities: Fishing, boating, water sports, swimming, picnicking, and photography
Restrictions: Portable toilets required when camping more than 200 yards from an established bathroom facility
Season: Year-round
Finding the campground: From the north entrance fee station, about 63 miles south of Hanksville, travel south on UT 276 for 0.2 mile, then make a left (east) onto a maintained gravel road that turns to dirt. Continue another 2 miles to the campground.
About the campground: Dispersed, shadeless sites are abundant along this inlet, across from Halls Crossing. From here, campers enjoy fishing for various game fish, such as largemouth, smallmouth, and striped bass. Broad bays offer plenty of space for waterskiing and for the houseboats that ply the lovely waters of Lake Powell.

281 Bullfrog: Glen Canyon National Recreation Area

Location: About 2 miles southwest of the north entrance station near Bullfrog
GPS: N37 31.316' / W110 43.272'
Facilities: Fire pits, BBQ grills, picnic tables, drinking water, ADA sites, flush toilets, dump station, and fish cleaning station; boat launch, marina, gas, gift shop, laundry, lodge, restaurant, and post office nearby

Sites: 78 basic sites
Maximum RV length: Any
Fee: $$ for basic sites
Maximum stay: 14 days
Elevation: 3,800 feet
Road conditions: Paved
Management: Glen Canyon National Recreation Area, PO Box 1507, Page, AZ 86040; (520) 608-6200; www.nps.gov/glca/index.htm
Reservations: None
Activities: Fishing, boating, water sports, swimming, picnicking, and photography
Season: Year-round
Finding the campground: From the north entrance fee station, about 63 miles south of Hanksville, travel south on UT 276 for 1.2 miles to the visitor center. Continue straight (southwest) for another 0.3 mile to the campground entrance, which is on the left (south).
About the campground: An assortment of deciduous trees provides some shade in the campground, which has three loops. Some sites have views of Lake Powell. There's a boat ramp a short drive away, as well as a marina where there are boat rentals and a store. There's also a ferry: The *John Atlantic Burr* travels between Bullfrog and Halls Crossing and saves 145 road miles. Lake Powell visitors have plenty to do—water sports, boating, fishing, and photography are perhaps the most popular activities.

282 Bullfrog RV: Glen Canyon National Recreation Area

Location: About 2 miles southwest of the north entrance station near Bullfrog
GPS: N37 31.704'/W110 43.679'
Facilities: Fire pits, picnic tables, flush toilets, showers, full hookups, and drinking water; boat launch, marina, gas, gift shop, laundry, lodge, restaurant, and post office nearby
Sites: 24 full-hookup sites
Maximum RV length: Any
Fee: $$$$$ for full-hookup sites
Maximum stay: 14 days
Elevation: 3,800 feet
Road conditions: Paved
Management: Glen Canyon National Recreation Area, PO Box 1507, Page, AZ 86040; (520) 608-6200; www.nps.gov/glca/index.htm
Reservations: Call (888) 896-3829; www.lakepowell.com
Activities: Fishing, boating, water sports, swimming, picnicking, and photography
Season: Year-round
Finding the campground: From the north entrance fee station, about 63 miles south of Hanksville, travel south on UT 276 for 1.2 miles to the visitor center. At the corner turn right (west) toward the marina; you'll see the RV campground about 0.5 mile down on your right.
About the campground: Full hookups, hot showers, and some shade trees will delight those who like plenty of amenities. On a hill overlooking the lovely waters of Lake Powell, the campground is

near the marina, where campers can sign up for a boat tour of the lake. If you have your own boat, you'll find a boat ramp nearby. There's also a ferry: The *John Atlantic Burr* travels between Bullfrog and Halls Crossing and saves 145 road miles. Activities abound here, with water sports, boating, fishing, and photography perhaps the most popular.

283 Lone Rock: Glen Canyon National Recreation Area

Location: About 63 miles east of Kanab
GPS: N37 0.985'/W111 32.741'
Facilities: Vault toilets, micro flush toilets, 1 comfort station (ADA), outdoor cold showers, off-road vehicle area, dump station, and potable water (seasonal)
Sites: Undeveloped beach camping; large RVs okay
Maximum RV length: Any
Fee: $ per night per vehicle
Maximum stay: 14 days
Elevation: 3,700 feet
Road conditions: Paved to the beach, then sand
Management: Glen Canyon National Recreation Area, PO Box 1507, Page, AZ 86040; (928) 608-6200; www.nps.gov/glca/index.htm
Reservations: None
Activities: Boating, swimming, waterskiing, fishing, photography, and picnicking
Season: Year-round
Finding the campground: From Kanab drive northeast on US 89 for 62.7 miles, then turn left (east) onto Lone Rock Road. The beach and campground are 2 miles farther.
About the campground: Dispersed camping is the norm here at Lone Rock Beach, which is along the southwest shore of Wahweap Bay at Lake Powell. It's a beautiful spot, and whereas the place is primitive, there are all sorts of amenities at Wahweap Resort, about 5 miles southeast across the Arizona border.

284 White House: Adjacent to Vermilion Cliffs National Monument

Location: About 45 miles east of Kanab and 32 miles west of Page
GPS: N37 04.815'/W111 53.433'
Facilities: Fire pits, picnic tables, and vault toilets
Sites: 5 walk-in sites
Maximum RV length: None
Fee: $ for walk-in sites
Maximum stay: 14 days
Elevation: 4,300 feet

Road conditions: Dirt

Management: Bureau of Land Management, Kanab Field Office, 669 S. Hwy. 89A, Kanab; (435) 644-1200; www.blm.gov/ut/st/en.html

Reservations: None

Activities: Hiking, photography, and picnicking

Season: Year-round, weather and road conditions permitting. (A four-wheel-drive or all-wheel drive vehicle may be needed to access the campground in inclement weather.)

Finding the campground: From Kanab drive east on US 89 for 42.6 miles. At this point turn right (south) at the sign for Paria Canyon–Vermilion Cliffs. There's a fee station and ranger station just after you turn. Continue 2 miles on the combination gravel and sand road to the campground. You'll have to park your vehicle and walk in to each site.

About the campground: Tucked up against vermilion cliffs, this campground is set in a beautiful spot and makes a good base from which to explore the area. Better yet, spend several days back-packing into Paria Canyon and be entranced by numerous narrow, twisting slot canyons. (**Note:** If you want to backpack, you'll have to obtain a hiking permit. Contact the managing agency for more information.)

Canyonlands

Utah is an outdoor kind of place, and the Canyonlands travel region is no exception when it comes to enjoying the great out-of-doors. There are many favored activities; some of the more popular use camera equipment, mountain bikes, rock climbing paraphernalia, hiking boots, fishing poles, rafts, kayaks, canoes, powerboats, and off-road vehicles.

Photographers will find a multitude of scenes worthy of their film, while mountain bikers will enjoy a wide range of terrain, including slickrock, a particular favorite. Rock climbers will find everything from traditional finger crack and crack climbs to bolted slab friction climbs, while hikers will enjoy just as much variety in trails—or even more. In addition, anglers will find many a fine fishing hole; rafters; kayakers, and canoeists will no doubt thrill to the likes of the Green, Colorado, and San Juan Rivers; boaters will enjoy the twisting canyons of Lake Powell; and off-road enthusiasts will discover many a track to follow.

In Canyonlands, visitors find it all. The countryside offers up everything from desert to mountains, narrow slot canyons, wide vistas, lengthy Lake Powell, and all things in between. Part of the geologic region known as the Colorado Plateau, it's a paradise for photographers and other artists; in fact, it's a paradise of sorts for all who come to visit.

Grand and San Juan Counties make up Canyonlands, the third largest of Utah's nine travel regions. Scattered over 11,414 square miles, the region is bordered on the north by Dinosaurland, on the west by the Green River, and on the east and south by the respective states of Colorado and Arizona.

Forty-five public campgrounds feature sites ranging from the lofty realms of the LaSal and Abajo Mountains, to the desert oasis at Sand Island (it's located on the banks of the San Juan River), to the natural-bridge-blessed kingdom of Natural Bridges National Monument. In addition, there are wonderful views from Dead Horse Point State Park, a maze of hiking trails and a bevy of climbing routes in and near both Canyonlands and Arches National Parks, and the water-sports-oriented waters of Lake Powell and the Colorado River. Ancient Indian ruins are common in this part of the country, with Hovenweep National Monument and Natural Bridges National Monument particularly nice spots from which to easily explore them. All campsites are managed by either the National Park Service, the Bureau of Land Management, the USDA Forest Service, or the Utah state park system.

The region can be visited at any time of year, though you'll find some of the higher campgrounds closed come winter. Still, you can always camp low and go high to cross-country ski in the LaSal and Abajo Mountains. Of course, even some of

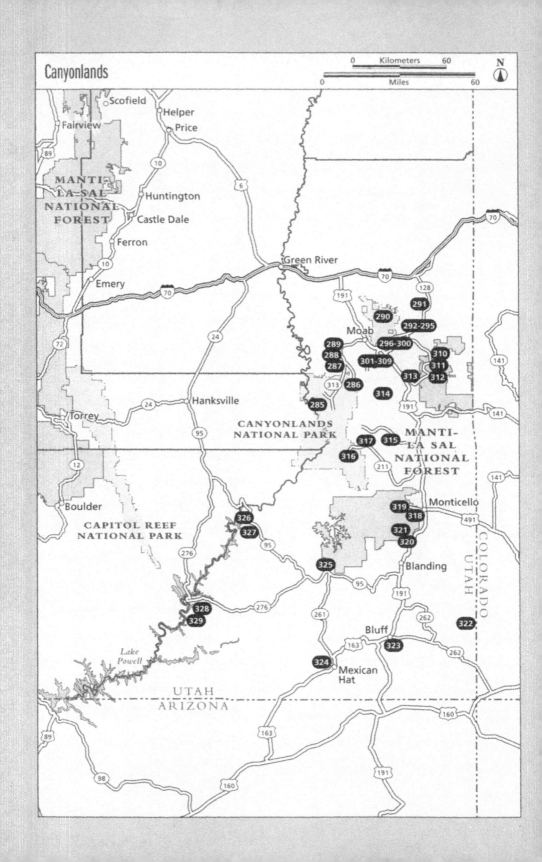

the lower-elevation campgrounds have the water turned off during winter months. Fortunately, camp fees are usually reduced; thus this is a good time to save money and avoid the summer crowds. Speaking of crowds, most of the national park campgrounds fill early from about March through October; plan accordingly.

For more information contact the Canyonlands Travel Region at PO Box 550, Moab, UT 84532; (435) 259-1370; or PO Box 490, 117 S. Main St., Monticello, UT 84535; (435) 587-3235 or (800) 574-4386; www.utahtravelcenter.com/travel regions/canyonlands.htm.

		Total Sites	Group Sites	Hook-up Sites	Hookups	Max. RV Length	Dump Station	Toilets	Showers	Drinking Water	ADA Compliant	Fees	Reservations	Recreation
285	Willow Flat	12				28		V				$		HMO
286	Dead Horse Point State Park	22	1	21	E	Any	•	F		•	•	$$$	•	HM
287	Cowboy Camp	7				None		V				$		HM
288	Horsethief	58				Any		V				$$		HM
289	Lone Mesa	5	5			Any		V				$$$$-$$$$$	•	HM
290	Devils Garden	50	2			40		F		•	•	$$	•	HCM
291	Dewey Bridge	9	3			34		V				$$-$$$$$		HMKLOB
292	Hittle Bottom	12				20		V				$$		KBLHM
293	Fisher Towers	5				18		V				$$		HC
294	Lower Onion	5	1			30		V				$-$$$$$	•	HKBLC
295	Upper Onion	2	2			40		V				$$$-$$$$$	•	HMRO
296	Upper Big Bend	8				18		V				$$		HMOCK
297	Big Bend Recreation Site	25	3			40		V				$$-$$$$$	•	HMOKC
298	Hal Canyon/Oak Grove	18				24/18		V				$$		HMKO
299	Drinks Canyon	17				18		V				$$		HMKO
300	Granstaff	16				18		V				$$		HMKO
301	Goose Island	19	2			40		V				$$-$$$$$	•	HMKO
302	Jaycee Park	6				None		V				$$		HCM
303	Williams Bottom	18				24		V				$		HCM
304	Gold Bar	9	4			40		V				$-$$$$$	•	HCMKOL

Hookup: W = Water, E = Electric, S = Sewer
Recreation: H = Hiking, C = Rock Climbing, M = Mountain Biking, S = Swimming, F = Fishing, B = Boating, L = Boat Launch, O = Off-highway Driving, R = Horseback Riding, K = Kayaking and Canoeing, G = Golf
Toilets: F = Flush, V = Vault, C = Chemical
Per-night campsite cost: $ = $10 or less $$ = $11 to $20 $$$ = $21 to 30 $$$$ = $31 to $40 $$$$$ = $41 and higher

		Total Sites	Group Sites	Hook-up Sites	Hookups	Max. RV Length	Dump Station	Toilets	Showers	Drinking Water	ADA Compliant	Fees	Reservations	Recreation
305	Sand Flats Recreation Area	122	2			40		V				$-$$$$$		HCMO
306	King's Bottom	10				24		V				$$		HCMO
307	Moonflower	8				None		V				$		HCMO
308	Spring Site and Hunter Canyon	13				18		V				$		HCMO
309	Ledge	26	1			None		V				$-$$$$$	•	HMO
310	Mason Draw	5				20		V				$		HM
311	Warner Lake	21	1			20		V		•		$-$$$$$	•	FHMR
312	Oowah Lake	11				20		V				$		FHM
313	Ken's Lake	30	3			40		V				$$-$$$$$	•	FHMRKBL
314	Hatch Point	10				24		V		•		$$		HM
315	Windwhistle	16	1			24		V		•		$$-$$$	•	H
316	Squaw Flat	29	3			30		F & V		•	•	$$-$$$$$	•	CMOH
317	Hamburger Rock	10				25		V				$		CMH
318	Dalton Springs	16				30		V		•		$-$$		FH
319	Buckboard	13	2			25		V		•		$-$$$$	•	FH
320	Devils Canyon	42				45		V		•	•	$	•	H
321	Nizhoni	27	2			40		V		•	•	$-$$$$	•	HF
322	Hovenweep National Monument	30				35		F		•	•	$		MH
323	Sand Island	27	1			Any		V		•		$-$$$$$	•	HFBL
324	Goosenecks State Park	4				30		V				None		
325	Natural Bridges National Monument	13				26		V		•		$		H
326	Hite	*				Any	•	F		•		$-$$		FBLSK
327	Farley Canyon	*				Any		C & V				$		FBSK
328	Halls Crossing	45	2			None		F	•	•		$$-$$$$$	•	FBLSK
329	Halls Crossing RV	32		32	WES	60	•	F	•	•		$$$$$	•	FBLSK

Hookup: W = Water, E = Electric, S = Sewer   * = Dispersed Camping, no designated sites
Recreation: H = Hiking, C = Rock Climbing, M = Mountain Biking, S = Swimming, F = Fishing, B = Boating, L = Boat Launch, O = Off-highway Driving, R = Horseback Riding, K = Kayaking and Canoeing, G = Golf
Toilets: F = Flush, V = Vault, C = Chemical
Per-night campsite cost: $ = $10 or less $$ = $11 to $20 $$$ = $21 to 30 $$$$ = $31 to $40 $$$$$ = $41 and higher

Mesa Arch at sunrise

285 Willow Flat: Canyonlands National Park

Location: About 9 miles southwest of the Island in the Sky entrance station
GPS: N38 22.943' / W109 53.290'
Facilities: Fire pits, picnic tables, tent pads, and vault toilets
Sites: 12 basic sites
Maximum RV length: 28 feet
Fee: $ for basic sites
Maximum stay: 7 days
Elevation: 6,200 feet
Road conditions: Gravel
Management: Canyonlands National Park, 2282 SW Resource Blvd., Moab; (435) 719-2100; www.nps.gov/cany/Index.htm
Reservations: None
Activities: Hiking, mountain biking, off-highway driving, photography, and picnicking
Season: Year-round
Finding the campground: From Moab drive northwest on US 191 for about 10 miles, then make a left (southwest) onto UT 313. A sign points the way to the national park, as well as to Dead Horse Point State Park. Continue southwest on the paved road for 20.4 miles to the fee station. Follow the signs another 8.8 miles to the campground.

About the campground: Junipers and pinyon pines decorate this small campground, a good place from which to explore the Island in the Sky section of Canyonlands. A number of trails lead to striking vistas, delicate arches, and an assortment of geologic wonders. There's also a great mountain bike loop that travels through a section of the park. Check out Jughandle Loop in Gregg Bromka's book *Mountain Biking Utah*. (**Note:** There is no water in this section of the park.)

Island in the Sky is the best place to go for overwhelming vistas. On this broad, level mesa wedged between the Green and Colorado Rivers, you'll see not only what's close by but also the distant horizon about 100 miles away. Three jagged mountain ranges loom in the distance; to the east you'll see the LaSals, to the south, the Abajos, and to the southwest, the Henrys.

286 Dead Horse Point State Park

Location: About 31 miles southwest of Moab
GPS: N38 29.208'/W109 44.423'
Facilities: Covered picnic tables, electric hookups, ADA sites, tent pads, charcoal grills, drinking water, flush toilets and a dump station
Sites: 21 electric-hookup sites and 1 group campground (maximum 30 people)
Maximum RV length: Any
Fee: $$$ for electric-hookup sites; $ per person for group site
Maximum stay: 14 days
Elevation: 5,900 feet
Road conditions: Paved
Management: Dead Horse Point State Park, PO Box 609, Moab, UT 84532-0609; (435) 259-2614; www.stateparks.utah.gov/parks/dead-horse
Reservations: In the Salt Lake area, call (801) 322-3770; elsewhere, (800) 322-3770; http://utahstateparks.reserveamerica.com
Activities: Hiking, mountain biking, photography, and picnicking
Restrictions: Campground gate closed from 10 p.m. to 6 a.m.
Season: Year-round
Finding the campground: From Moab drive northwest on US 191 for about 10 miles, then make a left (southwest) onto UT 313. A sign points the way to the state park, as well as to Canyonlands National Park. After 14.7 miles there's a junction to the state park. Go left (east) for 6.5 miles on paved UT 313 to the fee station. The campground is 0.25 mile beyond. There's also a group site about 1.5 miles prior to the fee station.
About the campground: Junipers and pinyon pines grace this lovely campground, with its nice views and footpath leading 2.5 miles to Dead Horse Point. The view from the point, 2,000 feet above the Colorado River, is breathtaking. Many of Canyonlands' sculptured pinnacles and buttes are visible from this peninsula of rock set atop sandstone. When taking in the view, you'll probably notice the unnaturally blue waters to the east; those are mine tailings. Also check out the Intrepid Trail System, open to mountain bikers and hikers. It's a must-do!

The folks at the state park say water is at a premium here. It must be trucked in from Moab, so please use it sparingly.

287 Cowboy Camp

Location: About 25 miles west of Moab
GPS: N38 33.659'/W109 47.648'
Facilities: Fire pits, picnic tables, and vault toilets (trash receptacle at Horsethief Campground)
Sites: 7 basic sites (tents, truck campers, and vans only)
Maximum RV length: None (RVs not allowed)
Fee: $ for basic sites
Maximum stay: 14 days
Elevation: 6,100 feet
Road conditions: Dirt and gravel
Management: Bureau of Land Management, Moab Field Office, 82 E. Dogwood, Moab; (435) 259-2100; www.blm.gov/ut/st/en/fo/moab.html
Reservations: None
Activities: Hiking, mountain biking, and photography
Restrictions: No generators
Season: Year-round
Finding the campground: From Moab drive northwest on US 191 for about 10 miles, then make a left (southwest) onto UT 313. A sign points the way to Dead Horse Point State Park, as well as to Canyonlands National Park. After about 14 miles turn right (west) onto a gravel road (a sign points the way to the camping area) and follow it a few feet to the fee station.
About the campground: Junipers and pinyon pines decorate this small campground with its big, wide-open views of the Henry Mountains and the La Sals. The campground is a nice place for a base camp from which to explore both Dead Horse Point State Park and the Islands in the Sky District of Canyonlands National Park.

288 Horsethief

Location: About 23 miles west of Moab
GPS: N38 35.048'/W109 48.852'
Facilities: Fire pits, picnic tables, tent pads, and vault toilets
Sites: 58 basic sites
Maximum RV length: Any
Fee: $$ for basic sites
Maximum stay: 14 days
Elevation: 5,800 feet
Road conditions: Gravel
Management: Bureau of Land Management, Moab Field Office, 82 E. Dogwood, Moab; (435) 259-2100; www.blm.gov/ut/st/en/fo/moab.html
Reservations: None
Activities: Hiking, mountain biking, and photography
Restrictions: ATVs not allowed

Season: Year-round

Finding the campground: From Moab drive northwest on US 191 for about 10 miles, then make a left (southwest) onto UT 313. A sign points the way to Dead Horse Point State Park, as well as to Canyonlands National Park. After about 12 miles turn right (west) onto a gravel road (a sign points the way to the campground) and follow it 0.5 mile to the campground entrance.

About the campground: Junipers and pinyon pines decorate this nice campground with its wide-open views. There are large sites for any size RV. The campground is a nice place for a base camp from which to explore both Dead Horse Point State Park and the Islands in the Sky District of Canyonlands National Park.

289 Lone Mesa

Location: About 23 miles northwest of Moab
GPS: N38 38.182'/W109 48.273'
Facilities: Fire pits, covered picnic tables, BBQ grills, and vault toilets
Sites: 5 group sites (minimum 10 to 15 people; maximum 20 to 40 people)
Maximum RV length: Any
Fee: $ per person; $$$$ to $$$$$
Maximum stay: 14 days
Elevation: 5,400 feet
Road conditions: Gravel
Management: Bureau of Land Management, Moab Field Office, 82 E. Dogwood, Moab; (435) 259-2100; www.blm.gov/ut/st/en/fo/moab.html
Reservations: Call (435) 259-2102; sites not reserved available on a first-come, first-served basis
Activities: Hiking, mountain biking, and photography
Season: Year-round

Finding the campground: From Moab drive northwest on US 191 for about 10 miles, then make a left (southwest) onto UT 313. A sign points the way to Dead Horse Point State Park, as well as to Canyonlands National Park. After 8.5 miles turn right (west) onto a gravel road (a sign points the way to the campground) and follow it 0.2 mile to the campground entrance. You'll pass a reservation board here; continue on the gravel road an additional 0.4 mile to another reservation board and a fee station.

About the campground: The campground is wide open and spacious with nice views of the La Sal and Henry Mountains. It can accommodate any size RV. Site A has a divided horse corral for four to six horses. If you like to hike, check out both Sunrise and Sunset Trails. The campground is a nice place for a base camp from which to explore both Dead Horse Point State Park and the Islands in the Sky District of Canyonlands National Park.

Turret Arch

290 Devils Garden: Arches National Park

Location: About 18 miles north of the entrance station and visitor center
GPS: N38 46.822'/W109 35.460'
Facilities: Fire pits, picnic tables, ADA site, drinking water, and flush toilets
Sites: 48 basic sites and 2 group sites (maximum 35 and 55 people, respectively)
Maximum RV length: 40 feet
Fee: $$ for basic sites; $ per person for group sites
Maximum stay: 14 days
Elevation: 5,000 feet
Road conditions: Paved
Management: Arches National Park, PO Box 907, Moab, UT 84532-0907; (435) 719-2299; www
.nps.gov/arch/index.htm
Reservations: Call (877) 444-6777 or (877) 833-6777 (TDD); www.recreation.gov
Activities: Hiking, rock climbing, mountain biking, photography, and picnicking
Season: Year-round
Finding the campground: From the visitor center, about 5 miles northeast of Moab, travel north
through the park for about 18 miles.

About the campground: Campsites usually fill by early morning here at Arches National Park, a wonderful place for hiking, mountain biking, rock climbing, and scenic driving. More than 2,000 cataloged arches vary in size; some have a mere 3-foot opening, the minimum considered an arch, while the longest, Landscape Arch, measures 306 feet from base to base.

Flush toilets and water are available from mid-March through mid-October. In winter vault toilets are the norm, and you'll have to get water at the visitor center. Campfire programs are offered in season at the amphitheater.

291 Dewey Bridge

Location: About 31 miles northeast of Moab
GPS: N38 48.651' / W109 18.503'
Facilities: Fire pits, picnic tables, vault toilets, and boat launch
Sites: 6 basic sites and 3 group sites (maximum 30 people each)
Maximum RV length: 34 feet
Fee: $$ for basic sites; $$$$$ for group sites
Maximum stay: 14 days
Elevation: 4,100 feet
Road conditions: Paved to the campground, then gravel
Management: Bureau of Land Management, Moab Field Office, 82 E. Dogwood, Moab; (435) 259-2100; www.blm.gov/ut/st/en/fo/moab.html
Reservations: None
Activities: Hiking, mountain biking, canoeing and kayaking, rafting, off-highway driving, and picnicking
Season: Year-round
Finding the campground: From the junction of US 191 and UT 128, about 2 miles north of Moab, drive northeast on UT 128 for about 29 miles.
About the campground: Though you won't find much, there is some shade at this campground, with a mammoth cottonwood for those lucky enough to select the site close to it. The Colorado River flows nearby, with a boat ramp providing access for kayakers, rafters, and canoeists. Mountain bikers, horseback riders, ATVers, and motorcyclists will be interested in the Kokopelli Trail, which passes through here. About 142 miles long, it crosses Dewey Bridge, just a small part of the trail (a series of old roads and some singletrack), which extends from Moab to Loma, Colorado.

292 Hittle Bottom

Location: About 25 miles northeast of Moab
GPS: N38 45.608' / W109 19.493'
Facilities: Fire pits, picnic tables, vault toilets, and a boat launch
Sites: 6 basic sites and 6 walk-in sites
Maximum RV length: 20 feet
Fee: $$ for basic and walk-in sites

Maximum stay: 14 days

Elevation: 4,000 feet

Road conditions: Paved to the campground, then gravel

Management: Bureau of Land Management, Moab Field Office, 82 E. Dogwood, Moab; (435) 259-2100; www.blm.gov/ut/st/en/fo/moab.html

Reservations: None

Activities: Kayaking and canoeing, rafting, hiking, mountain biking, and picnicking

Season: Year-round

Finding the campground: From the junction of US 191 and UT 128, about 2 miles north of Moab, drive northeast on paved UT 128 for about 23 miles.

About the campground: Cottonwoods provide some shade in this campground, while the muddy Colorado River flows nearby. Once the site of the Hittle Bottom Homestead, a boat ramp provides access for kayakers, rafters, and canoeists who wish to travel down this wonderful water-carved canyon. Hikers should check out the 3-mile-long Amphitheater Loop Trail, which starts at the campground. The trail climbs about 250 feet in elevation and allows for wonderful views of the Colorado River corridor.

293 Fisher Towers

Location: About 24 miles northeast of Moab

GPS: N38 43.526'/W109 18.548'

Facilities: Fire pits, picnic tables, and vault toilet; no trash service (pack it out)

Sites: 5 basic sites

Maximum RV length: 18 feet (no trailers, RVs, or large vehicles; best for tents, truck campers, and vans)

Fee: $$ for basic sites

Maximum stay: 14 days

Elevation: 4,600 feet

Road conditions: Graded dirt

Management: Bureau of Land Management, Moab Field Office, 82 E. Dogwood, Moab; (435) 259-2100; www.blm.gov/ut/st/en/fo/moab.html

Reservations: None

Activities: Hiking, rock climbing, and picnicking

Restrictions: No generators

Season: Year-round

Finding the campground: From the junction of US 191 and UT 128, about 2 miles north of Moab, drive northeast on paved UT 128 for about 21 miles. A sign points the way to Fisher Towers. Turn right (east) and drive the graded dirt road for 2.1 miles to the campground, trailhead, and end of the road.

About the campground: Located at the trailhead for Fisher Towers, a popular rock climbing area, the campground offers amazing views. Be sure to hike the trail at Fisher Towers. It leads past the base of the Titan and then on to a ridge at 2.2 miles where there are great views of the Colorado River Basin, including Castle Rock. The campground is also an excellent place for nighttime star viewing opportunities.

294 Lower Onion

Location: About 23 miles northeast of Moab
GPS: N38 44.236' / W109 21.629'
Facilities: Fire pits, picnic tables, vault toilets, and boat launch; no trash service (pack it out)
Sites: 4 basic sites and 1 group site (maximum 40 people)
Maximum RV length: 30 feet
Fee: $ for basic sites; $$$$$ for group site
Maximum stay: 14 days
Elevation: 4,000 feet
Road conditions: Graded dirt to the campground, then gravel
Management: Bureau of Land Management, Moab Field Office, 82 E. Dogwood, Moab; (435) 259-2100; www.blm.gov/ut/st/en/fo/moab.html
Reservations: For the group site only, call (435) 259-2102
Activities: Hiking, kayaking and canoeing, rafting, rock climbing, and picnicking
Season: Year-round
Finding the campground: From the junction of US 191 and UT 128, about 2 miles north of Moab, drive northeast on paved UT 128 for about 21 miles. A sign points the way to Fisher Towers to the east. Do NOT turn here. Instead, turn left (northwest) directly across the road onto an unmarked graded road and drive 1 mile to the campground.
About the campground: Located along the Colorado River, this campground offers some trees for shade. Onion Creek flows nearby. The campground is an excellent place for star viewing opportunities.

295 Upper Onion

Location: About 22 miles northeast of Moab
GPS: N38 43.250' / W109 20.580'
Facilities: Fire pits and vault toilets; no trash service (pack it out)
Sites: 2 group sites (maximum 20 people each)
Maximum RV length: 40 feet
Fee: $$$ minimum for group sites; if not reserved, sites available first-come, first-served for $ per vehicle
Maximum stay: 14 days
Elevation: 4,200 feet
Road conditions: Graded dirt
Management: Bureau of Land Management, Moab Field Office, 82 E. Dogwood, Moab; (435) 259-2100; www.blm.gov/ut/st/en/fo/moab.html
Reservations: For group sites only, call (435) 259-2102
Activities: Hiking, mountain biking, horseback riding, ATVing, and picnicking
Season: Year-round

Finding the campground: From the junction of US 191 and UT 128, about 2 miles north of Moab, drive northeast on paved UT 128 for about 20.3 miles. Turn right (south) onto signed Onion Creek Road and drive 0.7 mile on the graded road to the fee station for the group sites.

About the campground: The campground, with its spectacular views, is a popular place from which to explore Onion Creek Road. Horse enthusiasts will thrill to site A because it has a corral for up to eight horses. If you decide to drive the road up Onion Creek, note that it crosses the creek twenty-something times in just over 5 miles. The crossings are shallow; however, the water is corrosive, so clean the undercarriage of your bike or vehicle when you return to Moab.

296 Upper Big Bend

Location: About 10 miles northeast of Moab
GPS: N38 38.959'/W109 29.293'
Facilities: Fire pits, picnic tables, and vault toilets
Sites: 8 basic sites
Maximum RV length: 18 feet (best for tents, truck campers, or vans)
Fee: $$ for basic sites
Maximum stay: 14 days
Elevation: 4,000 feet
Road conditions: Gravel
Management: Bureau of Land Management, Moab Field Office, 82 E. Dogwood, Moab; (435) 259-2100; www.blm.gov/ut/st/en/fo/moab.html
Reservations: None
Activities: Hiking, mountain biking, off-highway driving, bouldering, rafting, kayaking and canoeing, and picnicking
Season: Year-round
Finding the campground: From the junction of US 191 and UT 128, about 2 miles northwest of Moab, drive northeast on UT 128 for an additional 8.1 miles.
About the campground: Located along the Colorado Riverway, a colorful medley of towering sandstone spires, water-carved canyons, and striking cliffs, this campground is a popular place from which to canoe, kayak, and raft from late spring through fall.

The Porcupine Rim Bike Trail is just to the south, as is the Big Bend Bouldering Area.

297 Big Bend Recreation Site

Location: About 9 miles northeast of Moab
GPS: N38 38.919'/W109 28.787'
Facilities: Fire pits, picnic tables, and vault toilets
Sites: 22 basic sites and 3 group sites (maximum 20 to 40 people each)

Maximum RV length: 40 feet

Fee: $$ for basic sites; $$$$$ for group sites

Maximum stay: 14 days

Elevation: 4,000 feet

Road conditions: Gravel

Management: Bureau of Land Management, Moab Field Office, 82 E. Dogwood, Moab; (435) 259-2100; www.blm.gov/ut/st/en/fo/moab.html

Reservations: For group sites only, call (435) 259-2102

Activities: Hiking, mountain biking, off-highway driving, bouldering, rafting, kayaking and canoeing, and picnicking

Season: Year-round

Finding the campground: From the junction of US 191 and UT 128, about 2 miles northwest of Moab, drive northeast on UT 128 for an additional 7.4 miles.

About the campground: Located along the Colorado Riverway, a colorful medley of towering sandstone spires, water-carved canyons, and striking cliffs, this campground has both basic sites and three group sites, one of which (Group C) is located across the road.

Cottonwoods and oaks offer a limited amount of shade, and the Colorado River, a popular place for canoeing, kayaking, and rafting from late spring through fall, is close by.

The Porcupine Rim Bike Trail starts here (or ends, depending on which direction you choose to bicycle), and there's a beach with a cement ramp for wheelchair access, too. If you enjoy bouldering, check out the Big Bend Bouldering Area just up the road.

298 Hal Canyon/Oak Grove

Location: About 9 miles northeast of Moab

GPS: N38 38.518'/W109 28.597' (Hal Canyon)

GPS: N38 38.591'/W109 28.583' (Oak Grove)

Facilities: Fire pits, picnic tables, and vault toilets

Sites: 11 basic sites and 7 walk-in tent sites

Maximum RV length: 24 feet (Hal Canyon); 18 feet (Oak Grove)

Fee: $$ for basic and walk-in tent sites

Maximum stay: 14 days

Elevation: 4,000 feet

Road conditions: Gravel

Management: Bureau of Land Management, Moab Field Office, 82 E. Dogwood, Moab; (435) 259-2100; www.blm.gov/ut/st/en/fo/moab.html

Reservations: None

Activities: Hiking, mountain biking, rafting, canoeing and kayaking, off-highway driving, and picnicking

Restrictions: No generators at Oak Grove

Season: Year-round

Finding the campground: From the junction of US 191 and UT 128, about 2 miles northwest of Moab, drive northeast on UT 128 for about 7 more miles.

About the campground: Because Hal Canyon and Oak Grove are similar in appearance and a mere 0.3 mile apart, I've listed the two campgrounds together. Hal Canyon offers eleven sites, including three walk-in tent sites and some shade. Oak Grove offers seven sites, including four walk-in tent sites, in the same kind of setting. RVers beware: There is no trailer turnaround space at Oak Grove, so RVs are not recommended.

Both campgrounds are located along the Colorado Riverway, a potpourri of picturesque cliffs, river-carved canyons, and towering sandstone spires. The river is a popular place for rafting, kayaking, and canoeing from late spring through early fall.

299 Drinks Canyon

Location: About 8 miles northeast of Moab
GPS: N38 38.065' / W109 29.044' (Middle Drinks Camping Area)
Facilities: Fire pits, picnic tables, and vault toilets; no trash service (pack it out)
Sites: 12 basic sites and 5 walk-in tent sites
Maximum RV length: 18 feet (best for tents, vans, and truck campers)
Fee: $$ for basic and walk-in tent sites
Maximum stay: 14 days
Elevation: 4,000 feet
Road conditions: Gravel
Management: Bureau of Land Management, Moab Field Office, 82 E. Dogwood, Moab; (435) 259-2100; www.blm.gov/ut/st/en/fo/moab.html
Reservations: None
Activities: Hiking, mountain biking, kayaking and canoeing, rafting, off-highway driving, and picnicking
Season: Year-round
Finding the campground: From the junction of US 191 and UT 128, about 2 miles northwest of Moab, drive northeast on UT 128 for 6.3 more miles.
About the campground: Located along the Colorado River, Drinks Canyon Camping Area is composed of three separate sections—Lower Drinks, Middle Drinks, and Upper Drinks. Because the fee tube is located at Middle Drinks, my GPS reading was taken there.

All three areas are located along the Colorado Riverway, a potpourri of picturesque cliffs, river-carved canyons, and towering sandstone spires. The river is a popular place for rafting, kayaking, and canoeing from late spring through early fall.

300 Granstaff

Location: About 5 miles northeast of Moab
GPS: N38 36.809' / W109 31.882'
Facilities: Fire pits, picnic tables, tent pads, and vault toilets
Sites: 16 basic sites

Maximum RV length: 18 feet (best for tents, truck campers, and vans)
Fee: $$ for basic sites
Maximum stay: 14 days
Elevation: 4,000 feet
Road conditions: Gravel
Management: Bureau of Land Management, Moab Field Office, 82 E. Dogwood, Moab; (435) 259-2100; www.blm.gov/ut/st/en/fo/moab.html
Reservations: None
Activities: Hiking, mountain biking, kayaking and canoeing, rafting, off-highway driving, and picnicking
Season: Year-round
Finding the campground: From the junction of US 191 and UT 128, about 2 miles northwest of Moab, drive northeast on UT 128 for 3.3 more miles.
About the campground: Located along the Colorado River, Granstaff Campground has a tight turnaround, which means no trailers and no large vehicles. With sites along the Colorado Riverway, a potpourri of picturesque cliffs, river-carved canyons, and towering sandstone spires, it is a popular place for rafting, kayaking, and canoeing from late spring through early fall. If you are in need of a great hike, head up nearby Negro Bill Canyon, which leads 2.5 miles to Morning Glory Arch, the sixth-largest natural span in the country.

301 Goose Island

Location: About 3 miles north of Moab
GPS: N38 36.577'/W109 33.477'
Facilities: Fire pits, picnic tables, some tent pads, and vault toilets
Sites: 16 basic sites, 1 walk-in tent site, and 2 group sites (maximum 25 and 40 people, respectively)
Maximum RV length: 40 feet
Fee: $$ for basic and walk-in tent sites; $$$$$ for group sites
Maximum stay: 14 days
Elevation: 4,000 feet
Road conditions: Gravel
Management: Bureau of Land Management, Moab Field Office, 82 E. Dogwood, Moab; (435) 259-2100; www.blm.gov/ut/st/en/fo/moab.html
Reservations: For group sites only, call (435) 259-2102
Activities: Hiking, mountain biking, kayaking and canoeing, rafting, off-highway driving, and picnicking
Season: Year-round
Finding the campground: From the junction of US 191 and UT 128, about 2 miles north of Moab, drive northeast on UT 128 for an additional 1.4 miles.
About the campground: There are two group sites and room for RVs at this Colorado River camp, with cottonwood trees providing some shade. Located along the Colorado Riverway, a scenic blend of lofty spires, river-carved canyons, and colorful cliffs, this is a favorite place for kayakers, rafters, and canoeists. Look for water enthusiasts in the spring through early fall.

RVs at Goose Island Campground

302 Jaycee Park

Location: About 6 miles southwest of Moab
GPS: N38 33.398' / W109 35.436'
Facilities: Fire pits, picnic tables, and vault toilets
Sites: 6 walk-in tent sites
Maximum RV length: None
Fee: $$ for walk-in tent sites
Maximum stay: 14 days
Elevation: 4,000 feet
Road conditions: Paved to the campground, then gravel
Management: Bureau of Land Management, Moab Field Office, 82 E. Dogwood, Moab; (435) 259-2100; www.blm.gov/ut/st/en/fo/moab.html
Reservations: None
Activities: Hiking, rock climbing, mountain biking, and picnicking
Season: Year-round
Finding the campground: From the junction of US 191 and UT 279 (Potash Road), about 2 miles north of the north end of Moab, drive southwest on UT 279 for about 4 miles to the campground.
About the campground: Six walk-in sites are offered here, along with the Portal Trail. It climbs

1,000 feet in 1.5 miles and offers great views of the surrounding area, with distant views to the La Sal Mountains.

If you're looking for a wonderful place to climb, head southwest from the campground. There are more than a hundred routes along Wall Street, where climbers can work routes ranging from easy to difficult. It's also a grand place from which spectators can watch climbers scaling the vertical wall. While traveling along the highway, be sure to look for prehistoric rock art and dinosaur tracks. You can see both along the way.

303 Williams Bottom

Location: About 7 miles southwest of Moab
GPS: N38 32.315' / W109 36.225'
Facilities: Fire pits, picnic tables, and vault toilets
Sites: 18 basic sites
Maximum RV length: 24 feet
Fee: $ for basic sites
Maximum stay: 14 days
Elevation: 3,900 feet
Road conditions: Paved to the campground, then gravel
Management: Bureau of Land Management, Moab Field Office, 82 E. Dogwood, Moab; (435) 259-2100; www.blm.gov/ut/st/en/fo/moab.html
Reservations: None
Activities: Hiking, rock climbing, mountain biking, and picnicking
Season: Year-round
Finding the campground: From the junction of US 191 and UT 279 (Potash Road), about 2 miles north of the north end of Moab, drive southwest on UT 279 for about 5.5 miles to the campground.
About the campground: Located among cliffs and cottonwoods, the campground is a great place for tents and small RVs. While driving Potash Road be sure to look for prehistoric rock art sites and dinosaur tracks, and if you like to hike, check out the Portal Trail located at Jaycee Park. The trail climbs 1,000 feet in 1.5 miles and offers great views of the surrounding area, with distant views to the La Sal Mountains. If you're looking for a great place to climb, head to Wall Street, where climbers can work routes ranging from easy to difficult.

304 Gold Bar

Location: About 12 miles southwest of Moab
GPS: N38 34.436' / W109 37.976'
Facilities: Fire pits, picnic tables (some covered), some BBQ grills, vault toilets, and boat ramp
Sites: 5 basic sites and 4 group sites (maximum varies from 30 to 90 people)

Dinosaur tracks along Potash Road

Maximum RV length: 40 feet
Fee: $ for basic sites; $$$$$ for group sites
Maximum stay: 14 days
Elevation: 3,900 feet
Road conditions: Paved to the campground, then gravel
Management: Bureau of Land Management, Moab Field Office, 82 E. Dogwood, Moab; (435) 259-2100; www.blm.gov/ut/st/en/fo/moab.html
Reservations: For group sites only, call (435) 259-2102
Activities: Hiking, rock climbing, mountain biking, rafting, kayaking and canoeing, and picnicking
Season: Year-round
Finding the campground: From the junction of US 191 and UT 279 (Potash Road), about 2 miles north of the north end of Moab, drive southwest on UT 279 for about 10.5 miles to the campground.
About the campground: Located along the Colorado River, this is a great place for large RVs. En route to the campground off Potash Road, be sure to look for prehistoric rock art sites and dinosaur tracks. You'll also pass by Wall Street, a great place to climb. Across the road from the campground you'll find a trail leading 1.5 miles to Corona Arch and nearby Bowtie Arch. Hike the trail and you'll pass through a bighorn sheep lambing area.

305 Sand Flats Recreation Area

Location: About 3 miles east of Moab
GPS: N38 34.533'/W109 31.412'
Facilities: Fire pits, picnic tables, and vault toilets
Sites: 120 basic sites and 2 group sites (maximum 16 people each)
Maximum RV length: 40 feet
Fee: $ for basic sites; $$$$$ for group sites
Maximum stay: 14 days
Elevation: 4,600 feet
Road conditions: Gravel
Management: Bureau of Land Management, Moab Field Office, 82 E. Dogwood, Moab; (435) 259-2100; www.blm.gov/ut/st/en/fo/moab.html
Reservations: None
Activities: Hiking, rock climbing, mountain biking, off-highway driving, and picnicking
Season: Year-round
Finding the campground: From the junction of Main and Center in Moab, go east on Center for 0.5 mile, then turn right (south) onto 400 East. After another 0.4 mile turn left (east) onto Millcreek Drive. You'll reach a fork in 0.6 mile; keep left (east) on unsigned Sand Flats Road. A sign reading "Slickrock Bike Trail" points the way. Reach the entrance station after an additional 1.6 miles.
About the campground: Sand Flats Recreation Area is composed of designated sites spread out over nine lettered campgrounds—A to H. Campsites are spread out along several miles of slickrock and sage, with wonderful views. Because Clusters A and E are gravel and the others can be quite sandy, I recommend that RVs head to A (it has some sites for RVs 40 feet long) and E.

The Moab Slickrock Bike Trail is a challenging test for mountain bikers. Porcupine Pine Rim is also a must-do for experts, and if you want an all-day adventure, try the Whole Enchilada, a 26.5-mile-long ride with 7,000 vertical feet of downhill.

306 King's Bottom

Location: About 3 miles southwest of Moab
GPS: N38 33.444'/W109 35.075'
Facilities: Fire pits, picnic tables, tent pads, and vault toilets; no trash service (pack it out)
Sites: 10 basic sites
Maximum RV length: 24 feet
Fee: $$ for basic sites
Maximum stay: 14 days
Elevation: 4,000 feet
Road conditions: Paved to the campground, then gravel
Management: Bureau of Land Management, Moab Field Office, 82 E. Dogwood, Moab; (435) 259-2100; www.blm.gov/ut/st/en/fo/moab.html
Reservations: None

Activities: Hiking, rock climbing, mountain biking, off-road driving, and picnicking

Season: Year-round

Finding the campground: From the junction of Main (US 191) and Kane Creek Boulevard in Moab, head west on Kane Creek Boulevard for 2.8 miles to Kings Bottom Campground, which is on the right (west) or river side of the road.

About the campground: Located along the banks of the Colorado River, this campground is great for tents and small RVs. There are some small willow and cottonwood trees for shade, and access to all sorts of outdoor activities. There are nice rock climbs, hikes, and mountain bike rides just waiting for those who enjoy the great out-of-doors.

307 Moonflower

Location: About 3.1 miles southwest of Moab

GPS: N38 33.250'/W109 35.212'

Facilities: Fire pits, picnic tables, and vault toilets; no trash service (pack it out)

Sites: 8 walk-in sites

Maximum RV length: None

Fee: $ for walk-in sites

Maximum stay: 14 days

Elevation: 4,000 feet

Road conditions: Paved to the campground, then gravel

Management: Bureau of Land Management, Moab Field Office, 82 E. Dogwood, Moab; (435) 259-2100; www.blm.gov/ut/st/en/fo/moab.html

Reservations: None

Activities: Hiking, rock climbing, mountain biking, off-road driving, and picnicking

Season: Year-round

Finding the campground: From the junction of Main (US 191) and Kane Creek Boulevard in Moab, head west on Kane Creek Boulevard for 3.1 miles to Moonflower, which is on the left (east) side of the road.

About the campground: Located in a shaded canyon with cottonwood trees, this campground has an assortment of petrogylphs for campers to discover. Campers can also enjoy many outdoor activities here, including rock climbing, hiking, and off-road riding.

308 Spring Site and Hunter Canyon

Location: About 6.8 miles and 7.7 miles, respectively, southwest of Moab

GPS: N38 31.061'/W109 35.731' (Spring Site)

GPS: N38 30.599'/W109 35.794' (Hunter Canyon)

Facilities: Spring Site offers fire pits and nothing else, while Hunter Canyon offers fire pits, picnic tables, and vault toilets.

Sites: 4 walk-in sites (Spring Site); 5 basic sites and 4 walk-in sites (Hunter Canyon)

Maximum RV length: 18 feet (best for tents, vans, and truck campers)
Fee: $ for basic and walk-in sites
Maximum stay: 14 days
Elevation: 4,000 feet
Road conditions: Gravel
Management: Bureau of Land Management, Moab Field Office, 82 E. Dogwood, Moab; (435) 259-2100; www.blm.gov/ut/st/en/fo/moab.html
Reservations: None
Activities: Hiking, rock climbing, mountain biking, off-road driving, and picnicking
Season: Year-round
Finding the campground: From the junction of Main (US 191) and Kane Creek Boulevard in Moab, head west on Kane Creek Boulevard for 6.8 miles to Spring Site, which offers campsites on both sides of the road. Continue another 0.9 mile to Hunter Canyon, where sites are also on both sides of the road. Sites are suitable for tents and vehicles such as camper vans and truck campers.
About the campground: Hunter Creek flows through the area, some of which is shaded by cottonwoods. Hunter Canyon offers a nice hike up the canyon, with an arch and other rock formations visible along the way. Continue at least 3 miles up the canyon, and you'll see a wonderful hanging garden complete with maidenhair fern.

309 Ledge

Location: Four Ledge Camping Areas range from 10.3 to 11.3 miles southwest of Moab
GPS: N38 28.830' / W109 36.215' (Ledge A)
Facilities: Fire pits, picnic tables, and vault toilets
Sites: 6 basic sites at Ledge A; 13 basic sites at Ledge B; 6 basic sites and 1 group site (maximum 30 people) at Ledge C
Maximum RV length: 30 feet (Ledge A and group site); Any for Ledge B and C
Fee: $ for basic sites; $$$$$ for group site
Maximum stay: 14 days
Elevation: 4,100 feet
Road conditions: Gravel
Management: Bureau of Land Management, Moab Field Office, 82 E. Dogwood, Moab; (435) 259-2100; www.blm.gov/ut/st/en/fo/moab.html
Reservations: For the group site only, call (435) 259-2102
Activities: Hiking, mountain biking, off-road driving, and picnicking
Season: Year-round
Finding the campground: From the junction of Main (US 191) and Kane Creek Boulevard in Moab, head west on Kane Creek Boulevard. The road is paved for the first few miles then becomes gravel. RVers should note that en route there is a steep, windy section of road with 10 percent grades.
About the campground: The Ledge Camping Area consists of three regions—A, B, and C—along with a group campground. When visiting you'll first encounter Ledge A. As you continue 1 mile south on the gravel road, you'll pass the other camping areas. All the areas are in the open with no trees for shade.

310 Mason Draw

Location: In the Manti–La Sal National Forest, about 28 miles southeast of Moab
GPS: N38 32.575'/W109 18.190'
Facilities: Fire pits, picnic tables, BBQ grills, and vault toilet
Sites: 5 basic sites
Maximum RV length: 20 feet
Fee: $ for basic sites
Maximum stay: 14 days
Elevation: 8,300 feet
Road conditions: Gravel
Management: Moab Ranger District, 62 E. 100 North, PO Box 386, Moab, UT 84532; (435) 259-7155; www.fs.usda.gov/main/mantilasal/
Reservations: None
Activities: Hiking and mountain biking
Season: Late May through September
Finding the campground: From the center of downtown Moab, drive about 8 miles south on US 191 and make a left (east) onto Old Airport Road. A sign points the way to the La Sal Loop Road. After another 0.6 mile make a right (south/southeast) onto Spanish Valley Drive, which eventually becomes CR 175 (also known as the La Sal Loop Road). Travel another 19.3 miles to FR 4821 and go right (east) on the rough, dirt road an additional 0.2 mile to the campground.
About the campground: Thick aspens, conifers, and some oaks exist in this small campground located right off the La Sal Loop Road. There are trails to hike and bike along the La Sal Loop Road, too.

311 Warner Lake

Location: In the Manti–La Sal National Forest, about 28 miles southeast of Moab
GPS: N38 31.227'/W109 16.581'
Facilities: Fire pits, picnic tables, stove stands, drinking water, vault toilets, and a cabin
Sites: 20 basic sites, 1 group site (maximum 50 people), and 1 small cabin
Maximum RV length: 20 feet
Fee: $ for basic sites; $$$$$ for group site or cabin
Maximum stay: 14 days
Elevation: 9,400 feet
Road conditions: Gravel
Management: Moab Ranger District, 62 E. 100 North, PO Box 386, Moab, UT 84532; (435) 259-7155; www.fs.usda.gov/main/mantilasal/
Reservations: Call (877) 444-6777 or TDD (877) 833-6777; www.recreation.gov
Activities: Fishing, hiking, mountain biking, horseback riding, and picnicking
Season: Late May through September

Finding the campground: From the center of downtown Moab, drive about 8 miles south on US 191 and make a left (east) onto Old Airport Road. A sign points the way to the La Sal Loop Road. After another 0.6 mile make a right (south/southeast) onto Spanish Valley Drive, which eventually becomes CR 175 (also known as the La Sal Loop Road). Travel another 14.3 miles to FR 063, a narrow, gravel road, and go right (northeast) an additional 5.1 miles to the campground.

About the campground: Huge aspens grace this lovely campground, with its wonderful view of Warner Lake and Haystack Mountain in the background. There are a couple of trails in the area: Miners Basin Foot Trail and the Trans Mountain Trail. A cute cabin is available by reservation. Three Lakes and Burro Pass are mountain bike rides that you can enjoy from Warner Lake. For more information read *Mountain Biking Utah*, by Gregg Bromka.

312 Oowah Lake

Location: In the Manti-La Sal National Forest, about 25 miles southeast of Moab
GPS: N38 30.115'/W109 16.391'
Facilities: Fire pits, picnic tables, some BBQ grills, and vault toilets
Sites: 11 basic sites
Maximum RV length: 20 feet (trailers and RVs not recommended)
Fee: $ for basic sites
Maximum stay: 14 days
Elevation: 8,800 feet
Road conditions: Gravel
Management: Moab Ranger District, 62 E. 100 North, PO Box 386, Moab, UT 84532; (435) 259-7155; www.fs.usda.gov/main/mantilasal/
Reservations: None
Activities: Fishing, hiking, mountain biking, and picnicking
Season: Late May through September
Finding the campground: From the center of downtown Moab, drive about 8 miles south on US 191 and make a left (east) onto Old Airport Road. A sign points the way to the La Sal Loop Road. After another 0.6 mile make a right (south/southeast) onto Spanish Valley Drive, which eventually becomes CR 175 (also known as the La Sal Loop Road). Travel another 12.9 miles to a steep, narrow, gravel road (not recommended for trailers and RVs) and go right (northeast) an additional 2.9 miles to the campground.

About the campground: Aspens and conifers abound in this campground, which is near Oowah Lake. Site 4 has the only view of the lake. There are a couple of trails in the area, open for both hiking and mountain biking. Clark Lake Trail begins at the lake, while the Trans Mountain Trail, begins about half a mile prior to reaching Oowah Lake.

Castle Valley from La Sal Loop Road

313 Ken's Lake

Location: About 10 miles southeast of Moab
GPS: N38 28.616' / W109 25.350'
Facilities: Fire pits, picnic tables, vault toilets, horse corrals at group sites A and B, and boat ramp
Sites: 27 basic sites and 3 group sites (maximum 20 people each)
Maximum RV length: 40 feet
Fee: $$ for basic sites; $$$$$ for group sites
Maximum stay: 14 days
Elevation: 5,100 feet
Road conditions: Paved to the campground, then gravel
Management: Bureau of Land Management, Moab Field Office, 82 E. Dogwood, Moab; (435) 259-2100; www.blm.gov/ut/st/en/fo/moab.html
Reservations: Call (435) 259-2102
Activities: Fishing, boating, kayaking, hiking, mountain biking, horseback riding, and picnicking
Season: Year-round

Finding the campground: From the center of downtown Moab, drive about 8 miles south on US 191 and make a left (east) onto Old Airport Road. A sign points the way to the La Sal Loop Road. After another 0.6 mile make a right (south/southeast) onto Spanish Valley Drive, which eventually becomes CR 175. Travel 1.5 miles to a sign for Ken's Lake. Go left (north) and continue 0.9 mile to the campground. (***Note:*** Along the way the paved road turns to gravel.)

About the campground: Located in Moab's Spanish Valley, the campground has wonderful views of the La Sal Mountains and is a great place to stay, especially for those with large RVs, ones too big for the mountain campgrounds up high. Juniper trees and wide-open spaces grace the grounds. Fishing is popular in the 2,610-acre lake. There are three trails for hikers to enjoy, including one to Faux Falls. Although man-made, the falls are pretty. Horseback riders will enjoy the Red Rock Horse Trail, which is sparsely marked. The lake is stocked with fish; boats are limited to nonmotorized craft.

314 Hatch Point: Canyon Rims Recreation Area

Location: About 45 miles northwest of Monticello
GPS: N38 10.594'/W109 27.701'
Facilities: Fire pits, picnic tables, drinking water, and vault toilets
Sites: 10 basic sites
Maximum RV length: 24 feet
Fee: $$ for basic sites
Maximum stay: 14 days
Elevation: 5,900 feet
Road conditions: Maintained gravel
Management: Bureau of Land Management, Moab Field Office, 82 E. Dogwood, Moab; (435) 259-2100; www.blm.gov/ut/st/en/fo/moab.html
Reservations: None
Activities: Wildlife watching, picnicking, hiking, and mountain biking
Restrictions: ATVs not allowed
Season: Year-round
Finding the campground: From Monticello drive north on paved US 191 for 20.5 miles to a turnoff on the left (west) for both the Needles and Anticline Overlooks and the Canyon Rims Recreation Area. Take the paved road for 15.1 miles to a Y. The left (west) fork leads to Needles Overlook; you should keep right (north) on a maintained gravel road for another 8.4 miles to a road heading right (east). Take this for 1 mile to the campground.

About the campground: Junipers and pinyon pines decorate this scenic campground set on a high mesa with wonderful views of the La Sal Mountains to the east and a broad mesa below and to the north. If you're looking for wildlife, you might see pronghorn, mule deer, peregrine falcons, and collared lizards. This is an excellent base for hikers and mountain bikers, who will find plenty to do in the area.

315 Windwhistle: Canyon Rims Recreation Area

Location: About 26 miles northwest of Monticello
GPS: N38 10.594'/W109 27.701'
Facilities: Fire pits, picnic tables, BBQ grills, drinking water, and vault toilets
Sites: 15 basic sites and 1 group site (maximum 15 people)
Maximum RV length: 24 feet
Fee: $$ for basic sites; $ per person with 10-person minimum
Maximum stay: 14 days
Elevation: 6,000 feet
Road conditions: Paved to the campground, then gravel
Management: Bureau of Land Management, Moab Field Office, 82 E. Dogwood, Moab; (435) 259-2100; www.blm.gov/ut/st/en/fo/moab.html
Reservations: For the group site only, call (435) 259-6111
Activities: Hiking, wildlife watching, and picnicking
Restrictions: ATVs not allowed
Season: Year-round
Finding the campground: From Monticello drive north on paved US 191 for 20.5 miles to a turnoff on the left (west) for both the Needles and Anticline Overlooks and the Canyon Rims Recreation Area. Drive west on this paved road for 5.8 miles to the campground.
About the campground: Junipers and pinyon pines decorate this scenic campground, tucked up near the mouth of a canyon on a high mesa with nice views. There's also a group site, though it's available by reservation only. A nature trail begins at the group site. Wildlife watchers should look for mule deer, which are plentiful, as well as pronghorn, peregrine falcons, collared lizards, and a whole lot more. This is an excellent base for hikers and mountain bikers, who will find plenty to do in the area.

316 Squaw Flat: Canyonlands National Park

Location: 3.5 miles west of the Needles entrance station
GPS: N38 08.942'/W109 47.786'
Facilities: Fire pits, picnic tables, tent pads, ADA sites, drinking water, outdoor sink, and flush and vault toilets
Sites: 26 basic sites and 3 group sites (maximum varies from 15 to 50 people)
Maximum RV length: 30 feet
Fee: $$ for basic sites; $$$$ to $$$$$ for group sites
Maximum stay: 7 days
Elevation: 5,100 feet
Road conditions: Paved
Management: Canyonlands National Park, 2282 SW Resource Blvd., Moab; (435) 719-2100; www.nps.gov/cany/index.htm

La Sal Mountains from Slickrock Trail

Reservations: For group sites only, download application form from website and fax to (435) 259-4285 or send to Reservation Office, 2282 SW Resource Blvd., Moab, UT 84532.
Activities: Rock climbing, mountain biking, off-highway driving, hiking, photography, and picnicking
Season: Year-round
Finding the campground: From the Needles entrance station drive past the visitor center, located 0.4 mile from the entrance station, for a total of 3.4 miles to a fork. Campground A is straight ahead (south), while Campground B is to the right (west).
About the campground: A few trees provide some shade, as do the various rock formations, at both of these campgrounds. Larger RVs should try for a space at Campground A, which will hold longer rigs.

Activities abound in the area. Though mountain bikes are not permitted on any of the trails, there are roads for bicycling. Four-wheel-drive vehicles can take advantage of the jeep trails. There are also multitudes of trails to hike, with one of the most popular leading to the green realms and magnificent Needle formations in and around Chesler Park. Though the Cedar Mesa sandstone in the Needles is soft and unsuitable for rock climbing, there are places to climb on the way into the park.

317 Hamburger Rock

Location: About 43 miles northwest of Monticello
GPS: N38 11.517'/W109 40.168'
Facilities: Fire pits, picnic tables, some tent pads, vault toilets; no garbage service (pack it out)
Sites: 10 basic sites
Maximum RV length: 25 feet
Fee: $ for basic sites
Maximum stay: 14 days
Elevation: 4,900 feet
Road conditions: Dirt, some gravel in the campground
Management: Bureau of Land Management, Monticello Field Office, 365 N. Main, Monticello; (435) 587-1500; www.blm.gov/ut/st/en/fo/monticello/recreation.html
Reservations: None
Activities: Rock climbing, mountain biking, hiking, and picnicking
Season: Year-round
Finding the campground: From Monticello drive north on paved US 191 for 13.7 miles; at this point head west on UT 211, a paved Scenic Byway. Continue another 29 miles to a dirt road on your right. After you turn, a sign points the way to Lockhart Basin and Hurrah Pass. Proceed another 1.2 miles to the campground.
About the campground: Located 4 miles from Canyonlands National Park, sites at this campground sit around a huge rock appropriately named Hamburger. It really does resemble a hamburger, as do many other rocks found in the area.

If you don't mind the dirt and dust, this is a good place from which to make a base camp and then mountain bike or hike to your heart's content. En route to the campground you'll pass Newspaper Rock. Stop to see and photograph petroglyphs that may be as old as 1,500 years. There are also many rock climbing routes in the area, ranging in difficulty from 5.7 to 5.12.

318 Dalton Springs

Location: In the Manti–La Sal National Forest, about 5 miles west of Monticello
GPS: N37 52.457'/W109 25.882'
Facilities: Fire pits, picnic tables, drinking water, and vault toilets
Sites: 14 basic sites and 2 double sites
Maximum RV length: 30 feet
Fee: $ for basic sites; $$ for double sites
Maximum stay: 14 days
Elevation: 8,300 feet
Road conditions: Paved to the campground, then dirt
Management: Monticello Ranger District, 496 E. Central, PO Box 820, Monticello, UT 84535; (435) 587-2041; www.fs.usda.gov/main/mantilasal/home

Reservations: None
Activities: Wildlife watching, fishing, picnicking, and photography; hiking trails in the area
Season: Mid-May through end of September
Finding the campground: From Monticello drive west on paved Blue Mountain/Harts Loop Draw Road. A sign points the way. Continue 4.9 miles to the campground, which is on the left (south) side of the road.
About the campground: The campsites here are shaded by a number of oak trees and may be open early in the season, when the water is off and the fee is reduced. It's a nice place to sit and watch the wildlife, if you're one of the lucky ones. There are plenty of deer in the area, as well as turkeys and other critters. The campground makes a nice base from which to hike one of the nearby trails or fish in a nearby stream. Check with the forest service for more information.

319 Buckboard

Location: In the Manti–La Sal National Forest, approximately 6.5 miles west of Monticello
GPS: N37 52.878'/W109 26.959'
Facilities: Fire pits, picnic tables, drinking water, and vault toilets
Sites: 11 basic sites and 2 group sites (maximum 100 people each)
Maximum RV length: 25 feet
Fee: $ for basic sites; $$$ for groups of 50; $$$$ for groups of 51 to 100
Maximum stay: 14 days
Elevation: 8,800 feet
Road conditions: Paved to the campground, then dirt
Management: Monticello Ranger District, 496 E. Central, PO Box 820, Monticello, UT 84535; (435) 587-2041; www.fs.usda.gov/main/mantilasal/home
Reservations: Reservations for basic sites are accepted and are necessary for group sites. Call (877) 444-6777 or TDD (877) 833-6777; www.recreation.gov.
Activities: Wildlife watching, fishing, picnicking, and photography; hiking trails in the area
Season: Mid-May through end of September
Finding the campground: From Monticello drive west on paved Blue Mountain/Harts Loop Draw Road. A sign points the way. Continue 6.4 miles to the campground, which is on the left (south) side of the road.
About the campground: The campsites here are shaded by a number of oak, aspen, spruce, and willow trees. You may be able to camp early or late in the season, when the water is off and the fee is reduced. It's a great place to relax and enjoy the scenery, and a wonderful area to watch wildlife, if you're so lucky. There's an abundance of deer in the area, as well as turkeys and other critters. The campground makes a nice base from which to hike one of the nearby trails or fish in a nearby stream.

320 Devils Canyon

Location: In the Manti–La Sal National Forest, about 10 miles northeast of Blanding and 12 miles south of Monticello
GPS: N37 44.2007'/W109 24.710'
Facilities: Fire pits, stove stands, ADA site, picnic tables, drinking water, and vault toilets
Sites: 42 basic sites
Maximum RV length: 45 feet
Fee: $ for basic sites
Maximum stay: 14 days
Elevation: 7,400 feet
Road conditions: Paved
Management: Monticello Ranger District, 496 E. Central, PO Box 820, Monticello, UT 84535; (435) 587-2041; www.fs.usda.gov/main/mantilasal/
Reservations: Call (877) 444-6777 or TDD (877) 833-6777; www.recreation.gov
Activities: Hiking and picnicking
Season: Memorial Day through late September
Finding the campground: From Blanding drive northeast on US 191 for about 9 miles. Now make a left (west) onto FR 85, a paved road, where a sign points the way to Devils Canyon. Continue another 0.6 mile to the campground turnoff, which is on the right (east).
About the campground: Campsites are set amid a forest of juniper, pinyon pine, and stately ponderosa pine trees, as well as wild roses. Section A offers sites 1 through 16 and was designed with big RVs in mind. You'll find sites 17 through 42 in Section B; stove stands are not available in this section. An interpretive trail that starts near site 42 tells the story of humankind's life in the forest. You'll see some ruins along the 1,400-foot trail, too.

321 Nizhoni

Location: In the Manti–La Sal National Forest, about 13 miles northwest of Blanding
GPS: N37 46.955'/W109 32.383'
Facilities: Fire pits, picnic tables, ADA sites, drinking water, and vault toilets
Sites: 25 basic sites and 2 group sites (maximum 100 people each)
Maximum RV length: 40 feet
Fee: $ for basic sites; $$$ for groups of 50; $$$$ for groups of 51 to 100
Maximum stay: 14 days
Elevation: 7,000 feet
Road conditions: Gravel
Management: Monticello Ranger District, 496 US Hwy. 666, PO Box 820, Monticello, UT 84535; (435) 587-2041; www.fs.usda.gov/main/mantilasal/home
Reservations: Call (877) 444-6777 or TDD (877) 833-6777; www.recreation.gov
Activities: Hiking, fishing, and picnicking.
Season: Mid-May through end of September

Finding the campground: From the junction of US 191 and 100 East in Blanding, drive northwest on 100 East, also called Blue Mountain Road and later Johnson Creek Road, for 12.6 miles. The road is paved except for the last 4.4 miles, which is gravel. You'll pass Dry Wash Reservoir 1.4 miles prior to the campground.

About the campground: Ponderosa pines and Gambel oak trees provide a nice setting for this campground, with its close access to Dry Wash Reservoir. There's a dock there, but powerboats are not permitted. A great place to see wildlife, including Abert's squirrels, it's also a nice place to hike. Also check out the Abajo Loop State Scenic Backway, which passes by the campground, but is not recommended for large RVs or trailers.

322 Hovenweep National Monument

Location: About 45 miles southeast of Blanding
GPS: N37 22.983'/W109 04.280'
Facilities: Fire pits, picnic tables (some covered), ADA site, drinking water, and flush toilets
Sites: 23 basic sites and 7 RV-only sites
Maximum RV length: 35 feet (any combined length)
Fee: $ for basic and RV-only sites
Maximum stay: 14 days
Elevation: 5,300 feet
Road conditions: Paved
Management: Hovenweep National Monument, McElmo Route, Cortez, CO 81321; (970) 562-4282; www.nps.gov/hove/index.htm
Reservations: None
Activities: Hiking, mountain biking, photography, wildlife watching, and picnicking
Season: Year-round
Finding the campground: From Blanding drive south on US 191 for about 14 miles, then turn left (east) onto UT 262. Continue 8.4 miles to CR 414; head left and follow the signs to Hovenweep. Along the way you'll travel on CR 404, 414, and 413 for another 22.1 miles to the national monument and campground. The campground is located about 0.9 mile from the visitor center.
About the campground: Utah junipers decorate this delightful campground, with easy access to an array of ancient ruins. Ancestral Puebloans (formerly called Anasazi) built their homes here about 700 years ago; some of the homes are still standing and available for observation.

Several trails allow access to the ruins. A trail to the Holly Ruins, one of six villages protected by the monument, begins near campsite 10. Gnats can be a nuisance in May and June; bring insect repellent.

323 Sand Island

Location: Along the San Juan River, approximately 3 miles west of Bluff
GPS: N37 15.737'/W109 36.982'
Facilities: Fire pits, picnic tables, drinking water, vault toilets, and boat launch

Hovenweep Castle and Little Ruin Canyon attract visitors to Hovenweep National Monument.

Sites: 26 basic sites and 1 group site (maximum 25 people)
Maximum RV length: Any
Fee: $ for basic sites; $$$$$ for group site
Maximum stay: 14 days for basic sites; 3 days for group site
Elevation: 4,300 feet
Road conditions: Gravel
Management: Bureau of Land Management, Monticello Field Office, 365 N. Main, Monticello; (435) 587-1500; www.blm.gov/ut/st/en/fo/monticello/recreation.html
Reservations: For the group site only, call (435) 587-1504
Activities: Hiking, fishing, boating, wildlife watching, petroglyphs, and picnicking
Season: Year-round
Finding the campground: From downtown Bluff drive west on US 191 for about 3 miles. Turn left (east) and continue 0.3 mile to the campground.
About the campground: Stately cottonwoods provide some shade at this campground set along the San Juan River. The campground, which is a popular place for rafters and kayakers to put in, is set up in two sections: Area A and Area B. Area A is a place for vans or tents; RVs are not allowed. Big rigs will find plenty of space at Area B, where length isn't a problem.

Near Area B be sure to look for the famous Petroglyph Panel. Though Sand Island is a fine place for fishing and boating, it's probably most noted for its numerous Kokopelli figures. Kokopelli was the humpbacked flute player of ancient mythology.

324 Goosenecks State Park

Location: About 7 miles northwest of Mexican Hat
GPS: N37 10.477'/W109 55.624'
Facilities: Picnic tables and vault toilet
Sites: 4 basic sites
Maximum RV length: 30 feet
Fee: None
Maximum stay: 14 days
Elevation: 5,000 feet
Road conditions: Paved to the dirt parking area
Management: Goosenecks State Park, c/o Edge of the Cedars State Park Museum, 660 W. 400 North, Blanding; (435) 678-2238; www.stateparks.utah.gov/parks/goosenecks
Reservations: None
Activities: Photography and picnicking
Season: Year-round
Finding the campground: From Mexican Hat drive north on US 163 for 3.1 miles, then make a left (west) onto UT 261 for 0.9 mile; now continue west on UT 316. A sign points the way to the paved road that ends at the state park after another 3.4 miles.
About the campground: Primitive sites and a vault toilet are all that you'll find atop this lofty mesa, where the wind often blows and tent camping is not recommended. If you do camp here, you'll have a wonderful view into a 1,000-foot-deep chasm shaped through the Pennsylvanian Hermosa Formation compliments of the silt-laden San Juan River. The river zigs and zags, meandering more than 5 miles while advancing only 1 linear mile toward the Colorado River and Lake Powell.

325 Natural Bridges National Monument

Location: 0.3 mile west of the visitor center
GPS: N37 36.517'/W109 59.014'
GPS: N37 34.216'/W109 52.968' (BLM overflow camping area)
Facilities: Fire pits, picnic tables, and vault toilets; drinking water at the visitor center; no facilities in the overflow area (pack trash out)
Sites: 13 basic sites
Maximum RV length: 26 feet total length including tow vehicle; no maximum at overflow area
Fee: $ for basic sites; free for overflow area
Maximum stay: 14 days
Elevation: 6,500 feet
Road conditions: Paved in main campground; dirt in overflow area
Management: Natural Bridges National Monument, HC-60 Box 1, Lake Powell, UT 84533-0001; (435) 692-1234; www.nps.gov/nabr/index.htm
Reservations: None

Sipapu Bridge

Activities: Hiking, picnicking, and photography

Season: Year-round

Finding the campground: If coming from the south, you'll reach the BLM overflow area first. From Blanding drive about 4 miles south on US 191, then turn west onto UT 95 for 28.3 miles. Now turn left (southwest) onto Utah 261 and drive no more than 100 feet to a small sign pointing the way left (southeast) to the camping area, another 0.6 mile away. Beware that the dirt road may be rutted, and if it is rainy or looks like rain, you don't want to camp here. To reach the main campground, go back out to the highway and the junction of UT 261 and UT 95. Continue north on UT 95 for 1.8 miles to UT 275. Go right (northwest) on UT 275, traveling 4.4 miles to the visitor center. The campground is 0.4 mile farther.

About the campground: If there's one thing that needs to be stressed here, it's that there is a strict adherence to the park's 26-foot vehicle limit. There just isn't space for longer units. (***Note:*** This limit means a total of 26 feet—not 26 feet for a travel trailer or fifth-wheel trailer plus the tow vehicle—but a total of 26 feet.)

There's plenty to do from the pinyon- and juniper-blessed park campground. Bridge View Drive, paved and 9 miles long, leads to overlooks and trailheads for the park's three famous natural bridges—Sipapu, Kachina, and Owachomo. Trailers and towed vehicles should be left in the visitor center parking lot. There's also a wonderful loop trail that's nearly 9 miles long and passes under the three bridges. If you enjoy ancient ruins, you'll want to look for them here.

Hite Campground and Lake Powell

326 Hite: Glen Canyon National Recreation Area

Location: In the Glen Canyon National Recreation Area, about 49 miles southeast of Hanksville
GPS: N37 52.393'/W110 23.544' (upper area)
GPS: N37 52.349'/W110 23.725' (lower area)
Facilities: None in the campground, but a central building nearby offers drinking water, dump station, fish cleaning station, boat ramp, and flush toilets. Groceries and gas are available across the road.
Sites: Dispersed (those camping more than 200 yards from the restroom need to have their own bathroom facilities)
Maximum RV length: Any
Fee: $ per person; $$ maximum per vehicle
Maximum stay: 14 days
Elevation: 3,900 feet
Road conditions: Paved
Management: Glen Canyon National Recreation Area, PO Box 1507, Page, AZ 86040; (928) 608-6200; www.nps.gov/glca/index.htm
Reservations: None

Activities: Fishing, boating, water sports, swimming, picnicking, and photography
Season: Year-round
Finding the campground: From Hanksville drive south then southeast on UT 95 for about 49 miles, then turn right (west) at the sign for Hite Marina. Continue a couple of miles to the primitive sites.
About the campground: There's a nice view of Lake Powell from this location. (That's if there is water in this part of the lake. Call ahead if you plan on boating.) If you need a boat ramp or boat rental, you'll find it at the marina. Visitors can enjoy a variety of activities, including water sports, boating, fishing, and photography.

327 Farley Canyon: Glen Canyon National Recreation Area

Location: About 56 miles southeast of Hanksville
GPS: N37 49.249'/W110 23.646'
Facilities: Chemical and vault toilets
Sites: Dispersed
Maximum RV length: Any
Fee: $ for dispersed sites
Maximum stay: 14 days
Elevation: 3,800 feet
Road conditions: Maintained dirt
Management: Glen Canyon National Recreation Area, PO Box 1507, Page, AZ 86040; (928) 608-6200; www.nps.gov/glca/index.htm
Reservations: None
Activities: Fishing, boating, water sports, swimming, picnicking, and photography
Season: Year-round
Finding the campground: From Hanksville drive south then southeast on UT 95 for 53.5 miles, then turn right (west) at the sign for Farley Canyon. Continue 2.2 miles down a maintained dirt road to the primitive site.
About the campground: The vegetation may be sparse, but the views from this primitive site are abundant. Lake Powell visitors can enjoy water sports, boating, fishing, photography, and a whole lot more.

328 Halls Crossing: Glen Canyon National Recreation Area

Location: A few miles west of the east entrance fee station
GPS: N37 27.392'/W110 42.968'

Facilities: Fire pits, picnic tables, flush toilets, dishwashing sinks, and drinking water; laundry, showers, store, gas, phones and boat ramp nearby

Sites: 43 tent sites and 2 group sites (maximum 6 and 8 tents respectively)

Maximum RV length: None (RVs not allowed)

Fee: $$ for tent sites; $$$$$ for group sites

Maximum stay: 14 days

Elevation: 3,800 feet

Road conditions: Paved

Management: Glen Canyon National Recreation Area, PO Box 1507, Page, AZ 86040; (928) 608-6200; www.nps.gov/glca/index.htm

Reservations: For group sites only, call (435) 684-7008 or (435) 684-7000

Activities: Fishing, boating, water sports, swimming, picnicking, and photography

Season: Year-round

Finding the campground: From the east entrance fee station, east of Halls Crossing and about 95 miles southwest of Blanding, travel west a few miles to the campground, which is off UT 276 on the left (south).

About the campground: An assortment of deciduous trees provides some shade in the campground, which overlooks lovely Lake Powell. The campground is near a small store, where you'll also find hot showers and a self-service laundry. Just down the hill, at the marina, you'll find a boat ramp and boat rentals. There's also a ferry: The *John Atlantic Burr* travels between Halls Crossing and Bullfrog and saves 145 road miles. Lake Powell visitors have plenty to do—water sports, boating, fishing, and photography are perhaps the most popular activities.

329 Halls Crossing RV: Glen Canyon National Recreation Area

Location: A few miles west of the east entrance fee station

GPS: N37 27.403'/W110 42.839'

Facilities: Fire pits, picnic tables, BBQ grills, full hookups, flush toilets, showers, dump station, drinking water, store, self-service laundry and boat rentals; boat ramp 0.5 mile away

Sites: 32 full-hookup RV sites

Maximum RV length: 60 feet

Fee: $$$$$ for full-hookup sites

Maximum stay: 14 days

Elevation: 3,800 feet

Road conditions: Paved

Management: Glen Canyon National Recreation Area, PO Box 1507, Page, AZ 86040; (928) 608-6200; www.nps.gov/glca/index.htm

Reservations: Call (800) 528-6154; www.lakepowell.com

Activities: Fishing, boating, water sports, swimming, picnicking, and photography

Season: Year-round

Finding the campground: From the east entrance fee station, east of Halls Crossing and about 95 miles southwest of Blanding, travel west a few miles to the campground, which is just off UT 276 on the right (north).

About the campground: A few trees provide some shade in this full-amenity campground. If you need a boat ramp or boat rental, just head down the hill to the lake and marina. There's also a ferry: The *John Atlantic Burr* travels between Halls Crossing and Bullfrog and saves 145 road miles. Lake Powell visitors have plenty to do—water sports, boating, fishing, and photography are perhaps the most popular activities.

Appendix

Hunting and Fishing Information

Division of Wildlife Resources
1594 W. North Temple, Ste. 2110
Salt Lake City, UT 84114-6301
(801) 538-4700
http://wildlife.utah.gov

Recreation

Bicycle Utah (a statewide organization promoting on- and off-road cycling)
www.bicycleutah.com

Ski Utah (ski industry trade association)
150 W. 500 South
Salt Lake City, UT 84101
(801) 534-1779
www.skiutah.com

Utah Guides and Outfitters Association
PO Box 1412
Moab, UT 84532
www.utah-adventures.com

Roads, Weather, and Public Safety

Department of Transportation (UDOT)
4501 S. 2700 West
Salt Lake City, UT 84114
(801) 965-4000
www.udot.utah.gov/main/f?p=100:6:0::V,T:,1
Road report: 511 (within Utah)
Road report: (866) 511-8824 (outside Utah)

Emergency: 911

National Weather Service
www.weather.gov

Public Safety (UT Patrol)
4501 S. 2700 West
Salt Lake City, UT 84114
(801) 965-4518 (administration)
(801) 887-3800 (non-emergency)
http://publicsafety.utah.gov/highwaypatrol

Travel Information

Utah Travel Site
(800) 200-1160
www.utah.com

Websites

Bureau of Land Management
www.blm.gov

National Park Service
www.nps.gov

Public Lands Information Center (one-stop source for information on your public lands)
www.publiclands.org

US Fish and Wildlife Service
www.fws.gov

USDA Forest Service
www.fs.fed.us

USDA Forest Service Campground Reservations and Information
recreation.gov
reserveamerica.com

Utah State Parks and Recreation
www.stateparks.utah.gov

Reading Material

Bromka, Gregg. *Mountain Biking Utah* (Guilford, Conn: FalconGuides/Globe Pequot Press, 1999).
Green, Stewart. *Rock Climbing Utah*, 2nd (Guilford, Conn: FalconGuides/Globe Pequot Press, 2012).
Schneider, Bill. *Hiking Utah*, 3rd (Guilford, Conn: FalconGuides/Globe Pequot Press, 2005).

Index

Donna Ikenberry and Mike Vining at Goblin Valley State Park.

About the Author

Donna Ikenberry is a full-time freelance writer, photographer, and guidebook author who lives in South Fork, Colorado. A year-round traveler from 1983 to 1999, Donna married Mike Vining on January 6, 1999, and the two of them settled in Colorado later that year.

Donna and Mike travel about six months of the year, engaging in a variety of activities for Donna to write about and illustrate. Besides photography, favorite activities include rock climbing, mountaineering, hiking, skiing, kayaking, and mountain biking.

Donna is the author of thirteen books, with all of them except for *Camping Utah* related to hiking and biking. Titles include *Hiking Colorado's Weminuche and South San Juan Wilderness Areas, Hiking Oregon, Bicycling the Atlantic Coast,* and *Bicycling Coast to Coast.* She has also had nearly 900 magazine and newspaper articles published, as well as more than 5,000 photographs.

Your next adventure begins here.

falcon.com

CPSIA information can be obtained
at www.ICGtesting.com
Printed in the USA
LVOW13s0458240118
563794LV00008B/144/P